WOODWORKING BASICS

BASICS THE ESSENTIAL BENCHTOP REFERENCE

WOODWORKING
BASICS THE ESSENTIAL BENCHTOP REFERENCE

William P. Spence & L. Duane Griffiths

Sterling Publishing Co., Inc.   New York

Library of Congress Cataloging-in-Publication Data

Spence, William Perkins, 1925–
    Woodworking basics : the essential benchtop reference / William P.
Spence & L. Duane Griffiths.
        p.   cm.
    Updated ed. of: The woodworker's illustrated benchtop reference.
1989.
    Includes index.
    ISBN 0-8069-0941-2
    1. Woodwork.   2. Woodworking tools.   I. Griffiths, L. Duane.
II. Spence, William Perkins, 1925–   Woodworker's illustrated
benchtop reference.   III. Title.
TT180.S635   1995
684'.08—dc20
                                                            94-46907
                                                            CIP

10 9 8 7 6 5 4 3 2 1

Published 1995 by Sterling Publishing Company, Inc.
387 Park Avenue South, New York, N.Y. 10016
Originally published and © 1989 by TAB BOOKS Inc.
under the title *The Woodworker's Illustrated Benchtop Reference*
© 1995 William P. Spence and L. Duane Griffiths
Distributed in Canada by Sterling Publishing
℅ Canadian Manda Group, One Atlantic Avenue, Suite 105
Toronto, Ontario, Canada M6K 3E7
Distributed in Great Britain and Europe by Cassell PLC
Wellington House, 125 Strand, London WC2R 0BB, England
Distributed in Australia by Capricorn Link (Australia) Pty Ltd.
P.O. Box 6651, Baulkham Hills, Business Centre, NSW 2153, Australia
Manufactured in the United States of America
All rights reserved

Sterling ISBN 0-8069-0941-2

Contents

Preface

Woodworking is one of the most popular leisure-time activities, and it can be a very productive one. You can make many valuable projects, as well as save a great deal on home repairs. Many people make their livelihood working with wood. Woodworking projects can be simple and inexpensive, if you utilize basic hand tools and less costly wood, or can become very involved as you do advanced work and invest in power tools and imported woods.

This book was written in an attempt to consolidate in a single volume the technical information and "how-to" procedures woodworkers need. Knowledge gathered by reading this book will aid beginners, yet provide advanced procedures for those who wish to progress further into the craft.

Another motivating factor for writing this book was to try to advance the understanding of the safe operating procedures required when using woodworking tools and machines. If our suggestions are followed, the reader will have a safe and happy time working with wood.

Introduction

Woodworking is a creative activity for the novice, as well as the experienced craftsman. This book presents the basics in a clear, easy-to-understand manner so many people can enjoy the rewards of working with wood. It also presents in a thorough and detailed manner the safe and correct way to use hand and power woodworking tools and machines. This book is suitable for beginners of any age. Young people interested in woodworking can read it as they work with wood at home or at their school. Mature readers can benefit from the basic processes as well as the more advanced machining techniques that are presented. They can, using this book, produce quality furniture and cabinet units.

No previous knowledge of woodworking is needed to benefit from this book. The very simplest procedures are carefully covered. If you have some experience a review of basic procedures could prove beneficial. Quite often your early experiences with tools are learned on a limited background and through trial and error. Following the suggestions in this book will enable you to produce higher quality work in a shorter period of time and reduce chances for personal injury.

The experienced woodworker will benefit a great deal from the material relating to machining procedures. Eleven chapters are devoted to power woodworking machines; an entire chapter is devoted to each major machine. Each chapter includes information on selecting and buying the machine, safety regulations, and how to perform a wide variety of operations. The steps are well illustrated.

Finishing the project is an area where many skilled woodworkers lack adequate knowledge. Many well-built projects are ruined by improper finishing procedures, so several chapters are devoted to finishing procedures and materials. They explain how to prepare the surface for finishing, select the proper finishing materials, and apply them to the project.

It is important in woodworking to know which joint should be used and how it should be made. The various types of joints, their advantages and disadvantages, and ways to make them with both hand and power tools are included.

After the joints are made the project must be assembled. Most woodworking books do not provide a great deal of information on proper clamping and assembly techniques. In this book, however, an entire chapter is provided on assembly. It is followed by a chapter explaining the proper uses for various glues, adhesives, and cements. A good assembly with an improper bonding agent can produce disappointing results.

Sharp tools are safe tools. A sharp tool will cut without requiring excessive force or pressure. The procedures for sharpening hand tools are thoroughly covered.

Throughout the book emphasis is placed on safety. In addition to a general safety chapter, each chapter covering a tool or power machine also includes safety considerations specific to that tool or machine. Emphasis is placed on proper setup, use of guards, and personal attitudes toward the prevention of accidents.

A chapter is devoted to furniture and cabinet design, followed by a chapter that gives instruction as to properly laying out parts on the stock. This helps the craftsman produce a project that is pleasing in appearance, and proper layout reduces costs, produces stronger parts, and incorporates the grain pattern of the wood into the overall design.

A special chapter explains how to construct furniture and cabinets, complete with detailed construction drawings to make this easy for the beginner to understand. Construction details for doors, drawers, and shelves are explained in still another chapter, which describes the use of shop-made and commercial drawer slides and the procedure for making a drawer. Various door designs, as a flush, overlay, lipped and sliding are given. A variety of ways to build fixed and adjustable shelves is detailed, including the application of hardware to doors, drawers, and shelves.

An experienced woodworker will sometimes want to apply expensive, exotic wood veneers or high-pressure plastic laminates over a less costly substrate. The procedures for cutting, fitting, bonding, and cleaning up the surface after bonding are given in detail, using tools found in a typical woodworker's shop.

In conclusion, this book covers woodworking procedures from basic to advanced and provides information every woodworker will find valuable.

Chapter 1

Forestry and Lumbering

Our forests produce the raw materials used to build homes and furniture, as well as make paper, cardboard, and many other products used in our daily lives. Some of the forests in the United States are owned by private companies that manufacture wood and paper products. Others are owned by private citizens, while the federal government owns approximately 200 million acres of forest lands. The government forests are used for national parks, unspoiled wilderness areas, and limited lumbering.

Trees are a unique natural resource because after they are harvested new trees can be planted. In other words, they are a renewable resource.

In the United States there are about 750 million acres in forest. The eastern half of the United States is heavily wooded. The West Coast plus areas in the Rocky Mountain states have large forests. The Plains states in the Central United States have only scattered forest areas.

FORESTRY

Forestry involves preserving, improving, and controlling the use of our forests. A major activity in forestry is reforestation. After the trees have been harvested, the area must be reseeded. Leaving some mature trees behind will naturally reseed the area, but this is a rather slow process. Therefore seeds are often planted by airplane or by ground equipment. It will take 20 to 40 years or more for the seedlings to grow to be mature trees, depending on the type of tree.

HARVESTING

After trees in an area become large enough, they are harvested. *Harvesting* refers to cutting the trees and moving them to a mill.

The two common methods of harvesting are clear cutting and selective cutting. With *clear cutting*, every tree in the area is cut down. With *selective cutting*, only the mature trees are removed and the smaller trees left to continue to grow. Clear cutting is used primarily for softwoods such as pine and fir. This type of cutting makes it easier to replant the area. Selective cutting is used primarily with hardwoods. These trees take longer to grow, and a particular species, as walnut, will be scattered throughout the forest.

A logging crew cuts the trees with a chain saw and removes the branches. Smaller trees can be cut with shears mounted on a tractor. The top clamp grips the tree and the shear cuts it off at the ground, then the tree is lifted in the air and moved to an area for branch removal.

After the branches are removed from the logs, the logs are moved to a loading area. Sometimes they are moved by helicopter. Long cables are used to slide logs off of a steep hillside, or they can be skidded by tractors. Once they are assembled at a clearing, they are usually loaded on trucks or railroad cars for shipment to the mill.

When the logs arrive at the mill, they are stacked in large piles and sprinkled with water. If the mill is near a river or lake, the logs are stored in the water, which keeps the logs from drying out and free of insects.

PRODUCTION

The logs are cut into lumber at a sawmill. The steps that change a log into usable lumber include debarking, sawing, edging, and trimming.

A debarking machine strips the log of its bark. Sometimes the bark is broken into small pieces and sold for ground cover.

After the bark is removed, the log goes to the headrig. This large machine moves the entire log back and forth past a saw, cutting the log into slabs. Small rigs use circular saw blades, large rigs use a bandsaw. The sawyer controls the log on the carriage and decides the best way to cut each log.

Softwoods are cut into standard sizes such as 2 × 4, 2 × 6, and 4 × 4 inches. Hardwoods are cut to get the widest and longest boards possible. Because hardwoods are cut up into various pieces to make furniture, they are not cut into standard widths or lengths.

Next, the slabs go to the edger. It cuts the slab to width, removing the bark on the edges. Softwood is cut to a standard length on a trimmer, and is fed into the trimmer by a conveyor. The trimmer has many blades, which the operator raises and lowers to get the longest and best cuts possible from each slab.

The waste material is often sent to a chipper, which chops it up into small chunks. These are used for paper and particleboard or burned to make steam for drying the lumber.

GRADING

As the board comes from the trimmer it is graded. Grading involves inspecting the board for defects and deciding the level of its quality. The grader notes the size, location, and type of defects and the percentage of clear board is estimated. This information is used to fit the board into one of the standard quality levels established for the industry.

Softwoods and hardwoods are graded by different standards. Softwoods are based upon the American Softwood Lumber Standard PS 20-70, which was established by the United States Department of Commerce.

There are individual softwood associations grading lumber in various geographic areas. For example, the Western Wood Products Association covers most of the west, and the Southern Pine Inspection Bureau establishes grades for softwoods in the south.

Hardwoods are graded by the standards of the National Hardwood Lumber Association. Basically hardwoods are graded by the amount of clear area. When buying softwoods or hardwoods, choose not only the species but the grade. The better grades have fewer defects but cost more. (Chapter 3 discusses grading in more detail.)

DRYING

The boards must have most of the water in them removed. This is done by air drying or kiln drying. The boards are stacked with sticks between each layer to permit air flow.

If the boards are air dried, the stacks are left out of doors. Roofs are placed over them to shed the rain. Air drying is slow, requiring many months to get the boards to the required moisture content. Air-dried lumber should be used only on outdoor projects.

Kiln drying involves placing the stacked lumber in a large tunnel-like building called a kiln. Here it is exposed to carefully controlled moist heat. As the temperatures are slowly raised the moisture level is lowered. This is much faster than air drying and gives a more uniform moisture level in the board. Also, the wood has fewer surface checks and cracks, and has little warp. Any wood used indoors must be kiln dried.

MANUFACTURING FINISHED LUMBER

After the boards are dried to the proper moisture level, they are manufactured into lumber and other products. Much of the kiln-dried hardwood is sold to furniture and cabinet manufacturers as rough sawed boards. The purchaser surfaces and cuts them to the sizes needed for their products. Most softwood is surfaced to standard sizes and sold as dressed lumber. The 2-×-4-inch stud used in house construction is an example. When dried and surfaced, it is actually 1½ × 3½ inches. Some softwoods are cut to a particular design for tongue-and-groove siding and for moldings. (Standard hardwood and softwood lumber sizes are given in Chapter 3.)

Chapter 2

A Gallery of Wood

There are over one thousand species of trees in the United States. Of these about 100 are used for construction or manufactured products. These are divided into two groups: hardwoods and softwoods.

Hardwoods are from deciduous trees, which are those that have broad leaves and shed in the fall. In the world there are more than 99,000 different species of hardwood trees. About 200 of these are available in quantities large enough for the manufacturing of furniture and other products.

Most hardwoods are open grained or ring porous. Open grained woods have rather large porelike openings on the surface. Oak and ash have very large pores. Several hardwoods, such as maple and cherry, have small pores and are considered closed grain or diffuse porous. Popular American hardwoods include oak, maple, cherry, walnut, gum, and poplar. Mahogany, ebony, koa, limba, rosewood, teak, and satinwood are popular imported foreign hardwoods. The various woods are described in detail later in this chapter.

Softwoods come from coniferous trees, which have needles and remain green all year. About 25 species of soft woods are available in quantities large enough for commercial use. Softwoods find their largest use as lumber for building construction.

All softwoods have a closed grain. The pores are very small and not noticeable when a product is finished. Some commonly used softwoods include various kinds of cedar, fir, hemlock, larch, pine, spruce, and redwood.

PROPERTIES OF WOOD

When selecting a wood you need to have an understanding of the properties of the species you are considering.

You also need to know the conditions under which the wood will be used. For example, if it is to be exposed to the weather it will need to resist decay. If it is to carry a load, as a chair leg, it must be a species that is strong. Some woods produce stronger glue joints than others, some are easier to machine or more dimensionally stable.

The properties to be discussed are density, texture, ease of working, stability, durability, compressive strength, color, and appearance.

Density

As the density of a wood increases so does its weight. Weight indicates the relative strength. Heavier woods tend to be stronger than lighter woods. Dry woods are stronger than green, or wet, woods. Denser woods are also better at withstanding repeated blows. Hickory, birch, and oak are very shock resistant. Denser woods tend to be the hardest and can resist wear, dents, and scratches. This is important when choosing a wood for a tabletop or arms for a chair. Wood floors are usually made of oak or maple, which are very dense and hard.

Texture

Texture refers to the overall physical composition of the wood. The growth of each species affects the cell structure and size, which influences the condition of the surface. The texture can influence how a wood has to be finished.

Ease of Working

Some woods are soft and have straight grains. They cut easily with regular tools. Others are very dense or have unusual grain patterns due to the way the tree grows. They are harder to work and to smooth. Some have mineral content and hardness, which makes it necessary to use carbide-tipped cutting tools.

Stability

Stability is a measure of a wood's tendency to stay in place—to not change in size or flatness—before and after it has been worked.

Durability

Durability refers to the ability of a wood to resist rot under conditions, such as direct contact with the earth, where decay is possible. Decay ratings refer to the use of heartwood only. Remember, no wood will decay if it is kept dry.

Compressive Strength

Compressive strength refers to the ability of wood to resist breaking when under a load that is applied against its end, squeezing toward its center. This condition occurs in wood posts and chair and table legs. If you want to use a wood that is low in compressive strength for such projects, its cross sectional layer must be larger.

Color and Appearance

Woods vary in color, the heartwood usually being darker than the sapwood. The grain pattern varies considerably with the species. Some species have highly figured grains while others have little or no noticeable pattern. The appearance is also influenced by the pore structure. An open-grained (ring porous) wood has a totally different appearance than the closed-grain (diffuse porous) wood. Some types, such as oak and beech, have rays or flakes across the grain.

WOOD TYPES

Following are descriptions of some of the woods commonly used in furniture and cabinet construction and in building construction. These are presented in three groups: American hardwoods, American softwoods, and imported woods.

American Hardwoods

Most hardwoods grow in the eastern half of the United States. The following species are those most commonly used for commercial purposes. See summation of their properties in Table 2-1.

White Ash. There are 16 ashes native to the United States. Of these white, black, and green ash are commercially important. White ash is the largest and most common of the species. It grows up to 80 feet in height and develops trunks up to 3 feet in diameter. White ash is heavy, hard, and stiff and has good shock resistance. It can be satisfactorily kiln dried and holds its shape well after seasoning. White ash holds screws and nails well but does have a tendency to split.

White ash is widely used for handles, such as those on shovels and rakes. It is also used on furniture, especially on bent parts, and in sporting equipment such as bats and oars.

Ash heartwood is brown to dark brown. The large pores are clearly visible. The wood rays are visible on quarter sawn boards. The summerwood, which is darker, has white dots or lines that are clearly visible. The major difference between ash and hickory is that the large pores are more distinctive in ash.

Quaking Aspen. Quaking aspen is widely distributed in the North, from Canada down into Illinois, Ohio, and Indiana. The tree grows to a height of 20 to 60 feet and diameters of 2 to 3 feet. The wood is light, soft, weak, and limber. It is low in shock resistance, decay resistance, and nail-holding ability. It shrinks very little when seasoned. It is easily worked and does not split readily. It glues well and is among the best in ability to hold paint.

Most quaking aspen is made into pulp for the manufacture of paper and corrugated boards, and some grades are used for boxes and crates, or is shredded into excelsior.

Aspen heartwood varies from white to a very light brown. Pores are small and usually not visible. The growth rings are very faint, so it appears a uniformly composed material.

American Basswood. There are three species of basswood: American, white, and Carolina. They grow in the eastern part of the United States from Canada to the Gulf Coast. The American basswood grows in more abundance than the others. The tree grows to a height of 70 to 100 feet, and will have a trunk 3 to 4 feet in diameter. Basswood is light, weak, soft, and moderately stiff, and has low resistance to shock. Although it resists splitting, it has low nail-holding ability. It is very easy to work, holds paint well, and glues well. Because of its even grain it is a popular wood for wood carvers.

Table 2-1. Properties of American Hardwoods.

HARD-WOODS	COLOR	DENSITY	TEXTURE	EASE OF WORKING	STABILITY	DURA-BILITY	COMPRES-SIVE STRENGTH
White ash	white to tan	medium	coarse	moderate	high	moderate	high
Quaking Aspen	pale tan	soft	coarse	moderate	average	not durable	medium
American Basswood	white to pale brown	soft	fine	easy	high	not durable	low
American Beech	pale reddish brown	medium hard	medium	moderate	high	moderate	medium
Yellow Birch	pale brown	hard	fine to medium	moderate	average	not durable	medium
Black Cherry	medium reddish brown	medium	fine	moderate	high	moderate	high
Cottonwood	pale brown	soft	medium	easy	below average	not durable	low
American Elm	pale brown	medium	coarse	moderate	average	not durable	medium
Rock Elm	dark brown	medium	coarse	moderate	average	moderate	medium
Hickory	light brown	hard	medium coarse	difficult	average	not durable	high
Sugar Maple	cream	hard	fine	moderate	average	not durable	high
Red Oak	salmon pink	hard	medium coarse	moderate	average	not durable	medium
White Oak	pale tan	hard	medium fine	moderate	average	moderate	medium
Yellow Poplar	yellow brown	soft	fine	easy	average	not durable	low
Sweetgum	reddish brown	medium	fine	moderate	average	not durable	medium
American Sycamore	reddish brown	high	coarse	moderate	below average	not durable	medium
Black Tupelo	pale yellow brown	medium	fine	moderate	below average	not durable	medium
Black Walnut	dark brown	medium	medium	moderate	high	very	high

Basswood is primarily used to make crates and boxes. Higher grades are used for window sashes, doors, and millwork. Some basswood is used in furniture construction and as the core material in plywood, which is overlaid with high-quality veneers.

Basswood heartwood varies from white to a very creamy brown. The pores are small and the growth rings faint.

American Beech. The American beech grows 60 to 80 feet in height and has a trunk 2 to 3 feet in diameter. It grows best in bottomlands and moist soils.

It is a strong, heavy, shock-resistant wood. It is easily bent when steamed. It wears well and remains smooth under friction. It is difficult to work with tools and difficult to kiln dry. It holds nails well but has a tendency to split when nails are driven into it.

Beech is used for veneer, boxes, baskets, furniture, handles, flooring, millwork, and food containers.

Beech can be identified by its heavy weight, conspicuous rays and tiny pores. The heartwood is light with a reddish brown tone.

Yellow Birch. There are several types of birch. Most thrive in the northeastern states. One specie, the river birch, is found in the southeastern states.

Yellow birch trees will grow to heights of 80 feet and develop trunks up to 3 feet in diameter. The wood is heavy, hard, strong, stiff, and very shock resistant. It shrinks a great deal during seasoning and has low resistance to decay. While it is difficult to work with hand tools, it is easily shaped with machine tools. It has high nail-holding ability.

Major uses for yellow birch include furniture, boxes, crates, woodware, and plywood.

Yellow birch heartwood is reddish brown with very small pores. The pore lines can be seen on the surface as fine grooves. Growth rings are visible on plain-sawn surfaces.

Black Cherry. Black cherry has been a favorite wood for the construction of quality furniture for many years. The tree grows to a height of 50 to 60 feet and will develop a trunk 2 to 3 feet in diameter. Black cherry is strong and stiff, and has high resistance to shock. It is moderately heavy and hard. While it is a bit difficult to work with hand tools, it has good gluing properties and bending strength.

Black cherry is mainly used for the manufacture of high-quality furniture. It is also widely used for veneering. Because it is very stable, the lower grades are good to use on interior parts of furniture and for molding and trim.

Black cherry heartwood has a distinctive light to dark reddish brown color. The pores tend to follow the outline of the grain pattern. The wood rays produce a distinctive flake-like pattern on the surface of quarter-sawn boards. The sapwood varies from white to a yellow brown.

Cottonwood. Cottonwood is the fastest growing commercial forest species in North America. It will grow to heights of 200 feet and diameters of 4 and 6 feet. There are several species of cottonwood and their properties are similar. It is moderately light in weight, moderately soft, and moderately limber. It is rather weak in bending and low in shock resistance. Cottonwood has a low nail-withdrawal resistance, but it does not split easily. It is hard to work because it chips or develops a fuzzy grain. It will hold paint well.

Cottonwood is used for the manufacturer of containers and interior parts of furniture. In furniture it is the core stock over which high-quality veneers are glued. It is also a major source of pulpwood.

Cottonwood heartwood is a gray white to a light gray brown. The annual rings are wide and the pores are very small.

American Elm. American elm is an important ornamental and shade tree growing to heights of 80 to 120 feet. Trees with diameters of 4 to 6 feet and more have been found. It is moderate in heaviness, hardness, and stiffness. American elm has good shock resistance but is moderately weak. While it glues well, its nail-holding ability is rated as intermediate.

American elm is used to manufacture containers, such as boxes, crates and baskets, heavy crates, and furniture. Because it bends easily, it is used for bent parts on furniture.

American elm heartwood varies from brown to dark brown. The wavy lines formed by the summerwood pores are lighter in color than the background wood.

Rock Elm. Rock elm is one of several species of elms available. The others are American elm, winged elm, and cedar elm. The rock elm grows to 60 to 80 feet tall, having a trunk 1 to 2 feet in diameter. The wood is heavy and is stronger, harder, and stiffer than the other species of elms. It is difficult to work with hand or machine tools. Rock elm is easy to bend but has only moderate resistance to decay. It glues well but has intermediate nail-holding strength.

Rock elm is used for containers such as fruit and vegetable boxes and baskets, crating for furniture and appliances, and for bent parts on furniture.

Rock elm heartwood varies from brown to a dark

brown. The pores in the summerwood appear lighter than the background wood.

Hickory. There are 15 species of the hickory, eight of which have commercial use. They grow in the hardwood forests in the eastern states north of Tennessee. They grow to a height of 50 to 60 feet. The wood of true hickories is very hard, heavy, strong, and stiff. It has high resistance to shock. Hickory shrinks considerably when seasoned, so seasoning must be carefully handled.

Most hickory is used to manufacture tool handles, bats and other sports equipment, parts on agriculture tools, and interior furniture parts. It is an ideal wood for these items because of its combination of strength, stiffness, and hardness.

Hickory heartwood varies from a brown to a reddish brown. The pores are clearly visible on the surface.

Sugar Maple. There are 13 species of maple native to the United States, five of which have commercial value. These are the sugar, red, black, and silver maple, and the box elder. The sugar maple is one of the largest and most important hardwoods in the eastern forests. It grows to a height of 75 to 100 feet and develops a trunk 3 to 4 feet in diameter. The wood of these hard maples is heavy, strong, stiff, and has a high resistance to shock. While it has intermediate gluing properties, it has high resistance to nail withdrawal. Maple turns well on a lathe.

Maple is used for flooring, boxes, crates, handles, interior finish, cabinets, furniture, and woodenware.

Maple heartwood is a light reddish brown. The pores are very small and are not visible. The wood is usually straight grained although it will occasionally have a curly, wavy, or birdseye grain.

Red Oak. Oak is divided into two species: red and white. Both grow in the same area. Red oak will reach a height of 70 feet and have a trunk 3 or more feet in diameter. It has the same characteristics as the white oak except it is very porous.

Red oak is used for the same purposes as white oak.

Red oak heartwood is a brown with a reddish tint. The pores are very open and the outlines of the larger pores are clearly visible.

White Oak. White oak is one of the most important hardwoods found in eastern forests. The white oak tree grows to a height of 80 to 100 feet, with trunk diameters of 3 to 4 feet. All of the white oaks are heavy, hard, and strong. The wood shrinks a great deal during curing, so care is necessary to prevent cracks and warping. White oaks work well in machining operations (except shaping). The heartwood is relatively decay resistant.

White oak is used to make flooring, furniture, cooperage, millwork, timbers, handles, boxes, and crates.

White oak heartwood is a gray brown color. The pores and growth rings are clearly visible.

Yellow Poplar. Yellow poplar grows in most of the eastern states. It is a stately tree, reaching 150 feet or more in height, and has trunk diameters of 8 to 10 feet. Poplar is moderately light in weight, and moderately stiff but relatively low in shock resistance and bending. It is easy to kiln dry and retains its shape after drying. It has intermediate machining properties and is low in nail-withdrawal resistance. It will hold stain, paint, or enamel very well.

Yellow poplar is used for interior parts on furniture, boxes, crates, veneer core stock, and fixtures.

Yellow poplar heartwood is a yellow brown color and often has a green tint. The pores are small but cannot be seen visually.

Sweetgum. Sweetgum grows best in rich bottomlands and can reach a height of 100 to 120 feet or more, and can grow to 4 feet in diameter. It is moderately heavy, strong, and stiff, but has moderately high shock resistance. While it is low in decay resistance, it is intermediate in nail-holding ability and splitting point. If it is to be glued, special drying procedures are necessary. It shrinks a great deal when seasoned and the heartwood and sapwood require different drying processes. Sweetgum is good for turning, boring, and steam-bending, and is below average for basic machining operations.

Sweetgum wood is used for boxes, crates, interior parts for furniture, and interior woodwork.

Sweetgum heartwood is reddish brown with frequent streaks of darker brown colors. The pores are small and not visible. The growth rings are not easily seen.

American Sycamore. American sycamore has a white bark that tends to fall off in patches, exposing the bark below. It is a fast growing tree, sometimes attaining heights of 100 feet and diameters of 10 feet. It has moderate strength, stiffness, hardness, and heaviness. American sycamore is difficult to kiln dry and is not durable when exposed to the weather. It turns easily on a lathe and is easy to bend when steamed.

Sycamore is used for lumber, fencing, veneer, ties, unexposed parts of furniture, flooring, handles, and butcher blocks.

Sycamore is close textured and has an interlocking grain. The heartwood is a reddish brown to a light tan in color. Rays are visible and appear to be uniformly spaced.

Black Tupelo. Black tupelo grows in the eastern part of the United States, while water tupelo grows along the Atlantic and Gulf Coasts. The tree grows to 40 to 60 feet high and has a trunk up to about 4 feet in diameter. The wood is hard, moderately heavy but low in decay resistance. It is moderately weak but can resist shock. Black tupelo has considerable shrinkage during seasoning and a tendency to warp. It requires special seasoning before it can be glued. It is below average in machining ability, but intermediate in the ability to hold nails or resist splitting.

Black tupelo is used for shipping containers and furniture parts. It is also used as a veneer and as pulpwood.

Tupelo heartwood varies from a pale brown to a fairly dark brown or gray. Pores are small, not clearly visible. Growth rings may either be hard to see or easily visible.

Black Walnut. Black walnut is a favorite wood for high-quality furniture. The trees grow 70 to 100 feet in height and develop trunks 2 to 3 feet in diameter. It is a heavy, hard, stiff, strong wood and has good shock resistance. The heartwood is one of the most durable of the hardwoods. It works easily with hand and machine tools, takes stains well, and is easily glued.

Black walnut is an expensive wood most favorable for furniture making. It is also used for gunstocks and as veneer on interior paneling.

Black walnut heartwood is a rich chocolate brown. Occasionally it has dark brownish purple streaks. The pores are easily seen on the surface, usually as dark streaks.

American Softwoods

Most softwoods grow in the western half and southeastern section of the United States. Some prefer high altitudes and a cold climate, while others prefer the warm, moist southland. While many have characteristics that are similar, some have their own distinct properties. The following species are those most commonly used for commercial purposes. See a summation of their properties in Table 2-2.

Incense Cedar. Incense-cedar is a lightweight wood that is moderately soft, weak, and low in shock resistance. It shrinks little when seasoned, and therefore has little checking or warping. It is a decay-resistant wood, ranking with bald cypress and redwood. It is easy to work with hand and power tools. It holds paint well but can withstand weathering, even if unprotected.

Incense cedar is used for lumber, fences, and posts. Some is used in the manufacture of pencils and slats for blinds.

Incense cedar heartwood varies from a red brown to a brown. It has the characteristic cedar odor, and the growth rings are very prominent.

Western Red Cedar. Western red cedar has the same properties as described for incense cedar. It is light, soft, and decay resistant, but weak when used as a beam. It is one of the most durable woods.

A major use for western red cedar is as shingles. It is also used for siding, posts, boxes, crating, sashes, doors, and exterior millwork.

Western red cedar heartwood ranges from a pink brown to a red brown to a dull brown. It also has the characteristic cedar odor. It looks much like redwood but can be distinguished by its odor.

Baldcypress. Baldcypress live in watery areas such as swamps. They are found largely in the southeastern states. Baldcypress has unusual widespread roots which send up growths that protrude several feet above the water. These are often called cypress knees. The trees grow to heights of 100 to 125 feet. Baldcypress is moderately heavy, hard, strong, and stiff. The heartwood is unusual because it is very resistant to decay in moist conditions, and to termites.

Baldcypress heartwood is used anywhere resistance to decay due to moisture is important. Building construction consumes a lot of baldcypress. It is used for greenhouses, stadium seats, cooling towers, sashes, doors and exterior trim. It is also used for paneling, vats, tanks, tubs, pilings and fencing.

Baldcypress heartwood varies from a light brown to a black brown. It might have a reddish tint. It has a rancid odor and feels waxy to the touch.

Douglas Fir. Douglas fir is moderately heavy, very stiff and strong, and moderately shock resistant. It is a bit more difficult to work than the softer pines. It can be glued satisfactorily, holds fastenings well, and has moderate resistance to decay.

Most Douglas fir is used for construction purposes. It is manufactured into lumber, timbers, piling, and plywood. Some is used to make millwork, sashes, and doors. Fir plywood is widely used for wall and roof sheathing, subfloors, and concrete forms.

Douglas fir heartwood varies from an orange red, to red to yellow. The annual rings produce a prominent grain pattern. Douglas fir, while similar to yellow pine, has a distinctive odor.

Table 2-2. Properties of American Softwoods.

SOFT-WOODS	COLOR	DENSITY	TEXTURE	EASE OF WORKING	STABILITY	DURA-BILITY	COMPRES-SIVE STRENGTH
Incense Cedar	red	medium	fine	moderate	high	very	medium
Western Red Cedar	reddish brown	soft	medium	easy	high	very	medium
Baldcypress	orange brown	soft	medium coarse	easy	high	very	medium
Douglas Fir	reddish brown	medium	coarse	moderate	average	moderate	high
White Fir	off white to tan	soft	coarse	moderate	average	moderate	medium
Western Hemlock	grayish brown	medium soft	coarse	moderate	average	not durable	medium
Western Larch	pale brown	medium	coarse	moderate	average	not durable	high
Western White Pine	pale tan	soft	fine	easy	average	moderate	medium
Ponderosa Pine	light tan	soft	fine	easy	high	moderate	low
Shortleaf Pine	brownish yellow	medium	coarse	easy	average	moderate	high
Sugar Pine	light tan	soft	fine	easy	high	high	low
Redwood	reddish brown	soft	fine	easy	high	high	high
Englemann Spruce	light tan	soft	fine	moderate	high	moderate	low
Sitka Spruce	light tan	soft	fine	difficult	high	moderate	medium

White Fir. White fir is light in weight, moderately soft and weak, moderately low in shock resistance, moderately stiff, and low in nail-withdrawal resistance. It is difficult to season, which limits its use. It glues satisfactorily if it can be properly seasoned.

White fir is used mainly for construction lumber or high-quality paper pulp.

White fir heartwood varies from a white to a pale red brown. The annual rings produce a clear grain pattern.

Western Hemlock. Western hemlock is moderately light in weight, moderately weak, moderately hard, and low in shock resistance. The wood is easy to work with tools and can be glued.

Western hemlock is used mainly for construction lumber and pulpwood. It is also used for containers, plywood core stock, and crossties.

Western hemlock heartwood has a light red brown color. There is little color difference between the springwood and summerwood.

Western Larch. Western larch is a heavy wood, moderately hard, stiff, and strong, and has a moderately high shock resistance. It appears much the same as Douglas fir and is often sold mixed with fir under the name "larch fir." Larch has a large shrinkage in drying and is slow to give up its moisture. It ranks high in nail-withdrawal resistance.

Western larch is primarily used for construction purposes, including timbers, planks and boards. Because it is strong, much of it is cut into structural members. Some is used for sash, doors, flooring, and interior finish materials.

Western larch heartwood is a reddish brown. There is little difference between the color of the springwood and summerwood.

Western White Pine. Western white pine is moderately light in weight, moderately soft, moderately stiff, and moderately low in ability to resist shock. It is easy to kiln dry and is rather low in ability to resist decay. It works and glues easily, does not split easily, and has intermediate nail-withdrawal resistance.

Most western white pine is used for lumber. High-grade stock is used for siding, trim, and paneling, while low grades are used for sheathing and subflooring.

Western white pine heartwood varies from a light cream to a light brown. The annual rings are easily seen and are more prominent than those in sugar pine.

Ponderosa Pine. Ponderosa pine is lightweight, soft, moderately weak, and low in shock resistance. It has little tendency to warp. It glues easily, does not split, and has moderate nail-withdrawal properties. It has low to moderate resistance to decay.

Ponderosa pine is used mainly for lumber. The high-quality wood is used in millwork, cabinets, and paneling. The low-grade wood is used in crates and boxes.

Ponderosa pine heartwood is a light yellow to light red to an orange brown. Growth rings can be clearly seen on the surface of boards.

Shortleaf Pine. Shortleaf pine is one of 36 species of pine native to the United States. It is possibly the most important species of conifer. There are over 100 species worldwide. Pines are separated into two groups: The soft or white pines have soft, light-colored, close-grained wood, and the hard or pitch pines are coarse-grained and darker in color.

Shortleaf pines grow to heights of 80 to 100 feet and diameters of 2 to 3 feet. It is one of the hard pine species. The wood is moderately heavy and hard, and is moderately strong, stiff, and shock resistant. The heartwood is moderately resistant to decay. It has a good nail-withdrawal resistance.

Shortleaf pine and the other hard pines are used mainly for building materials such as studs, joists, siding, sheathing, and subflooring. They are also used in crates, boxes, and interior parts of furniture. Much is used for pulpwood. The trees are also used to produce turpentine, tar, and tar oils.

Shortleaf pine heartwood varies from light yellow and orange to light brown. The annual rings are very prominent. All hard pines appear much the same.

Sugar Pine. Sugar pine is lightweight, moderately soft, moderately weak, and low in shock resistance. It is low in decay resistance and seasons without any difficulty. It works easily with hand and power tools, and has moderate nail-withdrawal resistance.

Sugar pine is used mainly as construction lumber and for boxes and crates. Some is used for millwork, doors, and sashes. The high-grade material is used for interior and exterior trim, siding, and paneling.

Sugar pine heartwood varies from light brown to a pale red brown. The growth rings, while visible, are not prominent.

Redwood. Redwood grows in a small area along the California coast. It is a long-lived tree that is light in weight and moderately strong and stiff. Its outstanding feature is its ability to resist decay. It has intermediate nail-withdrawal resistance, but will hold paint well. It is highly resistant to termites. It is a softwood and easy to work with hand or machine tools.

Most redwood is used for construction. It is also used to manufacturing siding, sashes, blinds, millwork, outdoor furniture, and tanks.

Redwood heartwood is a uniform deep red brown. The grain pattern is clearly visible. It has no odor, as does western red cedar and baldcypress.

Engelman Spruce. Engelman spruce is lightweight, soft, weak, and low in the ability to resist shock. It is low in decay resistance but glues well.

Engelman spruce is used mainly for building construction and boxes. Some is used for pulpwood.

Engelman spruce heartwood is the same color as the sapwood, which varies from white to a pale yellow brown. All the spruces except sitka have almost identical appearance and are difficult to tell apart.

Sitka Spruce. There are seven species of spruce native to the United States. Five of these have commercial use. Spruce grow best in moist areas in cooler climates.

Sitka spruce is moderately lightweight, soft, and weak, and has a moderately low resistance to shock. It works easily and holds nails well. One advantage is that it is straight grained and produces long lengths of wood free of defects. The wood tends to develop a fuzzy surface when planed.

Sitka spruce is used mainly for lumber and pulpwood. The lumber is used for construction, boxes, and crates. Some is used for millwork, doors, and sashes.

Sitka spruce heartwood varies from a light pink yellow to a light brown. The annual rings are rather inconspicuous.

Imported Woods

There are over 100,000 different species of trees in the world, and many are unique to a geographic area. These woods are imported steadily to the United States. Following are some of the more common imported woods. See a summation of their properties on Table 2-3.

Ebony. Ebony is found in Africa and parts of Asia. There are several species of trees providing ebony wood in a variety of colors. It is very heavy and very hard.

Ebony is used in small amounts for items such as decorative inlays, turnings, and wood carvings. It is an expensive wood, and so is not generally used for furniture construction. It is very difficult to work.

Ebony from the East Indies is a dull brown with stripes ranging from dark brown to gray to brownish orange. Ebonies from Gabon, Central West Africa, and Sri Lanka are solid black.

African Mahogany. African mahogany is found in Ghana, Ivory Coast, and Nigeria. It has about the same characteristics as Honduras mahogany and is related to it botanically. It has a highly figured open grain, but is not as easy to work as Honduras mahogany. It is used for the same purposes and has the same color.

Honduras Mahogany (Genuine). Honduras mahogany is imported from the tropical regions of Central and South America. It is medium in weight, hardness, stiffness, and nail-withdrawal resistance. It has medium shock resistance and high resistance to decay. It has high resistance to warping and is easily worked with hand and power tools. It is an excellent turning and carving wood.

Mahogany is mainly used in the manufacture of furniture. It is also used for veneers.

Mahogany heartwood varies from a pale to a deep reddish brown. The sapwood ranges from white to a light brown in color. It has open pores and a clearly visible grain pattern. Quarter-sawn surfaces will have a ribbon or strip figure.

Table 2-3. Properties of Imported Woods.

IMPORTED WOODS	COLOR	DENSITY	TEXTURE	EASE OF WORKING	STABILITY	DURABILITY	COMPREHESSIVE STRENGTH
Ebony	solid black dull brown	very hard	fine	difficult	average	very durable	high
African Mahogany	pale reddish brown	medium	medium	moderate	high	moderate	medium
Honduras Mahogany	reddish brown	medium	medium	moderate	high	moderate	medium
Philippine Mahogany	medium to dark red	medium	medium to coarse	moderate	average	moderate	low
Limba (Korina)	pale yellow	medium	fine	easy	high	not durable	medium
Rosewood	deep reddish brown	medium	coarse	moderate	average	moderate	medium
Satinwood	golden yellow	hard	fine	moderate	average	moderate	high
Teak	medium brown	hard	coarse	carbide tools	high	very durable	high

Philippine Mahogany. Philippine mahogany is a term used to describe several species of wood that grow in the Philippine Islands and have similar characteristics. It has medium weight, hardness, stiffness, and nail-withdrawal resistance. It is low in shock resistance and high in resistance to decay. It has high resistance to warping and is easy to work with tools. Woods sold as Philippine mahogany have properties similar to true mahogany, but are coarser in surface texture and appearance. They are easy to glue and cost less than genuine mahogany.

Philippine mahogany is used largely for furniture and as veneers for plywood and paneling.

The two types of Philippine mahogany are described by color: dark and light. The dark type comes from the Red Luaun and Tanguile species. Their heartwood varies from a pale to a dark reddish brown color similar to genuine mahogany. The light type comes from the Almon and Bogtican species. Their heartwood varies from straw color to a light red. In both types the pores are visible and the grain prominent.

Limba (Korina). Limba grows in Zaire. It is often called "Korina," which is a copyrighted name. It works easily and is uniform in color. It is easily stained if darker colors are wanted. Limba is of medium weight, hardness, and strength, and is easy to finish.

Limba is mainly a furniture wood. Its pale blond color makes it a favorite for furniture requiring a blond or light tan color.

Limba heartwood is a light blond color with a straight grain and small pores.

Rosewood. Rosewood comes from Asia, Madagascar, Brazil, and Central America. It is the product of several closely related species of trees. The wood is very hard and dense and has an open grain. When it is being cut it gives off a pleasant fragrance, thus its name. It is easy to work and finishes very smoothly.

Rosewood is available in limited amounts, therefore it is used for only the highest-quality furniture. Much is cut into veneers and inlay material.

Rosewood heartwood generally is a deep reddish brown or purple tone with dark brown and black streaks. The wood has a heavy residue of oil.

Satinwood. Satinwood comes from two parts of the world. In the East Indies it comes from Sri Lanka and India. In the West Indies it comes from Puerto Rico, the Bahamas, the Dominican Republic, and southern Florida. It is very hard and brittle and tends to surface check.

Satinwood is very expensive and is mainly used as banding or inlays on fine furniture.

West Indies satinwood heartwood is a golden yellow in color and deepens to a light golden brown as it ages. The East Indies satinwood is paler and has a more highly figured grain. When it is cut it has an odor much like that of coconut, and has an oily appearance and feel.

Teak. Teak comes from Java, India, Burma, and Thailand. It is very heavy, hard, and so dense it will not float. It has high resistance to decay, is very strong, and will keep its shape even when exposed to moisture. It is best worked with carbide-tipped tools, because it will quickly dull standard steel cutting tools. It is difficult to glue.

Teak is widely used for furniture construction, as a veneer and on the outer surfaces of plywood.

Teak heartwood varies from a honey color to a rich brown. It tends to darken when exposed to the atmosphere. It has small pores and generally a straight grain. Teak feels oily to the touch.

Chapter 3

Woodworking Materials

The best material for the project must be carefully considered. The choice will depend upon many factors: Some woods are easier to work than others, some have a grain or color that better fit the design. The availability and cost is important. Some products, such as period furniture, must be made from the same wood as the originals. Solid wood, plywood with a hardwood veneer, and particleboard with a plastic laminate will each produce an appearance similar to solid species of woods. The correct wood must also be chosen for the parts that are not visible. For example, drawer sides and cabinet backs can be made from a variety of woods or wood products. Some materials, such as plywood, are strong and warp very little, while certain solid woods tend to warp easily. Most projects use a number of different woods plus metal hardware. The materials selected will influence the appearance, strength, and cost of the final product.

SOLID WOODS

Solid hardwoods have a large range of grain patterns, strengths, and colors, as listed in Chapter 2.

When you select a wood for a project, the color and grain must be suitable. For example, maple is light tan to white, while cherry is a strong red brown. The grain of each is highly figured. After you select the species, examine the actual boards that are available. The color and grain will vary from board to board. You will also have to watch for sapwood, which is strong but will have to be stained to match the color of the heartwood.

SAWING LUMBER

Logs are cut into lumber by plain-sawing or quarter sawing the log (Fig. 3-1). To produce plain-sawn lumber, the log is cut square, then the boards are cut tangent to the annual growth rings. This produces wider boards at less cost. Plain-sawn lumber warps and shrinks more across the face than quarter sawn.

Quarter-sawn boards are produced by cutting the log into quarters. Each quarter is cut into boards so the annual growth rays are 45 to 90 degrees with the face. While more costly to produce, quarter-sawn boards warp less and withstand hard wear. Wood flooring is quarter-sawn.

Softwood lumber is cut to standard nominal sizes. A nominal size is the rough-sawn size. When the boards are dried and planed smooth they are smaller than nominal size (Table 3-1).

Hardwood lumber is cut to standard thicknesses but random widths and lengths. Because hardwoods are more valuable and usually cut up into small pieces, as for furniture parts, it is not cut to standard widths or lengths. Standard thicknesses of hardwood lumber are shown in Table 3-2.

DEFECTS IN SOLID WOOD

Defects affect the appearance and strength of the wood. (Fig. 3-2). For many products, small pieces are needed and the defects can be cut out. In some cases the defects

Plain sawing

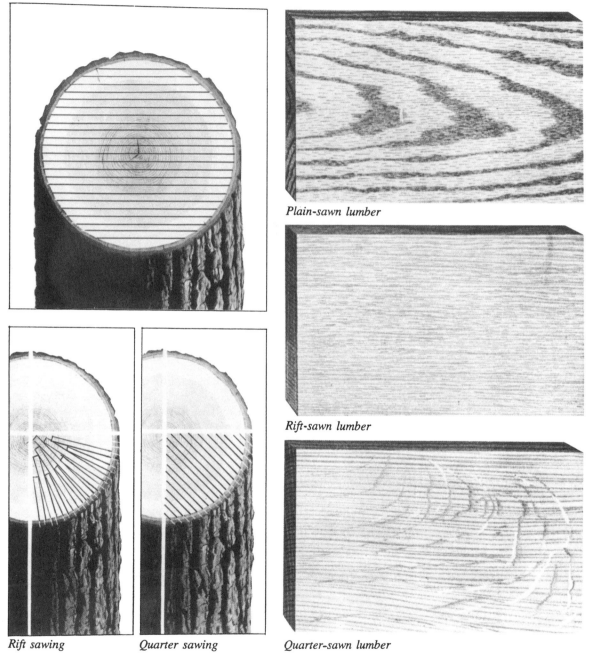

Plain-sawn lumber

Rift-sawn lumber

Rift sawing   *Quarter sawing*   Quarter-sawn lumber

Fig. 3-1. Various ways logs are cut into boards (Courtesy Architectural Woodwork Institute).

Table 3-1. Standard Thicknesses and Widths of Softwood Lumber.

	THICKNESS			WIDTH		
	NOMINAL (IN.)	DRESSED (IN.)	DRESSED (MM)	NOMINAL (IN.)	DRESSED (IN.)	DRESSED (MM)
	1	¾	16	2	1½	36
	1¼	1⅛	27	3	2½	62
	1½	1⅜	40	4	3½	88
Nominal	2	1½	36	5	4½	114
sizes and	2½	2	50	6	5½	140
dressed sizes	3	2½	62	8	7¼	190
of softwood	3½	3	76	10	9¼	233
	4	3½	88	12	11¼	290

add to the appearance of the product. A colonial chest of drawers with solid knots and a few worm holes is quite attractive and acceptable. Following are the commonly found defects:

- Knots are produced when a tree grows a limb. They are very hard and difficult to cut, and often drop out when the wood is dry. This produces a knot hole.
- Shakes are internal cracks that run with or across the grain. They are caused when the tree was suddenly rocked, as in a storm.
- Checks are small cracks on the surface of ends of boards. They are caused when the board dries out unevenly.
- Honeycombing refers to cracks on the inside of a board that do not appear on the surface. They are caused by improper drying.

Table 3-2. Standard Thicknesses of Hardwood Lumber.

THICKNESS		
NOMINAL (ROUGH)	SURFACED 1 SIDE (S1S)	SURFACED 2 SIDES (S2S)
3/8"	1/4"	3/16"
1/2"	3/8"	5/16"
5/8"	1/2"	7/16"
3/4"	5/8"	9/16"
1"	7/8"	13/16"
1 1/4"	1 1/8"	1 1/16"
1 1/2"	1 3/8"	1 5/16"
2"	1 13/16"	1 3/4"
3"	2 13/16"	2 3/4"
4"	3 13/16"	3 3/4"

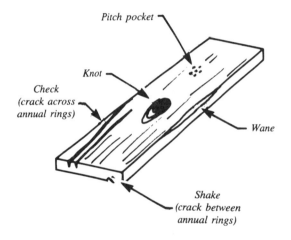

Fig. 3-2. Common defects in wood products.

- Pitch pockets are small depressions filled with tree sap. Insects tunnel into wood, forming holes.
- Case hardening refers to a condition when the surface of the board is in compression. The surface squeezes the core or inside of the board, and when the board is sawed it will develop a crook and will cup when planed.
- Wane refers to the edge of a board that is rounded on the edge and often has bark. It is part of the outside of the log.
- Warp describes a board that is no longer flat. It might have twist, cup, bow or crook (Fig. 3-3). These are caused by improper seasoning.

MOISTURE CONTENT

When a tree is cut down the cells forming the wood will be full of moisture and the fibers forming the walls of the

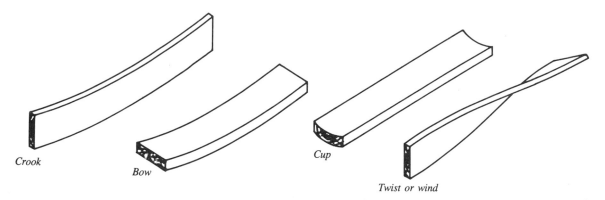

Fig. 3-3. A board can warp in various ways.

cells are completely saturated. After the tree is cut up into lumber it begins to lose some of this moisture. The purpose of kilns is to get the moisture content to a level where the wood is stable and will not warp or crack. It also affects the strength of the glue joints and the appearance of any finish that might be applied.

When softwood dries it shrinks an average of ¹⁄₃₂ inch for each inch of face width. Drying has minimal effect on the length. The actual amount of shrinkage varies considerably by specie. If a project is built of wood with a high moisture content, it will twist and crack and even break glue joints when it begins to dry.

The recommended percent of moisture remaining in wood used in interior and exterior locations is shown in Table 3-3. Hardwoods used for furniture and cabinet construction must be kiln dried to 6 to 8 percent moisture. Do not use air-dried wood for furniture, cabinets, or any other interior purpose.

Wood materials must be protected from excessive dampness or dryness, so the humidity in buildings where unfinished wood and wood products are stored must be controlled. Because normal humidity varies considerably across the country the required humidity in storage and work areas will vary. After the wood has been finished or painted the moisture changes occur slowly, so careful control of humidity is not as important. Knowing that moisture content does increase or reduce the size of wood, it is important for furniture and cabinets to have

Table 3-3. Recommended Moisture Levels for Wood Products.

	FOR INTERIOR USE		FOR EXTERIOR USE
GEOGRAPHICAL LOCATION	**OPTIMUM MOISTURE CONTENT OF WOOD**	**RELATIVE HUMIDITY NECESSARY TO MAINTAIN OPTIMUM MOISTURE CONTENT**	**OPTIMUM MOISTURE CONTENT OF WOOD**
Most of the United States, Ontario and Quebec	5-10%	25-55%	9-15%
Damp Southern Coastal Areas of the United States, Newfoundland, and Canadian Coastal Provinces	8-13%	43-70%	10-15%
Dry Southwestern States	4-9%	17-50%	7-12%
Alberta, Saskatchewan, Manitoba	4-9%	17-50%	10-15%

all surfaces finished, including the bottom of table tops, and drawer sides and bottoms. If left unprotected, a drawer can swell and stick or a top might shrink and break a joint.

Gluing

Moisture content of wood also influences gluing. Glues adhere well to wood with moisture contents up to 15 percent. However, if large changes in moisture content occur after gluing, the shrinking or swelling stresses might weaken the joints. Wood used for interior millwork is glued at 5 to 6 percent; for exterior millwork, 10 to 12 percent; for veneers 2 to 6 percent; for hardwoods for interior uses 6 to 8 percent.

Painting

When wood is wet it should not be painted. Ideally the moisture content of wood to be painted should be 16 to 20 percent. Wood painted at 16 to 20 percent holds paint better than wood at 10 percent.

Finishing

Wood to be finished, as staining and applying a transparent coating as used on furniture, should have a moisture content of 6 to 8 percent.

GRADES

The grade of lumber refers to its quality. This is based on the number, location, and size of defects, and the size of the board. These determine the amount or percentage of clear wood. The more clear wood in a board the higher the grade.

The grade of lumber to choose is sometimes a difficult decision. If visible defects are not objectionable the main consideration is strength. Using lower grades will reduce the cost. Some products use several grades of wood. For example, drawer fronts are very noticeable and will be a high grade. The framing behind the drawer, while still visible, is secondary and can be a lower grade.

Hardwood Lumber Grades

Different grading systems are used for hardwood and softwood. The hardwood system is simpler. The grading standards are set by the National Hardwood Lumber Association. Hardwoods are judged more on appearance than strength because they usually are cut up into small furniture and cabinet parts. Following are the standard grades for hardwoods.

- First and Second (FAS) are separate grades but are usually combined into one. Pieces are not less than 6 inches wide and 8 feet long. They give at least 83⅓ percent clear cuttings. These grades are best used when long clear boards are required.
- Selects have both faces graded. The best face must be a Second grade and the other face No. 1 Common. Selects must be 4 inches wide and 6 feet long.
- No. 1 Common must have more than 65 percent of the board clear on the poorest side. It must measure 4 inches by 2 feet or 3 inches by 3 feet. This is the grade commonly used for furniture and cabinet work.
- No. 2 Common, No. 3A Common, and No. 3B Common are often used by manufacturing companies where products require small pieces because they are cheaper. A No. 2 board should have at least 50 percent clear. A No. 3A Common comes in boards 3 inches wide and 2 feet long. A No. 3B Common must have 36 square inches of clear material.

Softwood Lumber Grades

Softwood lumber grades are based on the American Softwood Lumber Standard PS 20–70. It is a product standard published by the U.S. Department of Commerce. In addition, there are other grading associations that set additional standards in a particular area. The Western Wood Products Association covers woods grown in the western part of the United States. The Southern Pine Inspection Bureau sets standards for softwoods grown in southern states.

Softwood lumber grades are separated according to the product. Each division has a series of grades. The two divisions most likely to find use in woodworking projects are Finish and Boards S4S. See Table 3-4 for an explanation of these grades.

BUYING LUMBER

When buying lumber you have to specify the following:

- Specie (kind of wood)
- Rough or surfaced
- Thickness
- Width and length for softwoods
- Minimum acceptable width and length for hardwoods
- Kiln or air dried
- Grade
- Quarter or plain sawed
- Quantity in board feet

Table 3-4. Softwood Lumber Grades.

PRODUCT	GRADE	CHARACTER OF GRADE AND TYPICAL USES
Finish	B&B	Highest recognized grade of finish. Generally clear, although a limited number of pin knots permitted. Finest quality for natural or stain finish.
	C	Excellent for painted or natural finish where requirements are less exacting. Reasonably clear but permits limited number of surface checks and small tight knots.
	C&Btr	Combination of B&B and C grades; satisfied requirements for high-quality finish.
	D	Economical, serviceable grade for natural or painted finish.
Boards S4S	No. 1	High quality with good appearance characteristics. Generally sound and tight-knotted. Largest hole permitted is 1/16″. A superior product suitable for wide range of uses, including shelving, form, and crating lumber.
	No. 2	High-quality sheathing material, characterized by light knots. Generally free of holes.
	No. 3	Good serviceable sheathing, usable for many applications without waste.
	No. 4	Admit pieces below No. 3 which can be used without waste or contain usable portions at least 24″ in length.

(Courtesy Southern Forest Products Association).

Lumber is sold by the board foot. A board foot is equal to a piece 1 x 12 x 12 inches. The following formula shows how to calculate board feet (Thickness used is nominal size). A reference chart for board feet is in Table 3-5.

$$\frac{\text{T(inches)} \times \text{W(inches)} \times \text{L(inches)}}{144} = \text{board feet}$$

$$\frac{\text{T(inches)} \times \text{W(inches)} \times \text{L(feet)}}{12} = \text{board feet}$$

PLYWOOD

Plywood is made by gluing together layers of veneer. Each layer has its grain perpendicular to the one next to it. Plywood can be made with a veneer core, solid lumber core, particleboard, or medium-density fiberboard core. The core is the center section of the sheet. A veneer core usually has three to nine veneer plies. It is the strongest of all the cores. A lumber core panel has many strips of lumber glued edge to edge to form the core. Two veneer crossbands are on each side. This type of plywood is often used for cabinet doors where the edge is exposed. Particleboard and medium-density fiberboard cores have a single veneer ply glued to each side.

The outer veneers are called the face and back. The highest quality veneer is the face side. Inner layers of veneer are called crossbands. These increase the strength and stability of the sheet. The number of crossbands may be two, four, or six. For example, a five-ply sheet has a one-ply core and two crossbands on each side.

The face veneer determines the type of plywood; it may be hard or softwood. Hardwood plywood is used for furniture and cabinet construction. Softwoods are used heavily in the construction industry.

The basic process of making plywood is as follows (Fig. 3-4): Most veneers are cut on a rotary lathe. The log rotates against a knife, which cuts the veneer. Some are cut with a slicer, which cuts individual pieces the width of the log. The logs are steam heated before cutting to make cutting easier. The veneers move to the clipper, which cuts them into various widths.

At this point, the dryer removes the moisture from the veneer. The sheets are graded by their quality, and defects are cut out and the openings plugged. The veneers are spliced on the edges to form larger sheets, and are then coated with an adhesive front and back and assembled into sheets. The heated, hydraulic press applies

Table 3-5. Board Foot Chart.

NOMINAL SIZE (IN.)	ACTUAL SIZE (IN.)	BOARD FEET PER FOOT OF LENGTH
1 × 2	¾ × 1½	.17
1 × 3	¾ × 2½	.25
1 × 4	¾ × 3½	.33
1 × 5	¾ × 4½	.42
1 × 6	¾ × 5½	.50
1 × 7	¾ × 6¼	.58
1 × 8	¾ × 7¼	.67
1 × 10	¾ × 9¼	.83
1 × 12	¾ × 11¼	1.00
1¼ × 4	1 × 3½	.41
1¼ × 6	1 × 5½	.62
1¼ × 8	1 × 7¼	.83
1¼ × 10	1 × 9¼	1.04
1¼ × 12	1 × 11¼	1.25
1½ × 4	1¼ × 3½	.50
1½ × 6	1¼ × 5½	.75
1½ × 8	1¼ × 7¼	1.00
1½ × 10	1¼ × 9¼	1.25
1½ × 12	1¼ × 11¼	1.50
2 × 4	1½ × 3½	.67
2 × 6	1½ × 5½	1.00
2 × 8	1½ × 7¼	1.33
2 × 10	1½ × 9¼	1.67
2 × 12	1½ × 11¼	2.00
3 × 6	2½ × 5½	1.50
4 × 4	3½ × 3½	1.33
4 × 6	3½ × 5½	2.00

pressure while curing the adhesive with heat. The cured sheets are cut to size, sanded when necessary, and stacked for shipping.

Construction and Industrial Plywood

The requirements for the manufacture of construction and industrial plywood are specified by U.S. Product Standard PS 1-83 for Construction and Industrial Plywood. The American Plywood Association assures the quality of plywood made by its members mills. Plywood of this type is used mainly for construction and industrial purposes, but some types are used for hidden parts of furniture and cabinets. APA Sanded and Touch-Sanded softwood plywood is used in furniture and cabinet construction.

Veneer Grades

The outer veneers of softwood plywood are classified into five appearance groups: N,A,B,C, and D. The best grade is N and the poorest is D. See Table 3-6. The grades are stamped on the sheet. A grade of A-B would mean the face is grade A and the back is grade B.

Softwood plywood is classified by species. The species of wood on the face and back are used to identify the plywood. About 70 woods are used to construct plywood. They are grouped into five groups: 1,2,3,4, and 5, depending upon their strength and stiffness (Table 3-7). The woods in group 1 are the strongest and group 5 the weakest. The group number is stamped on the sheet. The inner plies can be wood from any of the species in that group. The outer plies must be the same wood.

Exposure Durability

Softwood panels manufactured to American Plywood Association specifications have four exposure durability classifications: Exterior, Exposure 1, Exposure 2, and Interior. Exterior panels use a waterproof adhesive and are used whenever the panel will constantly be exposed to moisture. Exposure 1 panels are used where they will have severe weather exposure, as during delayed construction, but will eventually be protected. They use the same adhesive as exterior, but permit the use of lower grades of veneer. Exposure 2 panels are identified as interior and use an intermediate adhesive. They are used where they will be exposed to moisture for a short time, as during construction, but will eventually be protected. Interior panels use an interior adhesive and are intended for interior use only, such as furniture or cabinet backs.

Softwood Plywood Grade Stamp

Each plywood panel has a grade stamp that describes its characteristics. It gives the group number, grade of face and back plies, exposure durability, where the panel was made, and the fact that it was made to American Plywood Association and PS 1-83 specifications (Fig. 3-5). Grade marks for two sanded panels are in Fig. 3-6.

Sanded and Touch-Sanded Panels

This type of plywood panel is used in furniture and cabinet construction.

Panels with B-grade or better veneer faces are sanded smooth during manufacture. They have good strength and stiffness, and excellent face veneers.

Touch-sanded panels come in three types: Underlayment, C-C Plugged, and C-D Plugged. These panels are sanded only to assure uniform panel thickness. They do not have the smooth, high-quality veneers that would allow them to be visible in furniture or cabinets. They are

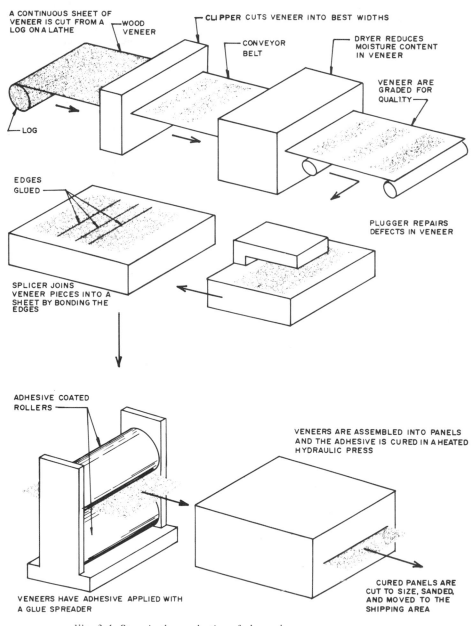

A CONTINUOUS SHEET OF VENEER IS CUT FROM A LOG ON A LATHE

WOOD VENEER

CLIPPER CUTS VENEER INTO BEST WIDTHS

CONVEYOR BELT

DRYER REDUCES MOISTURE CONTENT IN VENEER

VENEER ARE GRADED FOR QUALITY

LOG

EDGES GLUED

PLUGGER REPAIRS DEFECTS IN VENEER

SPLICER JOINS VENEER PIECES INTO A SHEET BY BONDING THE EDGES

ADHESIVE COATED ROLLERS

VENEERS ARE ASSEMBLED INTO PANELS AND THE ADHESIVE IS CURED IN A HEATED HYDRAULIC PRESS

VENEERS HAVE ADHESIVE APPLIED WITH A GLUE SPREADER

CURED PANELS ARE CUT TO SIZE, SANDED, AND MOVED TO THE SHIPPING AREA

Fig. 3-4. Steps in the production of plywood.

used as a layer over a subfloor, or for pallets, bins, and building soffits.

Buying Plywood

Plywood is normally sold in panels 4 x 8 feet. A panel contains 32 square feet. Plywood is priced by the square foot, so if it sells for $.75 a square foot, a panel would cost $24.00. The difference in thickness is reflected in the price. Plywood ¾ inch thick will cost more per square foot that ¼-inch panels.

When buying plywood, you must tell the supplier what characteristics you need the plywood to contain. He will match your requirements with the information found on the grade stamp.

Table 3-6. Veneer Grades for Softwood Plywood.

N	Smooth surface "natural finish" veneer. Select, all heartwood or all sapwood. Free of open defects. Allows not more than 6 repairs, wood only, per 4' × 8' panel, made parallel to grain and well matched for grain and color.
A	Smooth, paintable. Not more than 18 neatly made repairs, boat, sled, or router type, and parallel to grain, permitted. May be used for natural finish in less demanding applications.
B	Solid surface. Shims, circular repair plugs and tight knots to 1 inch across grain permitted. Some minor splits permitted.
C Plugged	Improved C veneer with splits limited to 1/8-inch width and knotholes and borer holes limited to 1/4 × 1/2 inch. Admits some broken grain. Synthetic repairs permitted.
C	Tight knots to 1½ inch. Knotholes to 1 inch across grain and some to 1½ inch if total width of knots and knotholes is within specified limits. Synthetic or wood repairs. Discoloration and sanding defects that do not impair strength permitted. Limited splits allowed. Stitching permitted.
D	Knots and knotholes to 2½ inch width across grain and ½ inch larger within specified limits. Limited splits are permitted. Stitching permitted. Limited to interior (Exposure 1 or 2) panels.

(Courtesy American Plywood Association).

Hardwood Plywood

The standards for the manufacture of hardwood plywood are set forth in the publication *American National Standards for Hardwood and Decorative Plywood, ANSI/HPMA HP 1983*. These standards include both hardwood plywood and decorative plywood (which can be either hardwood or softwood).

Veneer Grades for Hardwood Plywood

Hardwood plywood is manufactured with six grades of veneers. These grades and their identifying symbols are shown on Table 3-8.

A Grade (A) is the best. The face is made of hardwood veneers carefully matched as to color and grain. This grade is sometimes called premium.

B Grade (B) is suitable for a natural finish but the face veneers are not as carefully matched as on the A grade. This grade is sometimes called good.

Sound Grade (2) provides a face that is smooth. All defects have been repaired. It is used as a smooth base for a paint finish.

Industrial Grade (3) face veneers can have surface defects. This grade permits knotholes up to 1 inch in diameter, small open joints, and small areas of rough grain.

Backing Grade (4) uses unselected veneers having knotholes up to 3 inches in diameter and certain types of splits. Any defect permitted does not affect the strength of the panel.

Specialty Grade (SP) includes veneers having characteristics unlike any of those in the other grades. The characteristics are agreed upon between the manufacturer and the purchaser. For example, species such as wormy chestnut or birdseye maple are considered Specialty Grade.

Species Used in Hardwood Plywood

Many species of wood are used in hardwood plywood (Table 3-9). These species are divided into four categories: A,B,C, and D. The categories reflect the modulus of elasticity (stiffness) of each species. These data are used when establishing the maximum thickness of the veneer.

The species for the face of a panel can be any hardwood species. If the face veneer is to be a decorative face it could be any of the species in Table 3-9. The species of the back and inner plies may be any hardwood or softwood species.

Table 3-10 lists the four types of hardwood plywood in descending order of the water-resistance capacity.

Constructions. The construction of hardwood plywood is based on the core. Following are the recommended constructions:

- Hardwood veneer core with an odd number of plies, as 3-ply, 5-ply, etc.
- Softwood veneer core with an odd number of plies, as 3-ply, 5-ply, etc.
- Hardwood lumber core with 3-ply, 5-ply and 7-ply constructions.
- Softwood lumber core with 3-ply, 5-ply and 7-ply constructions.
- Particleboard core with 3-ply and 5-ply constructions.
- Medium-density fiberboard core with 3-ply construction.

Table 3-7. Classification of Species for Softwood Plywood.

GROUP 1	GROUP 2	GROUP 3	GROUP 4	GROUP 5
Apitong	Cedar, Port	Alder, Red	Aspen	Basswood
Beech, American	Orford	Birch, Paper	Bigtooth	Poplar, Balsam
Birch	Cypress	Cedar, Alaska	Quaking	
Sweet	Douglas Fir 2[a]	Fir, Subalpine	Cativo	
Yellow	Fir	Hemlock, Eastern	Cedar	
Douglas Fir 1[a]	Balsam	Maple	Incense	
Kapur	California Red	Bigleaf	Western Red	
Keruing	Grand	Pine	Cottonwood	
Larch, Western	Noble	Jack	Eastern	
Maple, Sugar	Pacific Silver	Lodgepole	Black	
Pine	White	Ponderosa	(Western Poplar)	
Caribbean	Hemlock, Western	Spruce	Pine	
Ocote	Lauan	Redwood	Eastern White	
Pine, South	Almon	Spruce	Sugar	
Loblolly	Bagtikan	Engelmann		
Longleaf	Mayapis	White		
Shortleaf	Red			
Slash	Tangile			
Tanoak	White			
	Maple, Black			
	Mengkulang			
	Meranti, Red[b]			
	Mersawa			
	Pine			
	Pond			
	Red			
	Virginia			
	Western White			
	Spruce			
	Black			
	Red			
	Sitka			
	Sweetgum			
	Tamarack			
	Yellow-Poplar			

(Courtesy American Plywood Association).

- Hardboard core with 3-ply construction.
- Special cores with 3-ply construction. Special cores are those made of any other material than those listed above.

Veneer Thicknesses. The thickness of the veneers varies with the intended use. These are specified in the standard. They range from ½ inch to ⅛ inch. Face veneers on decorative plywood are usually ⅛ inch.

Panel Sizes. Hardwood plywood is made in panels 48 x 84 inches, 48 x 96 inches, and 48 x 120 inches. The 48-x-96-inch is the most popular size. Other size panels can be had by special order.

Standard thickness for veneer core panels are ¼, ⅜, ½, and ¾ inch. Lumber core and particleboard core panels are ¾ inch thick.

Specifications. Hardwood plywood is manufactured to specifications provided by the Hardwood Plywood Manufacturers Association. The panel specifications are indicated with a grade stamp. It identifies the glue bond, the product standard under which it is manufactured, the type, the species of wood, the mill number and the ve-

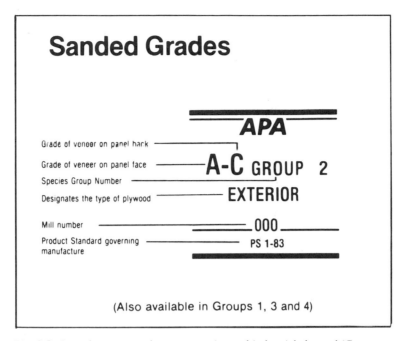

Sanded Grades

Grade of veneer on panel back —————— **APA**

Grade of veneer on panel face —————— **A-C** GROUP 2

Species Group Number ————————

Designates the type of plywood —————— **EXTERIOR**

Mill number ———————————————— 000

Product Standard governing ————————— PS 1-83
manufacture

(Also available in Groups 1, 3 and 4)

Fig. 3-5. A grade stamp used on construction and industrial plywood (Courtesy American Plywood Association).

APA

A-C GROUP 1

EXTERIOR

000

PS 1-83

APA

A-D GROUP 1

EXPOSURE 1

000

PS 1-83

APA A-C

For use where appearance of only side is important in exterior applications such as soffits, fences, structural uses, boxcar and truck linings, farm buildings, tanks, trays, commercial refrigerators, etc. EXPOSURE DURABILITY CLASSIFICATION: Exterior. COMMON THICKNESSES: 1/4, 11/32, 3/8, 15/32, 1/2, 19/32, 5/8, 23/32, 3/4.

APA A-D

For use where appearance of only one side is important in interior applications, such as paneling, built-ins, shelving, partitions, flow racks, etc. EXPOSURE DURABILITY CLASSIFICATIONS: Interior, Exposure 1. COMMON THICKNESSES: 1/4, 11/32, 3/8, 15/32, 1/2, 19/32, 5/8, 23/32, 3/4.

Fig. 3-6. Typical grade stamps for sanded softwood plywood panels.

Table 3-8. Hardwood Veneer Grades.

GRADE	SYMBOL
A Grade	A
B Grade	B
Sound Grade	2
Industrial Grade	3
Backing Grade	4
Specialty Grade	SP

Table 3-10. Types of Hardwood Plywood.

Technical—Exterior—Waterproof
Type 1—Exterior—Waterproof
Type 2—Interior—Water resistant
Type 3—Interior—Moisture resistant

neer grade of the face (Fig. 3-7). The backstamp used on prefinished hardwood plywood wall panels is shown in Fig. 3-8. It indicates the flame spread rating (the lower the number the slower the flame spread) as well as formaldehyde emission requirements. A similar backstamp is used on prefinished particleboard panels.

Industrial panels used by furniture manufacturers are shipped in large bundles. Rather than stamp each panel, a bundle grade stamp is used (Fig. 3-9). These panels are usually cut up into smaller sizes as required for furniture and cabinet construction.

Hardwood plywood used in kitchen cabinets for mobile homes and conventional houses must meet flame spread ratings set by ASTM E162. All exposed parts of the cabinets must have a flame spread rating of 200 or less (Fig. 3-10). Manufacturers are also meeting the HUD requirements for formaldehyde emissions in cabinets as well as wall panels.

Buying Hardwood Plywood. When buying hardwood plywood you must specify the following:

Table 3-9. Wood Species Used for Hardwood Plywood.

CATEGORY A	CATEGORY B	CATEGORY C	CATEGORY D
Ash, white	Ash, black	Alder, red	Aspen
Apitong	Avodire	Basswood, American	Cedar, Eastern red
Beech, American	Birch, paper	Butternut	Cedar, Western red
Birch, yellow, sweet	Cherry, black	Cativo	Fuma
Bubinga	Cypress	Chestnut, American	Willow, black
Hickory	Elm, rock	Cottonwood, black	
Kapur	Fir, Douglas	Cottonwood, Eastern	
Keruing	Fir, white	Elm, American (grey,	
Oak (Oregon, red or	Gum, sweet	red or white)	
white)	Hemlock, Western	Gum, black	
Paldao	Magnolia, Cucumber	Hackberry	
Pecan	Sweetbay	Hemlock, Eastern	
Rosewood	Maple, sugar (hard)	Lauan	
Sapele	Mahogany, African	Maple, red (soft)	
	Mahogany, Honduras	Maple, silver (soft)	
	Maple, black (hard)	Meranti, red	
	Pine, Western white	Pine, ponderosa	
	Poplar, yellow	Pine, sugar	
	Spruce, red, Sitka	Pine, Eastern white	
	Sycamore	Prima-vera	
	Tanoak	Redwood	
	Teak	Sassafras	
	Walnut, American	Spruce, black, Engelmann,	
		white	
		Tupelo, water	

(Courtesy Hardwood Plywood Manufacturers Association)

Fig. 3-7. A grade stamp used on hardwood plywood (Courtesy Hardwood Plywood Manufacturers Association).

- The veneer grade
- The face species
- The type
- The construction
- Panel size
- Flame spread rating
- Formaldehyde emission requirements

PARTICLEBOARD

Particleboard is made from wood chips held together with a binder. The binder joins the chips together under heat and pressure. The chips are not broken down into fibers.

Particleboard is made in two types. Type 1 is available in grades H, M and L. Type 2 is available in grades H and M (Table 3-11). The type 1 is manufactured with urea-formaldehyde resins and is used in furniture manufacturing. Type 2 is made with phenolic resins and is water resistant. It is used in construction. The grades H, M and L indicate densities. M (medium density) grades are above 50 pounds per cubic foot. H (high density) grades are 40 to 50 pounds per cubic foot. The third number in the grade indicates the strength classification: The higher the number the stronger the material.

Buying Particleboard

Particleboard is usually sold in 4-x-8-foot sheets. It is available in thicknesses from ⅛ inch to 1⁷⁄₁₆ inches,

with the ½- and ¾-inch thicknesses the most common. It is priced by the square foot.

HARDBOARD

Hardboard is made from fine wood fibers that are pressed together under heat and pressure. They are held together by the lignin that is found in all raw wood.

Hardboard is available in five grades: Standard, Tempered, Service, Service-Tempered, and Industrialite.

Table 3-11. Types of Particleboard.

TYPE 1 UREA FORMALDEHYDE	TYPE 2 PHENOLIC RESIN
GRADES	GRADES
1-H-1	2-H-1
1-H-2	2-H-2
1-H-3	
	2-M-1
1-M-1	2-M-2
1-M-2	2-M-3
1-M-3	
	2-MW*
1-L-1	
	2-MF**

*Made from wafers
**Made from flakes

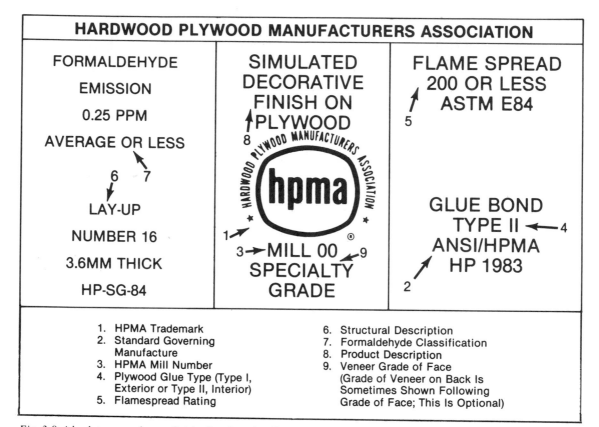

Standard grade is most widely used, often for drawer bottoms and cabinet backs. Tempered grade has chemicals added to increase its hardness, strength, and water resistance. It is used for exterior work in building construction. Service grade is the weakest and least water resistant. It is used for interior work in construction. These are available smooth one side (SIS) or smooth both sides (S2S).

Buying Hardboard

Hardboard is sold in 4-x-8-foot sheets, in thicknesses of ⅛, ³⁄₁₆, and ¼ inch. For special use it is made in thickness from ¹⁄₁₆ inch to 2 inches and widths from 2 to 5 feet and lengths from 4 to 16 feet. Hardboard is priced by the square foot.

VENEERS

Veneers are very thin layers of wood that have been sliced from logs. Standard veneer thickness is ¹⁄₂₈ inch, but furniture manufacturers sometimes use even thinner layers.

Veneers are available in all species of costly woods. They are glued to a core of inexpensive solid wood, plywood, or particleboard, which produces an expensive-looking surface at less cost.

Buying Veneers

Veneers are sold by the square foot and the pieces vary in size. For large jobs it is bought by the flitch. A *flitch*

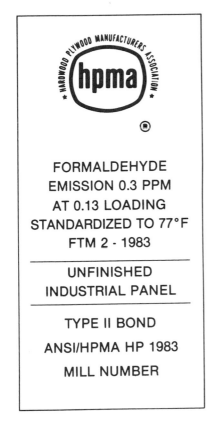

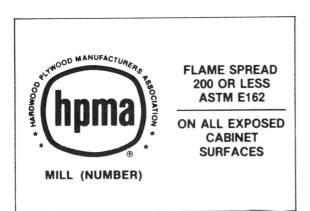

is a bundle of veneer cut from the same tree. The pieces are stacked in the order they were cut from the tree.

Wood Moldings

Wood moldings are available in a wide range of sizes and shapes. They are cut from both hardwoods and softwoods (Fig. 3-11). They are available in lumber yards but can be easily made with a shaper or a router. Moldings are used on furniture and cabinets for decorative purposes, and are sold by the lineal foot.

HIGH-PRESSURE PLASTIC LAMINATES

Plastic laminates are made from five to seven sheets of kraft paper treated with phenolic resin. The top layer of kraft paper has the color and design printed on it, and it is then covered with a translucent topcoat of melamine. Heat and pressure form a sheet. The laminates are available in a wide range of colors and patterns.

The grade of plastic laminates is related to the thickness and type of raw materials utilized. The general-purpose grade is $\frac{1}{16}$ inch thick. It's main use is on counter and furniture tops. It is the most stable and has high impact resistance. Walls and cabinet fronts are laminated with a $\frac{1}{12}$-inch vertical surface grade. For covering tops with rounded edges, a .050 inch postforming grade is used. All of these are bonded to solid wood, plywood, or particleboard.

Buying Plastic Laminates

Plastic laminates are sold by the square foot. They are available in several standard widths and lengths. Widths commonly available include 24, 30, 36, 48, and 60 inches. Some companies make the sheet $\frac{1}{4}$ inch wider so it can be cut into several pieces in even dimensions. For example, a 24-inch piece can be cut into two 12-inch pieces. Standard lengths are 60, 72, 84, 96, 120, and 144 inches.

OVERLAYS AND INLAYS

Overlays and inlays are used to provide surface decoration on furniture tops and doors. The inlay is made from wood veneers cut and assembled into a design, which is then set into a recess in the wood or surrounded by veneer. Overlays are glued on top of the surface. They are three-dimensional and protrude from the surface, and are sold as individual items.

Fig. 3-9. A grade stamp used on bundles of hardwood plywood (Courtesy Hardwood Plywood Manufacturers Association).

Fig. 3-10. Stamp used on kitchen cabinets of hardwood plywood, meeting code specifications for flame spread (Courtesy Hardwood Plywood Manufacturers Association).

Fig. 3-11. A few of the many commercially available wood moldings.

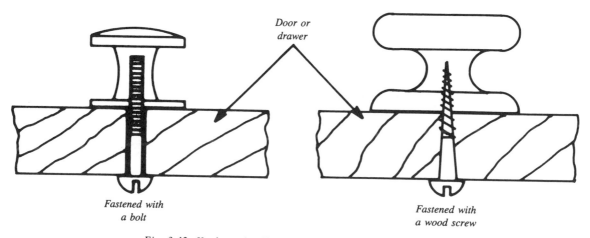

Door or
drawer

Fastened with
a bolt

Fastened with
a wood screw

Fig. 3-12. Knobs and pulls are fastened with bolts or screws.

UPHOLSTERY FABRICS

Upholstery is widely used in furniture manufacture. Chair seats and backs and entire sofas or chairs are covered with fabric. Any number of colors and patterns are avilable. Upholstery material is sold by the square yard.

HARDWARE

Hardware must be carefully chosen. Some types, as handles and pulls, become part of the overall design. They must be of good quality and reflect the design of the furniture.

Knobs and drawer pulls are used on doors and drawers. They are made from wood, metal, porcelain, and plastics, and are held in place with screws or bolts from the back side of the door or drawer (Fig. 3-12). Sliding doors use recessed fingercups and pulls that are inserted in a recess that is cut in the door. The unit is held in the recess with wood screws or a press fit.

Hinges are used to mount doors to cabinets; they permit the door to swing open. Some hinges are surface mounted and are decorative, while others are hidden or semihidden. Three commonly used types of hinges are: surface mounted, butt, and semiconcealed. The surface-mounted hinge (Fig. 3-13) is installed on the door first, then the door is placed on the cabinet. The hinge is screwed to the cabinet frame (Fig. 3-14).

A butt hinge (Fig. 3-15) is usually set in a gain. A *gain* is a recess cut in the door and frame. The hinge fits into this recess (Fig. 3-16).

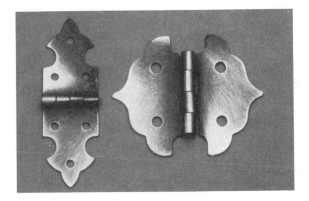

Fig. 3 13. A surface-mounted hinge.

A semiconcealed hinge (Fig. 3-17) is used for plywood doors. The screws in the door enter the face of the plywood, because if they were put into the edge they would break loose (Fig. 3-18). Some semiconcealed hinges have a built-in spring, which makes the hinge self-closing and does not require a catch.

Locks and hasps serve to hold a door or drawer closed. They may be used to secure the door or drawer so it cannot be opened without a key. There are many types available.

Door catches are also available in many types. Roller and magnet types are common. The roller catch is installed with the roller on the door and the catch on the frame (Fig. 3-19). The catch can be adjusted so the roller fits against it properly. The magnet catch has the magnet installed on the cabinet frame. It is the most common catch used on cabinets and furniture. A flat steel plate is screwed to the door and the magnet is adjusted until it touches the metal plate when the door is closed (Fig. 3-20).

The bottoms of legs on chairs, tables, and stools should have furniture glides. A furniture glide is a smooth, rounded metal unit that is nailed to the bottom of the leg (Fig. 3-21). It keeps the wood leg from splitting when it slides on the floor and helps the furniture slide easily along the floor.

A metal ferrule can be used in place of a glide (Fig. 3-22). These fit on the end of round legs and are decorative and are available in a variety of sizes. The leg must be shaped to fit the ferrule, so purchase the ferrules before making the legs.

Some furniture and cabinets have shelves. Generally, it is best to make the shelves adjustable. One way to do this is to use shelf standards (Fig. 3-23). Shelf standards are metal units with evenly spaced slots that are fastened to the sides of the cabinet with screws. They may be surface mounted or recessed into the side. Supports (metal clips) fit into the standards and hold the shelf.

Another type of shelving uses metal standards that screw to the back of a cabinet or on a wall. Shelf brackets fit into the standard and hold the shelf (Fig. 3-24).

Another option is adjustable shelving with plastic or metal shelving clips. To use these, ¼-inch (6 mm) holes must be bored into the side of the cabinet (Fig. 3-25).

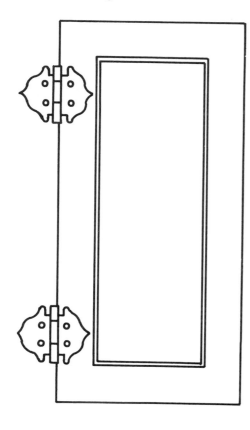

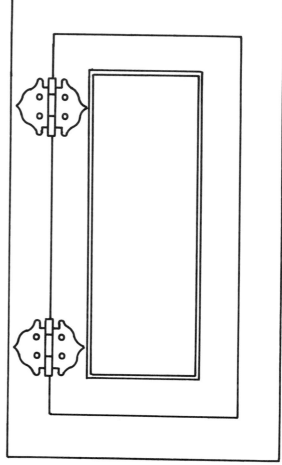

1. *Fasten the hinges*
   to the door

2. *Set door in*
   frame. Screw hinges
   to frame.

Fig. 3-14. How to mount a door with a surface-mounted butt hinge.

Fig. 3-15. A butt hinge.

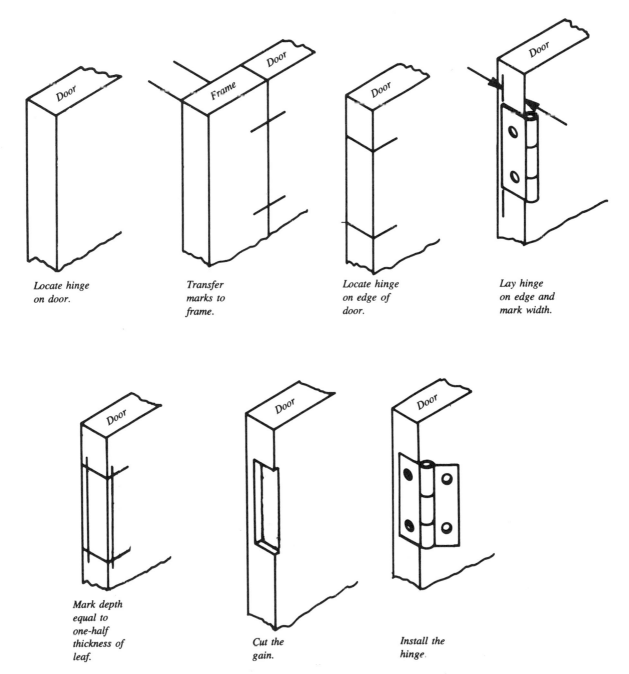

Locate hinge
on door.

Transfer
marks to
frame.

Locate hinge
on edge of
door.

Lay hinge
on edge and
mark width.

Mark depth
equal to
one-half
thickness of
leaf.

Cut the
gain.

Install the
hinge.

Fig. 3-16. The steps to install a butt hinge in a gain on a door.

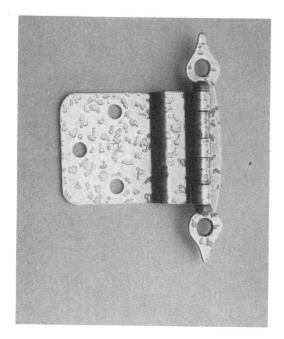

Fig. 3-17. A semiconcealed hinge.

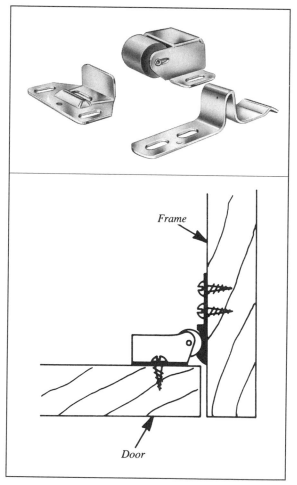

Fig. 3-19. A roller-type door catch is shown on top, installation on bottom (Courtesy Stanley Tools).

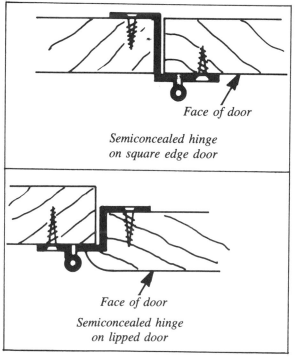

Face of door

*Semiconcealed hinge
on square edge door*

Face of door

*Semiconcealed hinge
on lipped door*

Fig. 3-18. Two types of semiconcealed hinges.

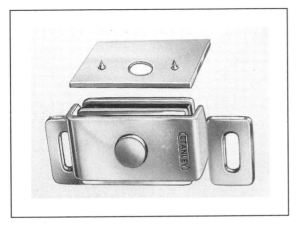

Fig. 3-20. A magnet door catch is shown on top, installation on bottom (Courtesy Stanley Tools).

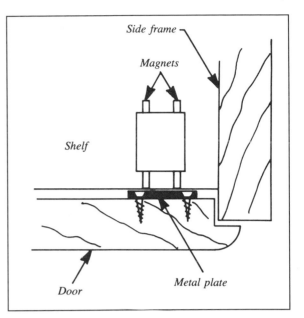

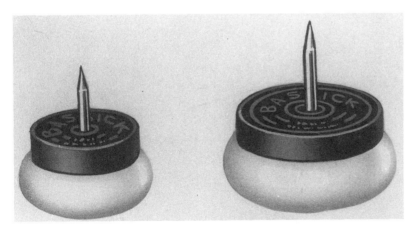

Fig. 3-21. Furniture glides.

Fig. 3-22. A metal ferrule.

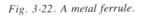

Fig. 3-23. Metal shelf standards are used to provide adjustable shelves (Courtesy Knape and Vogt Manufacturing Co.).

Fig. 3-24. Shelf brackets are mounted on the wall. Standards project out to hold the wood shelf boards (Courtesy Knape and Vogt Manufacturing Co.).

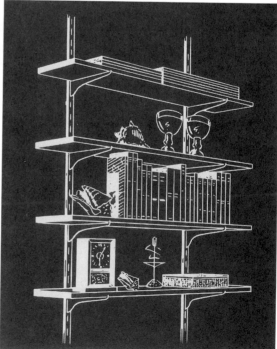

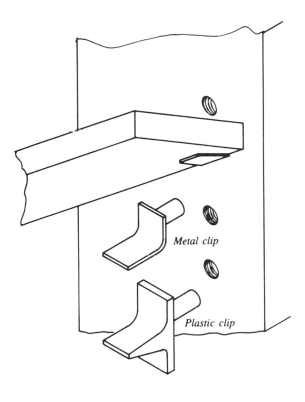

Metal clip

Plastic clip

Fig. 3-25. Bore ¼-inch (6 mm) holes to hold the shelving clips.

Chapter 4

Safety in the Shop

After an accident occurs it is usually easy to see what safety measures you should have taken. A safe worker knows the safe way to use tools and how to work in a shop. Safety is of the utmost importance.

PLANNING YOUR WORK

Before starting to work, secure the necessary tools and materials. Check to see that the tools are in good repair. Then arrange the workplace so it is clean and free of wood scraps and sawdust. Plan your first cuts or other operations. Be aware of possible hazards.

For example, know where your hands will be and where the saw, knife, or other tool will go if it slips. Be certain you and those working around you will be clear if the unexpected occurs. Do not work under crowded conditions.

Safety-conscious workers know the proper way to use the tools. If they do not, they ask for instructions before using them. They think safety. They look for unsafe conditions in the shop. They anticipate accidents that might happen. Personal safety as well as the safety of others is important to them.

Many different activities go on in a shop, each requiring different safety procedures. Learn as much as you can about the safety practices for each area before starting to work.

PERSONAL SAFETY

Never work alone in a shop. You might need help in case of an accident.

Never work in someone's shop without their permission.

Always wear approved eye protection. For general shopwork, wear safety glasses. Use goggles or face shields for more dangerous work, such as grinding or turning on a lathe (Fig. 4-1).

Remove loose clothing. This means rolling up sleeves, and removing scarfs and all jewelry. Wear a shop coat or apron to contain clothing. Loose clothing easily gets caught in machinery.

If you have long hair, wear a hair net or tie it up behind your head. Long hair is also easily caught in moving machinery.

Wear a respirator when sanding or performing other dust-producing operations. Also use a respirator when spraying finishes (Fig. 4-2).

Wear shoes with closed toes. Sandles or thongs are not allowed. In industrial shops, steel-toed shoes are often required.

If you are working in an area with loud noise, wear ear protection.

To lift a heavy object, bend your knees but keep your back straight. Lift with your legs, not your back. If it is too heavy get someone to help you. Also, do not try to move long boards or sheets of plywood by yourself. Keep the boards horizontal. If you carry them vertically, you might hit a ceiling light.

If you see a dangerous situation, do what you can to call it to the attention of those involved. It is much better to prevent an accident than to have to take emergency action after one occurs.

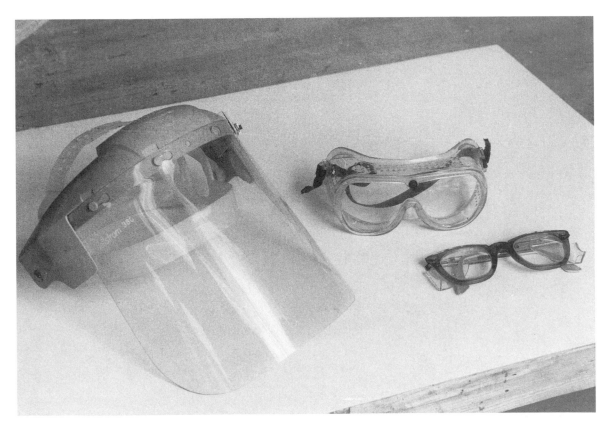

Fig. 4-1. Goggles, safety glasses, and face shields provide eye protection.

HOUSEKEEPING

Keep all machines free of dust and wood scraps that could get in the way when operating the machine.

Keep the floor swept clean. Sawdust on floors is very slippery.

Keep all tools and machines in good operating condition.

A safety-conscious worker watches for ways to help others. Safety requires cooperation.

HAND TOOL SAFETY

Do not use a tool until you know how to use it. Use the correct tool for each job. For example, do not open paint cans with a wood chisel. It will break the chisel and possibly cause an injury. A chisel is designed to cut wood, not to pry.

Carry tools carefully. Keep the cutting edges down so you do not hit someone. Do not place them in your pockets. When finished with a tool, return it to its storage place.

Keep tools sharp. Dull tools require extra pressure to cut and they could slip. (See Chapter 11 for information on sharpening tools.)

Clamp the stock to the workbench. Use either a bench vise, C-clamps, or hand screws. Do not try to hold it steady with your hand (Fig. 4-3).

Do not force a tool if it does not cut easily. Set it to take a lighter cut and check to see if the tool is dull. If it is dull, sharpen it before you continue to use it.

Push edge tools (chisels, knives) away from you and keep both hands behind the cutting edge (Fig. 4-4). This way you will never cut yourself.

Before starting to work, be certain your feet are solidly on the floor. Stand so you can keep your balance.

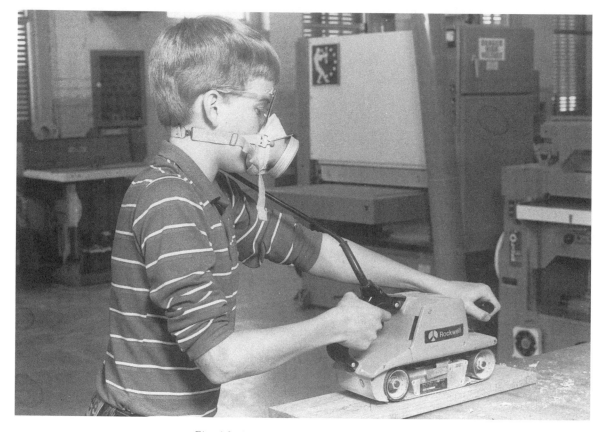

Fig. 4-2. A respirator filters dust from the air.

Pay close attention to your work. Do not try to work and talk with those about you. Accidents are caused by lack of attention.

ACCIDENTS AND FIRST AID

Any accident that leads to an injury, even a slight cut, should be treated immediately to prevent infection. Accidents causing considerable bleeding will require immediate treatment. Know the telephone number of the local ambulance or paramedics.

Do not try to remove something from a person's eye. Seek professional help.

FIRE SAFETY

Know the telephone number of the fire department. Keep oily rags in a fire-resistant metal container.

Learn to use the fire extinguishers and what types of fires they can extinguish. Type A is used on combustible materials, such as wood and paper. Type B is used on volatile finishing materials. Type C is used on fires in electrical equipment. Extinguishers marked ABC can be used on all three types of fires.

FINISHING SAFETY

There must be no flames or sparks in the finishing area.

Store all finishes in approved containers and place them in fireproof safety cabinets.

Clean up any spilled material immediately and place the rag in a flameproof metal container. Keep covers on all materials not being used at the moment.

Fig. 4-3. Before working on stock, clamp it to the workbench.

Apply finishes in a well-ventilated area.

Do not pour waste material down the sink.

Portable Power Tools

Follow the safety rules when using any portable power tools. Because they are small, it is easy to believe portable tools do not have much power. Quite the opposite is true. They must be treated with the same respect as the larger stationary power machines.

Operator Protection

Always wear eye protection, because chips and other objects can be thrown by the cutter (Fig. 4-5).

Some woodworkers are allergic to dust. If you are, wear a proper respirator or filtered mask. The mask will remove the harmful dust and allow you to breath clean air.

Position of Hands and Guards

All portable power tools have handles for controlling the machine (Fig. 4-6). You must keep your hands on these handles whenever the power is on. If the tool should jump or slip, your hands will not be in the path of the cutter. Be careful that your hands do not block the motor vents; this will cause the motor to overheat and shorten the life of the tool.

Once the power is turned on, never place your hands under the tool or board. There is always a danger of the cutter running out of control. If the waste part of the board must be supported with your hands, the cutter must not come any closer than 6 inches (152 mm) to your hand.

For those portable power tools that have guards, be certain that they are operating properly. If the guards are spring-loaded, they must snap back to cover the cutter (Fig. 4-7).

PORTABLE POWER TOOL SAFETY

☐ Wear eye protection at all times.
☐ Keep clothing and hair away from the tool and cutter. Long hair should be confined by a hair net.
☐ Know the safety rules for each machine before plugging in the power cord.
☐ Inspect the tool, power cord, and cutter to be certain they are in proper working order.
☐ Never operate a tool with a dull or broken cutter.
☐ Always clamp the material to a bench or sawhorses before starting the cut.
☐ Never operate tools near water or flammable gases or vapors.
☐ If a tool is not running correctly, shut it off and do not use until the problem is found.
☐ Never make adjustments if the cutter is turning.
☐ Do not talk to anyone who is operating a tool.
☐ Never place your hands under the tool or board.
☐ Allow the cutter to gain full speed before starting the cut.
☐ Do for force the tool; take light cuts.
☐ Arrange the power cord so that it does not interfere with the cut.
☐ Keep your hands on the handles of the tool.
☐ Turn off the power and wait until the cutter stops moving before removing the tool or board.

Positioning the Stock

Smaller pieces of material must be secured to a workbench, sawhorse, or some other large object. Never attempt to hold the material in your hands or in your lap while cutting it. For shorter pieces of material, use a bench vise or clamp attached to the workbench (Fig. 4-8). Longer pieces can best be handled by laying them across two sawhorses (Fig. 4-9). If the board tends to move as it is being cut, use a hand clamp to fasten it to the sawhorse. Always arrange the electrical cord so that it will not come close to the power tool.

When securing the material, plan your cuts. If possible, place the stock so the entire cut can be made without the cutter touching the workbench or sawhorse. Where this is not possible, cut within a few inches of the workbench and turn off the power. After the cutter stops moving, reposition the board and continue cutting.

Electrical Cords

Most portable power tools need electricity to do their work. This requires an electric cord. Because there is a danger of shock, be certain the cord is in good condition and that you do not use the tool near water or metal objects. Ideally, plug the cord into a grounded outlet that has sufficient power to run the tool. The amp rating on the power tool plate will indicate the amount of required electricity.

Only use an extension cord when the material cannot be moved next to an outlet. Unless the proper size of extension cord is used, the motor will overheat. As a general rule, the longer the extension cord the larger the gauge or diameter or wire required. Table 4-1 gives recommended sizes.

The plug on the power cord might have a third prong. This prong is designed to be used in a grounded plug (Fig. 4-10). A grounded plug contains a wire which will draw the electricity away from the tool if a short should occur. The exception to this is a double grounded power tool. These tools have a plastic housing that insulates the operator in case of an electrical short. Double grounded power tools only need a two-prong plug. This type of tool will be labeled "Double Grounded" on the identification plate.

Stationary Power Tools

Stationary power tools can make fast, accurate cuts. Because of their speed you must be careful to follow safety rules. An accident can happen so rapidly you might not even know that it has occurred. The cutters turn at a high speed and will cut anything in their path.

Safety Sense

You must learn the safety rules for each machine. These rules should become a natural part of every cut. This is

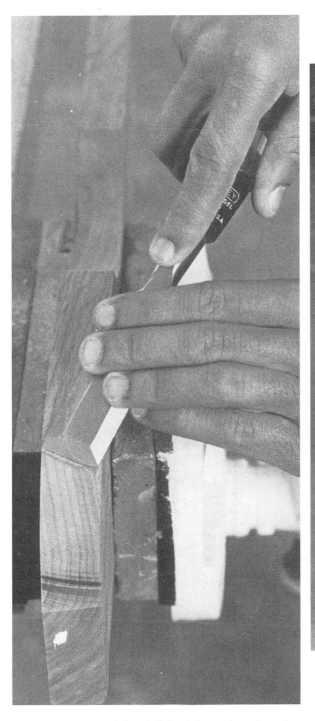

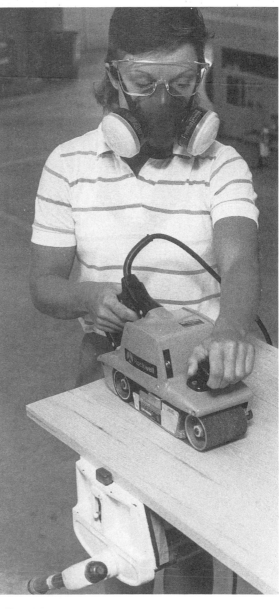

Fig. 4-5. *Wear eye protection at all times. A respirator will filter the dust.*

Fig. 4-4. *Keep both hands behind the cutting edges of sharp tools.*

Fig. 4-6. Use both handles to control the machine.

Fig. 4-7. Be certain the guard is working before plugging in the power cord.

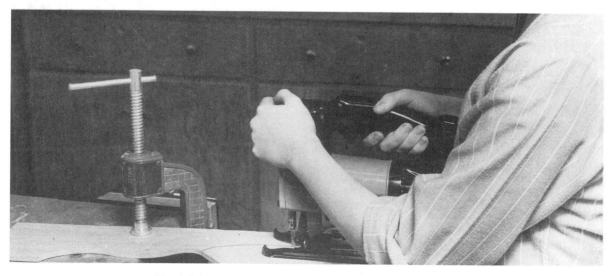

Fig. 4-8. Use a bench vise or clamp to secure smaller pieces.

Fig. 4-9. Use sawhorses to hold long boards.

called developing a safety sense. This safety sense can first be developed by learning how to properly operate the machines. Once you start using the equipment do not experiment. If a question occurs, refer to the machine manual.

Think through each operation before turning on the power. Do not rush your setup or cut. If the procedure is not followed correctly you might not only injure yourself but also bystanders. Do not become overconfident and careless; this will eventually lead to an accident.

Guards and Featherboards

Stationary power tools are designed to be operated with the proper guards. Unless your machine manual gives you permission, never make a cut unless the guard is

Table 4-1. Extension Cord Length Chart.						
AMPERE RATING ON TOOL NAMEPLATE	0 TO 2.0	2.1 TO 3.4	3.5 TO 5.0	5.1 TO 7.0	7.1 TO 12.0	12.1 TO 16.0
EXTENSION CORD LENGTH IN FEET	CORD WIRE SIZES					
25	18	18	18	18	16	16
50	18	18	18	16	14	12
75	18	18	16	14	12	10
100	18	16	14	12	10	8*
150	16	14	12	12	8*	8*
200	16	14	12	10	8*	6*

*Not normally available as flexible extension cord.

STATIONARY POWER TOOL SAFETY

☐ Understand and follow all safety rules for each power tool.
☐ Wear safety glasses, hair net, and other safety gear.
☐ Disconnect or unplug the power before changing or working near the cutter.
☐ Only the operator should be close to the machine.
☐ Use the proper guard and featherboards. Do not use the machine if the guards are missing or not operating properly.
☐ Remove any setup tools before turning on the power.
☐ Keep your hands and body out of the path of the cutter.
☐ Never reach over the top of or behind the cutter.
☐ Do not machine boards with paint or metal fasteners. Beware of cutting into knots, splits, or major defects.
☐ Have someone help with long or wide stock.
☐ Never adjust a machine once the cutter is turning.
☐ If the machine is not running correctly, turn off the power and correct the problem before machining any material.
☐ Give the machine your full attention; never talk to anyone while the power is on.
☐ Allow the cutter to achieve full speed before starting the cut.
☐ Take light cuts when possible.
☐ Keep the area around the machine free of excessive saw dust or scraps.
☐ Do not leave the machine until the cutter has stopped turning.
☐ Do not operate a machine until you have studied the operators manual.
☐ Do not wear gloves when operating power tools.

Fig. 4-10. A three-prong plug requires a grounded outlet.

properly installed (Fig. 4-11). The guard will cover the cutter and help keep the board against the table or fence.

Be careful that the guard does not give you a false sense of security. If the proper procedure is not followed, an accident still can occur. It is important that you keep your hands the recommended distance from the cutter.

Use featherboards (Fig. 4-12) whenever possible. They will cover the cutter and also aid in holding the material. Keep the clamps holding the featherboards out of the way of the operator.

Setting Up the Cut

Follow the step-by-step procedures given in this book for setting up the machine. Before setting it up however, be certain that the machine is designed to perform your type of cut. You can then make all the adjustments before turning on the power. If an additional adjustment is needed, allow the cutter to come to a complete stop.

Operating the Machine

Check that all guards are working and in place before

Fig. 4-11. Properly installed guard on the table saw.

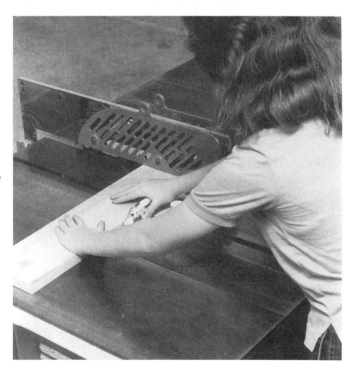

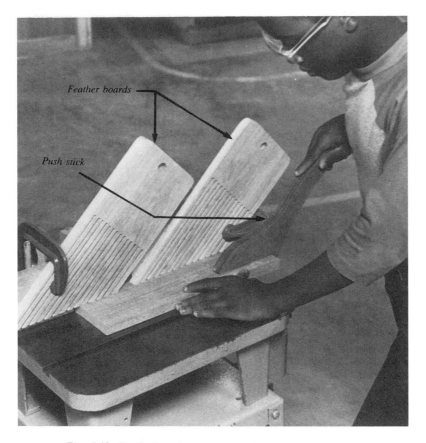

Fig. 4-12. Featherboards act as a guard and hold the material.

turning on the power. Also check that no one else is close to the machine. It might be helpful to have a safety zone marked on the floor surrounding each machine. Keep this area clean and free from sawdust and scraps. Have pushsticks or pusher blocks placed where they can easily be grasped (Fig. 4-13). If these safety devices become worn, throw them away and use a new one.

Once the power is turned on, give the machine your full attention. Don't look away from the cutter or talk to anyone. Stand in a balanced position. Before starting the cut, allow the cutter to gain full speed and then feed the board forward with a smooth steady motion. Stand to one side of the path of the cutter. Keep your hands out of the path of the blade (Fig. 4-14). If the board is thrown backwards you will not be hit.

Push the board completely past the cutter. Never reach over the cutter or press the board down immediately over the top of the cutter. Once you have finished your machine and turned off the cutter, stay with the machine until the cutter has stopped turning.

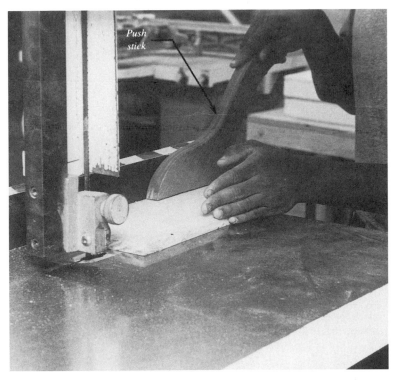

Fig. 4-13. Pushsticks are used to keep hands away from the cutter.

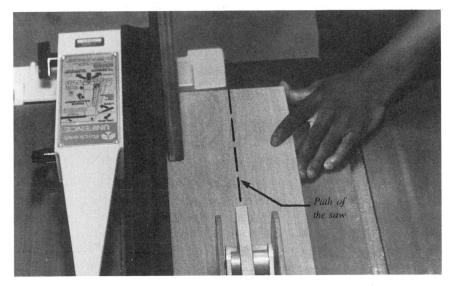

Fig. 4-14. Keep your body and hands out of the path of the blade.

Chapter 5

Design

Many products are manufactured from wood, each serving a special purpose. Principles of design are more important in some products than in others. For example, the color of the wood is more important for a piece of furniture than a window frame because the frame will be painted.

As you look at a product, you react to its size, shape, and color. Do you think it is attractive? As you examine it further, you begin to see other design features. Is it strongly constructed? Will it work as expected? Will it last a long time? Is it easy to use? As you can see, design includes beauty as well as usefulness and quality. The Danish furniture in Fig. 5-1 is a perfect example of beautiful furniture that is both strong and comfortable. This furniture displays the principles of good design.

ELEMENTS OF DESIGN

The design of a product is determined by the lines, geometric shapes, mass, tone, color, and texture and the way these are used.

Lines

Lines are either curved or straight. Regular curved lines are formed by swinging an arc from a point with a fixed radius. Irregular curves are drawn with the points on the curve at varying distances from a point (Fig. 5-2). The basic shape of a product is formed by some combination of these lines.

Shape

Shape is the contour or outline of an object. The basic geometric shapes include the square, circle, triangle, rectangle, hexagon, and octagon (Fig. 5-3), variations of which are used in product design.

Mass

Mass is the three-dimensional form of a product. The basic geometric masses are shown in Fig. 5-4.

Color

Different colors produce different reactions. Green and blue, for example, produce a cool reaction, red and orange, a warm reaction.

Examine the color wheel in Fig. 5-5. Notice the relationships among colors. The primary colors are red, yellow, and blue. Secondary colors are obtained by mixing equal amounts of primary colors and include orange, green, and violet. Intermediate colors are made by mixing a primary color and one of the secondary colors next to it on the wheel. These include yellow-orange, yellow-green, blue-green, blue-violet, red-violet, and red-orange. White is the presence of all colors. Black is the absence of all colors.

Tone

Tone is the effect produced by the combination of light, shade, and color. It is the light-to-dark gradations of color.

Fig. 5-1. This furniture exhibits all the characteristics of good design (Courtesy Association of Furniture Manufacturers in Denmark).

Texture

Texture is the character of the surface of a material, determined by the structure of the material. Wood has a grain and pores that provide a texture; fabric has threads woven in various ways to provide texture. Texture is the feeling of roughness or smoothness of a surface and greatly influences the design (Fig. 5-6).

EVALUATING A DESIGN

The viewers opinion of a finished piece is influenced by its design. This is a product of proportion, balance, harmony, rhythm, and emphasis.

Proportion

Proportion is the relationship of a part of a product to the whole. In Fig. 5-7, the lower drawers are in proportion to the overall size of the cabinet. The upper drawer is smaller and is in proportion to the total mass and the lower drawers.

Designers have established that the sides of a rectangular shape are in better proportion than those of a square. A rectangle with a shape five by eight units is considered ideal, and is called the *golden rectangle*. A person can enlarge or reduce these basic proportions by drawing lines perpendicular to each side until they meet at the diagonal (Fig. 5-8).

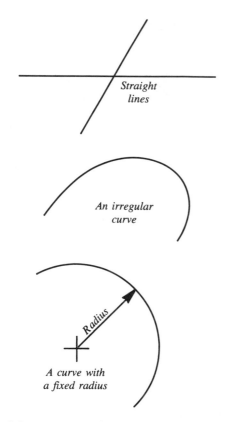

Straight lines

An irregular curve

Radius

A curve with a fixed radius

Fig. 5-2. Various types of lines are used in product design.

Balance

In a well-balanced piece, the elements in the design are at peace with surrounding lines. The piece must appear stable. If a cabinet has a large upper section of shelves and a small lower section, it appears top-heavy. It is out of balance.

There are two kinds of balance: formal and informal. Formal balance occurs when a product, if divided by a vertical centerline, is the same on both sides (Fig. 5-9). Informal balance occurs when the elements around the center are not equal but appear to be equal (Fig. 5-10). The various elements appear balanced, although they are not symmetrical.

Harmony

Harmony is a pleasing blending of elements such as color, size, and shape. If a wood product is made with many different woods of widely ranging colors, it is not in harmony if they do not blend together in a pleasing manner.

Rhythm

Rhythm is flow or movement produced by recurring design elements. It may be a small pattern, a decorative carving with a repetitive design, or repetitive use of a color.

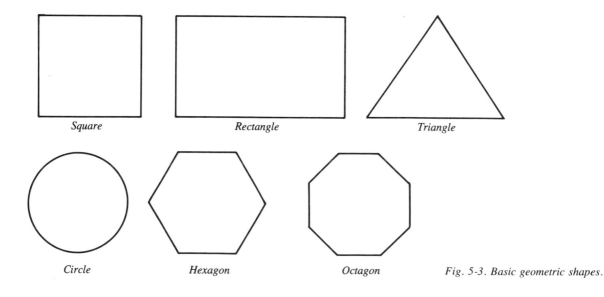

Square

Rectangle

Triangle

Circle

Hexagon

Octagon

Fig. 5-3. Basic geometric shapes.

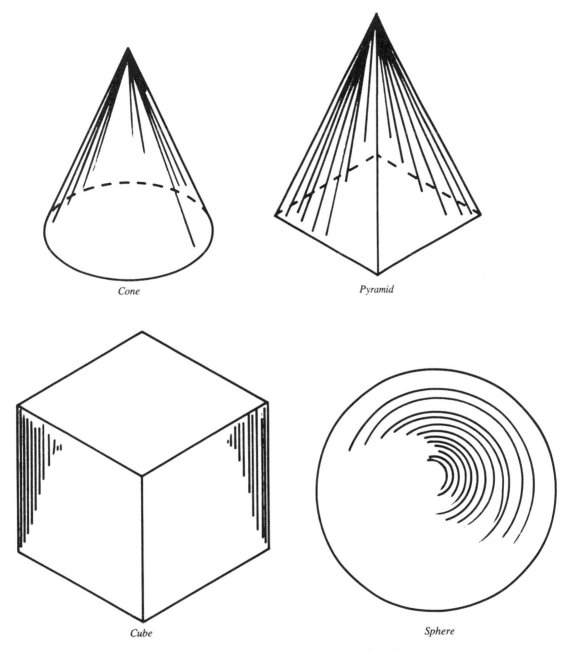

Fig. 5-4. Mass is the three-dimensional form of a product.

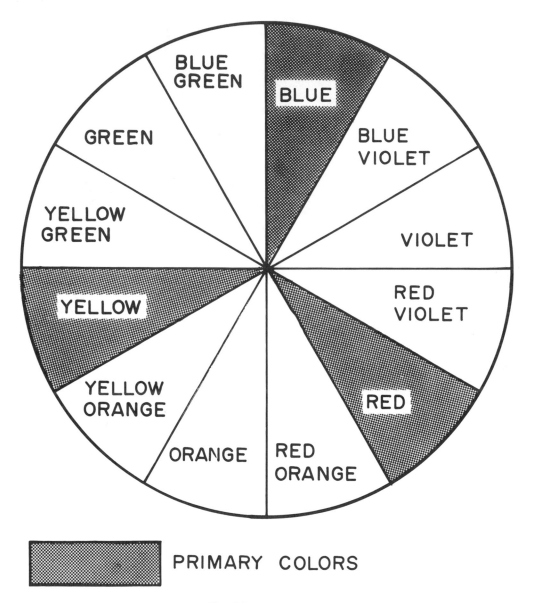

Fig. 5-5. A color wheel.

Emphasis

Emphasis refers to the point upon which attention is focused. On a television set the screen is the point of emphasis. On a china cabinet the glass doors tend to be the focal point.

DESIGNING A PROJECT

The first thing you must do is decide what to make. Do you want to build something for yourself, for your house, or as a gift for someone? Get ideas from a crafts or department store catalog. In many cases you'll have a

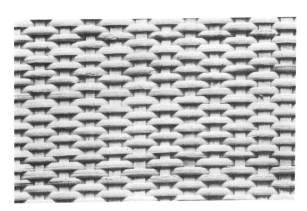

Fig. 5-6. *This caned chair seat has considerable texture (Courtesy The Woodworkers' Store).*

design problem to solve: For example, you have a dark corner in the den you'd like to brighten.

Next, study the problem and propose solutions. For example, you could solve the problem of providing general illumination in a den with a table lamp, wall lamp, floor lamp, or hanging lamp. Study the advantages and disadvantages of each, then select the best solution.

After choosing the best solution, note the specifications, the features of the product that has been chosen. These specifications might be changed as new ideas arise.

Fig. 5-7. *The parts of this low boy are in proportion (Courtesy Ethan Allen).*

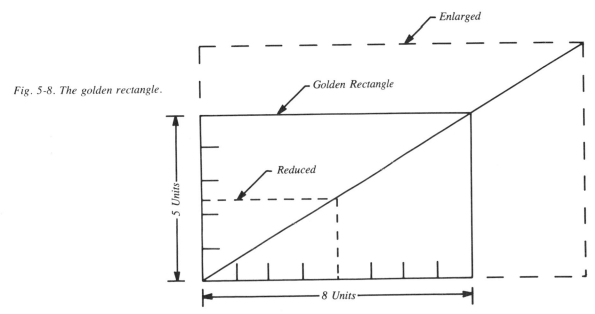

Fig. 5-8. *The golden rectangle.*

Enlarged

Golden Rectangle

Reduced

5 Units

8 Units

Fig. 5-9. This clock has formal balance (Courtesy Mark Kirkner and Stanley Tools).

Prepare the Design

In this instance, begin by examining table lamps in stores and catalogs for some ideas. Then make freehand sketches of several possible solutions (Fig. 5-11). Study each carefully. Alter or combine designs to improve appearance and function, always keeping in mind the principles of design. Get the opinions of others. Finally, choose one design.

It helps to use graph paper for sketches. The printed lines give guides for sketching straight lines. Change the sketches as often as needed. Keep the parts of the project in proportion by counting squares. For example, each square could equal 1 inch. This will help you set sizes and the relationships among parts.

PREPARING THE FINAL PLAN

After the design sketch is accepted, make the production plans. These include working drawings, a bill of material, and a plan of procedure. Production plans will help prevent mistakes. You save time and material if you have figured out beforehand how to do the job.

Working Drawings

The working drawings are based on the final design sketch. They show the size and shape of each part and the final assembled project. They have dimensions that give the location and size of every detail.

Working drawings show the project from several views—usually front, side, and top views are necessary. The back, bottom, and other side views can be drawn if they show some special detail. The steps to lay out a multiview drawing are illustrated with the spice rack in Fig. 5-12. The front view is the largest and most important view. The top and side views project off the front view.

Several types of lines are used on working drawings:

- Thick solid lines denote visible edges.
- Thin dashed lines denote hidden lines.
- Thin lines made of a long and short dashes denote center lines and locate the center of round features.
- Thin solid lines denote extension lines.
- Dimension lines are thin lines that carry the dimension. They run between extension lines and have an arrow on each end.
- Leaders are thin lines that connect notes to the feature to which they refer.

Fig. 5-10. This furniture unit with the mirror, vases, and other items exhibits the characteristics of informal balance.

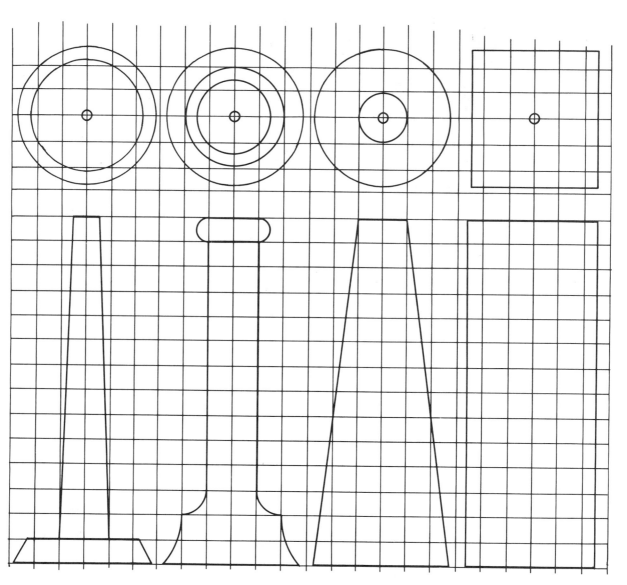

Fig. 5-11. Sketch proposed design solutions.

Working drawings are made to scale. They are drawn letting a fraction of an inch or a millimeter represent a larger or smaller number. For example, the scale ¼″ = 1″ will make a drawing one-fourth the actual size. The scale 1:2 (1 mm represents 2 mm) will make a drawing half the actual size. You must list the actual size of the dimension on the drawing, even when you are drawing to a smaller scale. If a project is very small, use a scale that enlarges it. For example 1″ could represent ¼ inch on the project. The drawing would be four times larger than true size.

In industry, full-size drawings are often used and they are therefore very large. The advantage is that they show the true size relationship among parts.

Dimensioning

When dimensioning a drawing, try to letter all the dimensions and notes off of the view. Record dimensions accurately because they give the finished size. Even if the drawing is a little out of scale, the project will be made correctly if the dimensions are correct. A project

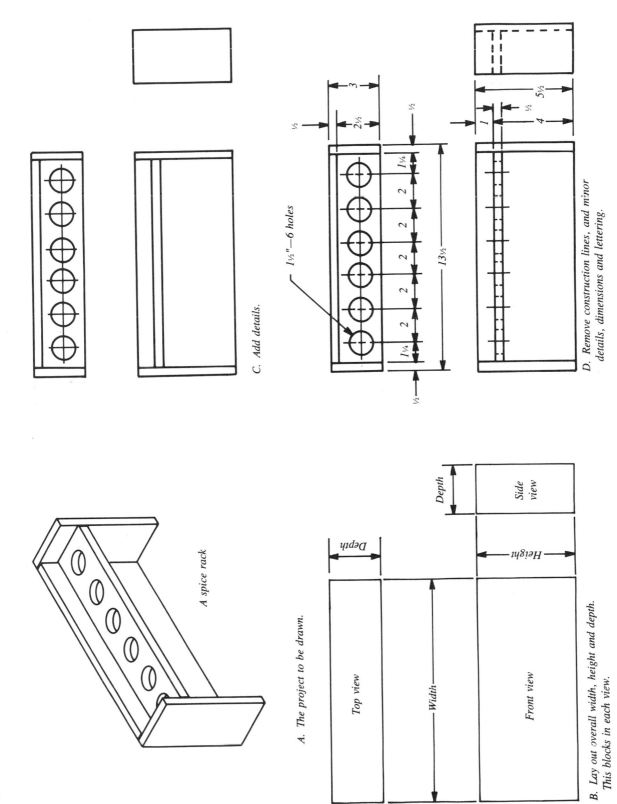

A spice rack

C. Add details.

$1\frac{1}{2}"$ — 6 holes

D. Remove construction lines, and minor
details, dimensions and lettering.

A. The project to be drawn.

B. Lay out overall width, height and depth.
This blocks in each view.

Top view

Side view

Front view

Width

Height

Depth

Depth

Fig. 5-12. The revised design of the final solution.

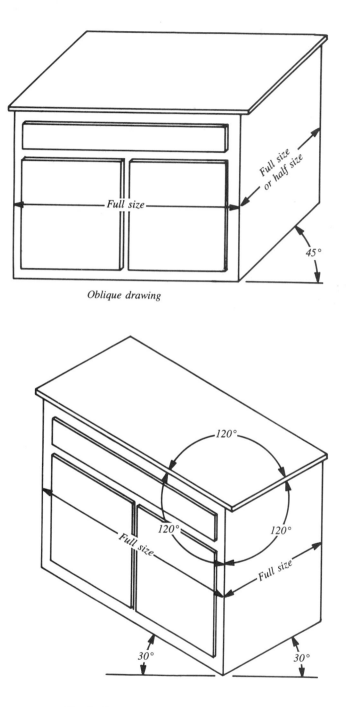

Oblique drawing

Fig. 5-13. Two types of pictorial drawings.

should be in all inches or all millimeters, do not mix these scales on a single project. (See Chapter 8.)

Pictorial Drawings

Industry uses pictorial drawings when designing products. These drawings show the product in a lifelike manner. Two of the pictorial drawings used are isometric and oblique (Fig. 5-13). An oblique drawing has the front view drawn in a normal way, and the side and top views are drawn on a 45-degree angle. The front view is drawn to scale the normal size. The top and side views are drawn either normal size or half size.

An isometric drawing is more lifelike. It is built around an isometric axis. The angle between the axes is 120 degrees. The front, top, and size views are drawn using the axes for sides. Measurements are made along the inclined axes.

Models

A *model* is a small copy of the planned project (Fig. 5-14). It is made to scale using the sketches or working drawings as a guide. Models can help you see how the finished project will look, and changes in design can be made easily on models. Simple projects usually do not require a model, but if there is any doubt as to how the finished project will look, a model is a good idea. It is especially helpful when checking proportions.

Models can be made from cardboard, wood, clay,

Fig. 5-14. Models can be built to check a proposed design.

plaster, or any other material. They can be rough if used to check proportions only.

Drawing Irregular Designs

Often it is necessary to enlarge or reduce an irregular design. First draw a grid of squares over the design. To enlarge it, draw a grid on a separate paper. These squares should be larger than those drawn over the design. For example, draw a grid with ¼-inch squares on the design. To double its size, draw the second grid with ½-inch squares. Then locate on the large grid points where the design crosses the small grid. Connect the points. A design can be reduced by making the squares on the second grid smaller (Fig. 5-15).

Grids are also useful for drawing irregular designs such as a lamp or table leg. They are usually full size. The design can be cut out and used as a template to check the part.

Bill of Material

After the working drawings are finished, complete a bill of material. A bill of material is a list of all materials (wood, hardware, and finishing materials) needed to complete a project. It includes the following information:

- ■ Number and name of each part
- ■ Finished and rough sizes
- ■ Kind of material
- ■ Amount of material
- ■ Cost of each part

Not all bills are this detailed, but the more information available, the less likely a mistake will occur. Also, the cost will be more accurate. The information for completing the bill of material is found on the working drawings. The bill is useful when you go to buy the material.

Waste Allowance

The finished size is shown on the working drawings. It is also listed on the bill of material. When cutting the rough stock, allow 1 inch (25 mm) extra on the length. Allow ½ to 1 inch (12 to 25 mm) extra on the width. If the stock has not been surfaced, it should be ⅛ to 3/16 inch (4 to 5 mm) thicker than the finished part. If it is surfaced, it should be the same thickness or slightly thicker than the finished part.

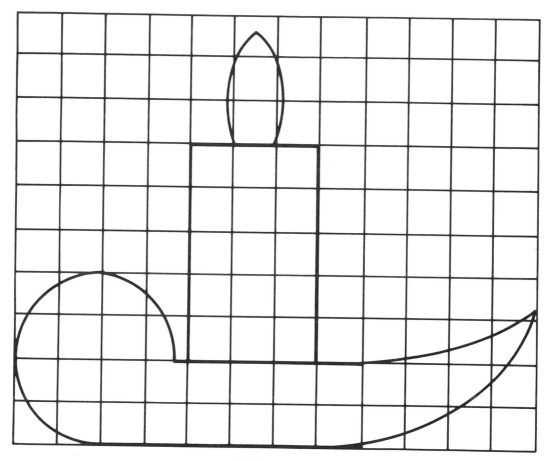

Full size

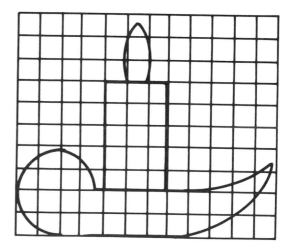

Fig. 5-15. A grid can be used to enlarge or reduce a pattern.   *Half size*

Figuring Lumber Quantities

Lumber is sold by the board foot. Plywood, particleboard and hardboard are sold by the square foot. Moldings are sold by the lineal foot. (Review Chapter 3.)

A board foot equals a piece 1 inch thick, 12 inches wide, and 12 inches long (Fig. 5-16). It contains 144 cubic inches. When figuring board feet, remember wood under 1 inch thick is counted as 1 inch. Wood over 1 inch thick is counted to the nearest ¼ inch.

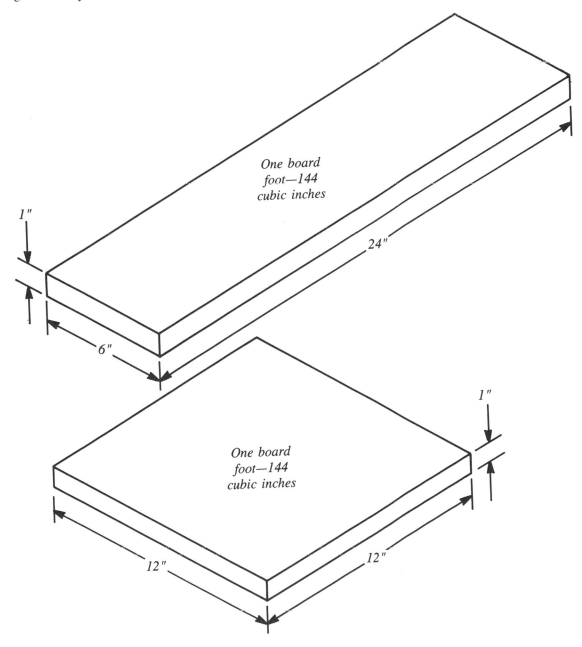

One board foot—144 cubic inches

1"

24"

6"

One board foot—144 cubic inches

1"

12"

12"

Fig. 5-16. A board foot contains 144 square inches of material.

To figure the number of board feet, multiply thickness × length × width (all in inches) and divide by 144.

$$\text{Bd Ft} = \frac{T'' \times W'' \times L''}{144}$$

If the board is long its length will be measured in feet.

Use the following formula:

$$\text{Bd Ft} = \frac{T'' \times W'' \times L' \text{ (in feet)}}{12}$$

Example: How many board feet are in a piece 1 × 9 × 18 inches?

$$\text{Bd Ft} = \frac{1'' \times 9'' \times 18''}{144} = \frac{162}{144} = 1.1 \text{ Bd Ft}$$

How many board feet in a piece 1½ inches × 10 inches × 8 feet?

$$\text{Bd Ft} = \frac{1.5'' \times 10'' \times 8'}{12} = \frac{120}{12} = 10 \text{ Bd Ft}$$

A square foot is a measure of surface area. It is equal to an area of 12 × 12 inches or 144 square inches. Thickness is not considered. The thickness is taken care of in the price per square foot. To figure square feet when the piece is measured in inches, multiply the width by length (in inches) and divide by 144. If the material is measured in feet, multiply width × length (in feet). To figure the cost, multiply the number of square feet by the cost per square foot.

A lineal foot is 12 inches long. Moldings and dowel rods are sold by the lineal foot. The thickness of the wood is not considered. Larger moldings cost more per lineal foot.

Miscellaneous Costs

The cost of screws, nails, and finishing materials are usually figured as a flat fee. This runs from 33 to 50 percent of the cost of the wood. Hardware, such as hinges, are priced by the piece.

PLAN OF PROCEDURE

The plan of procedure is a list of the steps to follow to make the project. These are listed in the order in which they should be performed. The plan also includes a list of the tools needed.

If you have limited experience in a shop, you will need help to write the plan. As you learn about tool processes, you will be able to plan with little help.

The plan of procedure is really a set of directions. It keeps you on an orderly course, which saves time and reduces mistakes. It also keeps you from forgetting something.

To plan a procedure, think through the job. What should be done first? Write it down. Go through the entire project step by step. Often you will have to go back and put steps between some already planned. Keep the steps rather general. A sample follows.

Plan of Procedure
SPICE RACK

Tools Required: Crosscut and rip saws, jack plane, try square, awl, twist drill, hand drill, screwdriver, expansion bit, brace.

Steps of Procedure:
1. Cut out stock to rough sizes.
2. Cut and plane sides to finished size.
3. Cut and plane back to finished size.
4. Cut and plane shelf to finished size.
5. Locate and bore holes in shelf.
6. Locate and bore holes for wood screws.
7. Sand each part.
8. Assemble parts with screws and glue.
9. Resand surfaces.
10. Apply finish.

Chapter 6

Measurement and Layout

The woodworker is constantly making measurements. Sizes are decided upon as the project is planned, and these are the measurements recorded on the working drawings. When the rough stock is cut, measurements must be correct, and when the stock is worked to finished size measurements must be very accurate. If they are not, the project might not fit together

MEASURING SYSTEMS

The two measuring systems used in the United States are the customary and the metric. The customary system has been in use for many years. The United States is one of the few countries in the world using this system. Most of the rest of the world uses the metric system. It is known as SI (The International System of Units).

The United States is slowly converting to the metric system, some industries, such as aerospace and automotive, have already changed. It is a simpler system and helps in the manufacturing of their products. The wood manufacturing and construction industries still use the customary system. Because many products other than wood are sold by metric measure, woodworkers should be able to use both systems.

The Customary System

In the woodworking shop the customary system is used to measure length, area, weight, and volume. Length is measured in feet and inches. Some materials are sold in yards. The foot is divided in common or decimal fractions. Both divisions are used by companies manufacturing wood products. If common fractions are used, the inch is divided in parts as $1/16$, $1/8$, $1/4$, and $1/2$. If decimal fractions are used the inch is divided into tenths and hundredths, 0.1 and 0.01. The decimal fraction is more accurate (Fig. 6-1). Linear measurements are made with bench rules, steel tapes, try squares, and folding rules. Area is measured in square inches, square feet, or square yards. A square inch is 1 inch on each side.

Materials are sold in ounces and pounds. Nails and some finishing materials are sold by the pound; these are weighed on a scale.

Materials in a liquid form are sold by volume. The units of volume are fluid ounces, pints, quarts, and gallons.

The Metric System

The metric system is also used to measure length, area, weight, and volume. The base unit of length is the meter, which is slightly longer than a yard. The meter is divided into decimeters, centimeters, and millimeters (Fig. 6-2). A decimeter is $1/10$ meter. A centimeter is $1/100$ meter. A millimeter is $1/1000$ meter. A dime is about 1 millimeter thick.

Area is measured by the square millimeter, square centimeter, square decimeter, or square meter. A square meter is one meter on each side.

The base unit for measuring volume is the liter. A liter is slightly more than a quart. The base unit for measuring weight (mass) is the gram. A paper clip weighs about one gram (Fig. 6-3).

The prefixes on metric units have special meaning. The prefix *deci* means $1/10$ (.1), *centi* means $1/100$

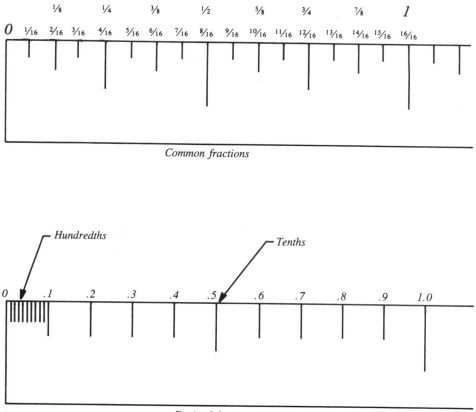

Fig. 6-1. Common fraction and decimal fraction scales.

(.01), and *milli* means ⅟₁₀₀₀ (.001). The prefix *kilo* means 1000. A centimeter is ⅟₁₀₀ meter. A kilogram is 1000 grams. They are used on length, weight, and volume base units (Table 6-1).

Metric measuring tools are available. Many include both customary and metric units on the same tool.

Conversion

When designing a product, use one system from the beginning. Once in a while it is necessary to convert sizes from one system to another. Some conversion factors are shown in Table 6-2. For example, to convert inches to millimeters multiply the inches by 25.4.

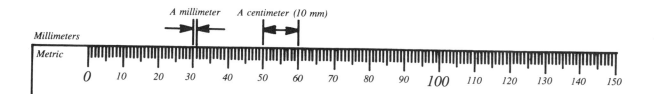

Fig. 6-2. A metric rule divided into millimeters.

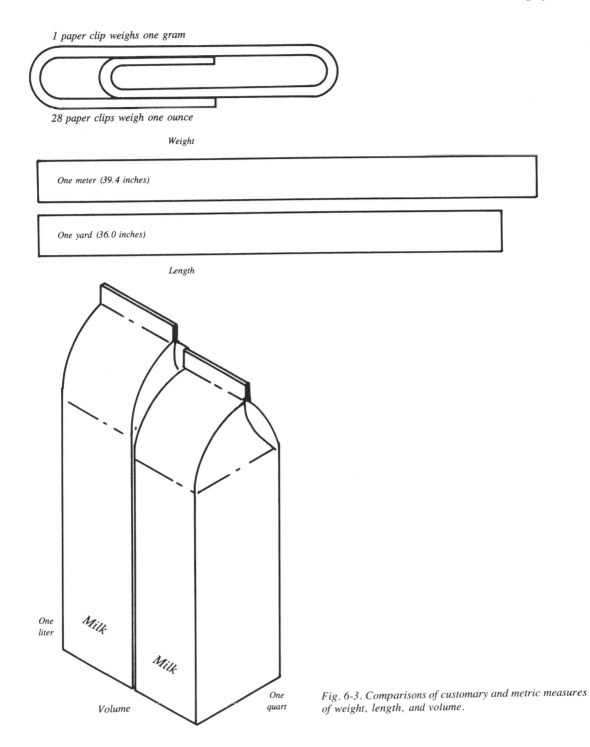

1 paper clip weighs one gram

28 paper clips weigh one ounce

Weight

One meter (39.4 inches)

One yard (36.0 inches)

Length

Milk

Milk

One
liter

One
quart

Volume

Fig. 6-3. Comparisons of customary and metric measures
of weight, length, and volume.

Table 6-1. Decimal Fractions.

UNITS OF LENGTH

Prefix	+ Base Unit	Metric Term	Term Means
Milli (m)	+ meter (m) =	millimeter (mm)	1/1000 of m
Centi (c)	+ meter (m) =	centimeter (cm)	1/100 of m
Kilo (k)	+ meter (m) =	kilometer (km)	1000 m

UNITS OF WEIGHT

Prefix	+ Base Unit =	Metric Term	Term Means
Milli (m)	+ gram (g) =	milligram (mg)	1/1000 of g
Centi (c)	+ gram (g) =	centigram (cg)	1/100 of g
Kilo (k)	+ gram (g) =	kilogram (kg)	1000 g

UNITS OF VOLUME

Prefix	+ Base Unit =	Metric Term	Term Means
Milli (m)	+ liter (l) =	milliliter (ml)	1/1000 of l
Centi (c)	+ liter (l) =	centiliter (cl)	1/100 of l
Kilo (k)	+ liter (l) =	kiloliter (kl)	1000 l

SETTING UP

After the production plan is ready, it is time to get out the stock. Lay out the various parts of the project on boards, plywood, or other materials. Layout is important because it determines the grain, color of wood, strength, and the amount of waste. A good project begins with good stock layout. This involves proper use of layout tools, careful measurements using geometric layout techniques, and proper stock layout techniques.

LAYOUT TOOLS

Many tools can be used for stock layout. Some are used to measure distances, others mark the lines to be cut. Angles of various kinds as well as regular and irregular curves must be drawn. The following layout tools are commonly used in woodworking.

Table 6-2. Conversion Factors.

APPROXIMATE CONVERSIONS FROM CUSTOMARY TO METRIC			APPROXIMATE CONVERSIONS FROM METRIC TO CUSTOMARY		
WHEN YOU HAVE	MULTIPLY BY	TO GET	WHEN YOU HAVE	MULTIPLY BY	TO GET
Length					
inches	25.4	millimeters	meters	39.37	inches
inches	2.5	centimeters	meters	3.28	feet
feet	300	millimeters	centimeters	.393	inches
feet	30	centimeters	millimeters	.039	inches
feet	.3	meters			
Area					
square inches	65	square millimeters	square millimeters	1.6	square inches
square inches	6.5	square centimeters	square centimeters	0.16	square inches
square feet	0.09	square meters	square meters	1.2	square yards
square yards	0.8	square meters			
Weight (mass)					
ounces	28	grams	grams	0.035	ounces
pounds	0.45	kilograms	kilograms	2.2	pounds
Volume					
cubic inches	16	milliliters	milliliters	0.03	fluid ounces
fluid ounces	30	milliliters	milliliters	0.06	cubic ounces
pints	0.47	liters	liters	2.1	pints
quarts	0.95	liters	liters	1.06	quarts
gallons	3.8	liters	liters	0.26	gallons
cubic feet	0.03	cubic meters			
Temperature					
degrees Fahrenheit	subtract 32° then multiply by 5/9	degree celsius	degree celsius	multiply by 9/5 and then add 32	degrees Fahrenheit

Rules

A rule is used to measure the length, width, and thickness of stock. Rules are divided into inches or millimeters. Those in inches are usually divided into sixteenths or tenths of an inch. If using a metric rule, it should be divided into millimeters. Some rules have both inch and metric markings (Fig. 6-4).

Bench rules are available in 1-, 2-, and 3-foot lengths. They are made from wood, and the scale is stamped into the wood. They usually have protective brass ends. To get an accurate measurement, place the rule on the edge then mark the distance. The rule should always parallel the edge being measured (Fig. 6-5).

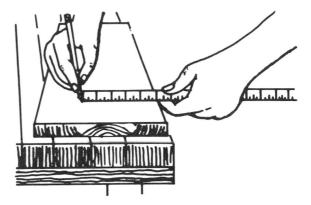

Fig. 6-5. When measuring a distance, stand the rule on edge.

Steel rules are much like the bench rule. They are available in inches divided into sixteens and tenths of an inch. The scale is stamped into the metal. Again, for greatest accuracy place the rule on edge when marking a distance.

The folding rule is available in 4-, 6-, and 8-foot lengths. When folded up, it is about 8 inches long. Unfold it carefully so the hinges do not become bent; this would reduce its accuracy. Some folding rules have an extension rule on the end, which is used to measure inside distances. The length of the extension is added to the length of the rule (Fig. 6-6).

Tape rules have a flexible metal blade upon which the markings are printed. They come in lengths 12 to 50 feet long for woodshop use. The blade is coiled into a case and held there with a spring. The blade has a hook on the end, which is hooked over the edge of the board as the tape is pulled out of the case. It is especially useful for large pieces, such as sheets of plywood. When using a tape rule to take inside measurements, remember to add the length of the case to the total measurement (Fig. 6-7). The tape rule can also be used to measure curved surfaces.

Squares

Squares have an inch or metric scale marked on the blade. They can be used to measure short distances, and are also used to lay out 90-degree angles, check surfaces for levelness, and check ends and edges for squareness. They are very accurate. Squares should be handled carefully so this accuracy is not destroyed (Fig. 6-8).

Try squares have a handle and a blade. The common blade lengths are 6 and 12 inches.

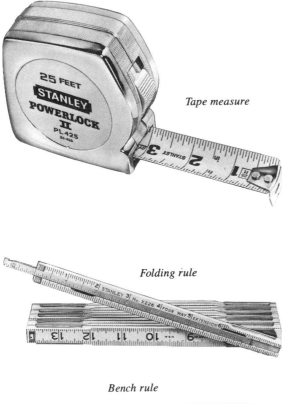

Tape measure

Folding rule

Bench rule

Fig. 6-4. Tools used to measure distances (Courtesy Stanley Tools).

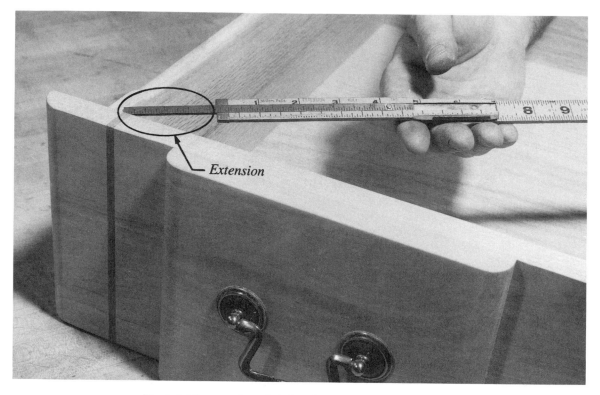

Fig. 6-6. The extension rule helps when measuring inside surfaces.

Steel squares are larger than try squares, and are made from a single piece of steel. The long blade is called the *body*. The short blade is the *tongue*. Inch or metric rule markings are on the tongue and body. These squares are used to measure distances, draw straight lines, and check for squareness. When laying out a square cut, let the tongue slide down over the edge of the board (Fig. 6-9).

A carpenters square is much like the steel square. It has a 24-inch body and a 16-inch tongue. It serves the same purposes as the steel square.

The combination square has a head designed to lay out 90- and 45-degree angles. The head slides along the blade, which permits it to be used to mark boards to width (Fig. 6-10). It is also used to check for levelness and squareness.

A sliding T-bevel is a layout tool with an adjustable blade. The angle desired is set between the blade and handle—usually this is set with a protractor—then the angle is marked on the wood (Fig. 6-11). It is also useful to transfer an angle from one board to another.

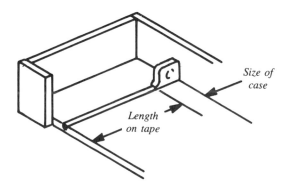

Fig. 6-7. When making inside measurements with a tape rule, remember to add the size of the case to the length shown on the tape.

Marking Tools

After measuring distances carefully, it is time to mark the lines with marking tools. The wood is cut to these lines, and they must be thin and sharp! A thick line will

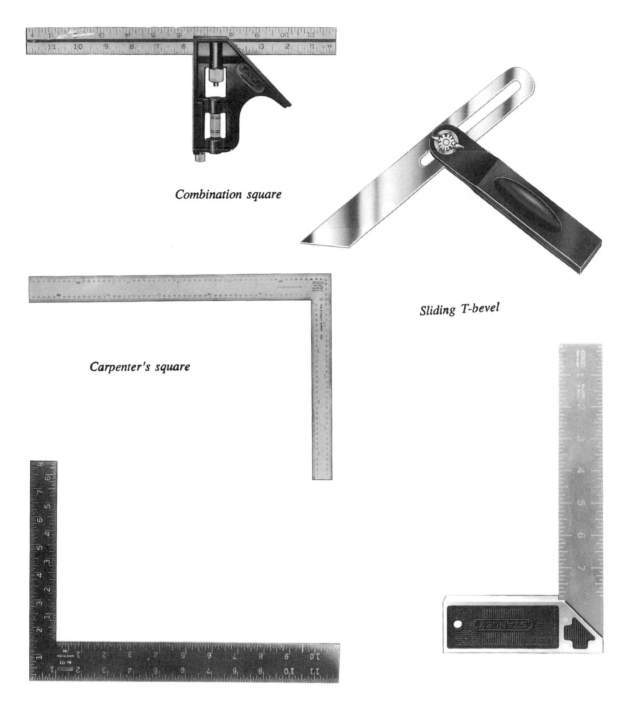

Combination square

Sliding T-bevel

Carpenter's square

Steel square

Try square

Fig. 6-8. There are many types of squares (Courtesy Stanley Tools).

Fig. 6-9. Squaring a line with a framing square.

Mark to width
by sliding square
on the edge with
a pencil at the
end.

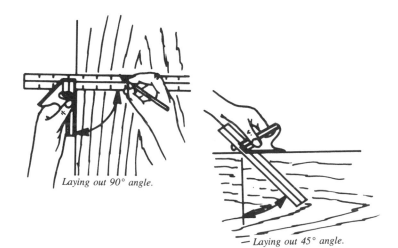

Laying out 90° angle.

— Laying out 45° angle.

Fig. 6-10. Laying out with a combination square.

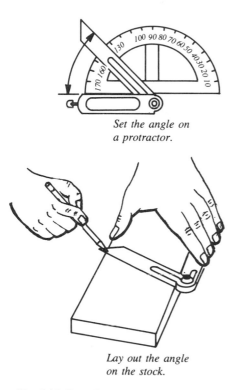

Set the angle on a protractor.

Lay out the angle on the stock.

Fig. 6-11. Transferring an angle to stock.

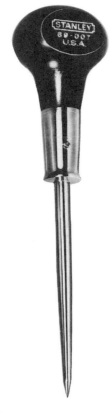

Fig. 6-13. Hole locations are marked with an awl (Courtesy of Stanley Tools).

produce an inaccurate cut. The grain of the wood can cause difficulty in marking; if it is very irregular a crooked line can result. A sharp knife is a good tool in this case.

Pencils are frequently used as layout tools. The point should be sharp, and the lead hard. A soft lead wears down quickly, and the width of the line might vary from one end to the other. One advantage to using a pencil is that it can be erased.

Knives make good marking tools. While any sharp knife will do, a utility knife is especially good (Fig. 6-12). It produces a thin, sharp line, and the handle is easy to hold. Because the blade does not taper in thickness, it slides easily along the straightedge.

Scratch awls are available in several sizes, and are used to mark the center of holes. The punch mark helps the drill start and stay in the center (Fig. 6-13).

A marking gauge is used to mark boards to width. It has a head that slides on a beam. Inches are marked on the beam. At the 0 mark is a sharp metal point. The head

Fig. 6-12. Utility knife (Courtesy Stanley Tools).

is slid away from the point a distance equal to the width desired (Fig. 6-14).

To use a marking gauge, place the head on the edge of the board. Roll it until the pin strikes the board, then push it away from you. The pin will scribe a line on the surface of the wood (Fig. 6-15).

Dividers and compasses are used to lay out circles and for transferring measurements (Figs. 6-16 and 6-17). Dividers have two sharp pointed metal legs. A compass has a pencil lead in one leg. Set the distance between the points to equal the radius by measuring on a rule. Locate the center of the arc. When drawing the arc, lean the dividers or compass in the direction you are turning them (Fig. 6-18).

Trammel points are used to draw large circles. They have two points that clamp to a wood bar. The bar can be any length desired. One point is placed at the center, the other scribes the arc. It might be necessary to have someone help when scribing large circles (Fig. 6-19).

Fig. 6-14. A marking gauge (Courtesy of Stanley Tools).

LAYOUT TECHNIQUES

Following are some layout techniques that will help produce accurate parts. If you have had some drafting experience, you will recognize the procedures.

Dividing into Equal Parts

It is often difficult to divide a board into equal parts: For example, a 6¾-inch board that must be cut to four equal parts. An easy method of laying out the four parts is to

Fig. 6-15. Push the marking gauge away from you.

Fig. 6-16. A compass (Courtesy Stanley Tools).

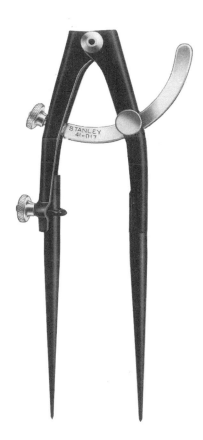

Fig. 6-17. Dividers (Courtesy Stanley Tools).

place a rule across the board on a diagonal. Move it until the scale from one edge to the other can be easily divided into four parts. In this case, 8 inches. Mark each of the four parts (2, 4, 6) on the diagonal. Draw lines through these marks (Fig. 6-20).

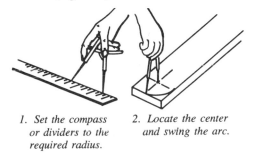

1. *Set the compass or dividers to the required radius.*

2. *Locate the center and swing the arc.*

Fig. 6-18. Arcs can be drawn with a compass.

Laying Out Equal Distances

Often it is necessary to lay out a number of equal distances. The most accurate way is to set dividers on this distance, then step off each distance by walking the dividers down the board (Fig. 6-21).

Laying Out Duplicate Parts

Often a project has several parts of the same size. These should be laid out at the same time. Place the pieces together and clamp in a vise or with handscrews, then mark all of them (Fig. 6-22).

Lay duplicate curved parts out with a template. Draw the part full size on heavy cardboard and cut it out carefully. Then place it on the wood and mark around it. With careful placement, waste can be reduced.

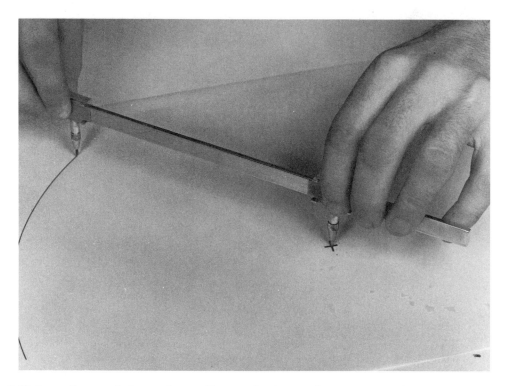

Fig. 6-19. Large diameter circles are drawn with trammel points or a beam compass. A beam compass is used here.

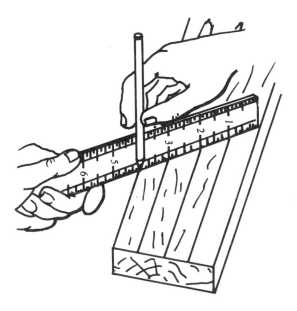

Transferring Designs

Many projects have scrolls and other irregular designs. It is necessary to lay these out on the wood. If the scroll is full size on the working drawing, it can be traced on the wood using a piece of carbon paper below. If it must be used many times, make a full-size template.

If the scroll is drawn to scale, it will have to be enlarged to full size. This process is explained in Chapter 5.

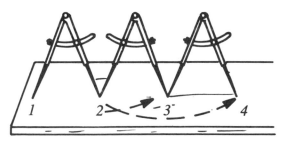

Fig. 6-20. A board can be divided into equal parts with a ruler placed on a diagonal.

Fig. 6-21. Dividers are used to step off equal distances.

Fig. 6-22. Duplicate parts are clamped together and marked at the same time.

Laying Out a Hexagon

A hexagon is a figure with six equal sides. To lay out a hexagon follow these steps (Fig. 6-23):

   1. Draw a circle with a diameter equal to the distance across the corners.

   2. With compass on this radius, step off distances around the circle.

   3. Connect these points with straight lines.

Laying Out an Octagon

An octagon is a figure with eight equal sides. To lay out an octagon, follow these steps (Fig. 6-24):

   1. Draw a circle with a diameter equal to the across the flats distance.

   2. Draw vertical and horizontal lines tangent to the center lines.

   3. Draw lines 45 degrees to the horizontal lines and tangent to the circle. Tangent means they just touch the circle.

Laying Out an Ellipse

An ellipse is shown in Fig. 6-25. It has a major axis and a minor axis. To draw an approximate ellipse:

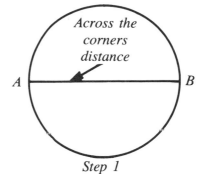

Step 1
Draw a circle with a diameter equal to the across the corners distance of the hexagon.

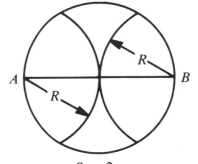

Step 2
Swing arcs from A and B using the radius of the circle.

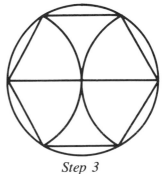

Step 3
Connect the points located on the circle.

Fig. 6-23. Drawing a hexagon when you know the distance across the corners.

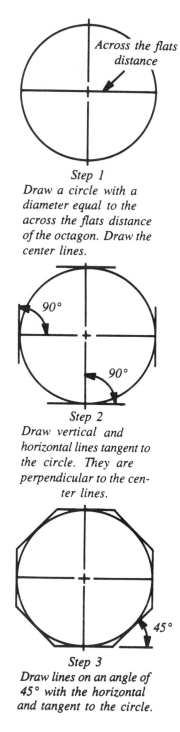

Step 1
Draw a circle with a diameter equal to the across the flats distance of the octagon. Draw the center lines.

Step 2
Draw vertical and horizontal lines tangent to the circle. They are perpendicular to the center lines.

Step 3
Draw lines on an angle of 45° with the horizontal and tangent to the circle.

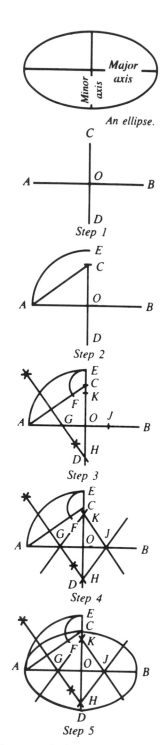

An ellipse.

Step 1

Step 2

Step 3

Step 4

Step 5

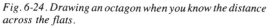

Fig. 6-24. Drawing an octagon when you know the distance across the flats.

Fig. 6-25. The steps to laying out an approximate ellipse.

1. Draw the major and minor axes perpendicular to each other.

2. Draw a line connecting one end of each axis. This is line AC. Set a compass on radius OA. Swing an arc from point O to locate point E.

3. Set the compass on radius CE. Swing an arc from point C to locate point F. Draw a line that bisects AF and is perpendicular to it. This crosses the axes at G and H.

4. Set the compass with a radius equal to HC. From points H and C, swing arcs until they touch lines GH and HJ.

5. Set the compass with a radius equal to AG. From points G and J, swing arcs until they touch lines GH and HJ.

STOCK LAYOUT

Wood products require parts of various sizes. Wood itself varies from board to board. The color, grain, and defects must be considered as parts are laid out.

Defects

It is natural for wood to have defects, such as a split. Most are undesirable and parts should be located to avoid them. Study the size and shape of the parts, and fit them on the board so waste is reduced (Fig. 6-26). In some cases sound knots, worm holes, and even pitch pockets are acceptable because they provide an "antique look." A sound knot has a variety of colors and grains, and can be very attractive when correctly finished. Splits and checks must be cut out because they will get larger with time and damage the project.

Use the best wood for visible parts such as drawer fronts or doors. Hidden parts such as drawer sides and drawer runners can be of poorer quality or cheaper wood.

Grain

The direction of the grain on each piece determines its strength. A board is weak when under pressure with the grain. It is strong when under pressure across the grain (Fig. 6-27). The direction of the grain should run parallel to the long dimension of the part.

Also examine the grain pattern. Use the pieces with the best color and pattern for the more important parts, such as a table top.

Laying Out On Solid Stock

Before laying out parts on solid stock, get an edge straight and square. Work your parts from this edge. Be certain to allow room for the saw kerf. A saw can remove 1/8 to 3/16 inch (3 to 5 mm) with each cut, called the *kerf*. (Fig. 6-28). If in doubt, allow 1/4 inch (6 mm) or more.

Consider warp when laying out parts. A board in crook can only give a long narrow piece. If it is to be cut in short pieces, cut them wider to reduce waste. If a board is cupped, it will have to be cut thin in order to get a flat board. If it is ripped, it will give thicker but narrower pieces (Fig. 6-29).

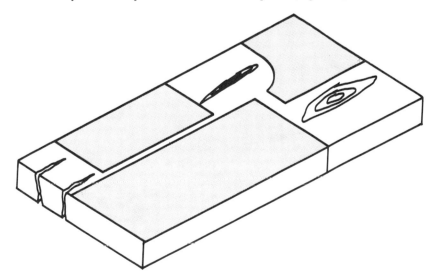

Fig. 6-26. Work around the natural defects in the board.

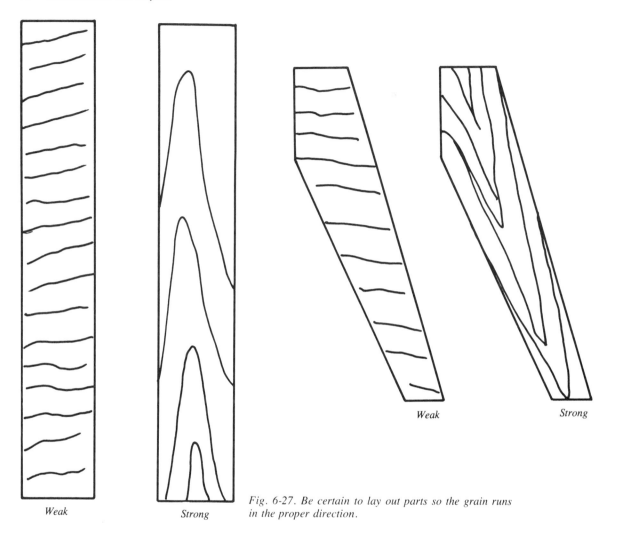

Fig. 6-27. Be certain to lay out parts so the grain runs in the proper direction.

Weak

Strong

Weak

Strong

Laying Out on Sheet Stock

Plywood is strong in both directions. However, it is generally stronger in the direction of the grain. This could influence how you lay out a part on the plywood panel. Also consider the direction you want the grain to run on your project for the sake of appearance, then lay out the parts accordingly. Watch for good color and pretty grain patterns.

Particleboard and hardboard have no grain pattern and can be used in any direction.

When locating parts on a sheet, work from the outer edges. These are usually smooth and square. Place pieces close together, but allow room for the saw cut.

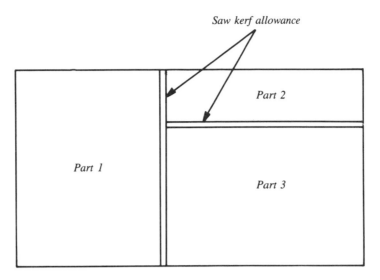

Fig. 6-28. When laying out on stock, remember to allow for saw kerfs.

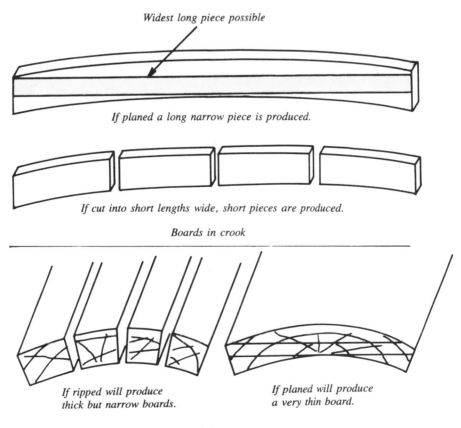

Widest long piece possible

If planed a long narrow piece is produced.

If cut into short lengths wide, short pieces are produced.

Boards in crook

If ripped will produce
thick but narrow boards.

If planed will produce
a very thin board.

Boards in cup

Fig. 6-29. Warped boards can be used for small parts by proper layout and cutting.

Chapter 7

Hand Saws

One of the first steps in building is laying out the parts and saw them to their rough size. Two types of cuts are required—straight and curved—and different saws are used for each. Straight cuts are made with crosscut, rip, dovetail, and backsaws. Curved cuts are made with key-hole, compass, and coping saws.

A saw is basically a blade with teeth and a handle (Fig. 7-1). The shape and size of the teeth vary with the saw. The teeth are sharp, and when they move across the board, they cut the wood fibers.

The number of points per inch on a blade also varies. A fine-cutting saw will have small, fine, teeth and many points per inch. A fast, rough-cutting saw will have larger teeth and fewer points per inch. Saws are specified by the number of points per inch. This is stamped on the heel of some saws. There is one less tooth than points: For example, An eight-point saw has seven teeth.

The teeth on a saw are set, which means they are bent alternately right and left. One tooth is bent left and the next right. This continues the length of the blade. The teeth of the saw are set so that the kerf—the groove the saw cuts—is wider than the blade, which keeps the saw from binding in the kerf.

CROSSCUTTING

A crosscut saw is used to saw across the grain of a board. When cutting a board to length, use a crosscut saw. It can be used to cut with the grain but it cuts slowly. A rigsaw cuts faster with the grain.

The crosscut and ripsaw appear the same, the only difference is the shape of the teeth (Fig. 7-2). The teeth on the crosscut saw are filed to sharp points. When set they form a series of sharp cutting edges. These edges cut the wood fibers. The slanted tooth bottom clears out wood between the two cuts made by the cutting edges.

For general use, a crosscut saw with 8 to 10 points

SAFETY

☐ Be certain your hands and legs are clear of the path of the saw.
☐ Wear safety glasses or goggles.
☐ Work in a clear area where you will not be bumped by others.
☐ Saw blades get hot; do not touch them after sawing.
☐ Do not handle the saw by the teeth; they are very sharp.
☐ Clamp or hold the stock firmly.
☐ Place the stock at a comfortable height so you can saw and keep your balance.

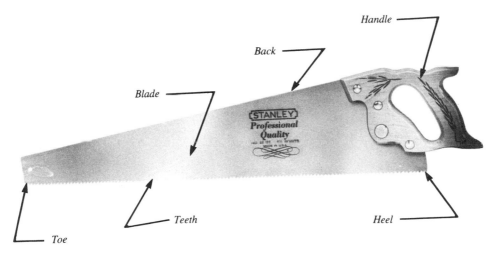

Fig. 7-1. A typical hand saw (Courtesy Stanley Tools).

to the inch is good. A 26- to 28-inch blade is normal. A 20-inch saw called a *panel saw* is available. It is easier to use because of its shorter length.

Using a Crosscut Saw

1. Mark the cuts on the board with a square.
2. If it is a long board, place it on a pair of sawhorses. If it is short, clamp it to a bench or in a vise.
3. If on a sawhorse, place your knee on the board. Be certain the saw will not hit the sawhorse. Hold the board with your left hand if you are right-handed (Fig. 7-3). Place your left thumb on the side of the blade. This serves as a guide when starting the cut.
4. Place the saw on the waste side of the line. When the cut is finished, the line should remain on the good piece (Fig. 7-4).
5. Pull the saw toward you a time or two to start a kerf. Then move it back and forth gently to make the cut. Do not press down on the saw. If it is sharp it will cut under a very light pressure.
6. Keep the saw at a 45-degree angle with the wood.

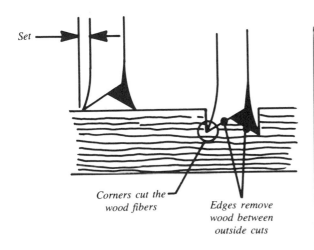

Fig. 7-2. Saw teeth are set to cut a kerf wider than the thickness of the blade. This crosscut saw produces a cutting action like a series of knives.

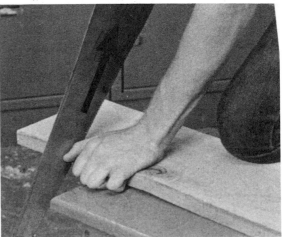

Fig. 7-3. To start the saw, steady the blade with your thumb and pull back on the handle.

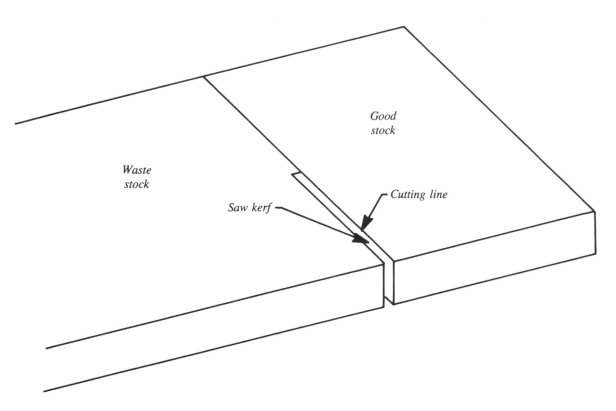

Fig. 7-4. Cut on the waste side of the line.

7. You will learn to keep the cut square by sighting down the blade. You can check for squareness with a try square (Fig. 7-5). Remove the square before starting to cut.

8. Complete the cut by taking long, steady strokes. Keep your arm and shoulder in line with the saw. If the saw moves away from the line, twist the handle a little. This will twist the blade and bring the cut back to the line.

9. As you near the end of a cut, hold the waste piece. It should not fall on the floor. If you just cut it off and let it drop it could split a piece off the bottom of your good board. If the waste piece is large, get someone to hold it.

Cutting Plywood

The crosscut saw should be used to cut plywood. Its fine, sharp teeth make a clean cut and leave a smooth edge. Cut plywood with the face veneer up, so if there is

Fig. 7-5. Use a try square to check the saw for squareness. Stop sawing when you make this check.

any splintering, it will be on the bottom. The angle of the saw can be lowered. Some put masking tape on the surface, then they draw the line on the tape and saw through it. This helps prevent splintering.

RIPPING

A ripsaw is used to cut with the grain of a board. If used to crosscut, the kerf will be rough and ragged.

The teeth on the ripsaw are filed so they are flat on the bottom. The outer edges cut the wood fibers. The flat bottom removes the wood in chips rather than fine sawdust (Fig. 7-6). A ripsaw with 5 ½ points per inch is a common type.

Using a Ripsaw

1. Mark the cut on the board.
2. Place the board on one or more sawhorses. Let one end stick out a foot or so beyond the sawhorse.
3. Hold the board with your knee and hand. Start the cut by pulling the saw back a few times. Keep it perpendicular with your thumb (Fig. 7-7).
4. Make full, even strokes. Hold the saw at 60 degrees to the board. Keep the saw on the waste side of the line. Move it out so you do not cut into the sawhorse. The saw cuts on the down stroke. Do not push down hard on the blade, it will cut as designed under very light pressure.
5. If it is a long board you will need someone to hold the cut part level. Long cuts tend to bind the saw. If this happens, place a small wood wedge in the kerf.

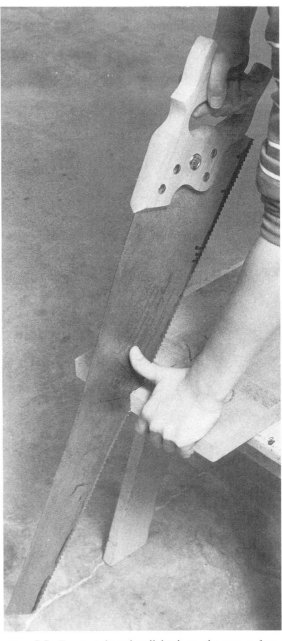

Fig. 7-7. To rip a board pull back on the saw a few times. Keep the saw at 60 degrees to the board.

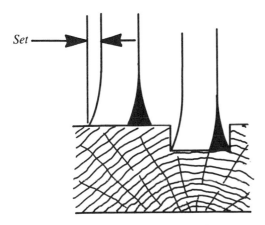

Fig. 7-6. Ripsaw teeth are flat on the bottom.

MAKING FINE CUTS

Fine cuts are made with a backsaw or dovetail saw (Fig. 7-8). They are used to cut joints, which require a smooth

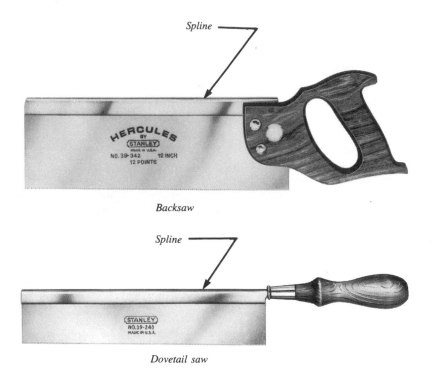

Fig. 7-8. Backsaws and dovetail saws are used for fine cuts.

cut. Both have a stiff blade with a heavy metal spine. Backsaws usually have 13 points to the inch, and have a 14-inch blade.

Dovetail saws have 15 points to the inch and have a 10-inch blade. They are used to cut angles and 90-degree cuts. The dovetail saw produces a very fine cut. It has a thin kerf. It is used to cut wood joints, and is named after the dovetail joint (Fig. 7-9).

Using Back and Dovetail Saws

1. Mark the cuts to be made on the wood with a square.

2. If it is a square cut, it can be cut with or without a guide block. Clamp the stock to the bench. Place the saw on the waste side of the line, slanting it 15 degrees. Pull it back several times to start the cut (Fig. 7-10).

3. Cut with steady strokes and lower the saw so it is horizontal. Cut to the depth mark on the edge of the stock.

4. If the cut is going through the board, place scrap beneath. This will keep you from cutting into the table.

5. A piece of scrap can be clamped along the line to serve as a guide for the saw.

6. Angles and 90-degree cuts can be made with a miter box.

Using the Adjustable Miter Box

The adjustable miter box has a table and fence set at 90 degrees. The miter saw is made like a backsaw, but is larger. The saw is mounted in a metal frame. The frame with the saw can be rotated 45 degrees right and left (Fig. 7-11).

1. Mark the cut line on the board.

2. Adjust the miter box to the desired angle. To do this, squeeze the locking lever and move it until the pointer reaches the angle on the scale. Release the lever.

3. Place the board on the table. Push it against the fence.

4. Lower the saw and line it up on the waste side of the cut line.

5. Hold the board in place with one hand. Some mi-

Fig. 7-9. Cutting a dovetail joint with a dovetail saw.

ter boxes have clamps to help hold the boards. You can also use C clamps or handscrews.

6. Start the cut by lightly pushing the saw forward. Take uniform strokes to complete the cut. Keep the saw parallel with the face of the board.

Wood miter boxes can be easily made in the shop. A suggested design is shown in Fig. 7-12.

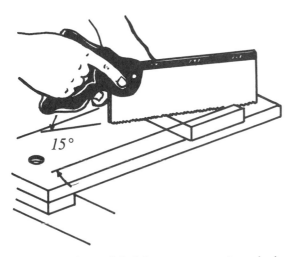

15°

Fig. 7-10. This stock is being cut square using a back saw and a bench hook.

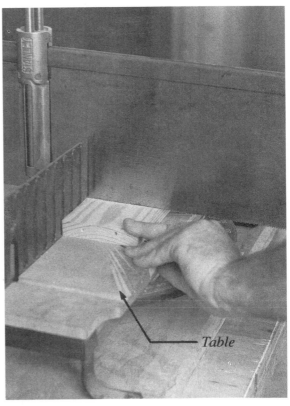

Table

Fig. 7-11. A square cut can be made with a miter box.

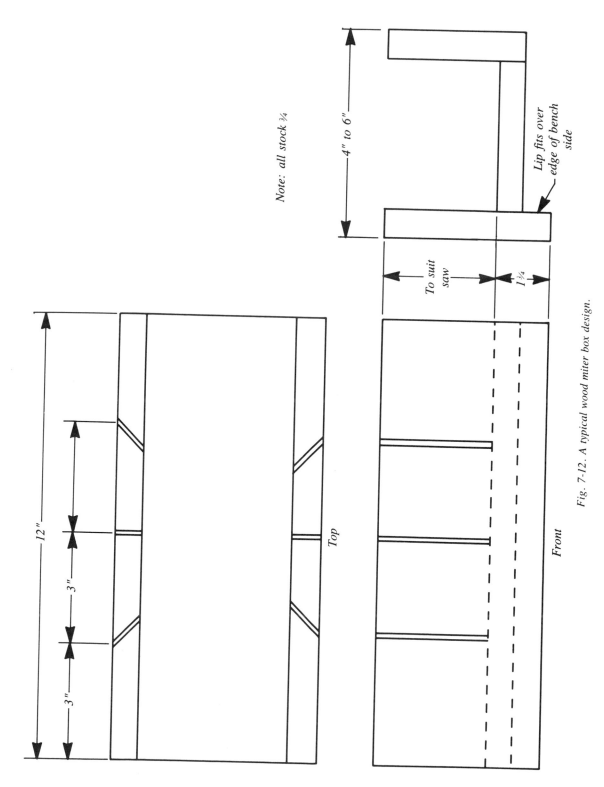

Note: all stock ¾

4" to 6"

Lip fits over edge of bench side

To suit saw

1¾

Top

Front

12"

3"

3"

3"

Fig. 7-12. A typical wood miter box design.

CUTTING CURVES

Curves are cut with the compass, keyhole, or coping saw. These saws have narrow or very thin blades, which help them turn as they cut along a curve.

Compass and keyhole saws are used to cut curves having a large radius. The compass saw is larger than the keyhole. It is 14 inches long and has 8 points to the inch. It will cut curves with a radius of 6 inches or larger. The keyhole is smaller, about 12 inches long, with 10 points to the inch (Fig. 7-13).

A coping saw is used to cut curves of all radii in thin wood. The saw has a metal frame and wood handle, and a very thin blade held in tension between the ends of the frame (Fig. 7-14). A wide variety of blades are available. The thinner ones have finer teeth and are used on sharp curves in thin wood; heavier blades are used for thicker wood.

Using a Compass or Keyhole Saw

1. Lay out the line to be cut.
2. Clamp the stock in a vise or to the bench.
3. Saw to the line, keeping the kerf on the waste side (Fig. 7-15). Keep the point of cutting close to the vise. If it gets too far away the board will vibrate, which makes cutting difficult.

4. If an internal curve is to be cut, bore a hole in the waste stock. The hole should be about ¾ inch (12 mm) in diameter. Clamp the stock in a vise. Insert the tip of the saw in the hole. Cut on the waste side of the line.

Using a Coping Saw

1. Lay out the line to be cut.
2. Clamp the stock in a vise. Keep the point of cutting close to the vise. If it gets too far away the board will vibrate, which makes cutting difficult and could break the blade. Move the piece as you cut to keep it in a good position.
3. Thin woods, such as ¼ inch or less, are best cut using a bracket. A bracket is a shop made tool that has a V cut in one end. It is clamped to the bench top (Fig. 7-16). The board is placed on it and the saw works vertically in the V cut.
4. When sawing, use a smooth, uniform stroke. Do not force the saw or the blade will break. The blade gets very hot, so stop and let it cool periodically or it will break.
5. When cutting a sharp curve, saw with gentle strokes, slowly turning the saw to follow the line. If the saw sticks, stop, back it up, and try again. If a cut is deeper than the frame, sometimes it can be finished by turning the blade sideways in the frame.

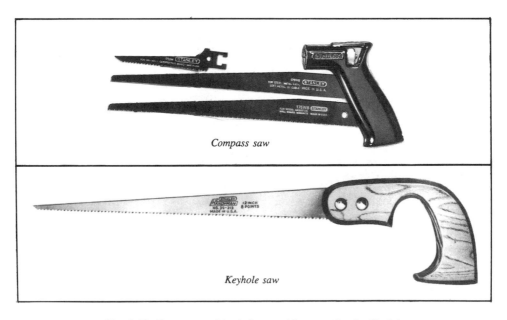

Fig. 7-13. Compass and keyhole saws (Courtesy Stanley Tools).

Fig. 7-14. A coping saw has a thin, fine-tooth blade (Courtesy Stanley Tools).

6. To make internal cuts, bore holes ⅜ inch in diameter at each sharp corner. Remove the blade from the frame, slide the blade through the hole, and put the blade back in the frame (Fig. 7-17).

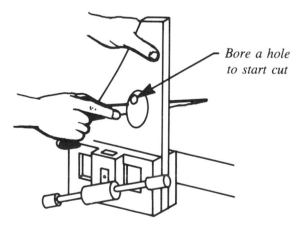

Bore a hole to start cut

Fig. 7-15. Internal cuts can be made with a keyhole or compass saw.

7. To replace a blade, unscrew the handle. This releases the tension on the blade. Remove the blade from the notches in the handle and top of the frame, and insert a new blade with the teeth pointing toward the handle. Tighten the handle, which will set the blade so it cuts on the pull stroke.

CARE OF SAWS

The teeth on saws are very sharp and rather small. It does not take much of a blow to bend or break one. Don't use a saw to cut into metal. When not using the saw, place it on the bench where other tools will not rest on top or against it. Better still, replace it on the tool rack. The tool rack is designed to protect the teeth.

Keep the blade free of rust. Coat it with a light oil and never get it wet. Rust makes the blade bind in the wood.

Do not use a dull saw. With a dull saw, you have to push hard to make it cut, which is hard on the saw. It is also more likely to slip and cause injury. Do not try to sharpen your own saw; this is a skilled operation that requires a professional saw sharpener.

Fig. 7-16. A shop-made V bracket is helpful when cutting with a coping saw.

Fig. 7-17. Using a coping saw.

Chapter 8

Planing and Scraping

Wood is rough cut to size at the saw mill, then smoothed by a power operated planer. The planer leaves small ridges on the surface, called *mill marks* (Fig. 8-1). Large mill marks are removed by smoothing the surface with a hand plane, small ones can be smoothed with a scraper.

HAND PLANES

A hand plane has a sharp blade that cuts a thin layer from the surface of the wood. It is much like a wood chisel. The blade can be adjusted to control the depth of cut. For successful operation the blade must be kept sharp and the cutting edge square. (The steps for sharpening a plane iron are given in chapter 11.)

Planes may be divided into two types: bench planes and specialty planes. Bench planes are all very much alike, the major difference being size. Specialty planes vary considerably in size and design.

Bench Planes

The types of bench planes include the smooth, jack, fore, and jointer. The blade is set on an angle with the bottom. The width of the blade varies from 1¾ to 2⅜ inches (44.5 to 60.3 mm). In length planes range from 9 to 24 inches (228.6 to 609.6 mm). The long planes are used on longer and wider boards. They are heavier and more difficult to use, but they make it easier to get the board flat.

Smooth planes are the shortest of the bench planes (Fig. 8-2). They are made in 9-inch lengths, and because they are short, they are used for planing short stock.

Jack planes are made in 14-inch (355.6-mm) lengths (Fig. 8-3). A smaller version, the junior jack, is 11½ inches (292 mm) long—enough for rough cutting and also for smooth final finishing. It can do the same work as the smooth and jointer planes.

Fore planes are 18 inches (457.2 mm) long (Fig. 8-4). They are used for long boards.

Jointer planes are made in lengths 22 and 24 inches (558.8 and 609.6 mm). They are used to plane very long surfaces and edges and are especially good for smoothing long rough stock (Fig. 8-5).

Specialty Planes

Specialty planes are each designed to serve a special purpose. The blades are set on a variety of angles and one

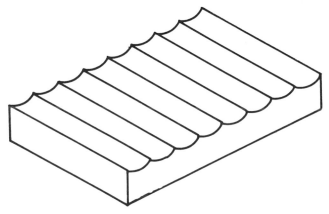

Fig. 8-1. Mill marks left by the planing mill are removed with a hand plane.

Fig. 8-2. Smooth plane (Courtesy Stanley Tools).

Fig. 8-3. Jack plane (Courtesy Stanley Tools).

type has an adjustable frame. Some are held with one hand and others require two hands. While they are not used a great deal, they are invaluable for the purpose for which they are designed.

Block planes are the most commonly used of the specialty planes (Fig. 8-6). They are made from 6 to 7 inches (152.4 to 177.8 mm) long. The blade is set on a smaller angle, 12 or 21 degrees, than the bench plane. The bevel is set up instead of down as on bench planes. Block planes are designed to plane end grain (Fig. 8-7).

Rabbet planes are used to cut rabbet joints on the

Fig. 8-4. Fore plane (Courtesy Stanley Tools).

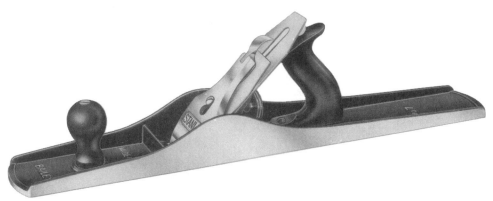

Fig. 8-5. Jointer plane (Courtesy Stanley Tools).

Fig. 8-6. Block plane (Courtesy Stanley Tools).

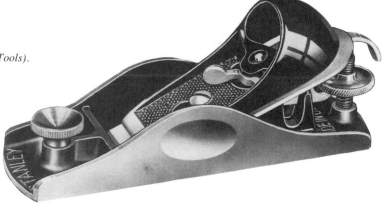

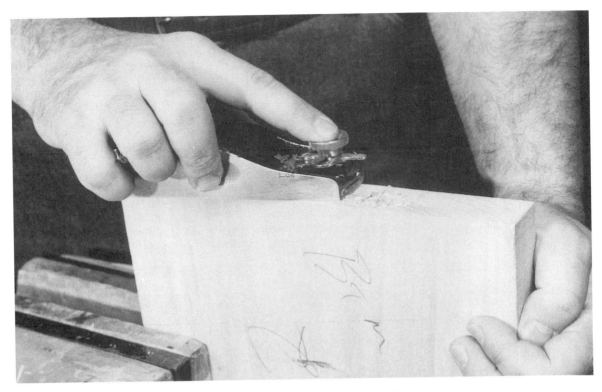

Fig. 8-7. Block planes are used to plane end grain.

Fig. 8-8. Rabbet plane (Courtesy Stanley Tools).

edge of boards (Fig. 8-8). The joint is cut with the grain as the blade cuts away layers of the wood. There are several types of rabbet planes, but they all operate in much the same way. The blade is set so it cuts even with the side of the frame, (Fig. 8-9).

Router planes are used to remove material between saw cuts forming dados, grooves, and other recessed area (Fig. 8-10). They have ¼-inch and ½-inch router blades and a ½-inch V shaped smoothing blade. The blade is square with the cutting edge formed on a foot set at right angles (Fig. 8-11).

Spokeshaves are a carryover from the days of wagon wheel manufacture (Fig. 8-12). They were used to form the large wood spokes. They have small blades similar to those on bench planes, and are used to shape wood and smooth curved surfaces (Fig. 8-13).

ASSEMBLING AND ADJUSTING A BENCH PLANE

Learning to use a bench plane to smooth wood surfaces requires some practice. A key to skilled use is an understanding of the purpose of each part and how to assemble and adjust the plane. A sharp, correctly adjusted plane is necessary for best performance.

Parts

The parts of a bench plane are shown in Fig. 8-14. The plane is held in both hands. Right-handed people hold the handle in the right hand the knob in the left. The *frame* is the large, heavy part to which the other parts are fastened. The *frog* is an inclined metal part that holds the plane iron, which does the actual cutting. The *plane iron*

Fig. 8-9. Rabbets are cut with a rabbet plane.

Fig. 8-10. Router plane (Courtesy Stanley Tools).

and the *plane iron cap* are fastened together with a bolt. This assembly is called the double plane iron (Fig. 8-15). The bevel on the plane iron is turned down. The plane iron cap is on the other side with the curved section up; it breaks the wood fibers as they enter the mouth and causes them to curl out of the opening. If it does not fit tightly, chips will slide underneath and clog the plane.

The plane iron sticks out through an opening in the bottom of the frame, called the *mouth*. The plane iron and cap iron are held to the frog with the lever cap. The depth of cut is controlled by the *adjusting screw*. It regulates how far the plane iron sticks out through the mouth.

The lateral adjusting lever is used to move the plane iron until the cutting edge is parallel with the bottom of the frame.

Assembly

The first step in plane assembly is joining the plane iron and the plane iron cap (Fig. 8-16). Place the plane iron with the bevel down. Place the plane iron cap on the other side with the curved section up. Slide the bolt in the plane iron cap through the hole in the plane iron and down the slot. Turn the plane iron cap until it is parallel

Fig. 8-11. Grooves and dadoes are smoothed with a router plane.

with the plane iron. Slide it toward the cutting edge until it is within $\frac{1}{16}$ inch (2 mm) from it. Tighten the plane iron cap screw with a large screwdriver.

To complete the assembly, place the double plane iron on the frog with the plane iron next to the frog. The head of the bolt must drop into the hole in the frog. The slot in the plane iron cap must fit over the end of the attachment from the adjusting nut. Place the lever cap over the long bolt, slide it down, and press down on the cam. This locks the double plane iron in place (Fig. 8-17).

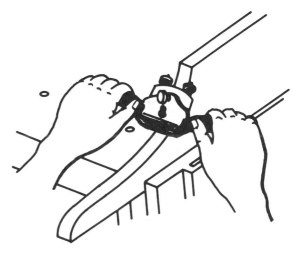

Fig. 8-12. Spokeshave (Courtesy Stanley Tools).

Fig. 8-13. Curves are smoothed with a spokeshave.

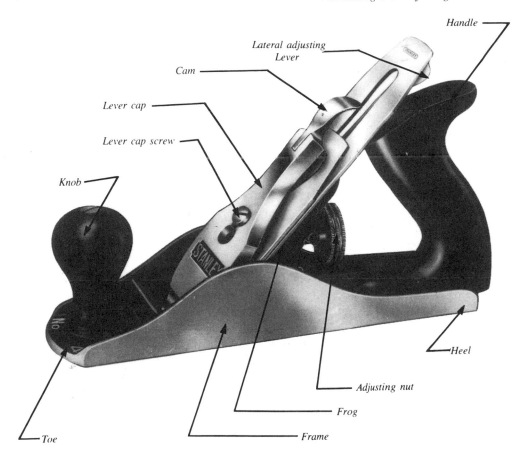

Fig. 8-14. The parts of a hand plane (Courtesy Stanley Tools).

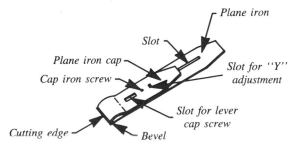

Fig. 8-15. The parts of a double plane iron.

Adjusting

Once the double plane iron is locked in the plane, its lateral position and depth of cut must be adjusted. To adjust the plane iron laterally:

1. Turn the plane over and sight down the bottom of the plane from the front (Fig. 8-18).

2. If the edge of the plane iron is not parallel with the bottom, move the lateral adjusting lever toward the low corner (Fig. 8-19). Adjust it until it is parallel.

3. Now adjust the depth of cut. Sight down the bot-

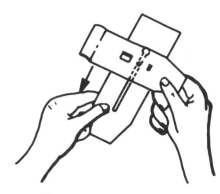 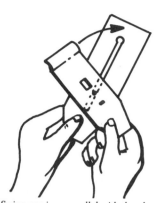 

Place cap iron and plane iron together with bolt in slot. Bevel must be down.

Swing cap iron parallel with the plane iron.

Slide cap iron within ¹⁄₁₆" (2mm) of the cutting edge. Tighten the bolt.

Fig. 8-16. The steps to assemble a double plane iron.

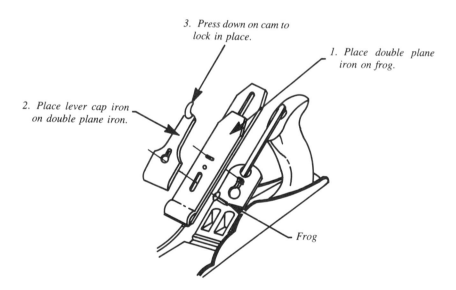

3. Press down on cam to lock in place.

1. Place double plane iron on frog.

2. Place lever cap iron on double plane iron.

Frog

Fig. 8-17. Placing and securing the double plane iron on the frog.

tom of the plane. Turn the adjusting nut until the plane iron sticks out about ¹⁄₆₄ inch (.4 mm).

4. Try the plane on scrap stock. Plane with the face grain. If the depth is too deep, the plane will stick and be hard to push. Reduce the depth of cut. If it slides easily but does not cut, increase the depth of cut.

5. If the plane begins to cut deeper on one side, re-adjust it with the lateral adjusting lever.

USING A PLANE

Before planing begins you need to get the work station ready. Remove all unnecessary tools and pieces of wood. Be certain the vise is in good condition and that its jaws will not mar the wood. Choose a bench the proper height: You should be able to plane at about waist level. Be certain the floor is free of scrap wood and shavings.

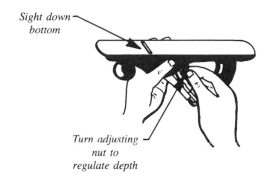

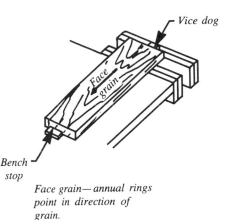

Fig. 8-18. Turn the adjusting nut to regulate the depth of cut.

Face grain— annual rings point in direction of grain.

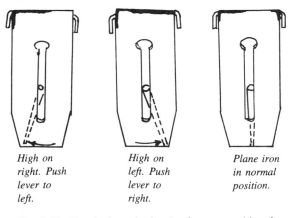

High on right. Push lever to left.

High on left. Push lever to right.

Plane iron in normal position.

Fig. 8-19. Use the lateral adjusting lever to position the plane iron parallel with the bottom of the plane.

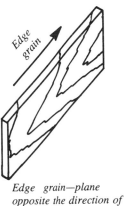

Edge grain—plane opposite the direction of the annual rings.

Fig. 8-20. Clamp the stock to the bench. Position so you plane with the grain of the board.

The following general procedures are used for all planing operations:

1. Examine the board carefully. Begin by planing the best surface first.

2. Check the stock with a square to find high spots or to see if it is warped. Mark the high areas with a pencil or chalk.

3. Clamp the stock in a vise or to the bench top with a clamp. Both hands must be free to hold the plane. Place the stock so you will be planing with the grain (Fig. 8-20).

4. Select the proper plane: Short pieces require a short plane as a smooth or jack plane, longer pieces require a fore or jointer plane.

5. Position yourself so you are standing in a comfortable position. Place the toe of the plane on the wood.

6. As you begin the forward movement of the plane, press harder on the knob. As the plane crosses the board, press equally on the handle and knob. As it finishes the cut, press harder on the handle (Fig. 8-21).

7. At the end of each stroke, lift the plane off the wood and move it back for the next stroke.

8. After every few strokes, check the wood with a try square. Stop planing as soon as it is square and surface defects have been removed. Do not overplane a surface.

Squaring a Face

The surface of a board may be rough or be warped. These faults can be corrected by planing. The thickness of stock is reduced by planing the surface. To plane a surface:

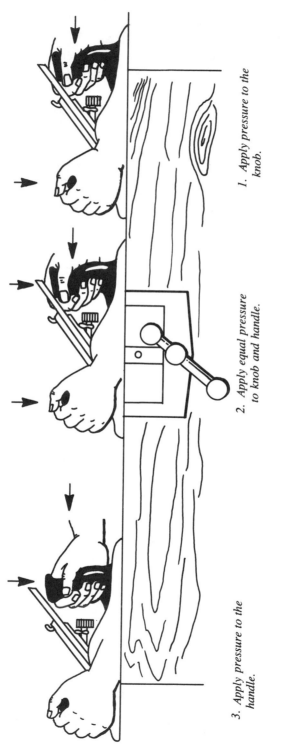

1. Apply pressure to the knob.

2. Apply equal pressure to knob and handle.

3. Apply pressure to the handle.

Fig. 8-21. The steps to plane an edge or surface.

Fig. 8-22. When planing a surface, slant the plane on the first cuts.

1. Select the best face. Plane it smooth and square. Use a very light cut, increasing the depth of cut as needed. Wide, flat surfaces are best planed if the plane is slanted slightly. This produces a slight diagonal cut. Make the final light smoothing cuts parallel with the edges of the board (Fig. 8-22).

2. Plane from one end of the board to the other in one continuous stroke. Stopping or starting somewhere in the middle will produce an irregular surface.

3. Check the surface for squareness (Fig. 8-23). Check it across the width, the length and the diagonals.

4. If the stock is to be reduced in thickness, mark this from the best face (Fig. 8-24).

5. Turn the stock over. Reduce the thickness by planing the back side until it reaches the line. Check the surface often for squareness.

Squaring an Edge

1. Edges are planed square after a face has been squared. Select the best edge.

2. Clamp the stock in a vise with the edge to be planed facing up.

3. Adjust the plane to take a light cut.

4. Keep the bottom of the plane perpendicular to the face. Plane the edge with long continuous strokes. Plane with the grain.

5. Check it for squareness with the face and along its length (Fig. 8-25).

6. If the board is to be squared to width, mark the width measuring from the square edge (Fig. 8-26).

7. If there is a lot of stock to be removed cut it away with a saw. Leave enough wood to smooth and square the edge. Proceed as just described for the first edge.

Squaring an End

End grain is difficult to plane because you are cutting across the fibers in the board. If you plane all the way across the end, the fibers will be torn away as the plane

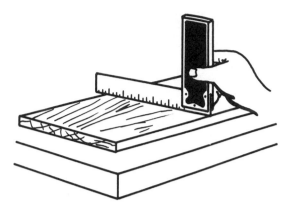

1. Check the width

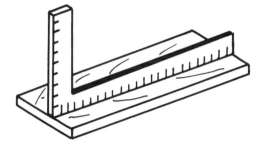

2. The length

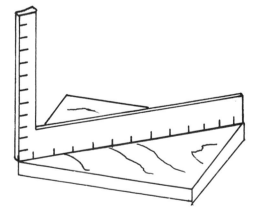

3. And the diagonals

Fig. 8-23. *When squaring a board, check the length, width and diagonals.*

finishes its stroke. The same is true for planing all edges of plywood.

To square an end (or edge on plywood):

1. Select the best end. Clamp the stock in a vise with the end up.

2. Check it for squareness and mark any parts out of square. If there are high parts they must be removed.

3. There are three ways to plane end grain. First, plane from each end toward the center (Fig. 8-27). Second, chamfer the corner on one end and plane toward it. Be certain to not plane after the chamfer has disappeared (Fig. 8-28). Third, clamp a piece of scrap stock against one side, then plane over the scrap and let it split (Fig. 8-29). Be certain the scrap stock is the same thickness as the piece being planed.

4. Check the end for squareness from each side and face (Fig. 8-30).

Squaring Stock

If you want to produce a board that has all sides square with each other, plane them in the order shown in Fig. 8-31. This order lets the newly squared surfaces be checked for squareness with those previously planed.

Planing a Chamfer

A *chamfer* is an angled surface cut along the corner of stock (Fig. 8-32). To plane a chamfer, lay out its depth on the face and edge (Fig. 8-33). Clamp the stock in a hand screw and clamp this in a vise, then position so the chamfer is cut parallel with the floor (Fig. 8-34). Plane the chamfer as you would an edge. Stop when you reach the depth lines. It can be checked with a T-bevel (Fig. 8-35).

Planing a Bevel

A *bevel* is an edge on a slope from the top to the back face of the board (Fig. 8-36). To plane a bevel, mark the depth on the face. Clamp and plane as explained for chamfers.

Planing a Taper

When a piece slopes from a given thickness at one end to a reduced thickness on the other, this is a *taper* (Fig. 8-37). Lay out the taper on the stock. Because you will plane toward the end with the most material to be removed, be certain the grain runs in that direction. Clamp the stock in the vise with the edge of the taper parallel

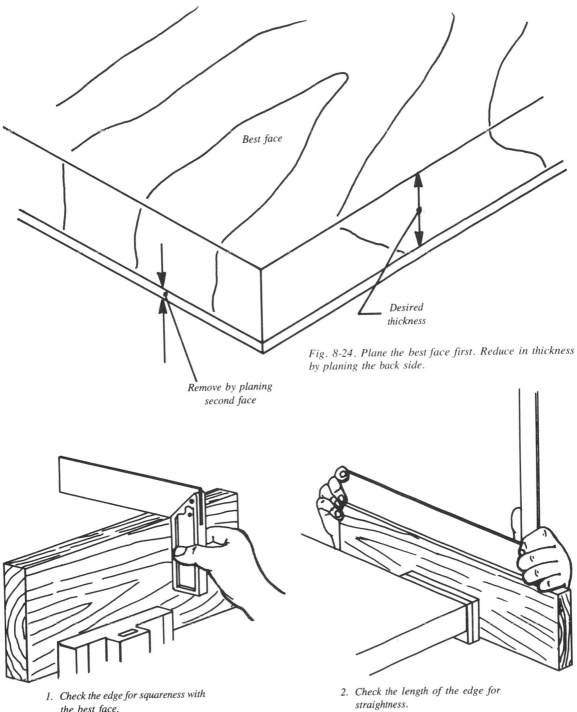

Fig. 8-24. Plane the best face first. Reduce in thickness by planing the back side.

Best face

Desired
thickness

Remove by planing
second face

1. Check the edge for squareness with
the best face.

2. Check the length of the edge for
straightness.

Fig. 8-25. When squaring an edge, check the length and width.

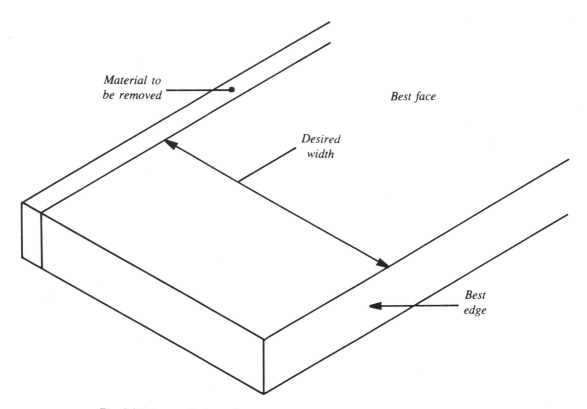

Fig. 8-26. Square the best edge, cut the board to width, and square the other edge.

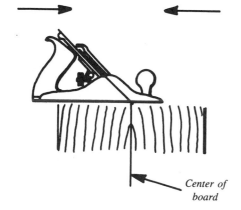

Fig. 8-27. One way to plane end grain is to plane from the ends toward the center.

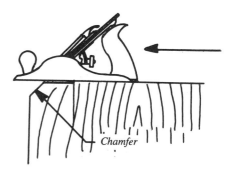

Fig. 8-28. End grain can be planed toward a chamfer on one side.

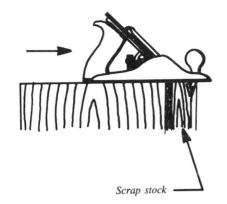

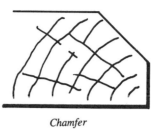

Chamfer

Fig. 8-32. Stock may be planed to have a chamfer.

Scrap stock

Fig. 8-29. Plane end grain by clamping a piece of scrap stock on one side and plane toward it.

1. Check from the best edge.

2. Check from the best face.

Fig. 8-30. When squaring an end check it from the best face and best edge.

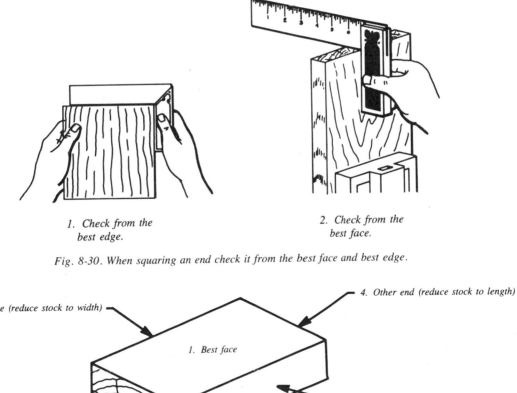

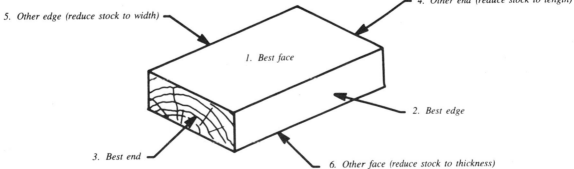

5. Other edge (reduce stock to width)

4. Other end (reduce stock to length)

1. Best face

2. Best edge

3. Best end

6. Other face (reduce stock to thickness)

Fig. 8-31. The recommended order for planing surfaces to square a board.

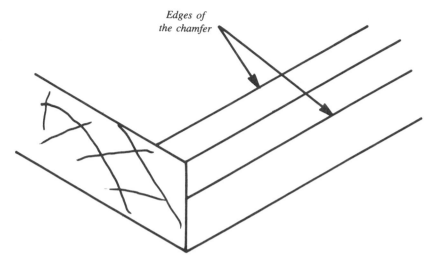

Fig. 8-33. Lay out the edges of the chamfer.

Fig. 8-34. To plane a bevel or chamfer clamp the stock in a hand screw. Then clamp the hand screw in a vise so the planing is parallel with the bench top.

Fig. 8-35. *Check the bevel or chamfer with the T bevel.*

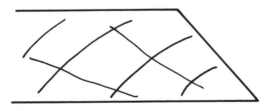

Fig. 8-36. *A bevel.*

with the bench top. Take light cuts, beginning on the end with the most material. Use longer strokes to reduce the material to the line (Fig. 8-38).

SCRAPERS

Scrapers remove very fine layers of wood from the surface of the stock. Mill marks and dents are removed by scraping. Scrape the surface after it has been planed and before it is sanded. Careful scraping can reduce the amount of sanding needed.

Hand scrapers are rectangular or irregularly shaped flat steel tools (Fig. 8-39). The edges have a fine, sharp burr that removes the wood. The rectangular scraper is used on flat surfaces, the irregular shaped scraper on curved surfaces, and the sharp scraper will cut small wood curls. If it only produces dust, the scraper is dull and must be sharpened. (The steps for sharpening a scraper are given in chapter 11).

To use the hand scraper, hold it in two hands. Because each edge can have two burrs, it can be pulled or pushed. It is slanted in the direction it is moved (Fig. 8-40).

Cabinet scrapers have a flat steel blade mounted in a frame that has two handles (Fig. 8-41). They are easier to use than the hand scrapers. The blade has a beveled cutting edge with a single burr, which is placed in the frame so the tool is pushed away from the user. The blade sticks out at the bottom just enough for the burr to scrape the surface.

Many other types of scrapers are available. They are used to remove glue, paint, and the old finish when a product is being restored and are not satisfactory for fine finishing of wood surfaces.

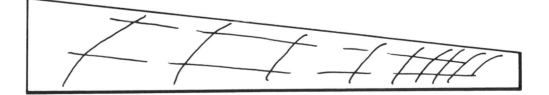

Fig. 8-37. *A taper.*

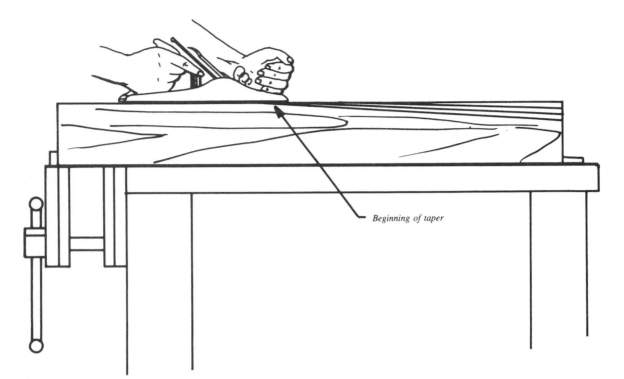

Beginning of taper

Fig. 8-38. To plane a taper, start on the end to be the smallest and take longer strokes until you get to the beginning of the taper.

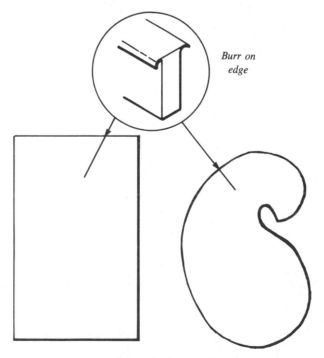

Burr on edge

Fig. 8-39. Hand scrapers.

Fig. 8-40. Hold the hand scraper in two hands. Bend it slightly, slant it, and push away from you.

Fig. 8-41. A cabinet scraper (Courtesy Stanley Tools).

Chapter 9

Drilling and Boring

Holes are drilled and bored in wood. Those under ¼ inch (6 mm) are considered "drilled" and are made with *drills*. Those over ¼ inch (6 mm) are considered "bored" and are made with tools called *bits*. Different types of tools can be used for each.

Holes are drilled in wood so metal fasteners can be installed. Some wood joints require bored holes. Holes also permit internal cuts with a saw for decorative purposes.

LAYING OUT HOLES

It is important that holes be accurately located. Proceed as follows:

1. Note the hole location on the working drawing. Carefully measure from two sides of the board (Fig. 9-1). Use a try square to draw lines through these measurements—where they cross is the center.

2. Punch the center with an awl; this gives a small dent into which to place the tip of the bit or drill, which keeps them from sliding on the wood as the hole is started (Fig. 9-2).

3. If holes in two parts must match and are the same diameter, consider clamping the two boards together. Then drill or bore the holes in both pieces at the same time. If they are different sizes, place the pieces together and mark through one hole with an awl (Fig. 9-3).

BORING TOOLS

The various types of boring tools have a square tapered *tang*, which fits in the brace. Boring bits are ¼ inch (6 mm) and larger.

Bit Brace

A bit brace has a chuck to hold the bit. The bit is held against the wood with the head of the brace and is rota-

---

SAFETY

☐ Wear your safety glasses.
☐ Clamp stock securely before drilling or boring; it can be held in a bench vise or clamped to the bench top.
☐ Keep your hands on the handles of the tools; this will keep your fingers out of the way of the cutting edges.
☐ Do not touch a bit or drill after making a hole; it is very hot.
☐ Do not work in crowded conditions; someone may bump you and cause an accident.
☐ Remove drills and bits from the drill or brace when carrying them in the shop; they are sharp and could stab someone.
☐ Be careful you do not bore or drill through a piece of wood and stab yourself or someone else.

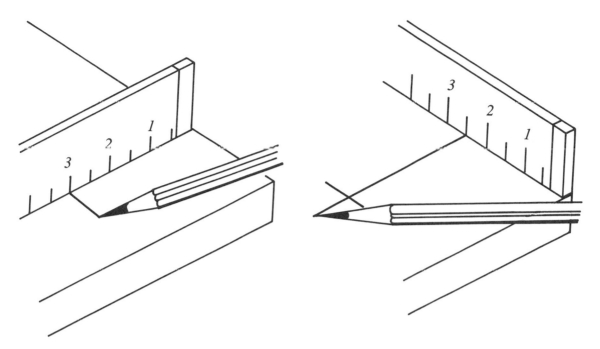

Fig. 9-1. Locate the center of a hole from two sides.

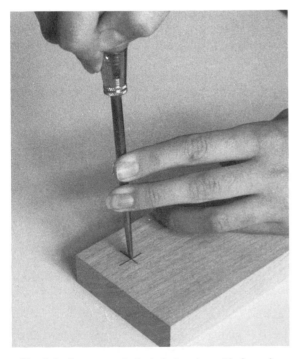

Fig. 9-2. Center punch the hole location with the awl.

ted by the handle. The chuck has jaws designed to hold the square, tapered tang on the bits (Fig. 9-4).

The size of the brace is given by the diameter of the sweep, which is the circle formed when the handle is rotated. Braces with larger sweeps have greater twist force. Large diameter bits are easier to turn with a brace that has a large sweep. Sweeps of 8, 10, 12, and 14 inches are common.

Braces have a ratchet mechanism located between the chuck and the bow. The ratchet permits a hole to be bored in tight places where the handle cannot rotate in a complete circle. The handle is turned clockwise, causing the bit to bore. When the handle hits something it is rotated counterclockwise. The ratchet slips so the bit does not turn. Then the handle is rotated clockwise again.

Bits

Bits are the boring tools used in the brace. They serve different purposes, depending upon the type of hole to be bored.

Auger bits are used only on wood. They are fast cutting and form a clean, smooth hole. The tang is designed to fit into the chuck on a brace. They should not be used in other hand or power boring devices; there are special boring bits designed for use in power tools.

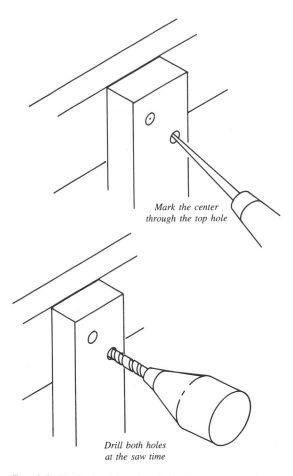

Mark the center
through the top hole

Drill both holes
at the saw time

Fig. 9-3. *Methods of locating holes in two parts where the holes must line up.*

shorter length (5½ inch) makes it easier to bore the holes. Dowel bits are used with a doweling jig. They are available in ¼-inch to ½-inch diameters.

Expansive bits are used to bore large-diameter holes. They have the screw, a spur, and cutting edges, but no twist (Fig. 9-7). Below the screw is a second cutting edge that forms a hole to clear the body. The blade can be adjusted to produce holes of various sizes. The bit is made in two sizes: One bores holes from ⅝ to 1¾ inch (13 to 38 mm) in diameter, the other holes from ⅞ to 3 inches (22 to 75 mm) in diameter (Fig. 9-8). The bits have a tang and are used in a brace. This tool requires more force to bore a hole than an auger bit. Use a brace with a large sweep. The expansive bit also clogs with chips and has to be drawn out of the hole and cleaned frequently.

Forstner bits are used to bore holes with flat bottoms, which is useful if the hole left by the screw on an auger bit is objectionable. Forstner bits will bore close to the lower surface without breaking through (Fig. 9-9). The bit has no screw so considerable pressure is required to make the cut. It has not twist so it must be removed from the hole and unclogged often.

Depth Gauge

When it is necessary to bore holes to a particular depth, a depth gauge is necessary. Commercial gauges are made of metal and clamp on the bit. You can also make one: Bore a hole through a block of wood; the amount of the auger sticking out is the depth of the hole (Fig. 9-10). If accuracy is not important, wrap a piece of tape around the auger and bore until you reach the tape.

BORING HOLES

To bore holes, proceed as follows:

1. Locate the center of each hole; mark the center using an awl.

2. Place the bit in the chuck of the brace and turn the shell counterclockwise to open the jaws. Place the tang in the jaws at least 2 inches (50 mm) and turn the shell clockwise to tighten (Fig. 9-11).

3. Clamp the board securely to a workbench. When the board is small, clamp it vertically in a vise and bore the hole horizontally—which is an easier method (Fig. 9-12).

4. Place the screw in the center punch mark. Hold the head in one hand and turn the handle in a clockwise direction. Apply only enough pressure on the handle

The hole is bored as the screw enters the wood when the chuck rotates and pulls the auger into the wood. The spurs touch the wood first and cuts the wood fibers in a circle. As the auger goes deeper, the lips remove the wood from inside the circle cut by the spurs (Fig. 9-5). The twist carries the wood chips from the cutters up and out of the hole. An auger with a solid center and a single twist is designed for general use. A double twist auger will bore smoother holes.

Auger bits come in sets, with sizes stamped on the tang (Fig. 9-6). The numbers represent 1/16 of an inch. For example, a No. 7 is 7/16 inches in diameter. Metric sizes range from 6 to 38 mm.

Dowel bits are made like auger bits, but are shorter. They are used to bore holes for dowel joints, and their

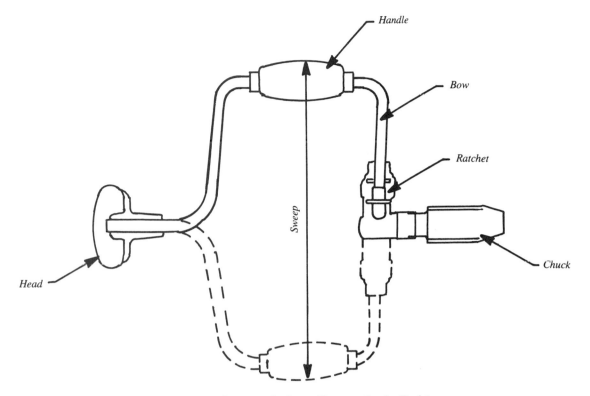

Fig. 9-4. The parts of a brace (Courtesy Stanley Tools).

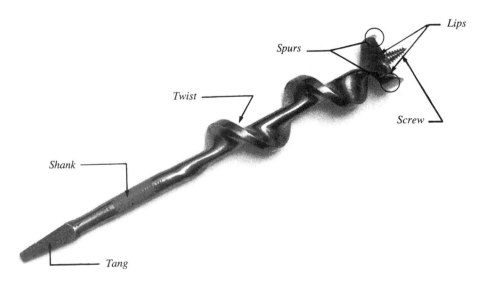

Fig. 9-5. A single twist general-purpose auger bit.

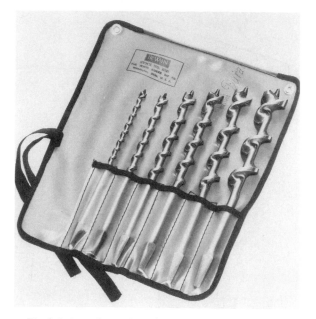

Fig. 9-6. A set of auger bits (Courtesy The Irwin Company).

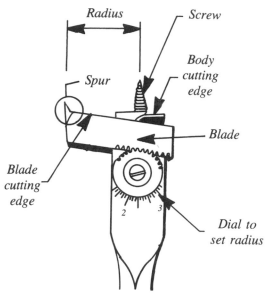

Fig. 9-8. Closeup of an expansion bit.

to get a steady cut. Do not turn the handle fast; use a smooth uniform motion.

5. Check the angle the bit makes with the wood. If it is to be 90 degrees, you can sight it or use a try square. Sight or check from the top and one side (Fig. 9-13). If boring on an angle use a T-bevel (Fig. 9-14). If many holes are to be bored on an angle, bore one correctly in a block of wood then clamp it on the work and use it as a guide (Fig. 9-15).

6. Bore into the wood until the screw just breaks

through the back side. Remove the bit from the wood and bore from the back side. If you bore straight through, the bit will splinter the wood around the hole. Another method is to clamp scrap wood behind the board and bore through into the scrap wood (Fig. 9-16).

7. If you are using a depth gauge, bore until the gauge lightly touches the surface then back out the bit. If you force the depth gauge against the wood it will make a circular scratch.

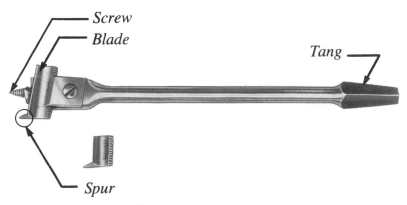

Fig. 9-7. An expansion bit.

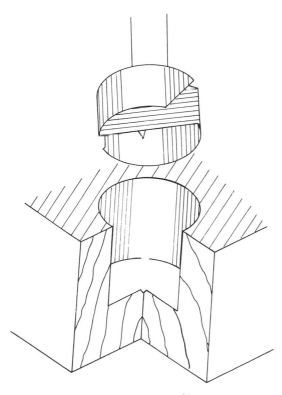

Fig. 9-9. Forstner bit.

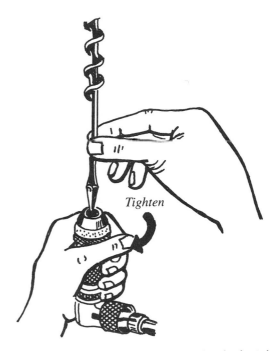

Fig. 9-11. Place the tang of the bit in the chuck of the brace.

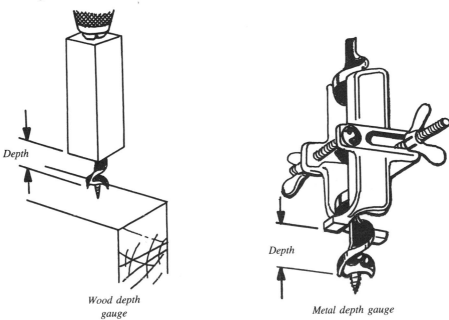

Fig. 9-10. Two types of depth gauges used with auger bits.

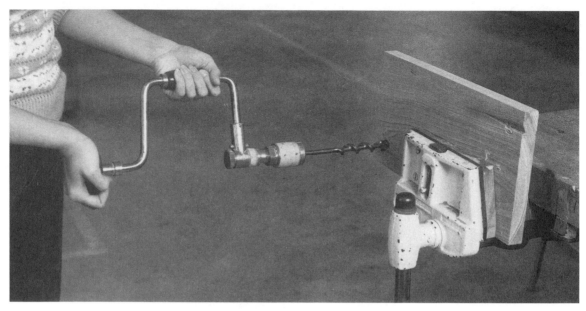

Fig. 9-12. It is easier to bore horizontally.

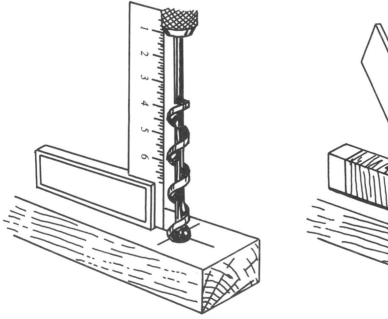

Fig. 9-13. Use a try square to keep the auger bit perpendicular to the surface.

Fig. 9-14. Angles can be bored by lining the auger bit up with a T bevel.

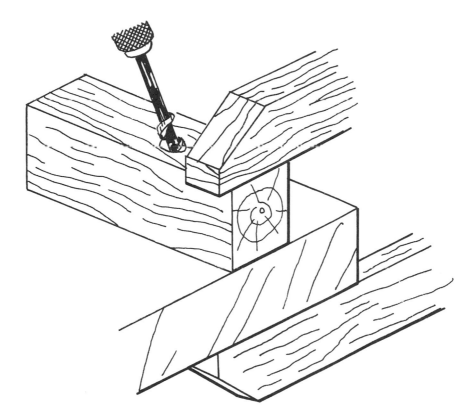

Fig. 9-15. *When many holes are to be bored at the same angle, bore one hole in a wood block and use it as a guide.*

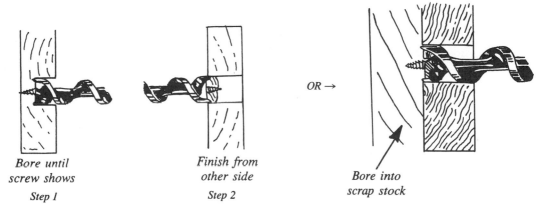

Bore until
screw shows

Step 1

Finish from
other side

Step 2

OR →

Bore into
scrap stock

Fig. 9-16. *Two ways to bore through stock without splitting the wood at the back side.*

DRILLING TOOLS

Drills are used to cut holes ¼ inch in diameter and smaller. They have a smooth round shank that fits into a three-jaw chuck. Larger-diameter drills are available for use in portable electric hand drills and drill presses.

Hand Drill

A hand drill has a handle, which is used to hold it upright. The three-jaw chuck holds the drill. The chuck is rotated by turning a crank in a clockwise direction. The crank turns a large gear that transmits power to the chuck through the pinions (Fig. 9-17).

To insert drills hold the large gear so it does not turn. Twist the outside shell of the chuck. Turn it counterclockwise to open the jaws, clockwise to close and tighten them. Open the jaws and insert the shank of the drill at least 1 inch (25 mm), then hand tighten the jaws—do not use a pliers or wrench. Drill as follows (Figs. 9-18 and 9-19):

1. Insert the straight shank drill in the chuck.
2. Place the tip of the drill on the center punch mark.
3. Turn the crank clockwise and press down lightly on the handle.

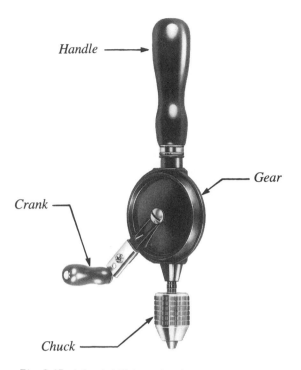

Fig. 9-17. A hand drill is used with straight shank twist drills (Courtesy Stanley Tools).

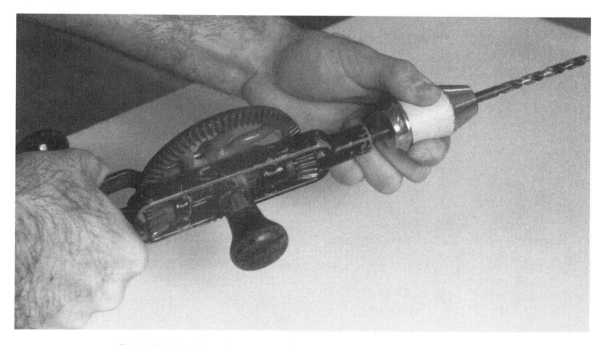

Fig. 9-18. To tighten the drill in the chuck, hold the gear and turn the chuck.

Fig. 9-19. Turn the gear to drill a hole.

4. Drill through into a block of scrap wood. This keeps the bottom of the hole from splintering. Be careful not to drill through the scrap piece and into the workbench.

Hand drills are made in several sizes and types. They are specified by the largest drill they will take.

Twist Drills

Twist drills drill small-diameter holes in wood, metal, and plastics. They have a smooth round shank, flutes to carry chips out of the hole, and two cutting edges on the tip. They can be used in hand drills, portable electric drills, and drill presses (Fig. 9-20).

A standard set, sizes range from $1/16$ through $1/4$ inch in diameter, although larger sizes are available. The difference in size between drills is $1/64$ inch. Metric twist drills range from 1 to 13 mm in diameter.

Push Drills

Push drills are used to drill holes from $1/16$ through $11/16$ inch in diameter. The drill points have two straight flutes with two cutting edges are at the tip. The drill points are stored in the handle (Fig. 9-21).

Operate the push drill as follows (Fig. 9-22):

1. Place a drill point in the chuck. It is spring-loaded, so you have to pull up on it to get the drill point in place.

2. Put the drill point on the center of the hole and push down on the handle. The chuck will rotate. Ease up on the handle and it will rise; push down again to rotate. Uniform push strokes will cause it to drill into the wood.

CARE OF TOOLS

Store tools so the cutting edges are protected. Twist drills are often placed in racks or in plastic cases. Auger bits should be stored in a wood rack so each is separate from the other. The points must be protected.

When using these tools, place them on the bench so they will not be hit by other tools or roll off on the floor. When you are finished using them, remove them from the chuck and return to the storage provided.

Drills and bits should be kept dry; rust makes them

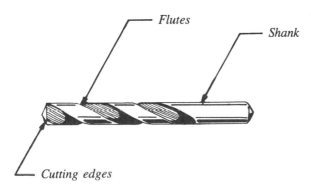

Fig. 9-20. A straight shank twist drill will drill holes in wood, metal, and plastics.

hard to use. Coat lightly with a thin oil to prevent rust, especially in a damp basement.

Keep the tools clear of wood chips. Sometimes the screw, twist, or flutes will clog. Use an old paint brush with short bristles to remove wood. If tree sap is on them, remove it with paint thinner.

Keep all tools sharp. Sharpening hand tools is explained in chapter 11.

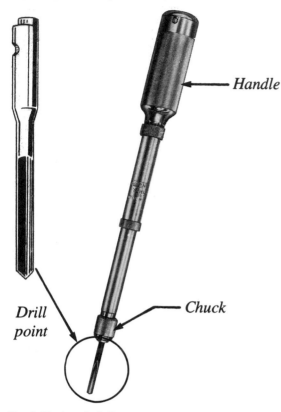

Fig. 9-21. A push drill uses fluted drill points (Courtesy Stanley Tools).

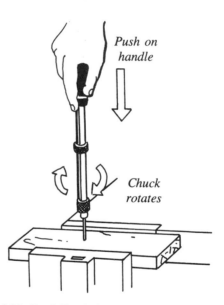

Fig. 9-22. To drill a hole with a push drill, move the handle up and down.

Chapter 10

Shaping, Smoothing, and Carving

After wood parts are cut they are carefully smoothed to the finished size. Files, rasps, and forming tools are used to finish curves and irregular shapes. Chisels are used to cut joints and recessed areas. Carving tools are used to cut designs into the wood surface.

FILES AND RASPS

Files and rasps are primarily used to smooth curves and irregular shapes. It is difficult to square an edge or end with a file; other tools work better.

Files and rasps have small teeth cut in rows on a hardened steel blade. One end of the file is pointed to form a tang, which is inserted into a handle (Fig. 10-1). Do not use a file without a handle. The tang is sharp and can pierce the skin.

The difference between files and rasps is the teeth.

A file has smaller teeth cut as rows of grooves. Rasps have larger, individual teeth (Fig. 10-2).

Files

Files are used to remove small amounts of wood and they produce a rather smooth surface. The teeth on files are very hard. Some types can be used to smooth plastics and metal as well as wood.

Files used in woodworking are made in flat, half-round, square, three-square (triangular), and round shapes. Two types of teeth—single-cut and double-cut—are available. Single-cut teeth have single rows of teeth cut on an angle across the face. Double-cut have two rows of teeth that are cut across each other (Fig. 10-3).

The coarseness of a file is specified by the cut. The degrees of coarseness from rough to smooth are: bastard,

---

SAFETY

- ☐ Wear your safety glasses.
- ☐ Always put a handle on the tang of a file or rasp before using it.
- ☐ Keep both hands behind the cutting edge of chisels, gouges, and carving tools.
- ☐ Do not cut or carve in crowded conditions; a slip can cut someone near you.
- ☐ Clamp the stock to the bench top or in a vise.
- ☐ Cut away from your body.
- ☐ Keep all edge tools sharp; a sharp tool is a safe tool.
- ☐ Carry tools with the cutting edges pointing toward the floor.
- ☐ Keep sharp tools in a safe place on the bench top so they do not cut someone.
- ☐ Do not place chisels or other tools in your pockets.

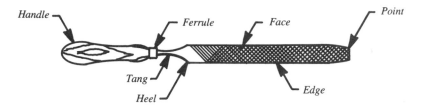

Fig. 10-1. The parts of a file or rasp.

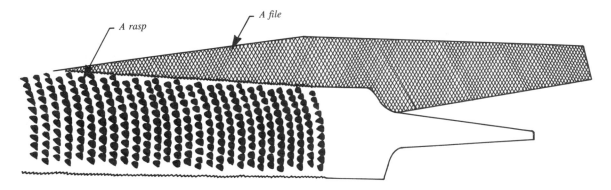

Fig. 10-2. Rasps have large individual teeth, while files have teeth cut in rows (Courtesy Simonds Cutting Tools).

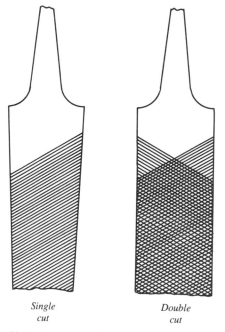

Single
cut

Double
cut

Fig. 10-3. Files are made with single and double rows of teeth.

second cut, and smooth. The longer the file, the coarser the cut of the teeth. For example, a 12-inch second-cut file is coarser than an 8-inch second-cut file. When buying files, specify the length, shape, cut, and coarseness of teeth.

Rasps

A rasp has a large, rough tooth and is used to rapidly remove large amounts of material. It is used primarily on wood. A rasp leaves a rough surface that must then be smoothed with a file or other tool.

Rasps are made in three shapes: flat, half-round and round. They come in two surfaces: bastard (very rough) and smooth.

When buying a rasp, specify the length, shape, and coarseness of teeth. For general use, lengths of 8 to 12 inches should serve the purpose.

Using Files and Rasps

The first task is choosing the right file. Examine the surface to be smoothed. If it is rather rough, start with a rasp or a coarser file. In most cases a second-cut file is a good choice. If it is a very rough surface, a rasp might

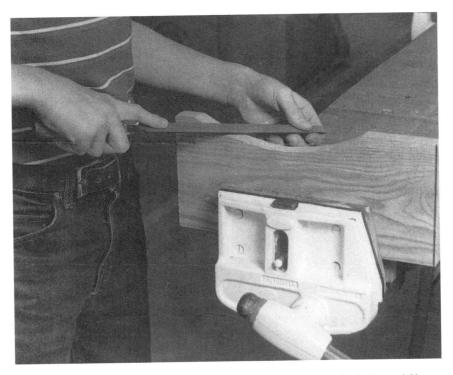

Fig. 10-4. Concave curves are smoothed with the curved surface of a half-round file.

be needed. Select a file that most nearly fits the shape of the surface. The half-round will be good on concave curves (Fig. 10-4), which are curves that turn inward like the inside surface of a sphere. A flat file works best on convex curves (Fig. 10-5), which are curves that turn outward. After the first file has removed the roughness from the saw, switch to a finer file. There is no need to continue filing with a coarse file; additional filing will not get the surface any smoother. After using the smoothest file available, finish the surface with abrasive paper and a sanding block.

Follow these steps when using a file or rasp:

1. Clamp the stock to the bench or in a vise. Keep it at a comfortable height. Keep the surface to be smoothed as close to the vise as possible; if it is too far away it will vibrate.

2. Hold the handle in the right hand and the point in the left. If you are left-handed, do the reverse.

3. Place the file flat on the wood near the point, slanted a little across the surface. Push it across the surface and forward at the same time (Fig. 10-6). Apply

enough pressure to make it cut but do not press too hard to try to force it to cut faster. Remember, cutting takes place on the forward stroke. Lift the file off the surface when making the back stroke.

4. If you are trying to keep the edge square, keep the handle parallel with the surface and avoid the tendency to rock the file.

5. When filing end grain, the file will sometimes split the edges of the wood. Avoid this by filing from the sides to the center with short strokes.

6. When the teeth become clogged the file will not cut. Stop and clean the teeth with a file card (Fig. 10-7).

Caring for Files and Rasps

Files and rasps have many fine teeth. They are cut of hardened steel but can be easily damaged. Following are some hints for their care:

1. Do not pile files on top of each other. Do not place other tools on top of files. This will damage the teeth.

Fig. 10-5. A convex surface is smoothed with a flat file.

Fig. 10-6. Hold the file flat on the surface and on a slight angle.

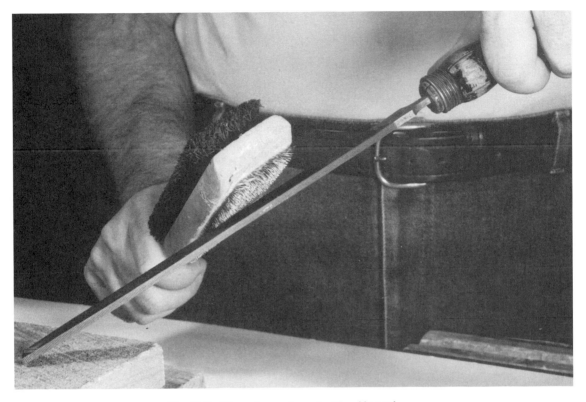

Fig. 10-7. File teeth are cleaned with a file card.

2. Keep them clean. A file card will remove most wood deposits. Lacquer thinner can be used to dissolve pitch that may be stuck in the teeth. Individual teeth can be cleaned with the point of a knife blade.

3. Coat the file with chalk or talcum powder to help prevent clogging.

4. Keep them dry; rust destroys files and discolors the wood.

5. Be certain handles are on tight.

6. Files and rasps are brittle and will snap if used as a pry bar.

MULTIBLADE FORMING TOOLS

A multiblade forming tool uses a steel blade that has cutting edges stamped into it. It comes in many sizes and forms (Fig. 10-8). Because there is a sizeable opening at each tooth, these forming tools do not often clog.

The tool is used the same as a file or rasp. It cuts on the push stroke and should be raised off the surface on the return stroke.

The amount of material removed varies with the angle at which the tool meets the wood. It takes a fast, rough cut when on a 45-degree angle with the surface. The smaller the angle, the finer the cut.

When the blade becomes dull, replace it with a new one from your local hardware store.

Using a Spokeshave

A spokeshave is used to shape wood. It has a small blade and two handles. The depth of cut is adjusted by moving the amount the blade sticks out at the bottom. It may be pulled or pushed (Fig. 10-9). Whenever possible, cut with the grain.

CHISELS

A wood chisel is an edge tool used to trim wood joints and cut recesses in wood. It also is used to smooth curves and irregular surfaces. It is a tool that requires some practice to use skillfully.

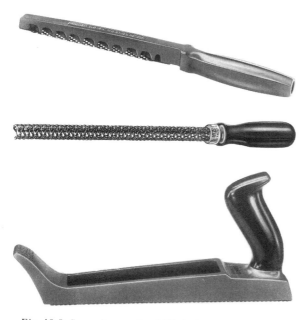

Fig. 10-8. Several types of multiblade forming tools (Courtesy Stanley Tools).

Fig. 10-9. A spokeshave can be used to smooth concave and convex curves.

Handles

A chisel has a strong steel blade that is attached to a handle (Fig. 10-10). The handle is attached to the blade with either a tang, socket, or shank (Fig. 10-11). The tang type has the tang forced into a hole in the handle and is used for hand work only. Never drive it with a mallet; the tang will split the handle. The socket type has the shank of the chisel formed into a cone (called a socket). The handle is made to slip into the socket. This type can be driven with a mallet. The shank type has the tang extend through the handle. It is the strongest of the three types. It is used for heavy duty work.

Handles are made of wood or plastic. They often have a leather or soft metal cap on the end to help keep the handle from splitting.

Types of Chisels

The basic types of wood chisels are the firmer, pocket, butt, and mortise. They differ in size and type of handle (Fig. 10-12).

A *firmer chisel* has a flat blade without a bevel. Widths range from ⅛ to 2 inches.

A *pocket chisel* has a beveled blade and is shorter than the firmer chisel. Widths range from ¼ inch to 1½ inches.

A *butt chisel* has a beveled blade. It is short and used for heavy work. It can be driven with a mallet. Blade lengths are from 2½ to 3 inches long, widths from ¼ inch to 2 inches.

A *mortise chisel* is a long heavy tool with thick square edges. Its main purpose is to hand cut mortises in table and chair legs. A mortise is a deep, rectangular hole into which the table or chair rails is glued. Common widths are ¼, ⁵⁄₁₆, ⅜, and ½ inch.

Using a Chisel

Before starting to cut with a chisel, be certain the work is clamped to the bench or is tight in a vise. Because a chisel is very sharp, remember to keep both hands on it. Never put a hand in front of the chisel. Always cut away from your body.

Follow these steps when using a chisel:

1. After clamping the stock select a chisel that is the same width or slightly narrower than the cut to be made.

2. Right-handed workers hold the blade of the chisel in the left hand and use the right hand only to apply pressure to the handle.

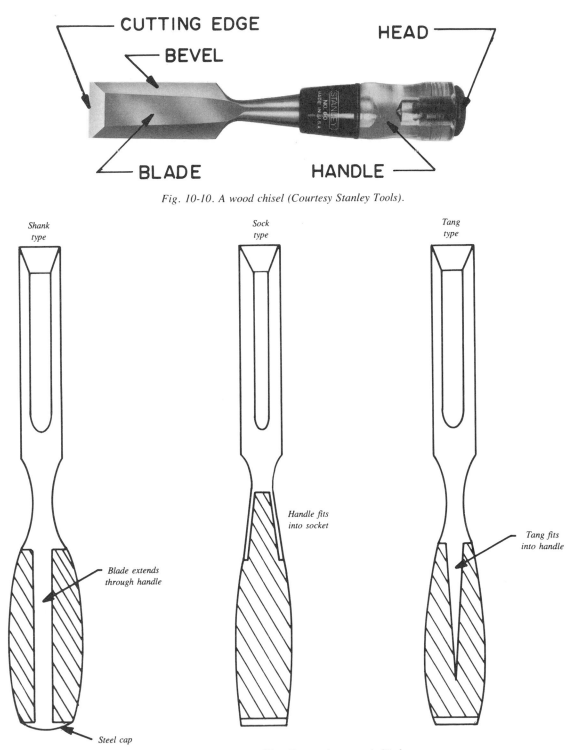

Fig. 10-10. A wood chisel (Courtesy Stanley Tools).

Fig. 10-11. Types of handles used on wood chisels.

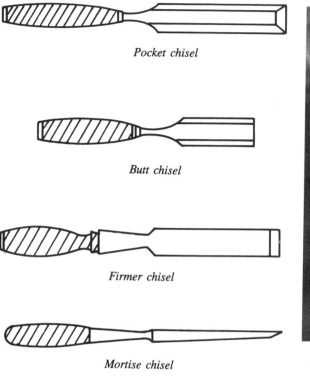

Pocket chisel

Butt chisel

Firmer chisel

Mortise chisel

Fig. 10-12. Types of wood chisels.

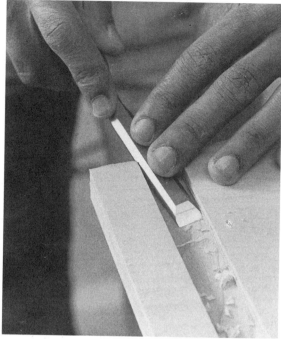

Fig. 10-13. Light finish cuts are made with the bevel up.

3. Make thin cuts by holding the blade flat on the work with the bevel up. Apply light pressure or tap the handle lightly with a mallet (Fig. 10-13).

4. Make deeper cuts by raising the handle on an angle with the work and turning the bevel down. Tap the handle with a mallet. Never strike a chisel a hard blow. If it does not cut with light blows, change the angle of the blade with the work.

5. Whenever possible, cut with the grain; this will produce a smoother finished surface.

Making Horizontal Cuts

1. Clamp the work to the bench.

2. Cut a saw kerf on each side of the area to be cut. You might prefer to cut on the lines with a chisel held vertically.

3. Place the chisel on the area to be cut. Take the rough cuts with the bevel down, the finish cuts with the bevel up.

4. If the cut is across the grain, cut halfway from each side. Alternate cuts from opposite sides until the cut

is finished (Fig. 10-14). If you cut all the way across, the side grain will split out when you finish the cut.

5. Check your work for squareness with a try square.

Making Vertical Cuts

1. Clamp the work to the bench.

2. Place the chisel vertically on the outline of the area to be cut. Keep the bevel facing into the area to be removed.

3. Tap the chisel with a mallet. Cut the entire outline of the area.

4. Cut out the wood inside the area using horizontal cuts.

5. Repeat these steps until the vertical cut is the proper depth.

6. Smooth the sides by placing the chisel flat against them. Take short slicing strokes.

Making Concave Cuts

1. Saw the curve, leaving material for smoothing.

2. Clamp stock to the bench.

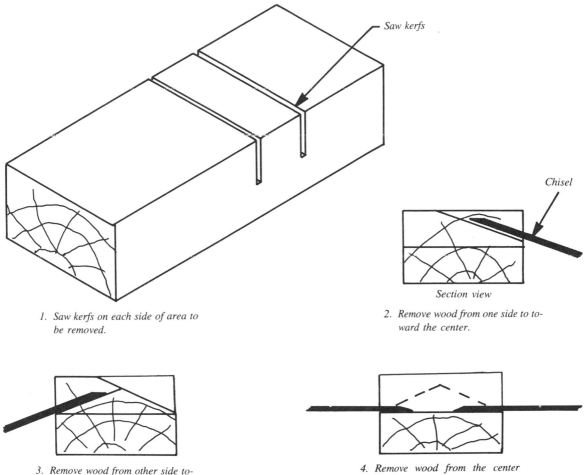

1. *Saw kerfs on each side of area to be removed.*

2. *Remove wood from one side to toward the center.*

Section view

3. *Remove wood from other side toward the center.*

4. *Remove wood from the center cutting from each side.*

Fig. 10-14. Horizontal cuts across the grain are made by cutting half way across from each side.

3. Place the chisel on the curve with the bevel down.

4. Starting at the top of the curve, take light slicing strokes, cutting to the bottom. First cut off the high spots, then go over the curve again, smoothing it and cutting it to the line (Fig. 10-15).

5. Use one hand to control the blade. Keep the strokes short.

Making Convex Cuts

1. Saw the curve leaving material for smoothing.
2. Clamp the stock to the bench.

3. Place the chisel on the curve with the bevel side up.

4. Starting at the top of the curve, take light cuts, moving along the curve. Remove the high spots, then go back and smooth the surface and cut to the line (Fig. 10-16).

5. Use one hand to control the blade. Keep the strokes short.

GOUGES

Gouges are much like chisels except their blades are curved. They are used to produce round-shaped grooves

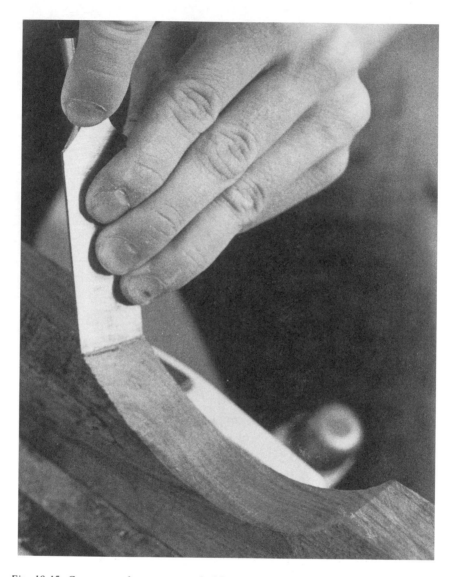

Fig. 10-15. Concave surfaces are smoothed by cutting down the slope with the bevel down.

and to hollow out things such as salad bowls. The two types of gouges are the inside bevel and the outside bevel. The inside bevel has the bevel on the cutting edge ground inside the blade. The outside bevel is ground on the outside of the blade (Fig. 10-17). They have the same types of handles as are used on wood chisels.

Using a Gouge

The outside bevel gouge is used to take deep cuts (Fig. 10-18). The depth of cut is controlled by changing the angle the blade makes with the work. To make heavy cuts, tap the gouge with a mallet.

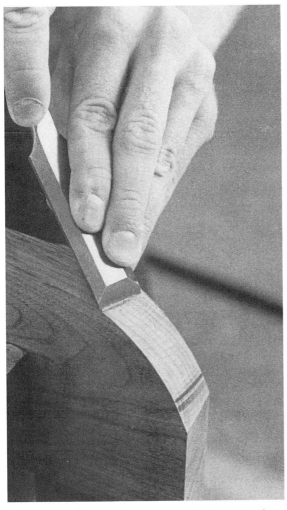

Fig. 10-16. Convex surfaces are smoothed by cutting down the slope with the bevel up.

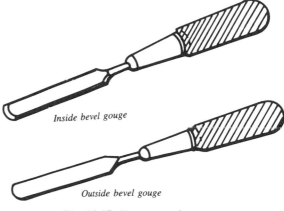

Inside bevel gouge

Outside bevel gouge

Fig. 10-17. Two types of gouges.

The inside bevel gouge is used for fine finishing cuts. Most of the time these cuts can be made with hand pressure. Use a mallet if needed, but tap the handle lightly.

To cut a concave groove, start with a small inside bevel gouge. Use larger sizes until the groove is the size desired.

Hold the gouge the same way as a chisel and follow the same safety precautions.

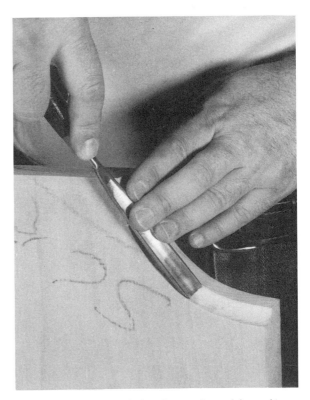

Fig. 10-18. The outside bevel gouge is used for making deep cuts.

Caring for Chisels and Gouges

These tools will only work properly if given basic care. Following are some suggestions:

1. Keep the tools very sharp. Sharpening is explained in the next chapter.

2. Store so the cutting edges are protected—in a wood or plastic box or a rack on a tool panel.

3. Do not place other tools on top of chisels or gouges.

4. Do not use the tools to pry open paint cans or remove screws.

5. Be careful when using used or dirty wood. Nails and grit can seriously damage the cutting edge.

6. Always tap the tools with a wood or plastic mallets; Never use a steel hammer.

7. Keep tools free of rust by wiping them with a light coat of oil occasionally. Remove rust with steel wool.

8. Check the handles to see that they are not loose. Do not use the tools if the handle is loose.

WOOD-CARVING TOOLS

Carving tools are used to produce decorative surfaces and form three-dimensional objects. They look like little chisels and gouges. A wide range of sizes and shapes are available. The blades are set in wood handles and are sharpened in the same manner as chisels and gouges (Fig. 10-19).

Using Carving Tools

Hold these tools in two hands, as you would chisels and gouges. It is important to keep both hands on the tool. Let one hand control the blade while the other hand pushes the handle. Most carving tools are the tang type and should not be driven with a mallet.

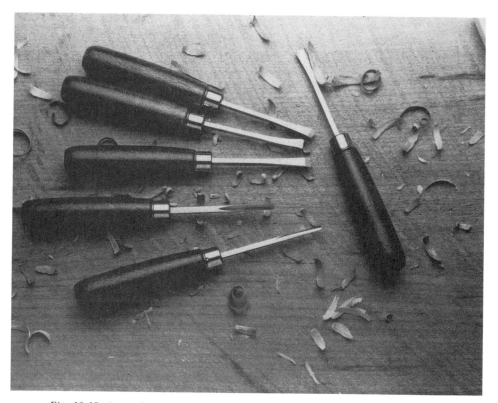

Fig. 10-19. A set of professional carving tools (Courtesy Woodcraft Supply Corp.).

Three-Dimensional Carving

Three-dimensional carving ranges from simple figures to large wood sculptures. The basic process involves first drawing the figure on a block of wood, cutting the basic outline with a saw, then using various types of knives to round and smoothed the object to final form (Fig. 10-20).

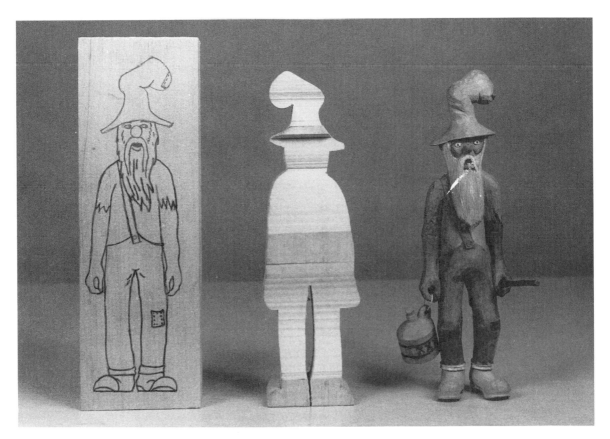

Fig. 10-20. The steps to produce a three-dimensional carving (Courtesy Dr. Fred J. Smith, Pittsburg, Kansas).

Chapter 11

Sharpening Hand Tools

Good-quality tools will hold their cutting edge for quite a while. Poor-quality tools will never get or hold a good cutting edge. It is better to regularly sharpen edge tools than to let them get badly worn and dull. It is also good practice to protect the cutting edges from damage. A chip in an edge will require the tool to be ground, which is much more difficult than just honing the edge and wears the tool out more quickly.

PLANE IRONS

If a plane iron is badly worn or chipped, the cutting edge must be ground and honed. If it is in proper shape but just dull, it only requires honing. It is not necessary to grind a plane iron every time it gets dull.

Grinding a Plane Iron

The cutting edge of the plane iron must be kept 90 degrees with the side. As the plane is used the plane iron must be reground to 90 degrees. This is very hard to do freehand; it is best to use a grinding attachment (Fig. 11-1). To grind a plane iron:

1. Wear safety glasses or, better still, a face shield.
2. Mount the plane iron in a grinding attachment. Adjust the attachment so the plane iron is ground on an angle of 25 degrees (Fig. 11-2).
3. Turn the attachment adjustment screw until the plane iron almost touches the wheel.
4. Start the grinder and turn the adjusting screw until the blade lightly touches the wheel. This will produce sparks. Immediately move the plane iron back and forth

across the wheel; do not let it sit in one place. Do not let either edge of the plane iron move off the edge of the wheel.

5. Pass the plane iron across the wheel and adjust it against the wheel some more. Do this until it has been ground entirely across the edge. Remove it from the attachment and check.
6. If more than a few passes are required, it is necessary to cool the plane iron. Dip it in water or let it air cool. Do not touch the cutting edge; it is very hot. Do not let the edge get so hot it turns blue because this destroys the temper in the edge and the tool will not stay sharp.
7. When the edge is ground uniformly it should be square with the side and the bevel concave (Fig. 11-3). Now hone the edge.

Honing a Plane Iron

In most cases, when a plane iron becomes dull it only needs honing. Examine the cutting edge for damage. If it is not damaged and still has a concave surface formed by grinding, a simple honing will resharpen it.

An oilstone is used for honing. Oilstones come in various degrees of coarseness. After grinding it is advisable to start honing with a coarse stone and finish on a fine stone. To resharpen without grinding, use a fine stone. To hone a plane iron:

1. Coat the oilstone with a layer of oil to serve as lubrication and keep the stone clean.
2. Place the ground bevel on the plane iron flat on

Fig. 11-1. A grinding attachment helps to grind the cutting edge of the plane iron square with the surface (Courtesy Delta International Machinery Corporation).

the stone. Then lift a little so it is at an angle of 30 degrees to the stone. Hold the plane iron in both hands and move it up and down on the stone. (Fig. 11-4).

3. After making several passes, place the plane iron flat on the stone, the bevel up. Move in a small circular pattern to remove the wire edge (Fig. 11-5). If the wire edge is not removed, hone it again on the bevel and then hone it flat. A wire edge can also be removed by cutting into a piece of wood.

4. Now repeat the honing again on a fine oilstone and remove the wire edge.

5. Test the blade for sharpness by slicing a piece of paper or wood. If it cuts easily it is sharp. Do not hone too much; you only need to touch up the cutting edge.

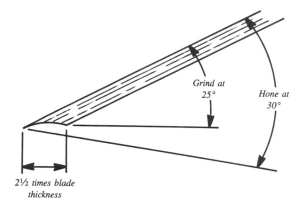

Fig. 11-2. The plane iron should be ground and honed at these angles.

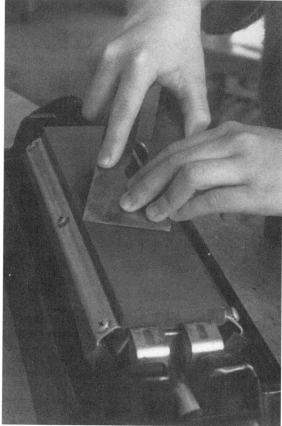

Fig. 11-4. To hone the plane iron, work it in a figure eight pattern.

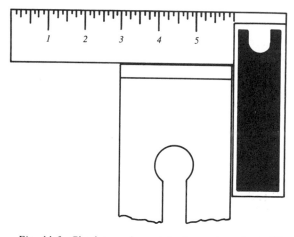

Fig. 11-3. Check to make certain the cutting edge is 90 degrees with the side.

CHISELS

The procedure for sharpening chisels is the same as explained for plane irons. If the chisel is not chipped or the concave surface worn off, the bevel only needs to be honed. If it must be ground, set the grinding attachment on 25 degrees (Fig. 11-6).

SPOKESHAVES

To sharpen a spokeshave, remove the blade from the frame. It is sharpened the same as a plane iron. If it must be ground, grind it on an angle of 25 degrees.

GOUGES

Gouges are ground when they are nicked or badly worn. Because the bevel is round, this job should be given to an expert. However, it is easy to hone a gouge:

1. Work the outside bevel against the concave surface of a slip stone. Roll it as you move it against the stone (Fig. 11-7).

2. Remove the wire edge by honing the inside of the gouge with a slipstone. A slipstone is a tear-shaped oilstone. Place it flat against the inside surface of the gouge. Push it off the end. Repeat honing the outside and inside until the wire edge is gone (Fig. 11-8). To hone an inside bevel gouge:

Fig. 11-5. Remove the wire edge by placing the plane iron flat on the oil stone with the bevel up.

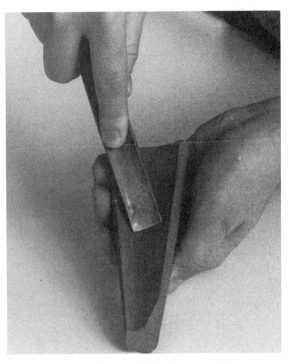

Fig. 11-7. Hone the outside bevel against the concave surface of a slip stone.

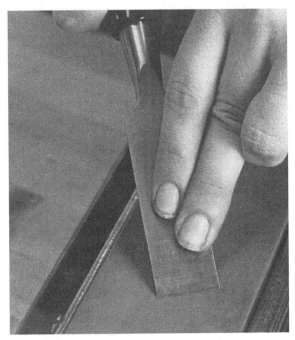

Fig. 11-6. Hone the chisel on an oil stone.

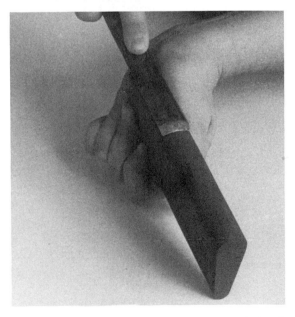

Fig. 11-8. Remove the wire edge on an outside bevel gouge with a slipstone placed flat on the inside of the gouge.

1. Hone the inside bevel with a slipstone. Hold it on an angle so it is flat against the surface of the bevel (Fig. 11-9).

2. Place the outside of the gouge flat on a flat oilstone. Push and roll it to remove the wire edge.

KNIVES

Seldom is it necessary to grind a pocket knife. If it has to be ground, grind on the angle originally on the blade. Keep the blade cool so it does not turn blue.

Most of the time a knife simply requires honing. Place the blade flat on an oilstone, raising the back of the blade off the stone a little. Move the blade in a circular pattern. Turn the blade over and hone the other side (Fig. 11-10).

SCRAPERS

A scraper has a burr on the edge. This burr is sharp and scrapes off a fine layer of wood. Because the burr is

Fig. 11-10. Hone a knife blade on each side.

formed by bending, it does not last very long (Fig. 11-11).

It is important that the edges of a scraper be straight. If they become concave or convex the scraper will not work properly. To sharpen a hand scraper:

1. Clamp the scraper in a vise. Using a fine flat file, draw file the edge flat and square (Fig. 11-12).

2. Remove the scraper from the vise and hone on an oilstone. First hold it vertically and move on the stone, then place it flat and hone both faces. Repeat until the wire edges are gone. This produces sharp corners on the edge.

3. Mount the scraper in a vise. Put a few drops of oil on a burnisher. Place it in the center of the edge and slope a little off the horizontal. Push down and forward on the burnisher; this bends the sharp corner over. Repeat on both edges, going from the center to each end.

Fig. 11-9. Hone the inside bevel on the convex surface of the slipstone.

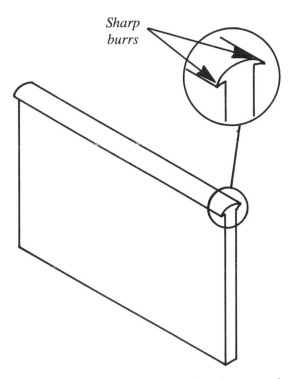

Sharp burrs

Fig. 11-11. A hand scraper has a sharp burr on each corner.

Fig. 11-12. File the edge of the scraper flat and square.

Then repeat lowering the handle on the burnisher some more. After two or three times you will be able to feel the burr with your finger. Do not burnish too much or you will turn under the burr (Fig. 11-13). To sharpen a cabinet scraper:

1. Clamp the blade in a vise. File the blade on a 45 degree angle, making certain it is straight.

2. Hone on an oilstone the same as a plane iron.

3. Clamp it in a vise and burnish the edge. Slant the burnisher on a 15-degree angle. Start in the center of the blade. Press down and slide the burnisher across the blade. Repeat for the other half. This will bend the sharp edge over, forming a burr (Fig. 11-14).

AUGER BITS

There are two parts to be sharpened: the spur and the lips. This is a delicate operation and should be approached carefully to avoid damage to the cutting edges. To sharpen an auger bit:

1. First sharpen the spurs. Place the bit firmly against the bench with the screw facing up. Using an auger bit file or a small three-square file, take one or two strokes on the inside of each spur (Fig. 11-15). Never file the outside: this will reduce the diameter of the bit and cause it to bind, and will ruin the bit.

2. File the lips. Place the bit with the screw down against the table. File on the bottom of each lip, being careful not to overfile. Take the same number of strokes on each lip (Fig. 11-16).

COUNTERSINKS

To sharpen a countersink, use a triangular file or fine stone to dress each cutting edge. One or two strokes on each edge is usually enough. Sharpen on the radial face only.

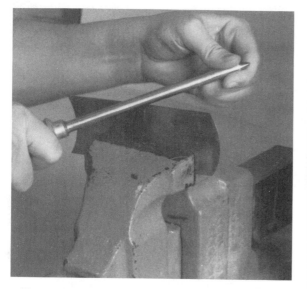

Fig. 11-13. Form the burr by pressing a burnisher against the edge.

Fig. 11-15. Lightly file the inside of the spurs.

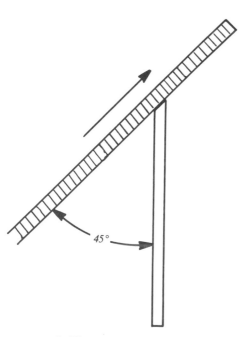

1. File cabinet scraper blade on 45° angle. Then hone it on an oil stone.

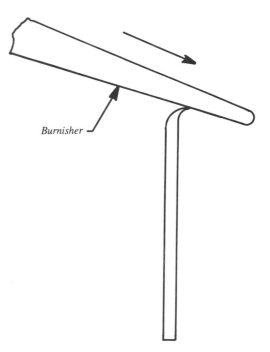

Burnisher

2. Bend a burr with the burnisher.

Fig. 11-14. Steps to form a burr on a cabinet scraper blade.

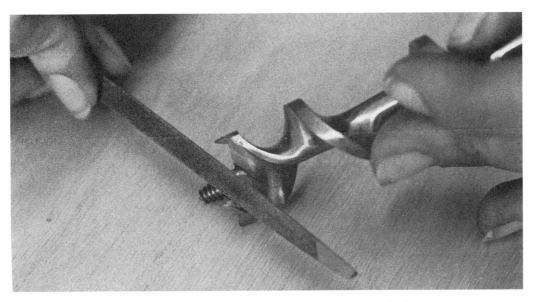

Fig. 11-16. Hold the auger bit like this when sharpening the lips.

SCREWDRIVERS

The tip of a standard screwdriver will become worn. To restore it to the square shape it was when you bought it, touch it lightly to a grinding wheel (Fig. 11-17). Grind the tip square. Lightly touch the sides to the wheel; this grinds them slightly concave. Be especially careful that the tip of the screwdriver does not catch in the wheel because this may throw the tool and will damage the tip.

The flats of a Phillips screwdriver are dressed on an oilstone. The inside of the flutes can be smoothed with a square stone.

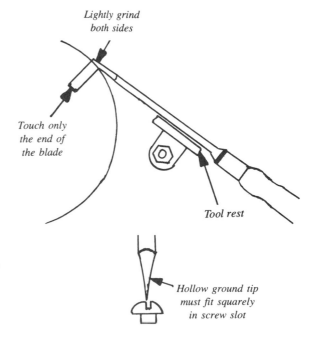

Lightly grind both sides

Touch only the end of the blade

Tool rest

Hollow ground tip must fit squarely in screw slot

Tool rest

1. Lightly press the screwdriver perpendicular to the grinding wheel to square the tip.

Fig. 11-17. The tip of the screwdriver is ground square and slightly concave on the faces.

2. Dress the faces to get the tip the desired thickness.

Chapter 12

Wood Joints

Furniture, cabinets, and other wood products require a variety of joints. Each joint has its advantages and disadvantages; it is important to choose the best joint for the job.

CHOOSING THE JOINT

The decision requires a knowledge of the various joints. Some are stronger than others; some are harder to make; some are hidden while others are visible. Consider each of these factors along with what equipment is available. For example, the frame for a chair must be very strong, so it would be wise to use the strongest possible joint, even though it is more difficult to make.

The strength of a joint depends upon:

- The size of the surface to receive glue.
- How well it is made.
- Whether it uses edge or end grain.
- The type of fasteners used.

The more glue area in a joint, the stronger it will be. If the glue area is small, wood or metal fasteners are used to increase the strength.

Joints that are glued using edge or face grain are stronger than those using end grain. A properly made and glued face-grain joint will be stronger than the wood. If you do use end grain, also use wood or metal fasteners to strengthen the joint.

The surfaces of a joint must fit properly. The two pieces should slide together with a small amount of hand pressure. Glue will not bridge gaps in a joint. When gaps occur, the actual glue area available is reduced.

Metal fasteners increase the strength of a joint. (Fasteners are explained in Chapter 15). Some are designed to hold boards together that are not under stress, while others will carry a considerable load.

Joints can also be used to simply add to the appearance of the product. A well-made dovetail joint is an example. Others, such as blind dadoes, are used because they are hidden. The wood parts meet with no indication as to how they are held together.

A skilled woodworker can make the stronger, more difficult joints. A beginner should consider using a less difficult joint: A well-made, simple joint might be better than a poorly made difficult one.

Choose a joint that will do the job; don't be tempted to overdo. If a joint, such as a corner in a picture frame, is under little stress, use a simple joint. When glued and nailed, it will hold quite well, so more complex joint is unnecessary. Following is a description of the more frequently used wood joints. The next chapter will provide instructions on making them.

BUTT JOINTS

Butt joints are the easiest to make. They are not very strong, so require reinforcement with wood or metal fasteners. The basic types of butt joints are as follows (Fig. 12-1):

- Face-to-face: Thin boards are glued face-to-face to make a thicker piece. Table legs and lamp bases are often made this way.
- End-to-edge: Table and cabinet frames use this joint,

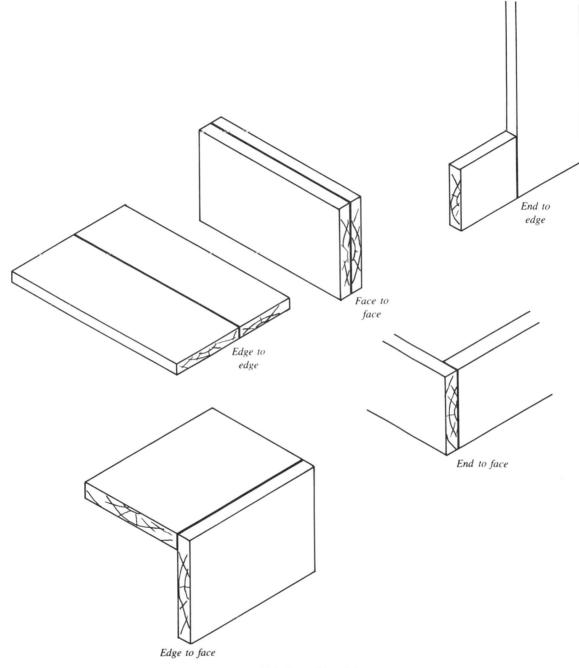

Fig. 12-1. Typical butt joints.

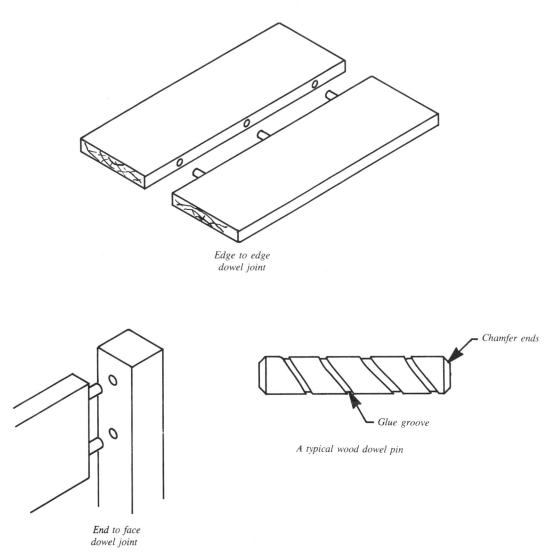

Edge to edge
dowel joint

End to face
dowel joint

Chamfer ends

Glue groove

A typical wood dowel pin

Fig. 12-2. Dowel joints add strength to butt joints.

and chair and table frames are joined to legs with this joint.

■ End-to-face: The top and sides of a cabinet or bookcase use this joint. It lets the end grain of one of the pieces show, which might not be desirable.

DOWEL JOINTS

Dowel pins are round wooden pegs used to reinforce butt joints. Holes are drilled in each piece and the wood

dowel pins glued in place. This is a fairly easy way to reinforce joints and makes the joint quite strong. The pins also help keep the pieces lined up while they are glued and clamped (Fig. 12-2).

MITER JOINTS

A miter joint is a type of butt joint. The ends of each piece are usually cut on a 45-degree angle, and form a 90-degree corner when joined. The advantage here is that

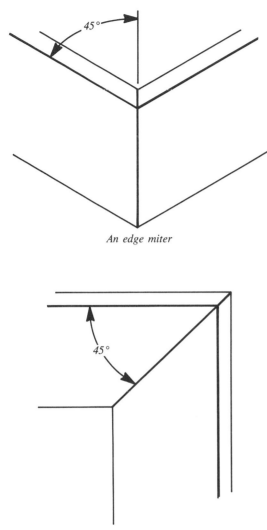

An edge miter

A flat miter

Fig. 12-3. Miter joints are used to form corners where no end grain is to show.

all end grain is covered. The grain pattern in the wood continues around the corner. Miters can be cut on edges or ends of stock (Fig. 12-3).

Miter joints are used on picture frames and whenever moldings are applied: For example, on furniture and cabinets or the trim around the doors and windows in a house.

Because a miter joint is comprised totally of end grain it is weak and requires wood or metal fasteners for strength.

RABBET JOINTS

Rabbet joints are cut on the end or the edge of boards. End rabbets are used to form corners for drawers and cabinets, while edge rabbets are used for the backs of cabinets. They are assembled with glue and nails or screws. (Fig. 12-4).

Rabbet joints hide more of the end grain than a butt joint. The lip also provides some vertical support. These joints help hold parts in place as they are being put together.

LAP JOINTS

There are many types of lap joints, each following the same principle: Half the thickness or width of each piece is cut away, so when the pieces are joined their surfaces are flush. A cross lap is used when two pieces meet and one stops at the meeting point. A middle lap is used when two pieces meet and one stops at the meeting point. An end lap is used to form a 90-degree corner. An edge lap allows two pieces to cross along their edges (Fig. 12-5). Because these joints have a large area of face grain exposed, they are strong when glued.

DADO AND GROOVE JOINTS

A *dado* is a rectangular slot cut across the grain of a board. It can be used, for example, to hold shelves in a bookcase. The joint often includes glue and metal fasteners.

A *groove* is a rectangular slot cut with the grain of a board. It is used, for example, to hold the bottoms of drawers to the sides. (Fig. 12-6). If the dado is to be hidden, it is cut short so it does not extend completely across the board. The board that is to fit into the dado has a notch to fit around the corner of the dado. This type is called a blind dado.

RABBET-AND-DADO JOINTS

The combination rabbet-and-dado is a popular joint. Such joints are used to form the corners of boxes and drawers. The tongue of the rabbet is glued in the dado, so the shoulder presses against the board and the dado strengthens the joint (Fig. 12-7).

TONGUE-AND-GROOVE JOINTS

Tongue-and-groove joints are used to glue narrow boards together. The tongue is in the center of one piece, the groove in the center of the other, and the surface of the

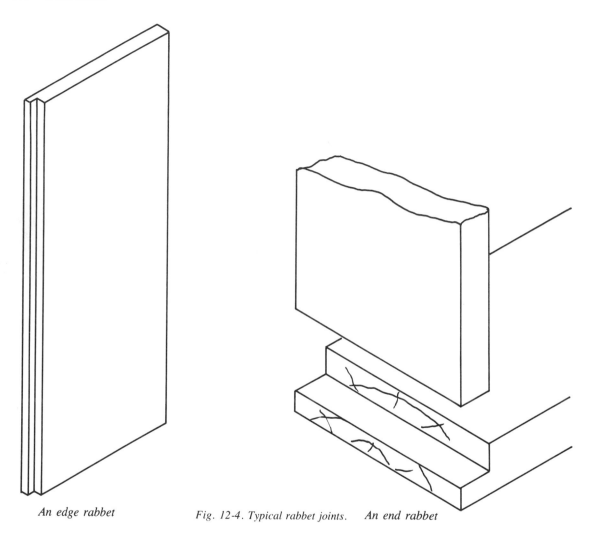

An edge rabbet   *Fig. 12-4. Typical rabbet joints.*   *An end rabbet*

boards flush. It is a difficult joint to make by hand, so it is usually cut with power tools. Because it has a large area of face grain, it can be glued. (Fig. 12-8).

MORTISE-AND-TENON JOINTS

Mortise-and-tenon joints are used to join chair and table rails to the legs. It is a very strong joint and is used on quality construction.

The blind mortise-and-tenon is most commonly used. It has the advantage of hiding the joint completely. The through mortise-and-tenon is glued and wedged in place. This joint adds a decorative appearance (Fig. 12-9).

Mortise-and-tenon joints are difficult to cut by

hand. The joint must fit tightly or the glue will not hold it properly.

DOVETAIL JOINTS

A dovetail joint is used to join corners of boxes, drawers, and cabinets. It is very strong and decorative, but is difficult to cut by hand. Careful layout is necessary, followed by accurate sawing. Use a chisel to trim the mortise and tenon to fit together (Fig. 12-10).

BOX JOINTS

A box joint is like a dovetail except that the fingers are rectangular. This joint is strong and decorative, and easier to cut and fit than the dovetail (Fig. 12-11).

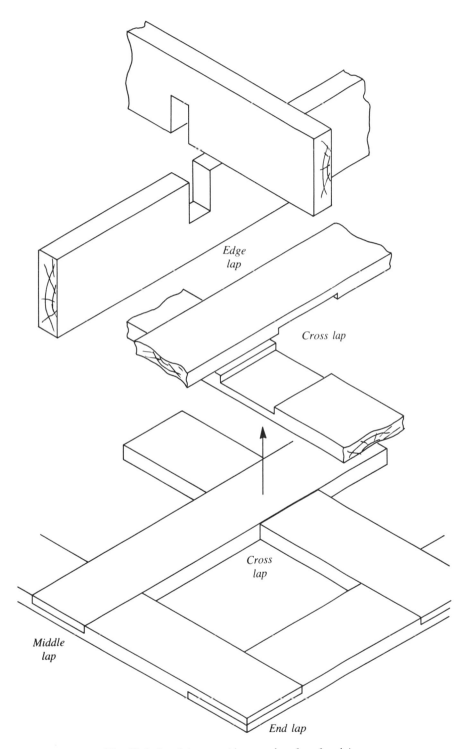

Fig. 12-5. Lap joints provide a good surface for gluing.

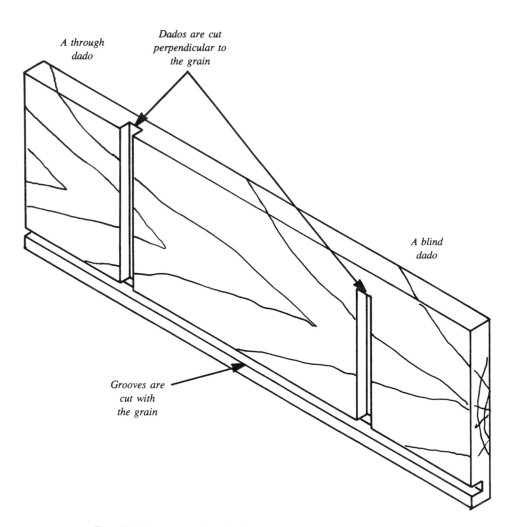

A through dado

Dados are cut perpendicular to the grain

A blind dado

Grooves are cut with the grain

Fig. 12-6. Grooves and dado joints are cut to support a joining piece.

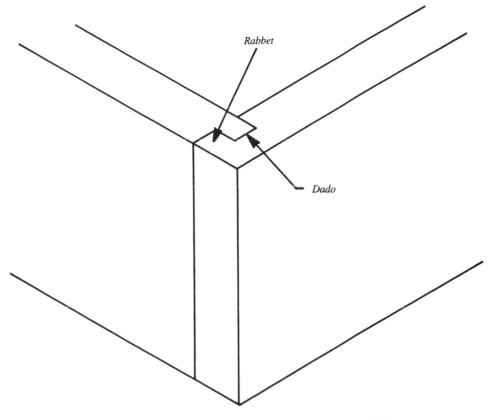

Fig. 12-7. A combination rabbet and dado makes a strong joint.

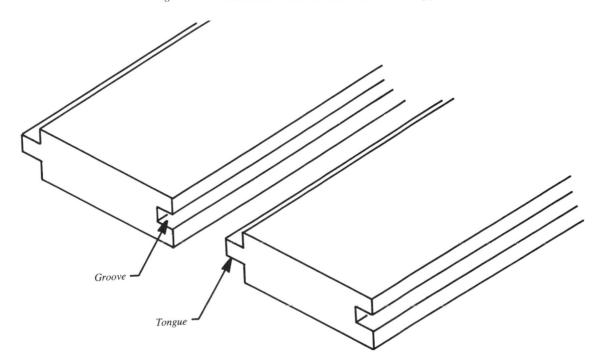

Fig. 12-8. A tongue-and-groove joint is used to join stock edge to edge.

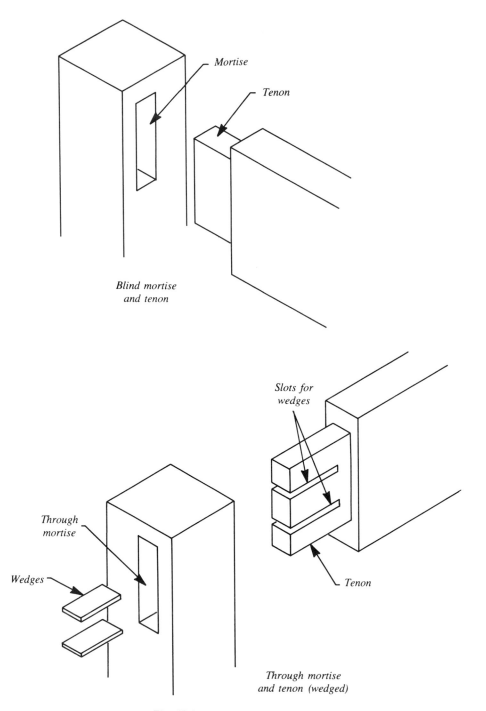

Mortise

Tenon

*Blind mortise
and tenon*

*Slots for
wedges*

Tenon

*Through
mortise*

Wedges

*Through mortise
and tenon (wedged)*

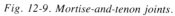

Fig. 12-9. Mortise-and-tenon joints.

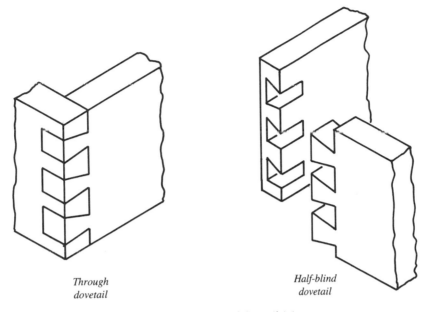

*Through
dovetail*

*Half-blind
dovetail*

Fig. 12-10. Two types of dovetail joints.

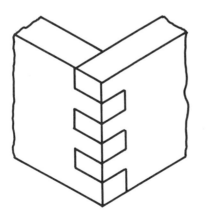

Fig. 12-11. A box joint.

Chapter 13

Cutting Wood Joints with Hand Tools

Cutting joints with hand tools requires skill and careful layout. It cannot be rushed. When a joint is finished and it fits properly, you can feel proud of this achievement. Practice first on scrap material before cutting the finished material. Your first attempts will not be perfect, but will improve with practice.

Joints can be cut with either power woodworking machinery or hand tools. The use of this equipment is covered in chapters 16 through 26.

LAYOUT TECHNIQUES

The key to success is an accurate layout of the joint. The sizes can be found on the working drawing of your project. Before making the layout, check the actual size of the wood pieces; they might be slightly larger or smaller than the sizes on the drawing. Lay out the joints to fit the sizes of the parts to be joined.

Use your layout tools properly. For best results, mark the sides of the joint with a sharp knife. A sharp, hard pencil will also work if it is kept sharp. You want a single thin line.

When cutting the joint, cut on the waste side of the line. Keep the cuts square. Do not cut beyond the depth mark.

After cutting the joint, put it together dry as a trial assembly. It should fit snugly yet not have to be forced together. You should be able to separate the pieces easily. Glue causes wood to swell, so you might not be able to get a joint that is too tight to fit together. If the trial assembly reveals that the joint is too tight, remove some

material with a chisel or a plane. Do not file the joint, because this tends to round the edges.

Be certain all surfaces of the joint are flat: Glue will not bridge gaps between pieces. The joint will be weakened if the surfaces do not touch lightly.

BUTT JOINTS

Butt joints are made by placing two squared pieces together. They must cut straight and square. They can be fastened with glue and dowels or fasteners (See chapter 15).

End-to-End Joint

To make an end-to-end joint:

1. Cut each piece to rough width, length, and thickness.
2. Plane each piece to the proper width and thickness, then cut each piece to length. The miter box is the most accurate tool to use here.
3. Check the fit by placing the end to the edge. If they do not fit tightly, check each for squareness with a try square. Plane carefully until they fit (Fig. 13-1).
4. This joint is usually secured with wood dowels, which are explained later in the chapter.

End-to-Face Joints

End-to-face joints are made as listed above, the only difference is that the end of one piece is fitted to the face of the other (Fig. 13-2).

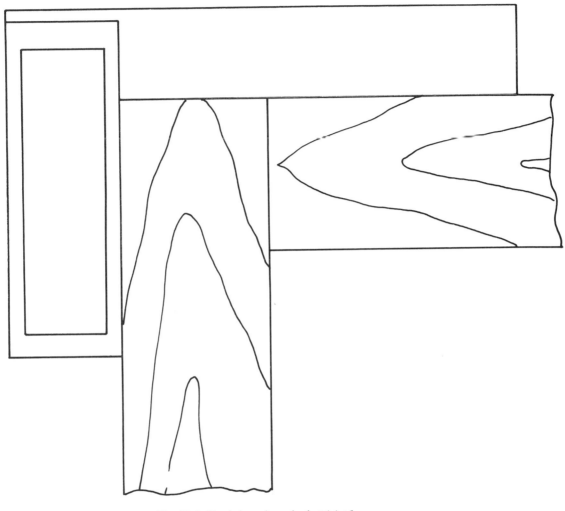

Fig. 13-1. Check the end-to-edge butt joint for squareness.

Edge-to-Edge Joint

Edge-to-edge joints are used to join narrow boards. Dowels are sometimes used to strengthen the joint and hold the boards in place while they are being glued. To make an edge-to-edge joint:

1. Cut each piece to rough width, length, and thickness. Usually pieces under 4 inches (100 mm) are used, because wider pieces might warp. If the boards are wide they are sometimes cut into narrower strips and glued together.

2. Place the boards side by side on the workbench. The grain on the face of each should run in the same direction (Fig. 13-3). Alternate the end grain. Wood cups opposite the direction of the growth rings, so if the pieces are alternated, the amount of cup will be small.

3. After arranging the boards, mark the joints.

4. Take two adjoining boards and place them together, keeping the face with marks out. Clamp in a vise with the edges flush. Plane both edges at the same time (Fig. 13-4). In this way, if the edge is a little out of square the joint will still close. Check the length with a framing square to be sure it is straight. Repeat for each pair of adjoining edges.

5. You can check each joint by placing it together and holding it to a light. If there is a gap, light will show

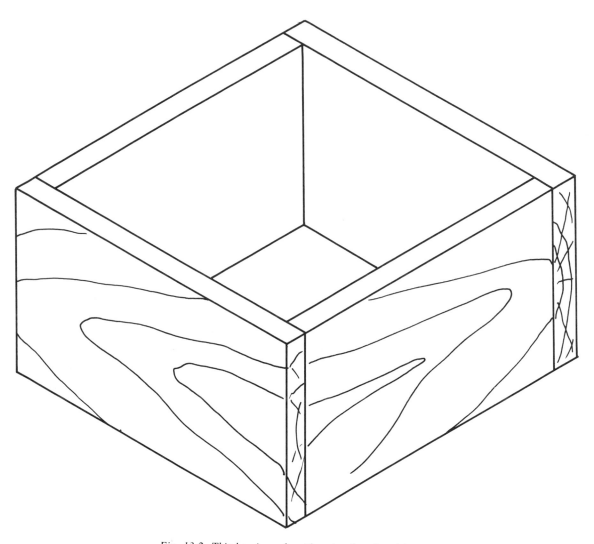

Fig. 13-2. This box is made with end-to-face butt joints.

through. Mark the high spots and plane them very carefully. Dowels are used to keep the parts in line as they are glued.

Face-to-Face Joints

To make a face-to-face joint:

1. Cut each piece to rough width and length.
2. Stack the pieces in the order they are to be as-

sembled. Keep the face grain in the same direction on each piece, alternate the end grain (Fig. 13-5).

3. Mark each face-to-face joint.

4. Plane the surface of each piece. Check it with a framing square (Fig. 13-6), it must be flat. Mark and plane the high spots. Hold the two pieces together and to the light. If no light shows through, they are flat. Repeat this for each of the other matching faces.

5. This joint can be secured with glue. Because it is face-to-face, it will be very strong.

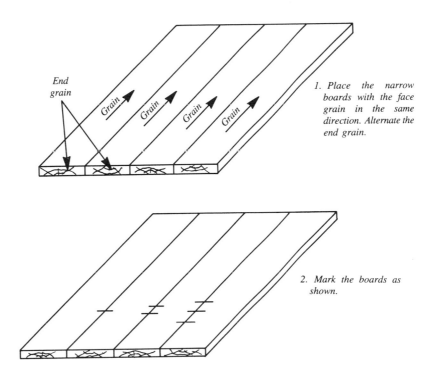

1. *Place the narrow boards with the face grain in the same direction. Alternate the end grain.*

2. *Mark the boards as shown.*

Fig. 13-3. To make an edge-to-edge joint, first arrange the boards and mark the joints.

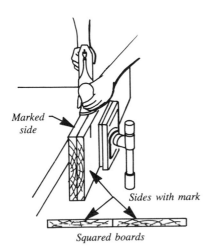

Fig. 13-4. Plane adjoining edges together with the marks out.

DOWEL JOINTS

Prepare the joint as explained for butt joints. Once it is true and square, mark the location of the dowels.

Dowel Pins

Dowel pins are short round pieces of wood. They can be purchased cut to length with glue grooves cut in them. They are available in diameters from ¼ to 1 inch. The ends of the dowels are chamfered (Fig. 13-7).

The diameter of the dowel pin should be one half the thickness of the wood. A ⅜-inch dowel is used on ¾-inch wood. Dowel pins 2 inches long are commonly used.

Laying Out the Dowel Holes

1. Hold the edges to be joined together in a vise. Keep the faces with the marks out.

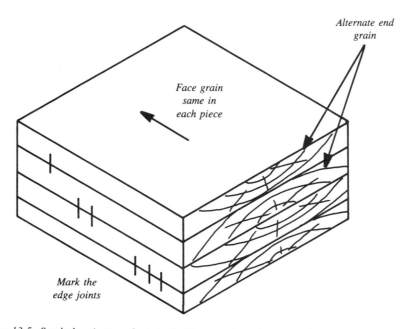

Fig. 13-5. Stack the pieces to be joined. Alternate the end grain and mark the edge joints.

2. Mark the location of each dowel with a try square. Edge-to-edge joints have dowels every 6 inches (Fig. 13-8). An end-to-edge dowel joint should have at least two dowels (Fig. 13-9).

3. After marking the location, mark the center of each using a marking gauge (Fig. 13-10). Mark the centers on each board from the outside face of the board, so if the center is missed, the holes will still line up.

Dowel centers can also be used to locate dowel holes. A dowel center is a metal cup with a pin on one side that is placed in the holes in one piece. The second piece can then be lined up and pressed against the points to locate the holes in that piece (Fig. 13-11).

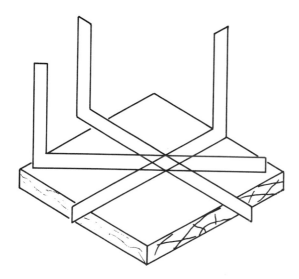

Fig. 13-6. Check each piece for squareness.

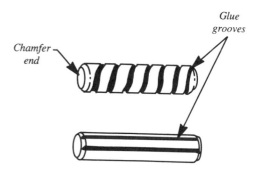

Fig. 13-7. Types of dowel pins.

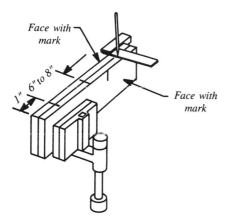

Fig. 13-8. Mark dowel locations on matching edges of each joint.

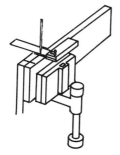

Fig. 13-9. Mark the edge-to-edge dowel locations of each joint at the same time.

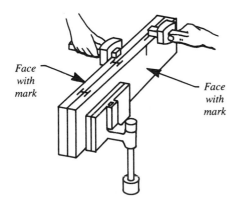

Fig. 13-10. Mark the center of each dowel hole from the faces with the marks.

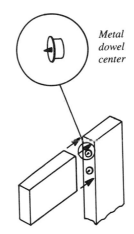

Fig. 13-11. Dowel centers can be used to locate dowel holes.

Boring the Dowel Holes

The best way to bore the dowel holes is with a dowel bit and dowel jig. The jig clamps on the edge of the board. It has a series of metal holes of different diameters.

Position the hole that is the same diameter of the dowel over the center mark. Place the dowel bit in a brace, and slide it in the hole in the jig. Bore each hole ⅛ inch deeper than one half the length of the dowel (Fig. 13-12). The dowel holes can be drilled with a hand drill or a portable electric drill. The dowel jig will help keep them perpendicular to the work.

Testing the Dowel Joint

After the holes are bored, insert the dowel pins in one side. Slide the second side over the pins and press them together. The joint should close up tightly. If it does not, take it apart and be certain the holes are free of chips. Check the pins to see if they are too long. Dowel pins should be about ¼ inch shorter than the depth of the holes (Fig. 13-13). Sometimes a slanted dowel will keep the joint from closing; try shaving a little off the dowel to permit the joint to close (Fig. 13-14).

MITER JOINTS

The most common miter joint is cut on a 45-degree angle. However, other angles can be cut; the procedure is the same (Fig. 13-15):

1. Work the wood to its finished thickness and width. The length should be 1 inch or more longer than

Fig. 13-12. Bore the dowel holes with a dowel jig.

the finished size. The stock can be molding or similar material.

2. Using a miter box, set the saw 45 degrees to one side. Cut one end on each piece, keeping the outside of the stock against the fence. The cut should slope toward the inside of the molding (Fig. 13-16).

3. Measure the length. If you know the outside size and the inside distance, measure these (Fig. 13-17). Careful measurements are vital to success.

4. Turn the saw 45 degrees in the other direction. Place the stock on the table and cut to the mark. Cut each piece to length. The cut will be more accurate if you clamp the molding to the table or frame of the miter box.

5. Assemble the pieces on the bench and press them together to see if all four joints close. If they do not, you can remove some wood with a block plane. If the joint is open a lot, clamp it to the table. Saw through it with a backsaw until it closes. Keep scrap wood under the joint so you do not saw into the table (Fig. 13-18).

Fastening Miter Joints

Because a miter joint is very weak it must be reinforced. The easiest way to do this is to apply glue to both surfaces and clamp them in a vise, then drive a finishing nail through the corner. Some prefer to cross-nail the corner (Fig. 13-19). A miter vise is a big help when fastening a miter joint (Fig. 13-20).

Another method of reinforcement is a spline. Cut a groove in each half of the miter. Cut a thin wood strip the size of the groove; this is called a *spline*. The grain

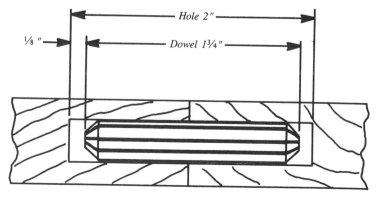

Fig. 13-13. The dowel pin must be shorter than the total depth of the holes.

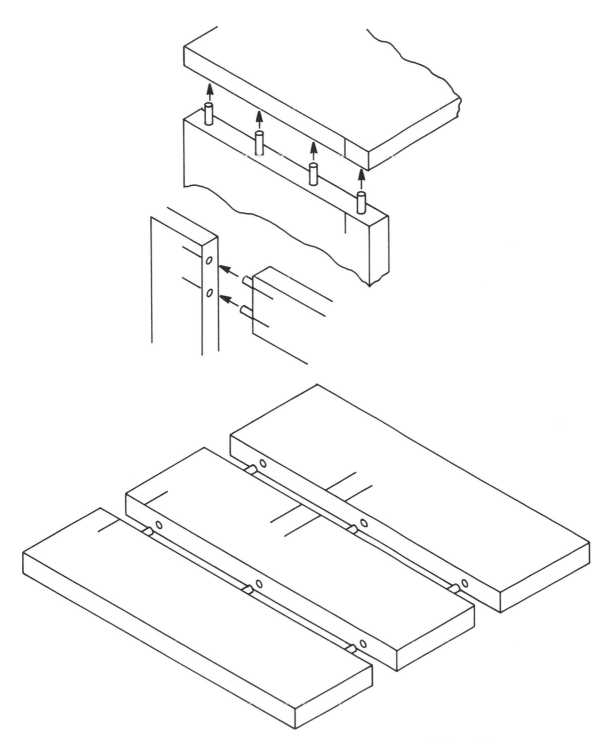

Fig. 13-14. Assemble the joint without glue. Adjust it to fit properly before gluing.

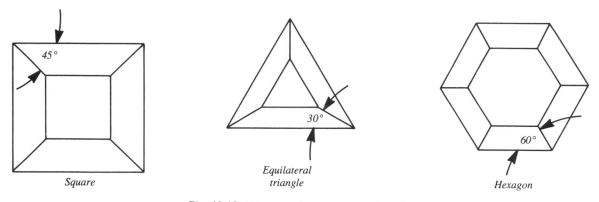

Fig. 13-15. Miters can be cut on several angles.

should run across it. Glue the spline into the groove in each side of the miter (Fig. 13-21). Miters can also be joined with metal fasteners.

RABBET JOINTS

An end rabbet joint can be made with two accurate saw cuts (Fig. 13-22). To make an end rabbet joint:

1. Square the stock to its final size.
2. Lay out the rabbet on one piece. This can be done by standing the matching piece on it and carefully marking the width.

3. Mark the depth with a marking gauge. Normally the depth is ⅔ the thickness of the stock (Fig. 13-23).
4. Clamp the piece in a vise. Cut each side with a dovetail or backsaw, making the end cut first (Fig. 13-24). To keep the saw square, clamp a block of wood along the line. Then make the shoulder cut on the waste side of the line (Fig. 13-25). The shoulder cut can also be made on a miter saw.
5. Place the two pieces together in a trial assembly. If they do not fit, trim the sawed faces with a chisel.
6. Fasten joints with glue and nails or screws.

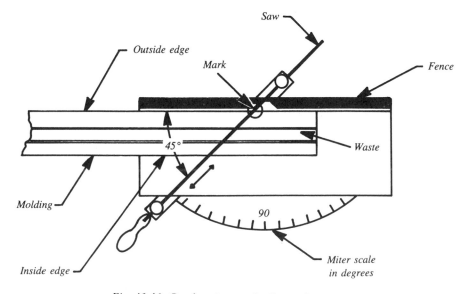

Fig. 13-16. Cut the miter on the first end.

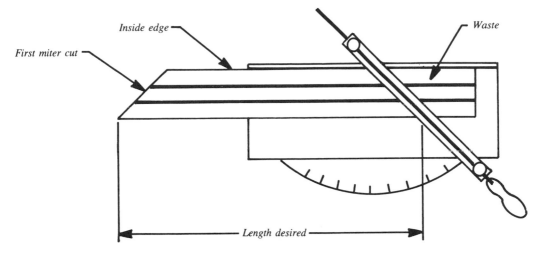

First miter cut

Inside edge

Waste

Length desired

Fig. 13-17. Measure the length, swing the saw to the other side, and cut the second angle.

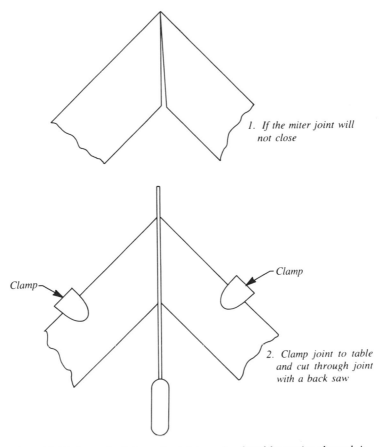

1. If the miter joint will not close

Clamp

Clamp

2. Clamp joint to table and cut through joint with a back saw

Fig. 13-18. A poorly fitting miter joint can be closed by sawing through it.

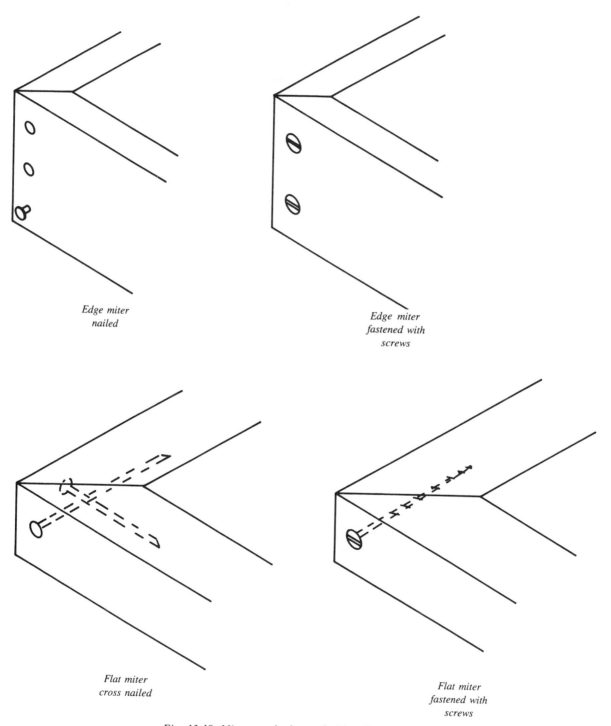

Edge miter
nailed

Edge miter
fastened with
screws

Flat miter
cross nailed

Flat miter
fastened with
screws

Fig. 13-19. Miters can be fastened with nails or screws.

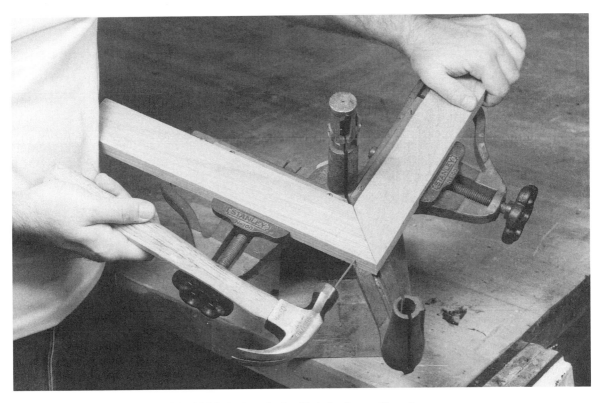

Fig. 13-20. A miter vise is a big help when nailing miters.

An edge rabbet joint is cut with a rabbet plane. To make an edge rabbet:

1. Lay out the rabbet using a marking gauge.
2. Set a rabbet plane to cut the width of the rabbet.
3. Clamp the stock to the bench and plane the rabbet along the edge (Fig. 13-26). Be careful not to cut too deep.

DADO JOINTS

A dado is a rectangular slot cut across the grain. To make a dado joint:

1. Square the stock to its final size.
2. Lay out the width of the dado. Locate one side by measuring with a rule, scribe a line there with a knife, then place the matching part against it (Fig. 13-27). Mark the second side carefully with a knife.
3. Mark the depth with a marking gauge. The depth is usually made one-third to one-half the thickness of the wood.

4. Place the piece on a miter box or use a back saw. Cut along each line in the waste material. Leave the line. Cut to the depth line and stop. Make a few extra cuts in the waste stock to remove this material.
5. Remove the waste material with a chisel. Cut from each side to prevent splitting the edge (Fig. 13-28).

RABBET-DADO JOINTS

To make a rabbet-dado joint:

1. Square the stock to finished size.
2. Mark the edges of the dado using a try square. The width of the dado is usually ¼ to ⅓ the thickness of the stock.
3. Measure and mark the depth of the dado, which is usually ½ the thickness of the stock (Fig. 13-29).

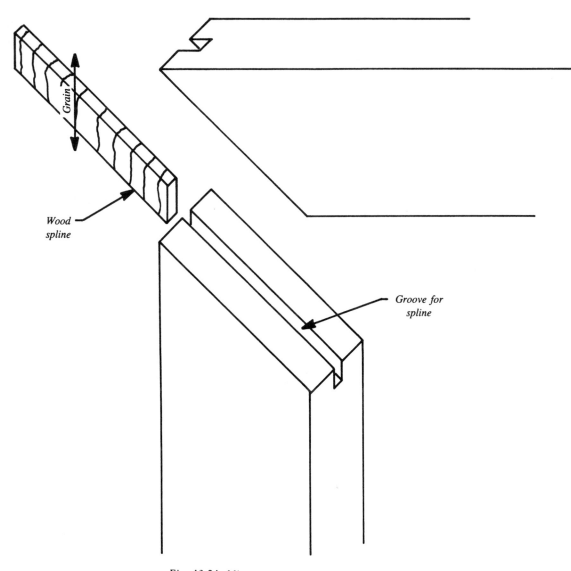

Fig. 13-21. Miters can be glued if a spline is used.

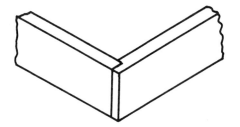

Fig. 13-22. A rabbet joint is made with two saw cuts.

4. Cut the dado with a miter saw and chisel, following the steps given earlier for cutting a dado.

5. Lay out the rabbet as explained earlier. The only difference here is that it is sized to fit the dado. It is about $\frac{1}{32}$ inch (.8 mm) shorter than the depth of the dado, which leaves a small glue pocket (Fig. 13-30).

6. Cut the rabbet as explained earlier. Smooth with a chisel until it fits the dado firmly and so the joint closes.

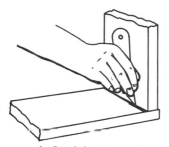

1. *Stand the piece to fit into the rabbet on the piece in which it will be cut. Mark the width.*

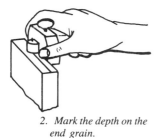

2. *Mark the depth on the end grain.*

Shoulder cut

End cut

3. *Producing this layout.*

Fig. 13-23. *Laying out an end rabbet.*

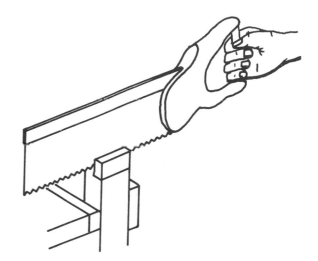

Fig. 13-24. *Make the end cut.*

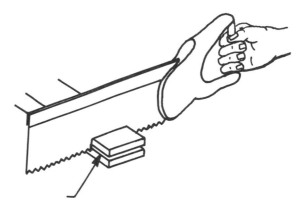

Fig. 13-25. *Make the shoulder cut.*

LAP JOINTS

Lap joints are strong. Because they have considerable face grain, glue is all that is needed (Fig. 13-31). The matching faces must be flat to achieve maximum strength. Work carefully and check for squareness. Be careful that you do not cut the joints too deep. The top surfaces should be flush. To make a lap joint:

1. Square the stock to finished size.
2. Lay the pieces together where the joint will be to make certain they are square with each other. Clamp together and mark the edges of the joint using a sharp knife.
3. Mark the depth of each half of the joint. This is ½ the thickness of the stock (Fig. 13-32).
4. Using a miter box or backsaw, cut just inside the layout lines. Cut to the depth mark. Take several more cuts in the waste stock to help in removing the waste stock.
5. Remove the waste stock with a chisel. Cut from each side toward the center (Fig. 13-33). Check to be sure the bottom is flat and square.
6. Place the two pieces together in a trial assembly. Use a chisel to trim until they fit snugly but can easily be taken apart.

Fig. 13-26. *The edge rabbet is cut with a rabbet plane.*

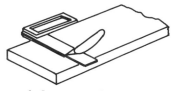

1. *Locate one side of the dado.*

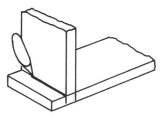

2. *Stand part to fit in dado in place and mark the width.*

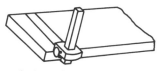

3. *Mark the depth with a marking gauge.*

Fig. 13-27. *Steps to laying out a dado.*

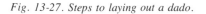

Waste material   *Saw kerfs*

1. *Mark saw cuts on each side in the waste material.*

2. *Remove the waste material with a wood chisel, work from each side to the center.*

Fig. 13-28. *Steps to cutting a dado.*

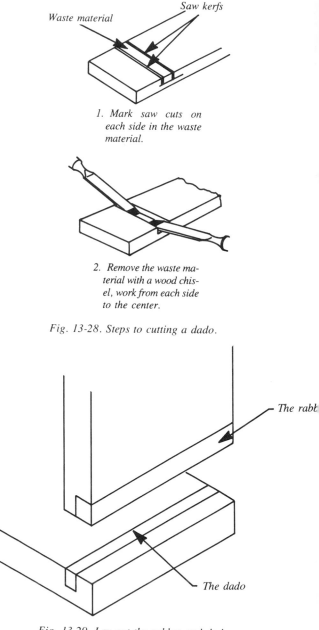

The rabb

The dado

Fig. 13-29. *Lay out the rabbet and dado.*

MORTISE-AND-TENON JOINTS

Mortise-and-tenon joints are used where great strength is needed. They are used in quality chair and table construction. It is a difficult joint to cut by hand and requires considerable skill. To make a mortise-and-tenon joint:

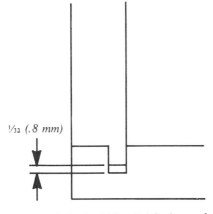

Fig. 13-30. The dado should be slightly deeper than the rabbet.

1. Square the stock to finished size.

2. Decide on the size of the mortise and tenon. The thickness of the tenon is ½ the thickness of the wood, and the top is ½ inch (12 mm) from the top of the piece, and the bottom is ¼ inch (6 mm) from the bottom of the piece. The mortise is the same size as the tenon.

3. Lay out the shoulder cuts for the tenon with a try square. Place all the pieces to have tenons together. Lay out all pieces at the same time (Fig. 13-34). Lay out the cheek cuts with a marking gauge. The length is 2½ times the thickness of the tenon.

4. Next lay out the mortise. Usually the mortise is cut no closer than 5⁄16 inch (8 mm) from the outer face of the leg. Using a marking gauge, lay out the sides of the mortise. Using a try square, lay out the top and bottom sides. Place the pieces to have mortises together. Lay out the length of the mortise on all pieces at the same time (Fig. 13-35).

5. First cut the mortises, then the tenon to fit the finished mortise. If the mortise ends up a little large, make an allowance for this when cutting the tenon.

6. Bore a series of holes in the waste material. The auger should not remove the layout lines. A doweling jig will help get the holes straight. Bore the holes ⅛ inch (3 mm) deeper than the length of the tenon.

7. Cut the remaining waste material with a chisel, keeping the sides perpendicular (Fig. 13-36).

8. Next saw the tenons. Make the cheek cuts first (Fig. 13-37). Do not cut beyond the depth marks. Cut on the waste side of the line. Then make the shoulder cuts using a miter box or backsaw.

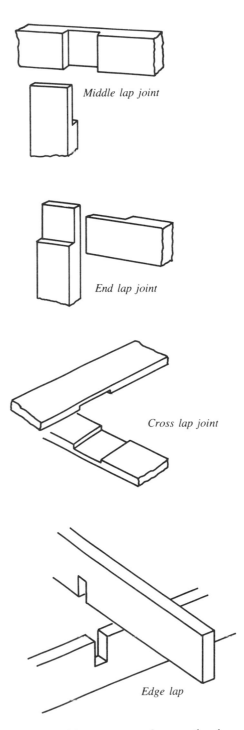

Fig. 13-31. Lap joints are strong because they have a lot of face grain exposed.

1. *Place the pieces to-
gether where the joint
will occur. Mark each
side of the joint.*

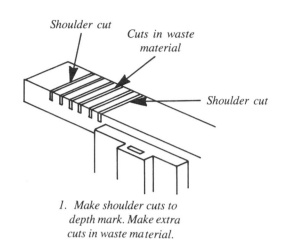

1. *Make shoulder cuts to
depth mark. Make extra
cuts in waste material.*

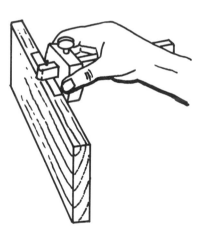

2. *Mark the depth.*

Fig. 13-32. *Mark the width and depth of the lap joint.*

2. *Remove waste materi-
al working from each
side toward the center.*

Fig. 13-33. *Saw to the depth mark and remove the waste
material with a chisel.*

1. Square the stock to finished size.

2. Lay out the pins on a cardboard template. The
size of the pins is usually the same as the thickness of the
wood, but this can be varied to make the pins come out
even.

3. Place the template on the wood and mark the
pins. Put an X on the parts to be cut away (Fig. 13-38).
Then mark the length of the pins.

4. Lay out the pins on the matching corner. Remember to cut away the pins opposite those on the first
piece (Fig. 13-39).

5. Saw the vertical cuts on the waste side using a
dovetail saw.

6. Saw the horizontal cuts with a coping saw. Use a
chisel to smooth up the pins.

7. Check each corner with a trial assembly. Mark
the matching pieces in each corner so they can be assembled.

9. Smooth and square the tenons using a wood
chisel. Work each one until it fits properly in a mortise,
then mark the tenon and mortise so they can be mated
during assembly.

BOX JOINTS

A box joint is a strong and decorative way to join corners. It is difficult to make with hand tools because of
the many accurate cuts required. To make a box joint:

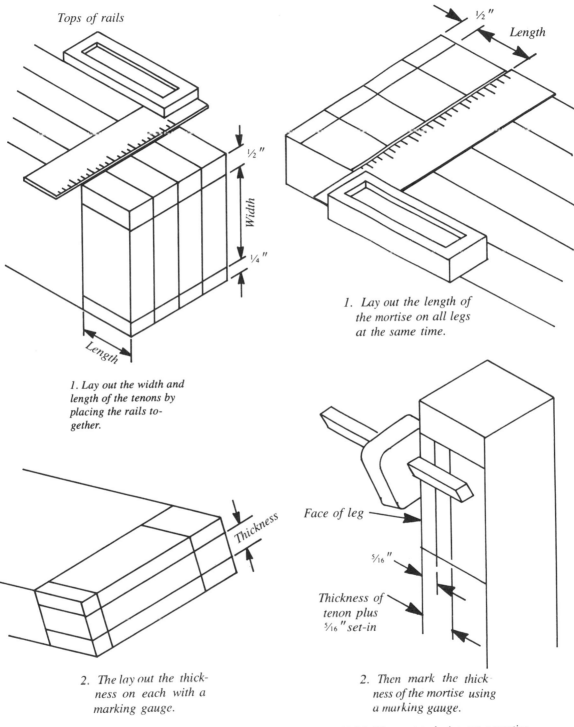

Tops of rails

½ "

Width

¼ "

Length

1. Lay out the width and
length of the tenons by
placing the rails to-
gether.

½ "

Length

1. Lay out the length of
the mortise on all legs
at the same time.

Thickness

2. The lay out the thick-
ness on each with a
marking gauge.

Fig. 13-34. The steps to laying out a tenon.

Face of leg

5/16 "

Thickness of
tenon plus
5/16 " set-in

2. Then mark the thick-
ness of the mortise using
a marking gauge.

Fig. 13-35. The steps to laying out a mortise.

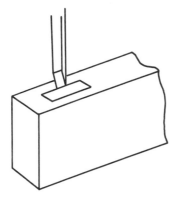

1. Cut the outline of the mortise with the bevel facing in.

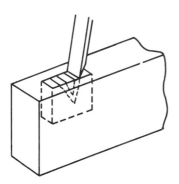

2. Remove the waste material with V-shaped cuts. Keep the bevel down.

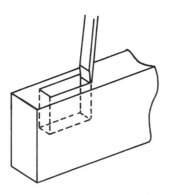

3. Straighten the sides by keeping the bevel facing in.

Fig. 13-36. The steps to cutting a mortise.

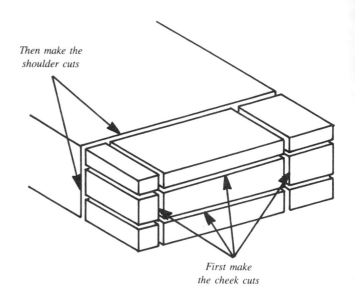

Then make the shoulder cuts

First make the cheek cuts

Fig. 13-37. The steps to cutting the tenon.

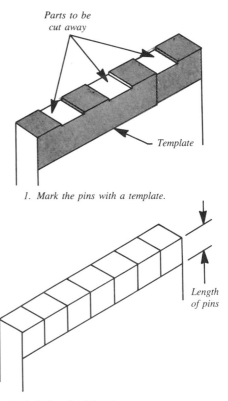

Parts to be cut away

Template

1. Mark the pins with a template.

Length of pins

2. Mark the length of the pins.

Fig. 13-38. The steps to laying out the box joint.

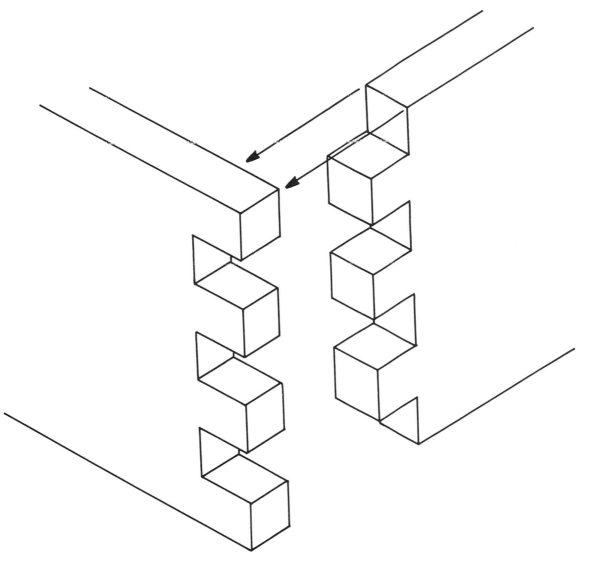

Fig. 13-39. Remember to alternate the pins on the matching side of the corner.

Chapter 14

Adhesives, Glues, Cements, and Mechanical Fasteners

Glues, adhesives, and cements are bonding agents used to hold wood products together. Adhesives are made from synthetic materials, glues from natural materials, cements from rubber-based materials. These products form an almost invisible bond between two pieces of wood, or between wood and other materials such as plastic laminates.

MECHANICAL AND SPECIFIC ADHESION

When wood pieces are bonded together a glue line is formed. The bonding agent is forced into the pores of the wood. When it hardens, it forms a mechanical bond. This is not the strongest bond. The bond gains additional strength by specific adhesion.

Specific adhesion bonds materials with or without pores such as glass, plastic, or wood. It works by the attraction of unlike electrical charges. The electrical charges existing in the bonding agent are attracted by the positive and negative charges on the wood. Specific adhesion is the strongest holding force in a glue joint.

Some bonding agents harden by evaporation; polyvinyl resins are an example. Others harden by a chemical reaction, such as when a catalyst is added to an epoxy resin.

CHOOSING THE CORRECT BONDING AGENT

There are many types of bonding agents; no one product can be used for all types of work. Consider the requirements for your job, then examine the qualities of the various bonding agents. For example, is a waterproof joint needed? How much time do you need to clamp the product together? Sometimes a product is complex and has many parts, so a slow-setting bonding agent is required. Table 14-1 will help in choosing the correct product.

SAFETY

☐ Study the instructions on the container containing the bonding agent and follow them carefully.

☐ Some materials are flammable; extinguish all sources of flame when using them.

☐ Some materials make fumes that are irritating to the eyes and lungs, so provide ventilation in the area.

☐ Some persons find their skin is irritated upon contact with these products. Wear rubber gloves when necessary.

Table 14-1. Characteristics of the Major Bonding Agents.

ADHESIVE	HOW SOLD	WILL BOND	CLAMPING TIME	ROOM TEMPERATURE	WATER RESISTANCE
Aliphatic	Ready mixed liquid	Wood Plywood Veneer Plastic laminates	Clamp within 10 minutes after application.	above 50°	Low water-resistance
Epoxy Resin	Two containers, mix as needed. Use immediately	All materials as wood, metal, ceramics, glass	Clamp immediately after application. Remove clamps in 8 hours.	above 32°	Waterproof
Hot Melts	Pellets that are placed in the gun	Overlay material moldings	Clamp immediately after application. Remove clamps in 2 minutes.		Water-resistant
Polyvinyl Resin	Ready mixed liquid	Wood Plywood Veneer Plastic laminates	Clamp within 10 minutes after application. Remove clamps in 30 minutes.	above 60°	Low water-resistance
Resorcinal-Formaldehyde Resin	Two containers, mix as needed. Use within 8 hours	Wood Plywood Veneer	Clamp within 20 minutes after application. Remove clamps after 24 hours.	above 70°	Waterproof
Urea-Formaldehyde Resin Glue	Powdered form, mix as needed. Use within 4 hours.	Wood Plywood Veneer	Clamp within 15 minutes after application. Remove clamps after 6 hours.	above 70°	Water-resistant
Casein	Powdered form, mix as needed. Use within 8 hours.	Wood Plywood Veneer	Clamp within 30 minutes after application. Remove clamps after 3 hours.	above 32°	Water-resistant
Liquid Hyde Cement	Ready mixed liquid	Wood Plywood Veneer Plastic laminates	Clamp within 30 minutes after application. Remove clamps after 3 hours.	above 70°	Low water resistance
Contact Cement	Ready mixed liquid	Plastic laminates to wood veneer	Allow to dry. Place pieces together. They grip immediately. No clamp time.	above 70°	Water-resistant

One important characteristic of bonding agents is their resistance to water. They are classified as: waterproof, water-resistant, and low water-resistant. Water-resistant agents will stand frequent wetting without failure, but will not stand constant wetting as in a boat hull. Low water-resistance agents will not stand frequent wetting or high humidity.

ADHESIVES

Adhesives are the most widely used bonding agents for wood products. Following are some of the commonly used types.

Polyvinyl Resin

Polyvinyl resin is often called "white glue" but is actually an adhesive. It is premixed and easy to apply. The joints should be clamped within 10 minutes after it is applied. It dries fast, allowing the clamps to be removed in 30 minutes. However, do not work the joint for 24 hours. This adhesive is not waterproof or heat resistant, so it must only be used for interior work and where temperatures do not exceed 150° F (65° C). Because it dries by evaporation, the wood should have a moisture content of 6 to 12 percent. Any more or any less will produce a weak joint.

Some brand names of this adhesive include Elmer's® Glue-All, Sobo® Glue, and Mighty Tacky™.

Aliphatic Resin

Aliphatic resin is a creamy yellow bonding agent that is sold ready mixed as a liquid. It is stronger and more heat-resistant than other polyvinyl resins. Aliphatic resin can be used at temperatures as low as 50° F (10° C). When it has set it will stand temperatures up to 250° F (120° C). It is not dissolved by lacquer finishes. While it has some resistance to moisture, its use is limited to indoor products. Some trade names for this adhesive include Titebond Wood Glue, Elmer's Carpenters Wood Glue, and Woodworkers Glue.

Small parts bonded with aliphatic resin need not be clamped. Apply the material to each part. Rub them together to get an even glue line. Hold for a few moments. The parts will remain in place without clamps. This material is superior to polyvinyl resin and is preferred by woodworkers.

Resorcinal-Formaldehyde Resin

Resorcinal-Formaldehyde resin is expensive, but is waterproof. Any product exposed to moisture should use this resin. It also resists high temperature. It is sold in two containers; the liquid resin and a catalyst are mixed together. The joint should be clamped within 20 minutes after the resin has been applied. It is slow curing, so a clamp time of 24 hours is recommended.

Urea-Formaldehyde Resin

Urea-Formaldehyde resin is moisture-resistant but not waterproof. It can be used outdoors but not in places where it is constantly wet. Urea-formaldehyde is sold in powdered form. When water is added a chemical reaction begins. The joint should be clamped within 15 minutes after the resin has been applied. It sets in about six hours.

Hot Melts

Hot melts are available in several types. They will bond wood, plywood, particleboard, paper, leather, and plastics. Glue pellets are heated in a hand-held applicator, which then produces the bonding agent in a hot, molten form. It is applied to only one of the surfaces to be joined. It sets quickly, so surfaces must be placed together rapidly. The pressure can be released in one to three minutes. Hot melts are not very strong. They are used to apply overlay and moldings to cabinets, but are not good for edge-to-edge joints.

Epoxy Resin

Epoxy is too expensive to use on most wood products, but is excellent for regluing wood joints on old furniture. It is sold in two containers; when it is time to use them, the epoxy resin and a hardener (catalyst) are mixed. The joint should be clamped immediately after the resin is applied and the clamp kept on for about eight hours.

GLUES

Glues are made from animal and vegetable products. The two popular types are: liquid hyde and casein.

Liquid Hyde Glue

Liquid hyde is a liquid form of animal glue that is good for furniture construction. Because it has a dark glue line, it is less noticeable on woods such as walnut and cherry. It is sold ready-to-use and applied with a brush to both surfaces to be joined. Because it has a long clamp time, it is good for joining complex projects.

Casein Glue

Casein glue is made from dried milk curd. It is sold as a powder and mixed with water. The mixture must stand for 15 minutes after mixing, then it is mixed again and is ready to use. Casein glue is water-resistant and can be used on outdoor items that are not continually exposed to moisture. One advantage is that it can be used in temperatures down to freezing. It does not dry fast, so assembly can be slow.

CEMENTS

Cements are made from rubber suspended in a liquid.

Contact Cement

Contact cement is the bonding agent generally used on wood products. It is used to bond veneers, plastic laminates, and other materials to wood. It is applied to both surfaces to be joined. The two pieces must be in perfect position before they are brought together, because they cannot be separated or slid after contact. Contact cement is usually applied to large surfaces with a roller.

APPLYING BONDING AGENTS

The way to apply bonding agents depends upon the agent itself. Liquid types such as polyvinyl, casein, and hyde glue can be applied with a brush. They are applied to only one of the surfaces to be joined, then the pieces are placed together in clamps. Apply only enough pressure to hold them together. Hot melts are applied with a special gum-like applicator, epoxies with a brush or roller. Following are some helpful hints for applying bonding agents:

1. Know the clamping time for the bonding agent. Clamping time is the number of minutes the joint can be left open before the bonding agent begins to set.
2. Stock should be bonded as soon as possible after it has been cut and surfaced.
3. Do not attempt to bend a poorly fitting joint.
4. Grease, oil, and wax weaken a joint. Keep the surfaces to be joined clean.
5. Let items bonded set for 24 hours before machining them.

CLEANUP

After the boards are clamped together, some of the bonding agent will be forced out of the joint. Let it set until it is semihard, then scrape it off with a metal hand scraper. If time will not permit this, wipe off the excess material with a damp cloth, which tends to work some excess into the pores of the wood. Extra sanding might be needed to clear the joint of adhesive so the stain will enter the wood.

MECHANICAL FASTENERS

Fasteners are used to attach hardware and join wood parts. Many kinds and sizes are available; it is up to the woodworker to pick the right one for the job. When making this decision, consider the following:

- Is it strong enough to hold?
- Will it remain securely in place?
- Can I install it properly?
- How will it affect the appearance of the product?

NAILS

Nails are used to hold wood parts together. To do a satisfactory job, the nails must be the correct type.

Nail Sizes

Nails vary in length and diameter: The longer the nail the larger the diameter. Nail lengths are identified by the term *penny,* which is abbreviated "d." Originally this term represented the weight in pounds of 1000 nails. It meant the 1000 8d nails weighed 8 pounds. Now the term is used to indicate length. Nails run from 2d to 60d in length. Up to 20d (4 inch), the length increases by ¼ inch. From 20d to 60d (6 inch), the length increases by ½ inch. *Gauge* refers to the diameter of the wire used to make the nail. The larger the wire, the smaller the gauge number. Wire nails, brads, and escutcheon pins are specified by length in inches rather than the penny size (Table 14-2).

Types of Nails

The basic types of nails are common, box, finishing, and casing (Fig. 14-1). They are made from mild steel. If used on exterior work, they are galvanized or made from aluminum. Galvanizing also increases their holding power. Common nails are large, strong, general-purpose nails. Their diameter in relation to their length is the largest of all the nail types. Sizes greater than 16d are called spikes. Because they are large, they tend to split stock. Spikes are generally used in building construction.

Box nails look much like common nails. They have

Table 14-2. Nail Penny Sizes.				
LENGTH AND GAUGE				APPROX. NUMBER TO POUND
SIZE	INCHES	MM	GAUGE	
20d	4	100	6	31
16d	3½	89	7	49
12d	3¼	83	8	63
10d	3	75	9	69
9d	2¾	68	10¼	96
8d	2½	62	10¼	106
7d	2¼	56	11½	161
6d	2	50	11½	181
5d	1¾	43	12½	271
4d	1½	37	12½	316
3d	1¼	31	14	568
2d	1	25	15	876

GAUGE DIAMETERS

15 14 13 12 11 10 9 8 7 6

a smaller diameter body and a larger, thinner head. They are used for box and crate construction. Because they do not split stock as easily as common nails, they are widely used in wood house framing.

Finishing nails have small heads slightly larger than the body. They are used where nail heads must be hidden. The head is set below the surface with a nail set, then filler is used to cover the hole. Typical uses include furniture construction and molding on cabinets.

Casing nails look much like finishing nails, but have a larger, cone-shaped head. This gives them more holding power than finishing nails. Their diameter is larger than finishing nails and the same size as box nails. Casing nails are used on interior trim and wood flooring.

Other nails commonly used include brads, wire nails, escutcheon pins, tacks, and staples (Fig. 14-2). These are made in a variety of lengths. Many other special purpose nails and staples are available, including some driven by power nailing and stapling equipment. (Fig. 14-3).

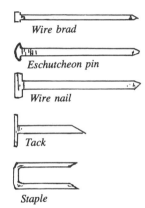

Fig. 14-2. Other types of nails often used on wood products.

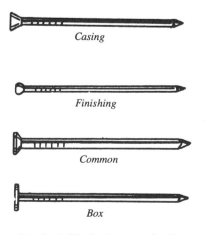

Fig. 14-1. The basic types of nails.

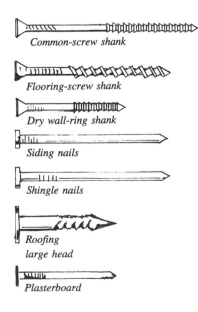

Fig. 14-3. Special purpose nails.

Choosing the Right Nail

The nail to use depends upon the job. For rough house framing, use a common nail. Use box nails if the common nail might split the stock. (Splitting can also be reduced by blunting the point. To do this, hit the point with a hammer.) If the nails are to be hidden, use a finishing nail or a wire brad. Outside work requires nails that are galvanized or aluminum. Follow this general rule: The length of the nail should be three times the thickness of the thinner board, and should not come closer than ⅛ inch to the back face (Fig. 14-4).

Fastening with Nails

Nails are driven with a claw hammer (Fig. 14-5). Hammers are specified by weight, and range in size from 7 to 20 ounces. Lighter hammers are used for brads and wire nails, while heavier hammers are used for nails up to 16d. The hammer handles may be wood, steel, or fiberglass.

Driving. The hammer is made to be held towards the end of the handle, where it is in balance. If you are driving a small nail and find you have to choke up on the hammer, get a lighter hammer.

Hold the nail between two fingers. Place it on the spot where it is to be driven. Give it a tap or two to set the point in the wood, keeping your eyes on the head of the nail. Now let go of the nail and drive it until it is almost flush with the wood. If you are doing general carpentry work, drive the head flush with the wood. If you are doing finish work set the head with a nail set. Drive small nails with a smooth movement of the wrist and

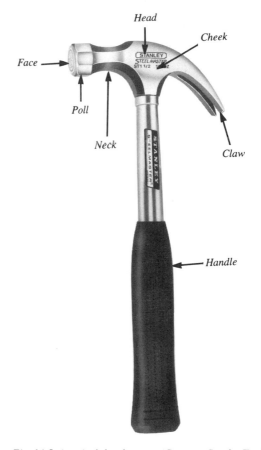

Fig. 14-5. A typical claw hammer (Courtesy Stanley Tools).

arm from the elbow, large nails with a swing from the shoulder.

Setting. Finishing nails and wire brads are usually set below the surface. Drive the nail until the head is almost flush, then place a nail set on the head and drive it ⅛ inch below the surface. Nail sets are made with different diameter points. Select one that is slightly smaller than the nail head. Finally, fill the hole with a filler (Fig. 14-6).

Toenailing. When boards meet in a butt joint, it is not always possible to nail through one into the end of the other. Toenailing solves this problem. *Toenailing* involves driving nails at an angle of 30 degrees from the vertical (Fig. 14-7). Stagger the nails from each side so they do not hit each other.

Clinching. Joints in boards joined by face nailing are stronger if the nails are clinched. *Clinching* involves driving the nail through the board, then bending the

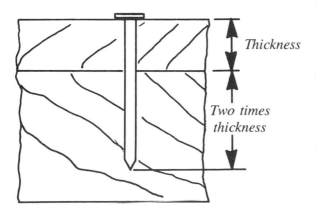

Fig. 14-4. The length of the nail should be three times the thickness of the stock.

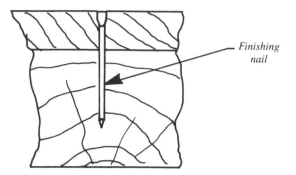

Finishing
nail

Fig. 14-6. After the nail is set, the hole is filled.

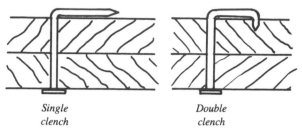

Single
clench

Double
clench

Fig. 14-8. Clinching the nail strengthens the joint.

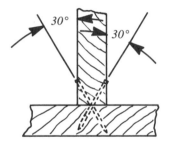

Fig. 14-7. Butt joints can be fastened by toenailing. Keep
the nails about 30 degrees from the vertical.

end sticking out and driving it on to the back face (Fig.
14-8).

Pulling. Most nails can be removed with the claws
of the hammer. If you are doing rough work, slip the
claws over the nail and pull back on the handle to remove the nail. If you do not want to mar the surface,
place a piece of wood, plywood, or hardboard under the
head of the hammer. Long nails are difficult to pull. After the hammer pulls the nail out as far as it can, place a
block of wood under the head and pull again (Fig. 14-9).

Avoiding Splitting. A big problem when nailing is
the danger of splitting the wood. Hardwoods are more
likely to split than softwoods. There are several techniques to avoid splitting:

1. Drill small holes about half the diameter of the
nail. Drill through the top piece and about half the length
of the nail into the second piece.

2. Stagger the nailing pattern; this keeps two nails
from lining up on the same section of grain (Fig. 14-10).

3. Keep the nails ¾ inch (18 mm) from the edge of
the board. If it is necessary to get closer to the edge, drill
holes for the nails.

Fig. 14-9. Put a block of wood under the hammer head
when pulling long nails.

4. Blunt the end of the nail by striking the nail on
the point with a hammer.

5. Use a nail with a smaller diameter. For example,
use a box nail instead of a common nail.

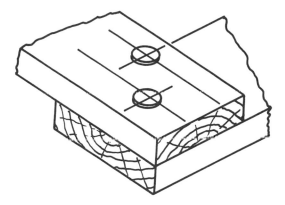

Fig. 14-10. Stagger the nails so you do not split the board.

Other Nailing Techniques

1. Increase holding power by slanting nails (Fig. 14-11).

2. When a nail bends as it is being driven, remove it and use a new nail.

3. Do not try to nail through knots or other defects.

4. Nails hold better in face grain than end grain.

5. The longer the nail, the greater is the holding power.

6. The larger the diameter of the nail, the greater is the holding power.

7. Nails that have annular or spiral shanks or have galvanized or cement shanks have greater holding power than smooth steel nails.

8. Nails in dry wood have greater holding power than in wet wood.

9. Nail through the thin piece of wood into the thick piece.

WOOD SCREWS

Wood screws provide an advantage in that they can be removed and reinstalled without damaging the wood.

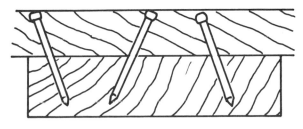

Fig. 14-11. Stagger the angle of the nails to strengthen the joint.

They also have greater holding power than nails, but are more difficult to install.

Types of Screws

Wood screws are made from steel, brass, and aluminum. Some are plated with chromium, brass, nickel, or are blued. The common head types are flat, round, and oval (Fig. 14-12).

Generally the heads are slotted or have a Phillips recess. Some other types include Pozidriv, clutch head, and Robertson head (Fig. 14-13). The types other than slotted are easier to drive straight; also, the screwdriver is less likely to slip off the screw.

Specifying Screws

Screws are specified by length, diameter, head type, recess type, and finish. For example: 2 inch No. 12 F.H. Steel. This will give a screw with a slotted head and no finish. Screws are sold in boxes of 100. Smaller packages are available in hardware stores.

Wood screws are made in lengths from ¼ inch to 6 inches. The length is the distance from the tip to the part of the head that is flush with the wood. The diameter is given in wire gauge numbers. These run from 0 to 24 (Fig. 14-14). Each length is made in several different diameters.

Choosing the Right Screw

When choosing a screw, consider the requirements of the job. If it is used outside, it must be rust resistant. The type of head should complement the appearance of the project. The length and diameter of the screw will depend upon the thickness of the material.

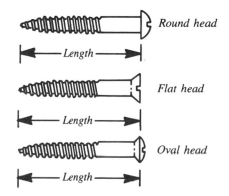

Fig. 14-12. The common types of wood screws.

Fig. 14-13. The types of screw head recesses.

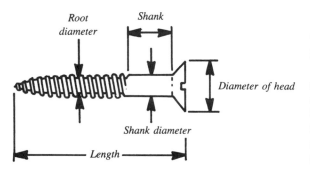

Fig. 14-14. Wire diameters are measured at the shank. Root diameters are measured at the thread.

For outside use, choose a brass, aluminum, or plated screw. If appearance is important, the oval or round head is more pleasing than the flat head. Consider using brass- or chrome-plated screws for a better appearance. When appearance is not important, use unplated steel screws.

If the screw must be flush with the surface, use a flat head screw.

The length depends upon the thickness of the stock. A screw should go through one piece and have all of its threads in the second piece. This is not always possible, but does provide maximum strength. The screw point should not come within 1/8 inch (3 mm) of the back face.

The wire diameter influences strength. Where strength is of greatest importance, choose the largest diameter. If strength is not important, choose a smaller diameter. The smaller diameters are less likely to split the wood and are cheaper. Thin stock will require small diameters. Also, use smaller diameters in hardwoods than in softwoods. Use larger diameters and longer screws in end grain. Screws do not hold as well in end grain as in face grain.

Fastening with Screws

The key to proper fastening with screws is an accurate layout and the proper size shank and pilot holes.

Shank and Pilot Holes. To properly install wood screws, drill two holes for each screw. In the top piece, drill a hole the same size as the shank of the screw. This is the *shank hole*. In the second piece, drill a hole about the size of the root diameter of the screw. This is the *pilot hole* (Fig. 14-15). The recommended sizes for the drills are shown in Table 14-3.

First mark the center with an awl, then drill the shank holes. Place the pieces together and mark through these with an awl to locate the pilot holes. Drill the pilot hole into the second piece of wood as deep as the screw will go (Fig. 14-16).

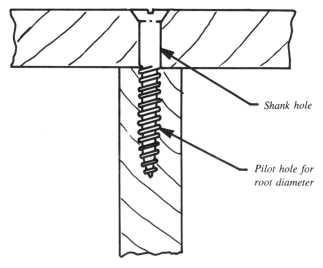

Fig. 14-15. Drill shank and pilot holes before installing a screw.

Table 14-3. Drill Sizes to Use for Counterbores, Shanks, and Pilot Holes.

WIRE GAUGE NUMBER	DRILL SIZE FOR COUNTERBORE FOR HEAD	DRILL SIZE FOR SHANK HOLE	DRILL SIZE FOR PILOT HOLE	
			HARD WOOD	SOFT WOOD
0	.119 (1/8)	1/16	3/64	
1	.146 (9/64)	5/64	1/16	
2	1/4	3/32	1/16	3/64
3	1/4	7/64	1/16	3/64
4	1/4	1/8	3/32	5/64
5	5/16	1/8	3/32	5/64
6	5/16	9/64	3/32	5/64
7	3/8	5/32	1/8	3/32
8	3/8	11/64	1/8	3/32
9	3/8	3/16	1/8	9/64
10	1/2	3/16	5/32	9/64
12	1/2	7/32	3/16	9/64

Countersinking. Flat head and oval head screws require that the shank hole be countersunk. *Countersinking* means cutting a cone-shaped depression in the top of the hole so the screw head fits into it (Fig. 14-17).

Special bits are available that drill the pilot and shank holes and prepare the countersink in one operation (Fig. 14-18).

Counterboring. A shank hole is counterbored when it is necessary to set the head of a screw or bolt below the surface. A *counterbore* is a round hole with vertical sides. Its diameter is slightly larger than the head of the screw (Fig. 14-19).

If a hole is to be counterbored, first locate the center of the hole. Drill the counterbore to its proper depth, then bore the shank hole.

There are special bits that will drill the pilot and shank holes and the counterbore in one operation (Fig. 14-20). The deeper the bit is drilled, the farther the screw is placed below the surface.

If you plan to make wood plugs to cover the screwhead make them from scrap stock from which the parts were cut so the colors will match. Plugs are cut with a plug cutter (Fig. 14-21). You may also purchase wood buttons to decorate the surface and cover the screwhead (Fig. 14-22).

SCREWDRIVERS

The three most commonly used screwdrivers are the standard, cabinet, and Phillips (Fig. 14-23). The standard and cabinet types are both used for straight slotted screws. The difference is that the standard has a larger stronger blade and tip, while the cabinet screwdriver is used for smaller screws. They are specified by the blade length. The longer the blade, the wider and thicker the tip. The Phillips screwdriver is used on screws with the Phillips recess. They are made with tip sizes 0 through 4, 0 being the smallest size.

Screwdriver bits are used in a brace. They have a tang that fits in the chuck of the brace (Fig. 14-24). They give considerable leverage and will drive screws you cannot turn with a screwdriver. They can also twist a screw in half, so use carefully.

The spiral ratchet screwdriver is used to rapidly drive small screws. It is especially useful when you have several to install. It comes with different size tips (Fig. 14-25).

Choosing the Proper Screwdriver

When driving slotted head screws, select a screwdriver that will fit snugly in the slot. It should be almost as wide as the head of the screw. Do not use the screwdriver if the tip is chisel-shaped; it should be flat and square on the bottom. (See chapter 11 for information on how to dress a screwdriver.)

The Phillips screwdriver should fit into the bottom of the recess and be snug. If it fits loosely, use the next larger size. If it does not go fully into the recess, use the next smaller size.

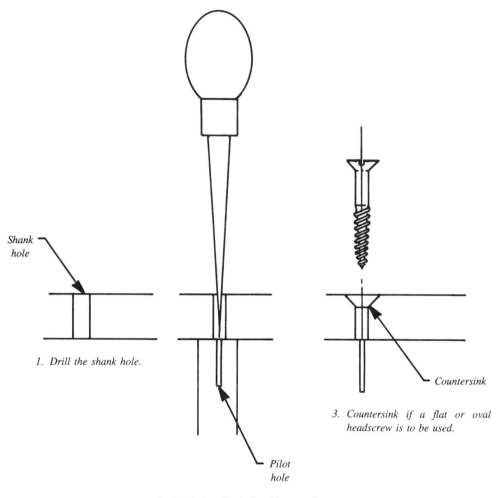

1. Drill the shank hole.

Shank hole

Pilot hole

2. Mark the pilot hole with an awl.
Drill it to depth.

Countersink

3. Countersink if a flat or oval
headscrew is to be used.

Fig. 14-16. Steps to locate and drill shank and pilot holes.

Driving Wood Screws

1. Prepare the shank and pilot holes.
2. Countersink or counterbore if required.
3. Select the proper screwdriver. The longer the blade, the more leverage you can produce.
4. In hardwoods wax or soap applied to the threads can make them easier to turn.
5. Place the screw in the hole. Line up the screw-driver with the screw. Apply light pressure and turn the handle clockwise. If the screw is hard to drive, apply additional pressure. Put a little soap on the screw if it is hard to drive.
6. Tighten until the screw is in place.

To use a spiral ratchet screwdriver, set the ratchet so the tip rotates clockwise. Place the tip in the screw slot and push down on the handle. This will rotate the

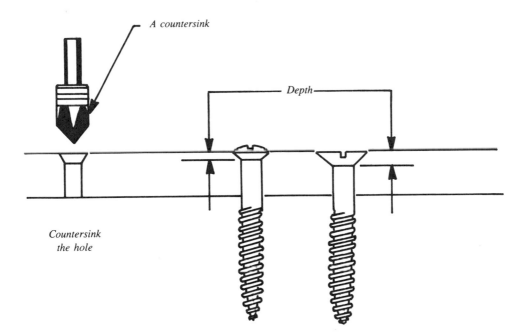

Fig. 14-17. Oval and flat head screws require the shank hole to be countersunk (Courtesy Stanley Tools).

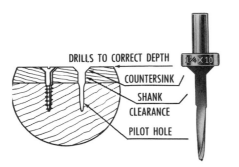

Fig. 14-18. A drill that makes the pilot and shank hole and a counterbore in one operation (Courtesy Stanley Tools).

tip. Ease up on the handle so it will rise, then push down again.

OTHER METAL FASTENERS

Manufacturers supply a wide variety of metal fastener and holding devices. Following are some of those most commonly used:

■ Lag screws have wood threads and a large square head. They require a shank and pilot hole, and are driven in place with a wrench (Fig. 14-26).

■ Hanger bolts and T nuts are used to join a wood member, such as a leg, to a frame. The frame has a hole drilled for the nut. The hanger bolt is screwed into the leg, and the leg is then screwed into the nut (Fig. 14-27).

■ Dowel screws are used for the same purposes as hanger bolts. They have threads on both ends (Fig. 14-28).

■ Hooked fasteners come in a variety of sizes and shapes (Fig. 14-29).

■ Screw eyes are made in the medium eye and small eye types (Fig. 14-30).

There are three types of special nails for forming corners: chevrons, clamp nails, and corrugated fasteners. They are used as a quick, easy way to form a corner. They are not strong, and they are used when appearance is not important.

Metal plates and angles are used to join wood members. They are secured with wood screws. Select a screw that will fit the countersunk hole properly. These are also used where appearance is not important (Fig. 14-31).

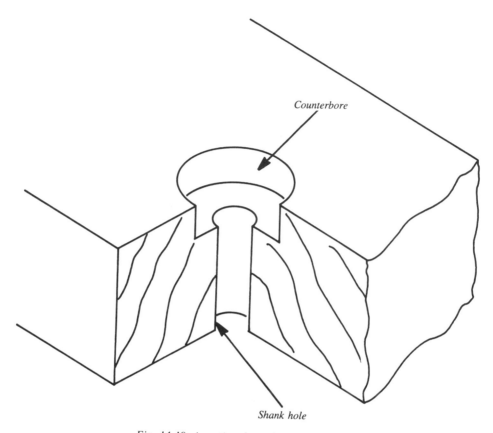

Fig. 14-19. A section through a counterbore.

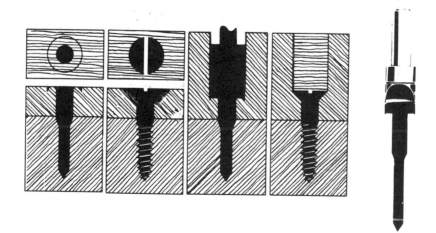

Fig. 14-20. A drill that makes the pilot and shank holes with countersink or counterbore in one operation (Courtesy Stanley Tools).

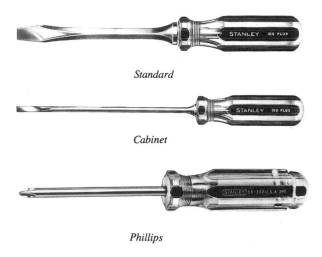

Standard

Cabinet

Phillips

Fig. 14-23. Common types of screwdrivers (Courtesy Stanley Tools).

In addition to these mechanical fasteners, an extensive variety have been developed for usc in assembling furniture and cabinets. Many units are now sold in a disassembled condition (called knocked down). Special fasteners are available to permit quick assembly by even inexperienced persons. Some examples are shown in Fig. 14-32. (Details can be found in chapter 30.)

Fig. 14-21. A plug cutter (Courtesy Stanley Tools).

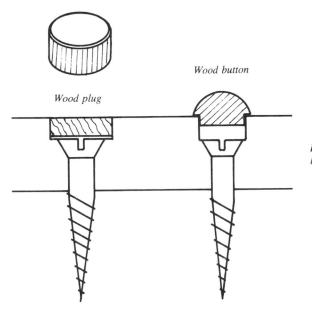

Wood button

Wood plug

Fig. 14-22. Counterbored holes can be covered with plugs or buttons.

Fig. 14-24. A screwdriver bit (Courtesy Irwin Auger Bit Company).

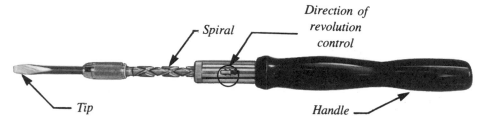

Fig. 14-25. A spiral ratchet screwdriver (Courtesy Stanley Tools).

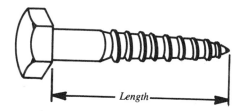

Fig. 14-26. Lag screws are large and strong.

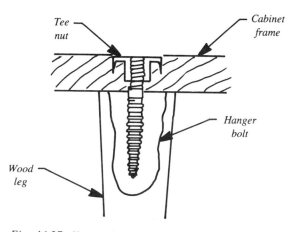

Fig. 14-27. Hanger bolts with T nuts are used to join legs to furniture.

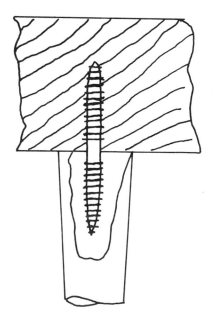

Fig. 14-28. Dowel screws have wood screw threads on both ends.

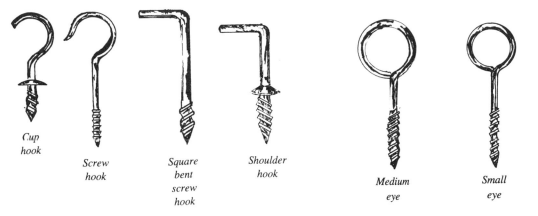

Cup hook

Screw hook

Square bent screw hook

Shoulder hook

Medium eye

Small eye

Fig. 14-29. Hook fasteners are made in a variety of shapes.

Fig. 14-30. Common types of screw eyes.

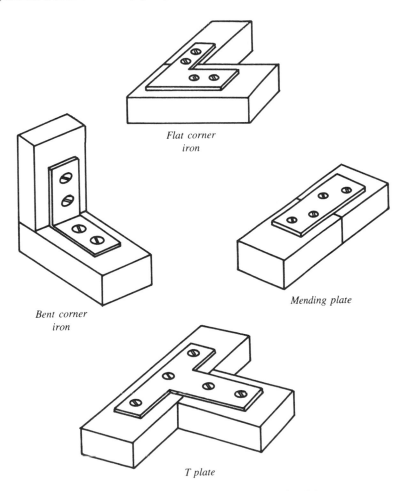

Flat corner iron

Bent corner iron

Mending plate

T plate

Fig. 14-31. Metal plates are used to strengthen butt joints.

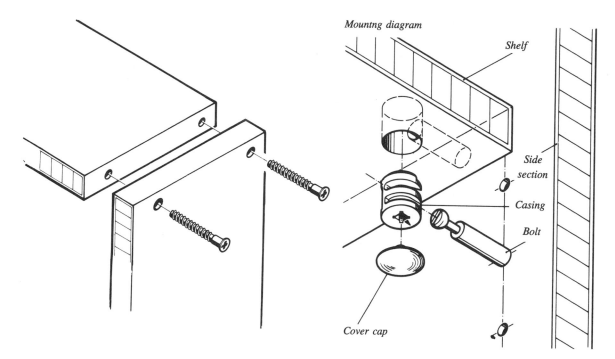

Fig. 14-32. Several of the many types of mechanical fasteners available for use in furniture and cabinet construction (Courtesy Hafele America).

Chapter 15

Clamping and Assembly

HAND-OPERATED CLAMPING TOOLS

It is necessary to choose the best clamping device for the job. Each has certain advantages. Often a job will require the use of several different types.

Hand Screws

Hand screws have two long wood jaws. The distance between them is adjusted by two handles that turn threaded shafts, called screws (Fig. 15-1). They are made with jaw openings from 2 to 14 inches. Jaw lengths range from 4 to 18 inches.

Hand screws apply pressure over a long area. To do this the jaws are kept parallel. To adjust a hand screw:

1. Turn the handles until the jaws are parallel.
2. Turn the handles to open the jaws wide enough to go over the product. Keep them parallel.
3. Place the clamp over the joint.

4. Turn the handles in the opposite direction to close the jaws. Keep the jaws parallel. Turn the inside handle a little then the outside handle, alternating until the jaws firmly grip the work. Do not overtighten. Once tightened, the entire area of the clamp face should touch the material.

Hand screws allow the application of pressure over a large area. Because the jaws are wood, they will not mar the surface. Be certain the jaws are clean and free of old glue before using them.

Hand screws can also be used to hold certain irregularly shaped objects. By adjusting the handles, the jaws can be made to clamp at an angle (Fig. 15-2).

C-CLAMPS

C-clamps come in a variety of sizes and shapes. Typical opening distances run from 2 to 12 inches, depths from 1 to 6 inches (Fig. 15-3).

SAFETY

☐ Wear eye protection.
☐ Tighten clamps carefully; do not catch your fingers or those of your helper in a clamp.
☐ Some assembled projects with many clamps are heavy; do not try to move them by yourself.
☐ Keep the bonding agent off your skin. Wash your hands immediately after finishing a job.
☐ Do not drip glue on the bench or floor; it is slippery and can cause an accident.
☐ Place the assembled project in storage in such a way that the clamps will not trip someone or hit them as they walk past.
☐ Put all waste paper, rags, and scrap wood in a fireproof waste can.

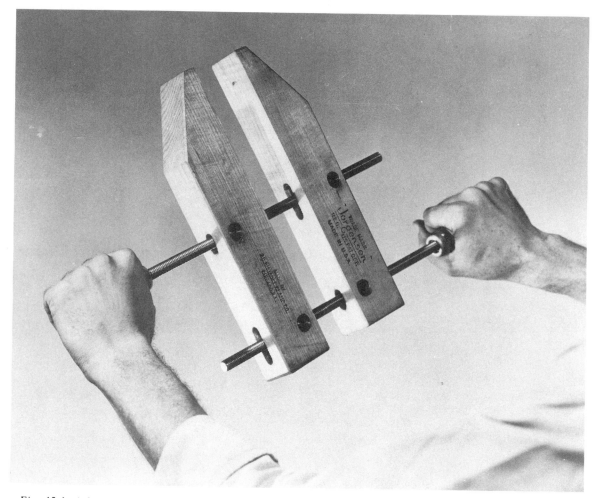

Fig. 15-1. A hand screw. (Courtesy Adjustable Clamp Co., Manufacturers of Jorgensen®, Pony® and Adjustable™ Clamps).

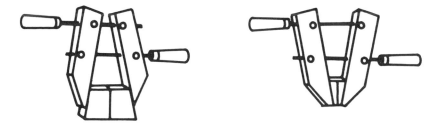

Fig. 15-2. Hand screws can be adjusted to clamp some irregularly shaped objects.

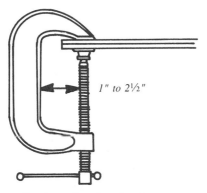

Regular and medium throat
C-clamp

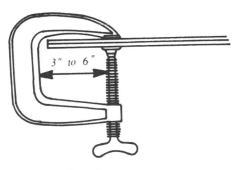

Deep-throat
C-clamp

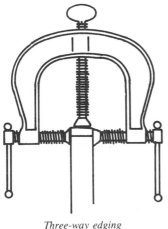

Three-way edging
C-clamp

Fig. 15-3. C clamps are made in many sizes.

To use a C-clamp, turn the handle to open the throat. Because they are metal, protect wood surfaces to be clamped with scrap wood blocks. The opening must be large enough to span the blocks and the parts to be clamped. Turn the handle until the stock is gripped firmly, but do not over tighten (Fig. 15-4).

Bar Clamps

Bar clamps are sometimes called "cabinet clamps." They have a long metal bar with an adjustable foot at one end, and a screw type clamp at the other (Fig. 15-5). They are available in lengths from 2 to 8 feet. Short bar clamps are made from 6 to 8 inches long (Fig. 15-6). These clamps are most commonly used to clamp stock edge to edge, as for cabinet assembly. A pipe clamp will perform the same job as the bar clamp and is similar, except that in place of a bar, a pipe is used.

Spring Clamps

Spring clamps have a strong spring that holds their two jaws together. They are made with jaw openings of 1, 2, and 3 inches. To use, simply squeeze the handles together, insert the wood, and release the handles (Fig. 15-7).

Web Clamps

Web clamps are used to clamp round or irregularly shaped products. They have a fabric band which is wrapped around the product, then a metal tightening device pulls in the band—similar to tightening the seat belt in an automobile (Fig. 15-8).

Miter Clamps and Vises

Miter clamps and vises are used to hold a miter joint as it is nailed or glued. The corner clamp holds stock up to 3 inches wide (Fig. 15-9). A miter frame clamp holds all four corners at one time (Fig. 15-10). The miter vise holds stock up to 4 inches wide (Fig. 15-11).

CLAMPING TECHNIQUES

There are many things to think about as you assemble and clamp your project. Here is a list of procedures:

1. Get everything ready before you begin to apply a bonding agent. This includes the proper clamps adjusted to the correct opening, scrap stock to prevent damaging wood surfaces, the bottle of adhesive, and someone to help you.

Fig. 15-4. Use scrap blocks to protect the product.

2. Assemble the project dry as a trial assembly to make certain the joints fit. This will let you adjust the clamps to the proper size. Now is the time to rework a joint or get extra clamps.

3. Take the project apart and carefully lay each piece so it can be easily reassembled. Some bonding agents set slowly, so you have working time, but others set quickly, so you must work quickly. Know how much time you have to assemble and clamp.

4. Apply the bonding agent to the parts you can clamp in the time available. Most bonding agents are applied to only one side of a joint. Know the requirements of the agent you are using.

5. Place the joints together and begin to tighten the clamps. Apply light pressure all around until the entire project is together. If you tighten too much, you might force too much of the bonding agent out of the joint. This will create a *starved joint*, which will hold but not

be as strong as it should. It is also possible to not tighten enough to bring the wood surfaces together, which will produce a brittle joint.

6. Quickly check the project for squareness. Use a try square to check corners. Measure diagonals to check overall squareness (Fig. 15-12). It might be necessary to loosen and move some clamps to get it square. Remember, this must be done before the clamp time of the glue is reached.

7. Some woodworkers prefer to wipe away the excess bonding agent that comes out of the joint. Use a wet cloth and wipe the surface clean. Do not let any get into the grain of the wood. Others prefer to let the agent set until it becomes semihard, then scrape it off with a hand scraper. This last method produces a stronger joint, and there is less chance of rubbing the glue into the wood.

8. Write the time and date you clamped the project on it with chalk. This will let others know when the

clamps can safely be removed so they can use them. Usual clamp time is 24 hours but this varies with the bonding agent.

FACE-TO-FACE ASSEMBLY

Stock is face-clamped when several boards are joined to make a thicker part. Stock joined this way is less likely to warp and check than a thick solid piece. To make a face-to-face joint:

1. Square the stock so the faces fit with no gaps.
2. Mark the edges so the proper faces fit together. Be certain the face grain in each piece is in the same direction.
3. Assemble the pieces dry. Alternate the clamps from both sides and space them about 6 inches apart. This helps achieve uniform pressure.
4. Take the joint apart. Apply bonding agent to one surface and place it on the joining face. Rub the two together to get an even coating.
5. Clamp them with hand screws, C clamps, or short bar clamps. Begin tightening in the center and work to each end (Fig. 15-13).

EDGE-TO-EDGE ASSEMBLY

Narrow boards joined together will warp less than one solid piece. Following these steps to make an edge-to-edge assembly:

1. Square the boards and place side by side on the bench top. Reverse the growth rings in every other board to reduce warping (Fig 15-14).
2. Mark the edges to be joined. Prepare dowel joints if needed.
3. Place the bar clamps on the bench top. Space 18 to 24 inches apart. Place the boards on the clamps and make a trial assembly, making certain the dowel pins permit the joints to close.
4. Remove the boards from the clamps and apply the bonding agent to the dowel pins. Insert them in the holes in one edge. Apply bonding agent to one edge and the dowel pin stocking out.
5. Place the boards on the bar clamps and hand assemble. Repeat this for each joint.
6. When all are in the clamps, tighten each enough to close the joint.
7. Check to make certain the boards are flat on the bar clamps, then install clamps on the top side. Scrap

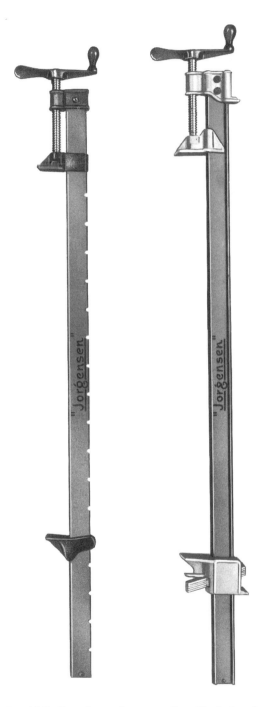

Fig. 15-5. Bar clamps have an adjustable foot and a screw type clamp on the other end. (Courtesy Adjustable Clamp Co., Manufacturers of Jorgensen®, Pony® and Adjustable™ Clamps).

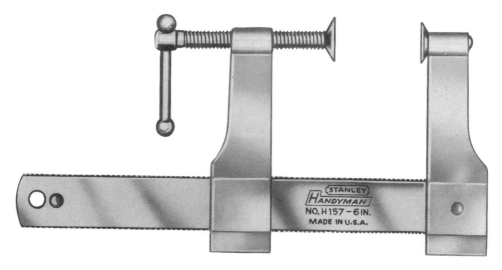

Fig. 15-6. A short bar clamp (Courtesy Stanley Tools).

Fig. 15-7. A spring clamp (Courtesy Stanley Tools).

Fig. 15-8. A web clamp has a fabric strip that is pulled tightly about the product (Courtesy Adjustable Clamp Co., Manufacturers of Jorgensen®, Pony® and Adjustable™ Clamps).

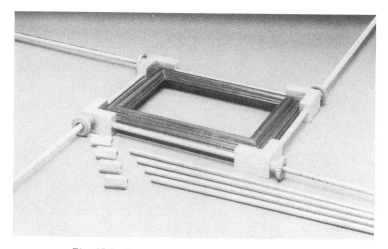

Fig. 15-9. Corner clamps (Courtesy Stanley Tools).

Fig. 15-10. Miter frame clamp (Courtesy Stanley Tools and Woodcraft Supply Corp.)

stock can be clamped on the ends to prevent warping. (Fig. 15-15).

8. Remove the glue and mark the time and date. Store in a manner so the boards will remain flat and not under stress.

Clamping a Miter Joint

Miter joints are usually cut on a 45-degree angle. Because they tend to slide when nailed or screwed, a miter vise or corner clamp is needed. To join a miter joint:

1. Cut the pieces to finished size.

2. Dry assemble the miter in the miter vise or corner clamp. If it does not close, saw through the joint. Mark each corner so the correct pieces are assembled.

3. Remove the pieces from the clamp. Apply the bonding agent. If it is a spline joint, glue the spline in its groove on one piece. Apply bonding agent to the rest of the spline.

4. Place the pieces in the vise and press the joint closed. Tighten the clamps to hold the pieces in position. (Fig. 15-16).

5. If the joint is to be nailed, drive nails in each corner.

6. Check the final joint for squareness.

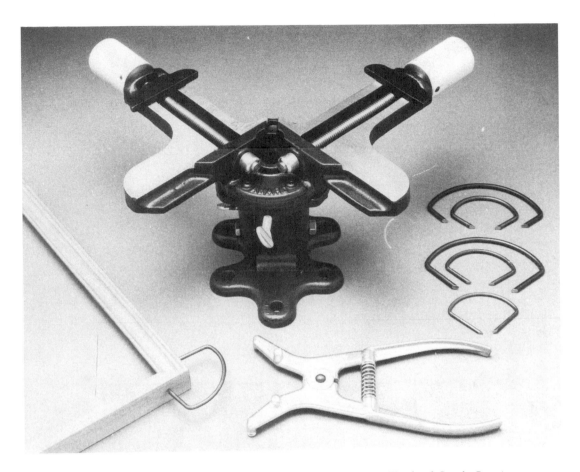

Fig. 15-11. The miter joint can be held with a miter vise (Courtesy Woodcraft Supply Corp.).

ASSEMBLING CABINETS
AND FURNITURE

Cabinets and furniture are large assemblies made from many parts. It is difficult to assemble an entire project at one time. Instead, divide it into subassemblies, which are small parts of a larger project. For example, a subassembly of a table could be two legs and a rail. After two such subassemblies have dried, they can be joined into the finished table frame (Fig. 15-17).

Bar clamps are most commonly used on cabinet and furniture assemblies. Band clamps are also a great help.

Sand the inside surfaces of furniture and cabinets before assembly. They can be easily sanded as individual pieces, but once they are assembled, sanding is very difficult.

Make a trial assembly. Usually you will need someone to help you. If it takes longer to make the trial assembly than the set time of the bonding agent you planned to use, choose one with a longer set time. Check the trial assembly to make certain all joints close easily, and that it can be clamped so it is square. The key to successful assembly is careful planning and thorough checking before the bonding agent is applied to the joints.

ASSEMBLING IRREGULARLY
SHAPED PRODUCTS

Irregularly shaped surfaces require a variety of clamps and special devices. The band clamp is especially useful because it will form itself around curved and inclined surfaces. Special blocks designed for a particular situation are often the best way to assemble an irregular product (Fig. 15-18).

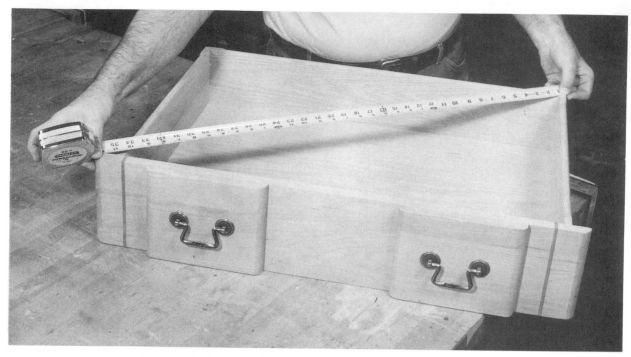

Fig. 15-12. *Measure the diagonals to make certain the product is square.*

Fig. 15-13. *Clamp the face-to-face joint with hand screws.*

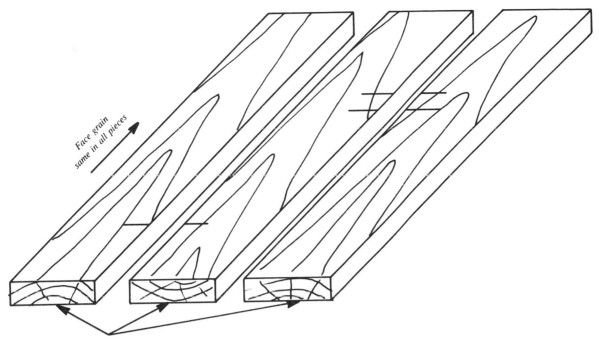

Face grain same in all pieces

Alternate end grain

Fig. 15-14. Alternate the end grain of stock to be glued edge to edge.

Fig. 15-15. End clamping helps reduce warpage (Courtesy Adjustable Clamp Co., Manufacturers of Jorgensen®, Pony® and Adjustable™ Clamps).

Fig. 15-16. Clamp the miter and nail it.

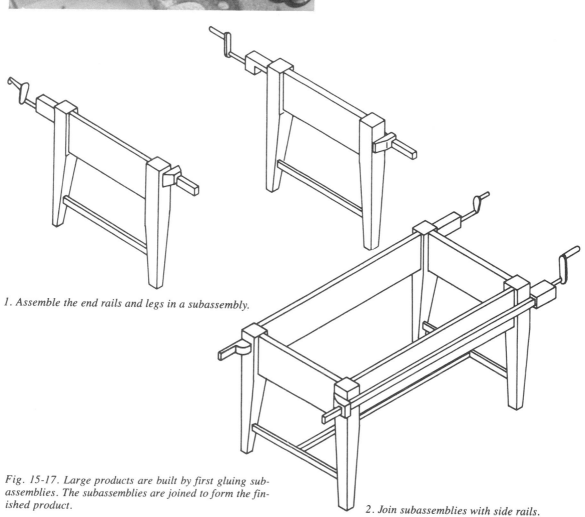

1. Assemble the end rails and legs in a subassembly.

Fig. 15-17. Large products are built by first gluing sub-assemblies. The subassemblies are joined to form the finished product.

2. Join subassemblies with side rails.

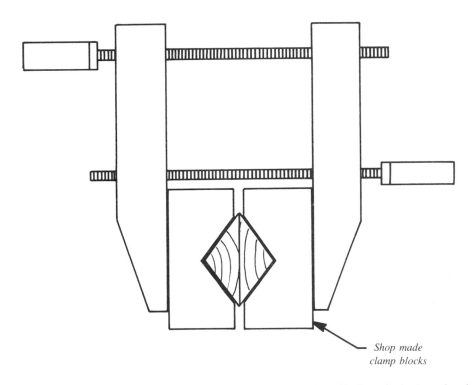

Fig. 15-18. Irregularly shaped objects can be assembled by making clamp blocks to fit the irregular shape.

Chapter 16

Portable Power Tools

The woodworker has many portable power tools available. These machines are easy to use, make accurate cuts, and are reasonably priced. Portable power tools can save a great deal of time, and make joints and perform other operations that are very difficult to do with hand tools. In addition to being light in weight and compact, they are easy to guide over your projects so are easier to use than stationary machines.

The tools discussed in this chapter include: the portable electric drill, saber and reciprocating saw, portable circular saw, portable sanders, portable electric plane, and portable router. Each section includes what to look for when purchasing these machines as well as rules of safety.

ELECTRIC DRILL

The portable electric drill can perform the same operations as the hand drill. This drill is driven by an electric motor, however, so boring holes is quite easy. Because it can be moved, it also has the capacity to bore holes in projects that are too large to fit on the drill press.

Parts

The drill is controlled by holding the *handle* (Fig. 16-1). It is activated by squeezing the *on-off power switch* located on the front of the handle. Some drills have *variable speed power switches*. The farther in the switch is squeezed, the faster the chuck will turn. Such a switch is needed when using a drill to install screws.

Also positioned in most handles is the *power lock button* and *forward-reverse switch*. The power lock keeps the power on without holding in on the power switch. To shut off the power, squeeze and release the power switch. Never use the power lock unless the drill can be easily controlled. Some drills have a forward-reverse switch that should be moved only when the chuck is not moving. It will reverse the direction the chuck will rotate. This feature is ideal when a bit becomes jammed and needs to be backed out or for removing screws.

The *chuck* holds the drill bit. The largest drill bit shank that can fit into the chuck determines the size of the drill. Chuck sizes include ¼, ⅜, and ½ inch (6, 10,

---

SAFETY WHEN USING AN ELECTRIC DRILL

☐ Unplug the power cord before changing bits.
☐ Never leave the chuck key in the chuck.
☐ Always clamp stock to the workbench.
☐ Arrange the power cord away from the drilling area.
☐ Hold the drill by the handle and motor housing. Do not block the motor vents.
☐ Keep hands and clothes away from the bit.

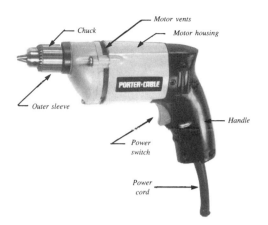

Chuck — Motor vents

Chuck — Motor housing

Outer sleeve

Handle

Power switch

Power cord

Fig. 16-1. Parts of a portable electric drill (Courtesy Porter-Cable Corporation).

and 13 mm). A ⅜-inch drill, for example, will accept any drill bit with a ⅜ inch or smaller shank.

Installing the Bit

Be certain the drill is unplugged. Select the bit according to the information given in the drill press unit. Insert the shank of the bit at least 1 inch (25 mm) into the chuck. Hand-tighten the outer sleeve on the chuck. Use the chuck key in each of the three chuck key holes to secure the bit. Failure to tighten the chuck with the chuck key will cause the bit to spin in the chuck. Always remove the chuck key once the bit is secured.

Boring through Holes

First find the center of the hole using two lines drawn at right angles with a square, then use an awl to mark the center point. Place the stock over a scrap piece to pre-

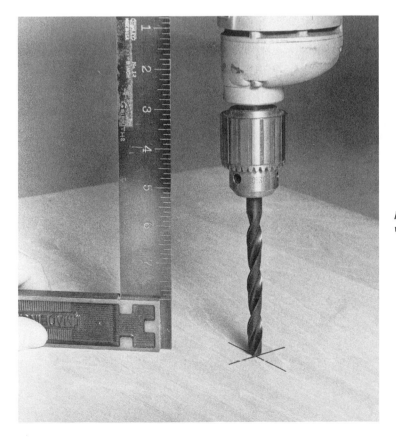

Fig. 16-2. Use a square to serve as a gauge when boring a hole at 90-degree angle.

Fig. 16-3. A gauge block holds the drill bit at the desired angle.

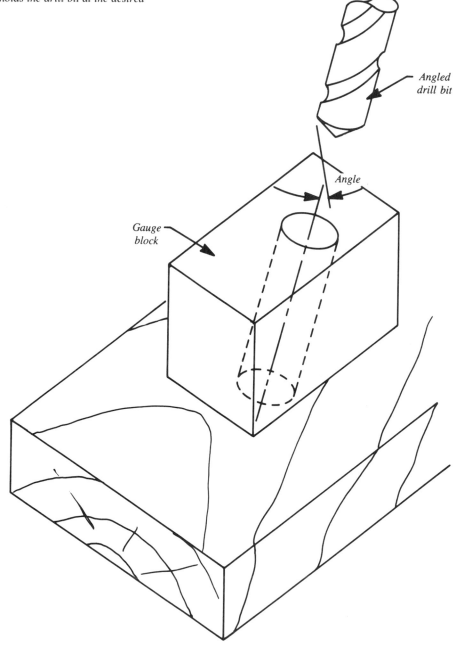

vent the back surface of the board from breaking out when the bit comes through. Be careful not to bore into the workbench or other surfaces. Clamp the stock to the workbench if there is a danger of it spinning loose.

Grasp the drill by the handle and motor housing. Keep your hands away from the motor vents, chuck, and drill bit. Position the center of the drill bit over the spot marked with the awl, making certain the angle of the drill bit is the same as the angle the hole is to be bored. Place a try square next to the drill to serve as a gauge for aligning the drill bit for a 90-degree hole (Fig. 16-2). A hold bored at the desired angle in a gauge block of wood can serve as a gauge for angled holes (Fig. 16-3).

Start the drill and apply light forward pressure. If the material is hard, rotate the chuck at a slow speed. Softer woods require a faster speed. For deep holes, back the bit out often to allow the bit to clean itself. Just before the bit breaks through the bottom surface, ease up on the drill pressure.

Boring Stopped Holes

Some holes might not extend all the way through the piece. These are called *stopped holes*. To bore a stopped hole, measure the depth of the hole from the tip of the bit. Apply a piece of masking tape around the bit at this point. Bore the hole using the same procedure as given for through holes. Just before the masking tape reaches the surface of the board, pull the bit back out. If you go past the edge of the tape, you will bore too deep a hole.

SABER AND RECIPROCATING SAW

The saber and reciprocating saws are used primarily to make curved cuts. A *saber saw* is the smaller of the two and can be used for furniture and cabinets. The *reciprocating saw* is much heavier and can make larger rough cuts for house construction and is not discussed in this text.

Parts

These saws are relatively simple in their construction. They contain a handle, motor, gear case, blade chuck, and base plate (Figs. 16-4 and 16-5). Inside the handle is the *power switch* which turns the motor on and off. The *gear case* changes the rotary motion of the motor to an up-and-down movement for the blade. The *base* is located towards the bottom of the saw. It is placed against the stock and allows the saw to slide along the surface.

Blades

Many different types of blades are available (Table 16-1). They are specified by length, width, and number of teeth per inch. The longer the blade, the thicker the material that can be cut. Wider blades will make straight cuts, while narrower blades are best for making curves. The more teeth per inch, the smoother the cut will be. The fine-toothed blades cut slower than those with larger teeth. Most blades have a universal top fitting so that they can be used on any saw. However, before purchasing the blade always check that it will fit the saw.

Mounting the Blade

Unplug the cord and place the saw on its side. Use either an Allen wrench or small screwdriver to remove the blade screw. Select the blade to perform the type of cut required. Place the blade on the blade chuck with the teeth pointing forward and the pointed end down. Replace the blade screw, making certain that it is tight. Check that the base plate is at the desired angle. A square can be used to check for a 90-degree angle, although most saws have an angle gauge to aid in the angle setting.

Operating the Saws

Lay out the desired pattern and clamp the material to the workbench or sawhorse. Because most patterns will ex-

---

SAFETY WHEN USING A SABER OR RECIPROCATING SAW

☐ Unplug the power cord when changing a blade.
☐ Always clamp the material to the workbench.
☐ Arrange the cord so it does not interfere with the cut.
☐ Hands must come no closer than 4 inches (102 mm) to the blade.
☐ Never reach under the stock.

Table 16-1. Saw Blades.

	TOOTH PER IN.	TOOTH TYPE	BLADE LGTH. IN.	BLADE WIDTH IN.	BLADE MATE-RIAL	RECOMMENDED USE
WOOD AND COMPOSITION CUTTING						
	12	Set	2-3/4″	5/32″	HC	Excellent for scroll cutting wood, plastics, etc.
	6	Set	3-1/8″	1/4″	HC	Fast cutting of wood, plywood and composition materials
	10	Set	3-1/8″	1/4″	HC	Smoother cutting of wood, plywood and composition materials
	6	Taper	3-1/8″	1/4″	HC	Excellent for pocket cutting and smooth, fast scroll cutting in wood
	12	Taper	3-1/8″	1/4″	HC	Smoothest scroll cutting and pocket cutting in wood
	6	Set	3-5/8″	1/4″	HC	For fast cutting of plywood, plastics and composition materials
	6	Set	3-5/8″	3/8″	HS	Deluxe blade for fast, straight cutting of wood, plywood, etc.
	6	Taper	3-5/8″	1/4″	HS	Deluxe blade for fast smooth cuts in all types of wood
	10	Taper	3-5/8″	1/4″	HS	Deluxe blade makes fast, smooth, deeper cuts in wood
	6	Taper	3-5/8″	3/8″	HS	Rugged, deluxe blade for straight, smooth and deeper cuts in wood, plywood and masonite
	10	Taper	3-5/8″	3/8″	HS	Longer lasting blade for deepest and smoothest cuts in wood, plastics, chipboard, etc.
SPECIAL PURPOSE CUTTING						
	8	Set	3-5/8″	1-1/8″	HC	For accurate flush cuts up to a vertical surface
	12	Taper	3-1/8″	1/4″	HC	Smooth, non-chip, down-cutting action on veneers, chipboard, laminated plastics, etc.
	8	Set	3-1/8″	1/4″	HC	For fast cutting of plaster, plaster board and abrasive materials
	Knife	Knife	3-1/8″	1/4″	HC	For smooth cuts in rubber, cork, leather, etc.
	12	Set	3-5/8″	5/16″	HS	Deluxe high speed steel all-purpose blade for cutting nail-embedded wood and abrasive materials
METAL CUTTING						
	12	Set	2-3/4″	5/16″	HS	High speed steel blade cuts ferrous and non-ferrous metals over 1/4″ thick. Also used on plastics, asbestos, and fiberglass
	17	Set	2-3/4″	5/16″	HS	For cutting ferrous and non-ferrous metals over 3/16″ thick. Suitable for pipe and tubing
	21	Set	2-3/4″	5/16″	HS	Easily cuts ferrous metals, aluminum, copper, brass, etc., over 1/8″ thick
	36	Set	2-3/4″	5/16″	HS	Cuts ferrous and non-ferrous metals, plastics, formica, fiberglass, etc., over 1/16″ thick

(Courtesy of Porter-Cable Corporation).

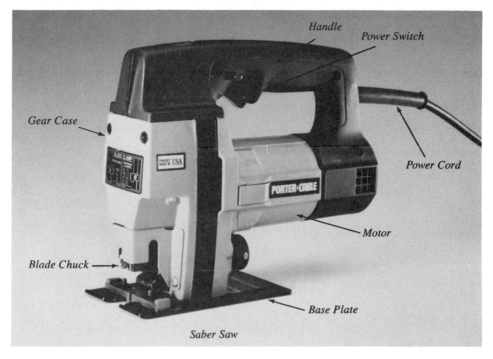

Fig. 16-4. Parts of saber saw (Courtesy of Porter-Cable Corporation).

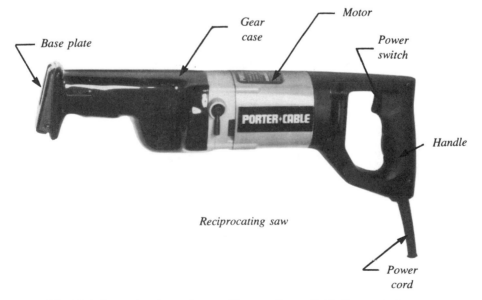

Fig. 16-5. Parts of reciprocating saw (Courtesy Porter-Cable Corporation).

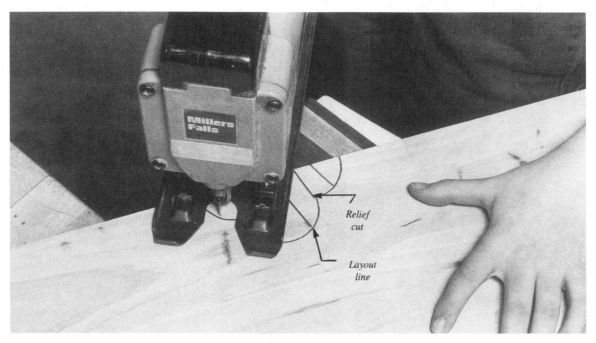

Fig. 16-6. Saw relief cuts just up to the layout line for small curves.

Fig. 16-7. A rip guide aids in ripping a board.

Fig. 16-8. A wooden straight edge can be used to make straight cuts.

tend over the top of the workbench, plan on cutting only the part of the layout line that extends off the workbench. Cut up to the edge of the workbench and then re position the board to continue the cut. Be careful not to cut into the bench.

If the pattern has small curves or any inside corners, first make relief cuts up to the layout line (Fig. 16-6). These short cuts divide the waste area into small pieces. Then cut on the layout line. As the pattern is cut, the small pieces will fall clear and prevent the blade from binding.

Grasp the handle of the saber saw with the right hand. The reciprocating saw must be controlled by holding it with both hands. Align the blade with the layout line. The blade must not touch the stock. Turn on the power switch and begin the cut. Use light forward pressure and stay on the outside of the layout line. Forcing the saw will cause the blade to break. Keep the base plate flat against the stock. Support the waste with the left hand as the cut is completed. Keep the hands at least 4 inches (102 mm) from the blade.

If the saw is used for ripping or making straight

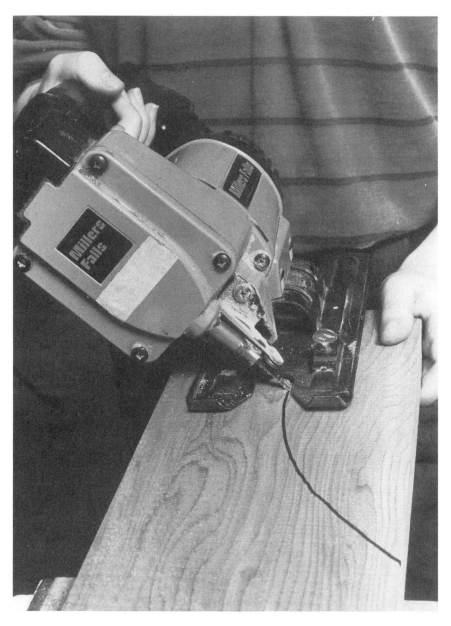

Fig. 16-9. Angle the base plate to make a bevel cut.

cuts, use a rip guide (Fig. 16-7). When a rip guide is not available, use a straightedge clamped to the material to guide the base along (Fig. 16-8). The base plate can also be angled to make a beveled cut (Fig. 16-9).

CIRCULAR SAW

The portable circular saw is a common portable power tool used by woodworkers and especially carpenters. Because this saw can easily be moved around, it is ideal

---

SAFETY WHEN USING A PORTABLE CIRCULAR SAW

☐ Unplug the power cord before installing a blade.
☐ Always clamp the stock to either sawhorses or a workbench.
☐ Hands must come no closer than 4 inches (102 mm) to the blade.
☐ Arrange the power cord so it will not interfere with the cut.
☐ Grasp the saw by the handles.
☐ Be certain the retractable guard is in working order.
☐ Adjust the blade to extend no more than ¼ inch (6 mm) below the stock.
☐ Never reach under the board.

---

for cutting large pieces of plywood and long boards to length.

Parts

Behind the blade is the *motor* and *handle* (Fig. 16-10). On the bottom side of the handle is the *on-off switch*. The *base plate* extends on either side of the blade and can be adjusted up or down with the depth adjustment knob. The base can also be tilted to any angle up to 45 degrees by using the angle adjustment knob. Below the base plate is the *retractable guard* to protect the blade. It is spring-loaded and must always snap closed and cover the blade once the cut is completed.

Consider these two items when determining the size of a portable circular saw: First, consider the largest blade diameter that can be safely mounted on the saw. A good general-purpose saw uses a 7¼-inch (184 mm) blade that has a maximum cutting depth of 2½ inches (64 mm). Second, consider the size of the motor. The larger the ampere rating for the motor, the more power it will have. A ten-ampere motor can make most cuts safely.

Changing the Blade

To change the blade, first be certain that the saw is unplugged. Secure the shaft of the saw with either the

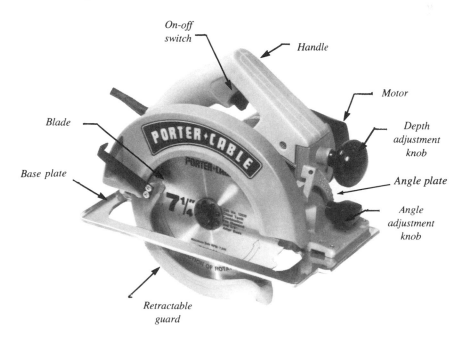

Fig. 16-10. Parts of a portable circular saw (Courtesy Porter-Cable Corporation).

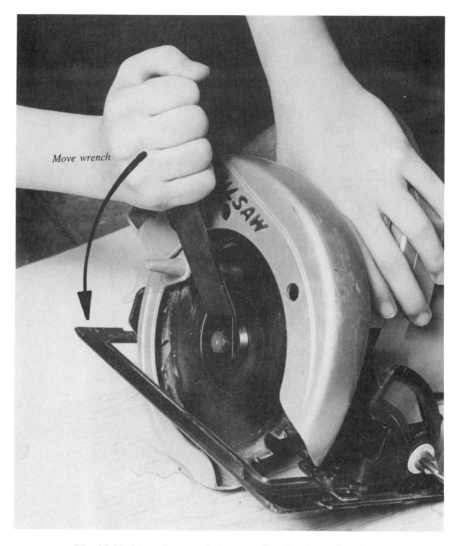

Fig. 16-11. Move the wrench the same direction the teeth point.

built-in blade lock or motor wrench. If neither is available, wedge a piece of wood between the blade and base. Using the blade wrench, loosen the arbor bolt (Fig. 16-11). Pull the wrench the same direction the teeth of the blade point. Remove the stabilizing washer and then the blade.

Slip the new blade under the retractable guard. Make certain the teeth are pointing in the same direction as the arbor turns. Replace the washer and arbor bolt, tighten the bolt, and check that the retractable guard is properly working.

Operating the Saw

Before picking up the saw, position the stock. The best face should be placed down to reduce chipping. Clamp the material to a pair of sawhorses, making certain the cut will not pass through the sawhorses. If the blades will touch the sawhorses, cut up to the sawhorses and stop the saw. Reposition the material and continue the cut. Using the depth adjustment knob, adjust the depth of cut so that the blade is ¼ inch (6 mm) below the bottom surface of the stock. Be sure the blade is at the desired angle by checking the angle plate.

Grasp the saw by the handles and place the base plate firmly against the stock. Align the blade with the layout line. Many saws have an alignment notch cut into the base to show the path of the blade. Check that the blade is not touching the stock. Turn on the power and slowly push the saw forward. *Never* reach under the board. Hands must stay at least 4 inches (102 mm) from the blade. Steady the piece that is being cut off to prevent pinching the blade. If the piece is large, have some one hold it for you.

Crosscutting

Crosscutting cuts a board to length. Using a square, draw a line where the piece is to be cut. For a fast cut, free-hand the saw along the line. Use the same procedure as given in the preceding operating section.

If an accurate cut is required, first measure the distance from the blade to the outside edge of the base. Clamp a straightedge this same distance away from the layout line. Run the edge of the base along this guide (Fig. 16-12). The cut will be parallel to the straight edge.

Ripping

Ripping is usually done to cut boards to width. Most portable circular saws have a *rip guide*. Adjust the rip guide the same distance away from the blade as the desired width of the board. This guide works well for material up to 6 inches (152 mm) wide. Be certain the edge the guide is to be run against is straight and true (Fig. 16-13).

Ripping can also be done using either freehand techniques or by running the base against a straightedge.

Fig. 16-12. A straightedge clamped to the stock acts as a guide for crosscutting.

Cutting Bevels

Bevels are angular cuts along the edge or end of a board. To make a bevel cut, tilt the base to the desired angle. Secure the base with the bevel adjustment knob. It is a good practice to unplug the saw before attempting to tilt the base. The angle plate will indicate the angle (Fig. 16-14). If a very accurate angle is required, cut a scrap piece and check the cut on the board with a protractor. Use either crosscutting or ripping techniques to complete the cut.

Cutting Plywood

Because of its size, a portable circular saw works well for cutting large 4- × -8-foot (1219- × -2438 mm) plywood sheets. The portable saw can make finish cuts or be used to cut a piece to rough size—making it easier to square on the table saw.

Cuts can be made either freehand or with a straightedge. The straightedge technique will require some time

to set up, but will give better results. Place the best face down to achieve the smoothest cut.

SANDING MACHINES

Portable sanders are lightweight machines that can be easily moved over your project. There are several types of portable sanders from which to select; the most common include the portable belt sander and the finish sander. The *portable belt sander* can remove a great deal of material with little effort. As the name implies, it uses a sanding belt to remove material. The *finish sander* produces a surface ready for finishing but removes the wood at a slower rate. This sander utilizes a piece of abrasive paper to sand the wood.

PORTABLE BELT SANDER

A portable belt sander removes deep mill marks and other major defects. It is a difficult machine to use, so it is best to practice on a scrap piece of material to learn

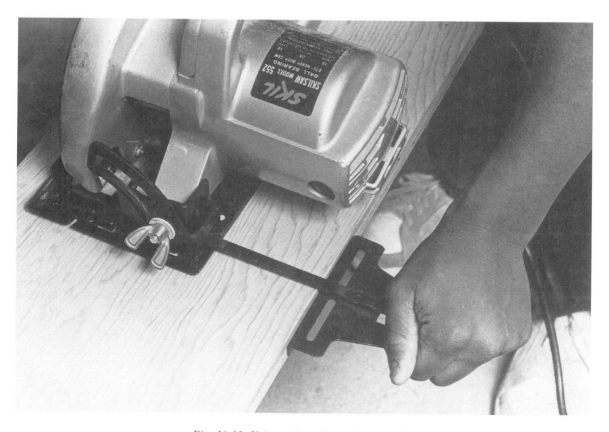

Fig. 16-13. Using a rip guide to rip material.

Fig. 16-14. The angle plate indicates the angle of the blade.

SAFETY WHEN USING PORTABLE SANDERS

☐ Unplug the sander when changing abrasive.
☐ Clamp stock to the workbench.
☐ Grasp the sander by both handles.
☐ Arrange the power cord away from the work area.
☐ Before plugging in the sander be certain the on-off switch is in the off position.
☐ Keep tools and other loose pieces out of the path of the sander.

how to best control the sander. If not properly controlled, it can quickly dig into the wood, creating deep scratches and grooves that are very difficult to remove.

Parts

The portable belt sander is made with a *front* and *rear handle* (Fig. 16-15). The rear handle contains the *on-off switch*. Below the motor unit is the *belt pulley*. The *power pulley* that rotates the belt is located to the rear of the sander. The *front pulley* provides tension to the belt and keeps the belt stretched tight between the pulleys. Between the pulleys is the *platen*, which keeps the belt flat on the board and allows a flat surface to be sanded. Some belt sanders have a *dust bag* attachment.

The size of the belt sander is determined by the width and length of the belt. Sizes range from 3 × 21 inches (76 × 533 mm) to 4 × 24 inches (102 × 610 mm).

Changing Belts

Most rough sanding is completed with an 80-grit belt. For general purpose sanding, however, a 100-grit belt is best. Sometimes a belt sander is used on smooth material and for removing smaller amounts of material. In this case, use a 120-grit belt. The grit number refers to the diameter of the individual abrasive particles: The larger the grit number, the finer the abrasive particles on the belt.

When a different belt is desired or when a belt becomes worn, it must be changed. To change a belt, first unplug the power cord. Push in the front pulley to release the belt tension. Some sanders have a compression lever to retract the front pulley to remove the old belt (Fig. 16-16).

Check the inside of the new belt to be certain it is the correct size and that the printed arrow points in the same direction as the rotation of the belt. Slide the belt onto the pulleys and center the belt on the platen.

Release the belt tension and plug in the power cord. Turn the sander over and quickly turn the switch on and off. If the belt moves off the platen, turn the tracking knob a small amount. Switch the sander on and off again and see if the belt moves back onto the platen. If it does not, turn the knob the opposite direction. Keep turning the tracking knob a small amount until the belt remains centered on the platen. Be careful the belt does not cut into the metal frame of the sander.

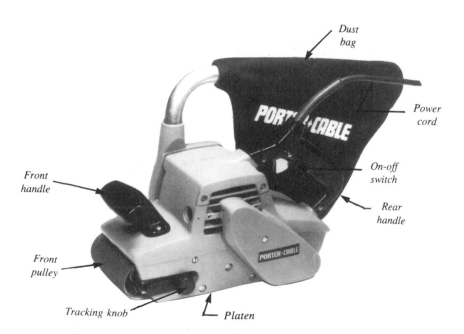

Fig. 16-15. Parts of a portable belt sander (Courtesy of Porter-Cable Corporation).

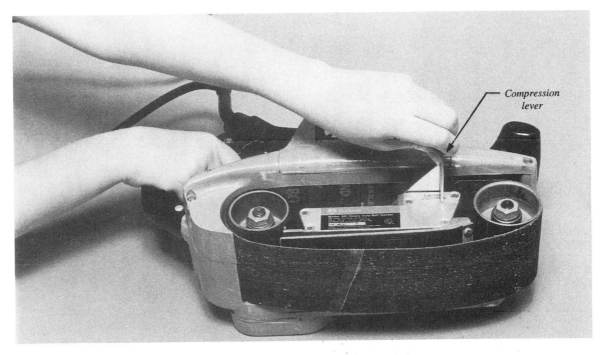

Fig. 16-16. Compress the front pulley by lifting the lever.

Operating the Belt Sander

To use the portable belt sander, first clamp your stock to the workbench. Check that you are using the right grit of sanding belt on the sander. Arrange the cord so that it will not come in contact with the moving belt. Wear a respirator or fabric mask over your nose if dust becomes a problem.

This sander should be run so the sanding belt rotates with the grain. Position the sander on the stock with the belt lying parallel to the grain. Sanding across the grain will place deep scratches in the wood. Place the sander flat on the wood. Grasp each handle and position your body so it is well balanced. Turn on the power and move the sander forward immediately. Don't allow the moving belt to remain in one spot or it will cause a low spot. Don't concentrate the sander over defects. Keep the sander moving back and forth over the entire surface, using the sanding pattern in Fig. 16-17.

PORTABLE FINISH SANDERS

Portable finish sanders are also sometimes called "pad sanders." They are very simple to operate. Many wood-

workers use these sanders to do all of their sanding. They save much hand sanding and produce a surface ready for finishing.

There are three major kinds of finish sanders; most shops will have at least one of these (Fig. 16-18):

The *orbital sander* is the most common. It moves the sanding pad in an eliptical pattern, which causes a portion of the pattern to be across the grain. The cross scratch will be slightly visible when the finish is applied.

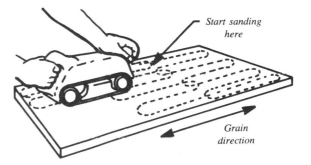

Fig. 16-17. Move the sander in the correct pattern.

Orbital sander   Vibrating sander   Straight-line sander

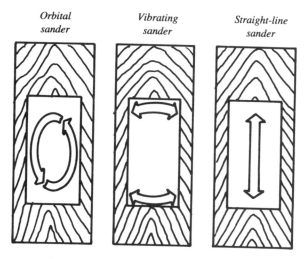

Fig. 16-18. Three types of finishing sanders.

The *vibrating sander* moves the pad back and forth across the grain, which causes cross scratches in the wood.

The *straight-line sander* is moved back and forth in a straight line. If run properly, it does not produce cross scratches. Material, however, is removed at a slower rate. Do not turn the sander sideways or it will make deep cross scratches.

Parts

Finish sanders are one of the simplest portable power tools. They have either one or two *handles* (Fig. 16-19).

Generally the handles are part of the *motor housing*. On the bottom side of the sander is the *sanding pad* to which the abrasive paper is mounted. It is generally covered with either cork or soft rubber. The spring-loaded *pad clips* located at each end of the pad hold the abrasive paper in place.

The size of the finish sander is determined by size of the pad and the number of strokes or movements per minute. Most sanders use a fourth, third, or half sheet of abrasive paper. The strokes per minute vary from 10,000 to 20,000.

Mounting the Abrasive Paper

Before starting to sand, select the abrasive paper. For most sanding jobs, start with 100-grit abrasive paper. After the major mill marks are removed, change to 120-grit. Finish sanding with 150 and then 180. Most plywood and other smooth boards can be sanded starting with 150-grit abrasive paper.

To cut the abrasive paper to size, use a straightedge and knife. Cut from the backside of the sheet. To save time cut an entire sheet, but place the unused pieces where they can remain flat.

Unplug the power cord before mounting the paper. Lift up on one of the spring-loaded pad clips located at the end of the sanding pad (Fig. 16-20). Slip one end of the abrasive paper under the clip and release the clip. Smooth the paper over the pad and insert the opposite end under the second spring clip.

Fig. 16-19. Parts of a finishing sander (Courtesy Porter-Cable Corporation).

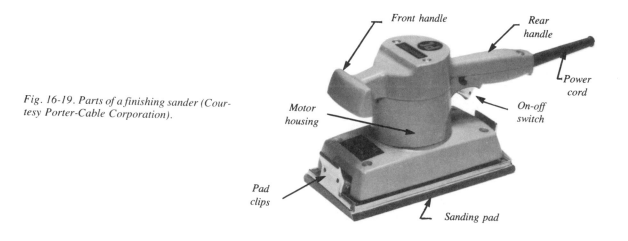

Fig. 16-20. Slide the abrasive paper completely under the spring clip.

Operating the Finish Sander

Place the material to be sanded on a flat surface such as a workbench. If there is a danger of the piece being scratched, pad the workbench top with a piece of carpet or cloth. Select and mount the best grit of abrasive paper for the job.

Position the sander on top of the board and plug in the power cord. After turning on the switch, start moving the sander over the entire surface. Allow the weight of the sander to do the sanding. Pushing down on the sander will cause the motor to overheat and do serious damage. If a scratch or major defect needs to be removed, do not sand only over the mark, because this will cause a noticeable low spot.

POWER PLANE

The portable power plane is designed to perform many of the same operations as the hand plane. Because it is powered, however, it makes removing material much easier.

SAFETY WHEN USING A PORTABLE POWER PLANE

☐ Unplug the power cord when working with the cutter.
☐ Clamp the stock to a workbench.
☐ Grasp the plane by the handles.
☐ Arrange the power cord away from the work area.
☐ Keep hands at least 4 inches (102 mm) away from the cutter.
☐ Remove no more than $1/32$ inch (1 mm) with each cut.
☐ Once the cutter has cleared the board, leave the plane in place until the cutter has stopped turning.

Parts

The plane contains a handle, front and rear beds, motor, and cutter (Fig. 16-21). The *handle* is used to control the plane and also houses the on-off switch. To control the depth of cut, the *front adjustable bed* is moved up and down by the depth adjustment knob. Located immediately behind the front bed is the *cutter*. It generally has two or three cutting edges and looks much like the cutter on a jointer. The *rear fixed bed* does not move and supports the weight of the plane. An *adjustable fence* is positioned to the left of the beds and holds the plane at the desired angle. By tilting the fence, angles from 90 to 45 degrees can be planed (Fig. 16-22). It might take several passes to complete the entire bevel.

Operating the Plane

Be certain the power cord is unplugged before making any adjustments. Set the depth of cut to no more than $1/32$ inch (1 mm). To remove more than $1/32$ inch, make multiple passes. The final pass might require a fine depth adjustment to make the desired depth of cut. Check the angle of the fence by using the angle gauge (Fig. 16-23).

Secure the stock to a workbench and plug in the power cord. Grasp the plane by the handle. Steady the plane on the stock, being certain that the bed and fence are flat against the board (Fig. 16-24). The cutter must not be touching the stock.

Turn on the power. When the cutter is running full speed, slowly push the plane forward. Use a slow, steady motion to feed the plane. Keep the bed and fence against the stock. Once the cutter has cleared the board, turn off the power. Allow the plane to stay on the board. Hold the plane in this position until the cutter has stopped turning. Never reach under the plane for any reason. Your hands must come no closer than 4 inches (102 mm) to the cutter.

ROUTER

There are probably more uses for the *router* than any other portable power tool. It can make accurate joints as well as shape decorating edges. Because there are many different router bits, the types of cuts are practically unlimited.

Parts

The router has only two main parts (Fig. 16-25). The *motor unit* powers the router and contains the chuck that holds the router bits. A *base* slides up and down the motor to adjust the depth of cut. On most routers two handles are also attached to the base to control the router.

The size of the router is determined by the horse-

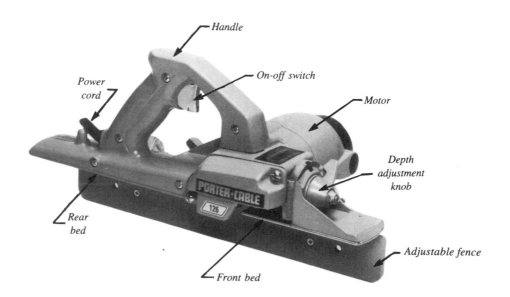

Fig. 16-21. Parts of a portable power plane (Courtesy of Porter-Cable Corporation).

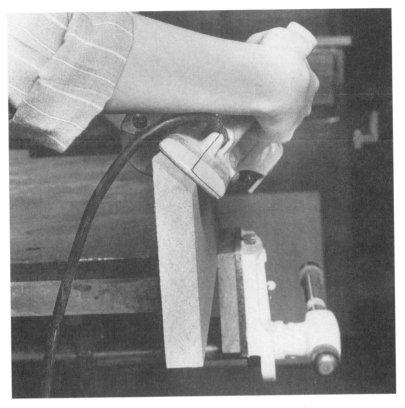

Fig. 16-22. Tilt the fence to plane a bevel.

power rating of the motor and the size of the collet. The horsepower rating can range from less than ½ horsepower to over 3 horsepower. A 1-horsepower router will perform most general-purpose cuts. The collet holds the router bit in the motor unit. Collet size determines the diameter of the shank of the router bit to be used (Fig. 16-26). Sizes are ¼, ⅜, and ½ inch (6, 10, and 13 mm). Some routers will only accept a ¼- or ½-inch collet, while others will take all three.

Router Bits

Router bits vary widely in shape and size (Fig. 16-27). The least expensive bits are made from high-speed steel. They work well for shaping solid wood and are easy to sharpen. Carbide-tipped router bits are most expensive but will last much longer. These bits do not burn as easily and can be used on more abrasive materials such as plastic laminates and particleboard. They need to be sharpened by a professional.

SAFETY WHEN USING A PORTABLE ROUTER

☐ Unplug the power cord when changing or working near the router bit.
☐ Stock must be clamped to the workbench before routing.
☐ Control the router by holding both handles.
☐ Do not reach under the stock or router.
☐ Move the router in the correct direction.
☐ Use light cuts.

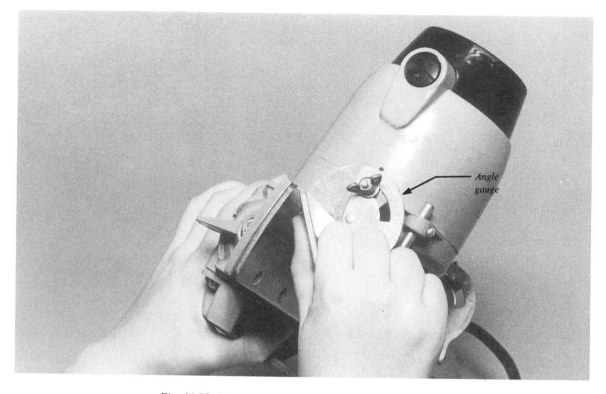

Fig. 16-23. The angle gauge indicates the angle of the fence.

All router bits have a shank and a cutting edge. Some bits also contain a pilot. The shank is either ¼, ⅜, or ½ inch (6, 10, or 13 mm) in diameter and fit into the matching collet. Most bits have a ¼-inch shank. The ½-inch shank, however, makes a stiffer bit, which is less likely to break.

Those bits containing a pilot are used to shape edges of stock. The pilot is either solid or a ball bearing. The pilot glides along the edge of the board and controls how far in the bit cuts. A solid pilot costs less but has a tendency to burn the wood. Ball bearing pilots do not turn with the bit and do not burn the edge.

Installing a Router Bit

Unplug the power cord and disassemble the motor unit from the base. Pick the bit that will produce the desired shape and the collet that fits the shank of the router bit. Insert the collet into the shaft of the motor. Loosely screw the collet nut onto the shaft. Slide the shank of the router bit at least ½ inch into the collet.

Using the router wrench, secure the shaft of the motor. Some routers might have another method of holding the shaft. Using a second wrench, finish tightening the collet nut. Move the second wrench clockwise to tighten while holding the first wrench still (Fig. 16-28). Reassemble the motor unit and base unit. Make certain the switch is off before plugging in the router.

Setting Up

The amount the router bit extends below the base determines the depth of cut. The farther the bit is lowered, the deeper the cut. To adjust this depth, slide the base up or down on the motor unit (Fig. 16-29). Tighten the depth lock once the depth is set. If the router is small or a heavy cut is required, consider taking a series of light cuts. Lower the bit after each pass until the desired depth is reached.

Operating the Router

The router is moved in the opposite direction the router bit turns. When an outside edge such as a tabletop is to

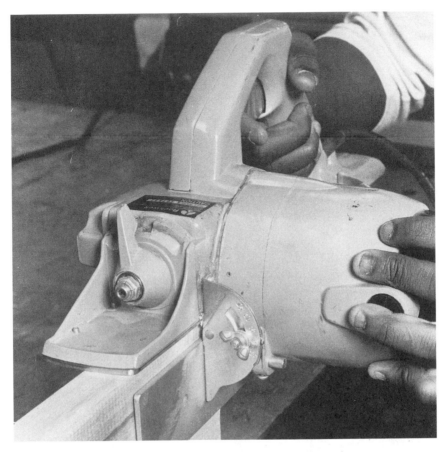

Fig. 16-24. Keep the bed and fence against the stock.

Fig. 16-25. Parts of a portable router (Courtesy of Porter-Cable Corporation).

Power cord

On-off switch

Motor unit

Base

Handle

Handle

be routed, move the router counter clockwise or from left to right. Inside cuts such as the inside of a circle should be made by guiding the router clockwise or right to left.

Each type of wood and each router bit requires a different feed rate. Too fast a feed rate will create a rough cut and wear out the router. Too slow a feed rate will burn the wood and router bit. When the router is being fed correctly, the motor will not pull down or lower greatly in sound.

Clamp a scrap piece to a workbench and practice routing it to check the cut. If the cut is incorrect, make any necessary adjustments. Control the router by using both handles located on base. *Never* reach under the router when it is running.

Edge Routing

A bit containing a pilot is generally used to rout an edge. Because the pilot is run against the edge, be certain that

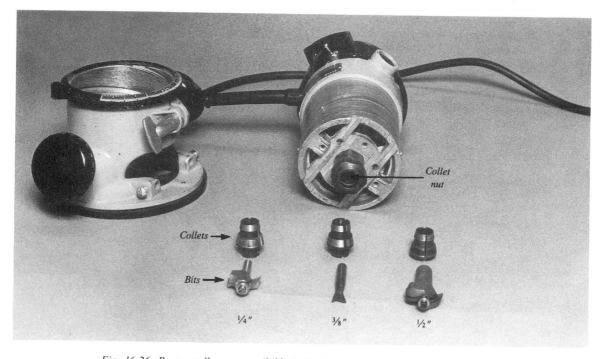

Fig. 16-26. Router collets are available in ¼, ⅜, and ½ inches (6, 10 and 13 mm).

the edge is smooth. Any low or high spots will be duplicated in the routed edge. Always rout the end grain first. Any splitting out at the ends of the cut will then be routed away when the edges are shaped. If the router is not large enough to make the cut in one pass, make multiple passes until the pilot is against the edge.

Joint Routing

Because the router makes a smooth cut, it is ideal for making rabbets, dados, or grooves. Straight cuts can be made by guiding the router with either a commercial fence or straightedge. Router bits without a pilot are used here.

Secure the commercial fence to the base of the router with screws. You can adjust it in or out depending on where the cut is to be placed. Guide the fence along the edge of the board to make the cut (Fig. 16-30).

Clamp the straightedge to the stock. Run the base against the straightedge as the cut is made. Be careful to not let the router move away from the guide. A second straightedge can be clamped against the opposite edge of

the router, which will form a trough in which to run the router.

Freehand Routing

Freehand routing is used primarily for making signs and other irregular cuts. A core box or straight bit works best. Trace or draw the pattern onto the surface using a pencil, then trace around the design with a router (Fig. 16-31).

Template Routing

Template routing is generally used to make inside cuts. It requires a bit without a pilot and a template guide. A template guide is an attachment that is screwed to the router base (Fig. 16-32). The template guide is run against a custom-made template. Make the template out of tempered hardboard or other hard material.

The template is clamped or screwed to the stock. Pivot the turning router bit into the material. Keep the outside edge of the template guide against the template

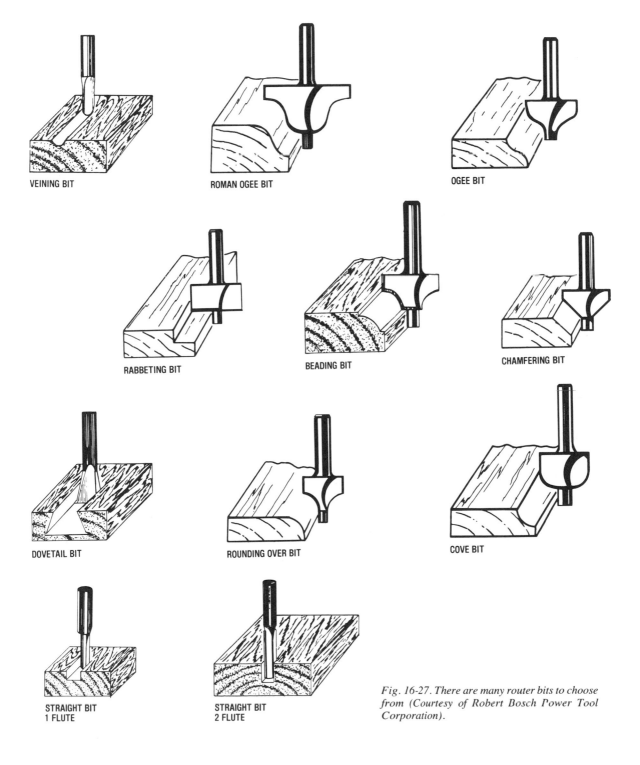

VEINING BIT

ROMAN OGEE BIT

OGEE BIT

RABBETING BIT

BEADING BIT

CHAMFERING BIT

DOVETAIL BIT

ROUNDING OVER BIT

COVE BIT

STRAIGHT BIT
1 FLUTE

STRAIGHT BIT
2 FLUTE

Fig. 16-27. There are many router bits to choose from (Courtesy of Robert Bosch Power Tool Corporation).

Fig. 16-28. Tightening the collet nut.

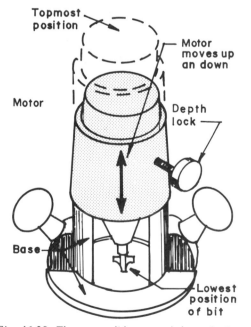

Fig. 16-29. The motor slides up and down the base to adjust the depth of cut.

or a true cut will not be made. Trace around the template to complete the cut (Fig. 16-33).

Dovetails

Dovetails are used primarily for quality drawer construction. They require the use of a template guide, dovetail bit, and dovetail fixture. Although the setup requires several steps, dovetails can be cut using a simple procedure.

Install the template guide, then the dovetail bit (Fig. 16-34). The bit must be set exactly $^{19}/_{32}$ inch (15 mm) deep. Use a depth gauge to aid in setting the depth. Secure the dovetail fixture to the workbench with either the bench vise or clamps. Prepare the drawer parts to the finished sizes. Also plane two pieces of scrap stock to the exact same thickness as the finished drawer material.

Place one of the pieces of scrap into the front of the dovetail fixture. It must be kept against and held in place with the front clamp. Slip the second piece of scrap under the top hold-down bar and against the other board and locating pin. Tighten the hold-down bar. If necessary, adjust the first piece so that the end is exactly flush with the top of the second piece (Fig. 16-35).

To rout the dovetails, place the router against the

Fig. 16-30. A commercial fence rides along the straightedge.

Fig. 16-31. Using the router to freehand a sign.

Fig. 16-32. Attaching the template guide with the template guide screws.

Fig. 16-33. Routing a design using a template guide and template.

Fig. 16-34. Adjust the depth of the dovetail bit.

template on the far left. Turn on the router and trace along the template. Never lift or raise the router base up off the template because raising the router will cause the bit to cut into the template. Once the cut is completed, turn off the router and leave it on the template until the bit stops turning.

Remove the two pieces of material and check the fit of the joint. If the joint is too tight, raise the bit $\frac{1}{64}$ inch. If it is too loose, lower the bit $\frac{1}{64}$ inch. Sometimes the fingers of the dovetail fit correctly, but are not flush. Move the template in or out. Make a trial cut after each adjustment and continue making adjustments and trial cuts until a perfect fit is achieved.

Only after a perfect cut is made on the scrap material can the finished drawer parts be routed. Use the left side of the dovetail fixture to dovetail the right front corner and the left rear corner of the drawer, and the right side of the fixture for the left corner and the right rear corner of the drawer. The outside of the drawer parts should be placed with the outside surface facing in.

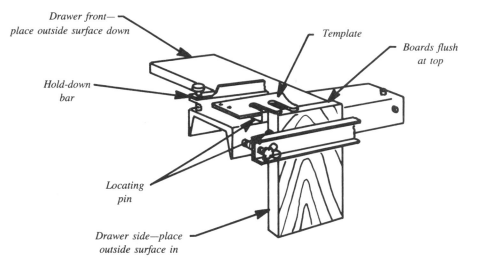

Fig. 16-35. Position the front board flush with the top of the second piece.

Chapter 17

Table Saw

The table saw is one of the most often used stationary woodworking machines. With the proper cutter it can cut boards to size, make jointery cuts, and even shape decorative moldings.

PARTS

The major parts of the table saw are the table, base, miter gauge, rip fence, and saw guard (Fig. 17-1). To cut a board first place the stock on top of the table and against either the miter gauge or rip fence. The *miter gauge* slides in one of the two miter gauge grooves milled into the table on each side of the blade. It is used for cross-cutting. The *rip fence* is moved along the *rip fence guide* bars and locked into place with the *fence lock*. It is used for ripping operations.

The *base* is located below the table. This metal base contains the handwheels to raise and tilt the blade. Inside the base is the saw arbor that holds the saw blade.

The size of the table saw is determined by the largest diameter of saw blade that is recommended by the manufacturer for the saw. The most common size is a 10-inch table saw.

SAFETY

☐ Unplug the saw whenever changing the blade or installing the guard.
☐ Your hands should never come any closer than 4 inches (102 mm) to the blade.
☐ Unless a special safe procedure is followed, always use the saw guard.
☐ Adjust the blade to ⅛ inch (3 mm) above the top of the stock.
☐ Do not place your body or hands in the path of the blade; stand to the left or right of the blade.
☐ Always use the rip fence or miter gauge to cut a board; never cut freehand.
☐ Allow the blade to come to a complete stop before removing scraps or loose material.
☐ Move the fence out of the way when crosscutting with the miter gauge.
☐ Do not use the saw if the blade is dull, cracked, or if it wobbles.
☐ When crosscutting, there must be at least 6 inches (152 mm) of stock in contact with the miter gauge.
☐ Material must be at least 10 inches (254 mm) long to be ripped.
☐ Always use a pushstick when ripping material less than 6 inches (152 mm) wide.
☐ Do not rip stock less than ½ inch (13 mm) wide.
☐ Push the stock completely past the blade and guard before releasing the board.
☐ Stock against the table must be flat. The edge against the miter gauge or rip fence must be straight.
☐ When finished with the saw turn off the power and lower the blade below the table.

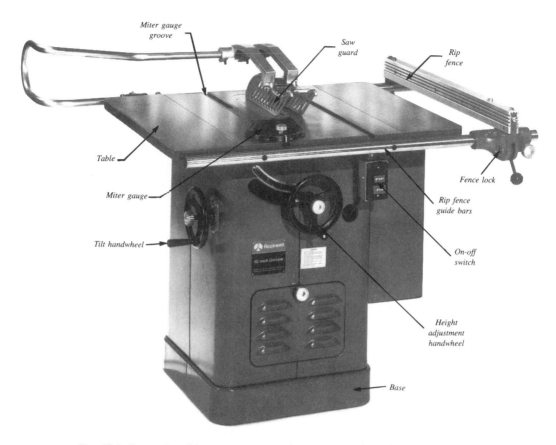

Fig. 17-1. Parts of a table saw (Courtesy Delta International Machinery Corporation).

The *guard* is one of the most important parts of the tablesaw (Fig. 17-2). Each guard should contain a blade guard, antikickback fingers, and a splitter. The *blade guard* covers the blade and keeps the hands of the operator from being cut. The *antikickback fingers* prevent the board from being thrown back towards the operator. To keep the board from pinching the blade a *splitter* is located immediately behind the blade. *Do not* operate the saw unless all parts of the guard are properly working and in place.

SAW BLADES, DADO HEADS, AND OTHER CUTTERS

Most generally a *saw blade* is used as a cutter on a table saw. It has teeth ground around the outside edge to remove the wood. A groove is made as the board is cut. It is called the *saw kerf*.

Some blades are made completely of steel. There are four basic styles of these blades. A *ripping blade* has large chisel-like teeth that are filed at a 90-degree angle. It should only be used to cut boards with the grain. The *crosscut blade* has smaller knife-shaped teeth. It words best for making a smooth cut across the grain. A *rough-cut combination* has teeth similar to a rip blade, but sharpened at a bevel. This blade can be used to saw either with or across the grain. It makes a rather rough cut. The *four-tooth combination* is the best blade for furniture and cabinetmaking. It makes a smooth cut.

Close inspection of a steel saw blade reveals that every other tooth is bent to the right, the others bent to the left. This bending is called *spring set*, and is important to making the wide saw kerf. Without set, the sides of the blade will rub against the board and burn, which will cause the board to kickback or to be thrown uncon-

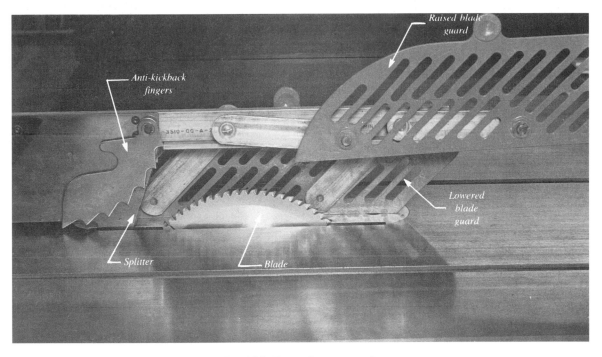

Fig. 17-2. Parts of a saw guard.

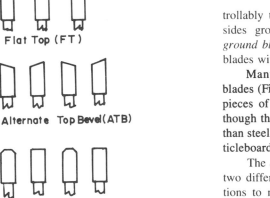

Flat Top (FT)

Alternate Top Bevel (ATB)

Triple Chip (TC)

Combination
(Alternate Top Bevels with
Rakers —ATB/R)

Fig. 17-3. Styles of carbide-tipped saw blades.

trollably to the rear of the saw. Some blades have the sides ground on an angle. These are called *hollow ground blades*. The tapered sides provide clearance like blades with the teeth set.

Many saws are equipped with *carbide-tipped* blades (Fig. 17-3). These are blades that have very hard pieces of metal attached to the tips of the blade. Although they cost more, the carbide stays sharper longer than steel. They also can cut abrasive materials like particleboard and plastics.

The *dado head* is used to make grooves. It contains two different types of cutters that are used in combinations to make various widths of cuts (Fig. 17-4). The *outside cutters* are shaped like a combination blade. When only one is used, it makes an ⅛-inch-wide (3 mm) groove. The two outside cutters together make a ¼-inch (6 mm) groove. To make a groove wider than ¼ inch, the second type of dado cutter, the *inside chipper*, is also used. Most dado head sets contain inside cutters that are either ¹⁄₁₆ or ⅛ inch (2 or 3 mm) wide. Different combinations of these chippers along with the outside cutters are used to make various widths of grooves. Adjustable dado heads only have one cutter, which is angled to make different cuts (Fig. 17-5).

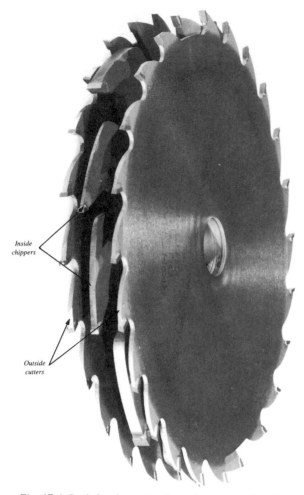

Inside chippers

Outside cutters

Fig. 17-4. Dado heads consist of outside cutters and inside chippers. (Courtesy D.M.L. Corporation).

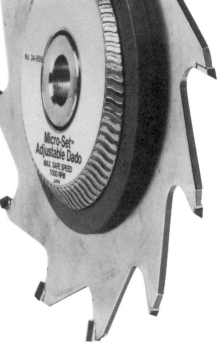

Fig. 17-5. Adjustable dado head (Courtesy Delta International Machinery Corporation).

The *molding head* is used primarily to make decorative cuts. It consists of a steel body on which different shaped cutters are mounted (Fig. 17-6). Before it is mounted on the saw arbor, three knives of the same shape are bolted to the body. It is important that the knives be securely tightened in place before using the molding head.

CHANGING A SAW BLADE

If a blade becomes dull or if a different type of cut is to be made, the saw blade must be changed. Start by disconnecting the power. After removing the guard and throat plate, raise the saw blade to its highest position. Wedge a scrap board against the front of the blade to keep it from turning (Fig. 17-7). Place the arbor wrench that came with the saw on the arbor nut, and pull the handle of the wrench forward towards the operator to remove the nut.

Remove the stablizing collar and blade. Be careful not to drop or place the blade against the metal table. Install the new blade with the teeth pointing towards the front of the saw. Replace the stablizing collar and nut, and secure the nut by wedging a board against the back

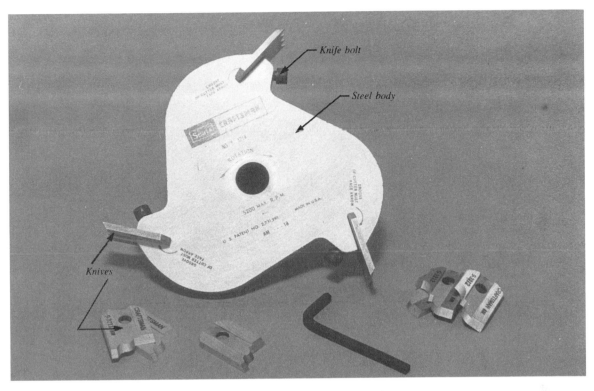

Fig. 17-6. Parts of a molding head.

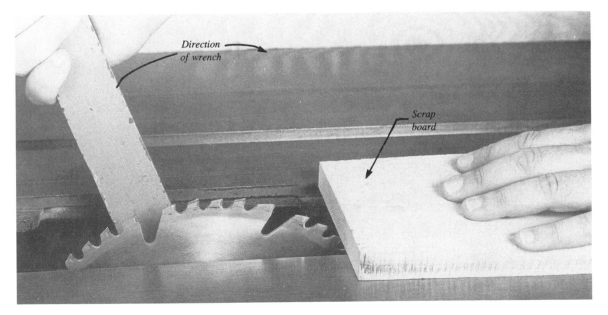

Fig. 17-7. Pull the wrench handle forward.

of the blade and tightening with the wrench. Finish the procedure by installing the throat place and guard. Reconnect the power.

RIPPING BOARDS TO WIDTH

Boards to be ripped are cut with the grain. They must have one straight edge and one flat face. Any piece ripped on a table saw must be at least 10 inches (254 mm) long. Do not rip any material less than ½ inch (13 mm) wide. Adjust the blade to ⅛ inch (3 mm) above the stock.

Always rip the stock with the widest part of the board between the blade and the rip fence. Using a ruler, set the rip fence the same distance away from the blade as the desired width of the board. Measure between the tooth leaning closest to the fence and the face of the rip fence. If the saw cut edge is to be jointed or planed, add 1/16 inch (2 mm) to this dimension. Replace the guard.

Standing to the left of the blade, turn on the power and place the straight edge of the board against the fence and the flat face against the table. Push the board for-ward always keeping it against the fence. The hands of the operator must not come any closer than 4 inches (102 mm) to the blade. Do not let the left hand go past the front edge of the blade. For boards less than 6 inches (152 mm) wide, always use a pushstick to push the stock between the blade and rip fence (Fig. 17-8).

Feed the board forward at a slow speed. Never pull the board back towards you. This will cause a kickback, where the board is thrown uncontrollably. Long boards must be supported on the back of the saw with either someone holding onto the boards or with a support roller.

RESAWING

To save material, thick boards can be ripped or resawn on edge to produce two or more thin pieces. Position the rip fence the desired distance from the blade. For most boards, this will be exactly half the thickness of the board. Place the stock along the fence and install a featherboard against the outside face of the stock. A *featherboard* is a shop-made holding device that is clamped to

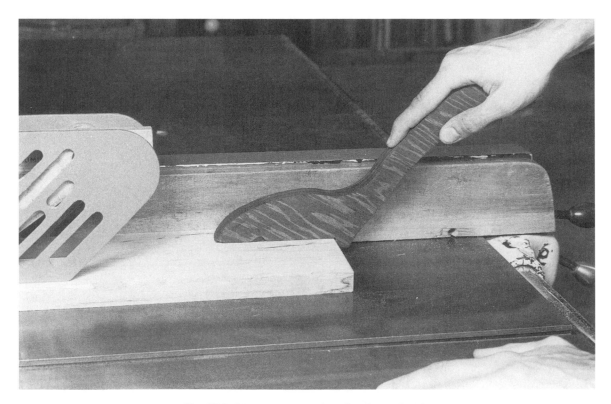

Fig. 17-8. Ripping a narrow board with a pushstick.

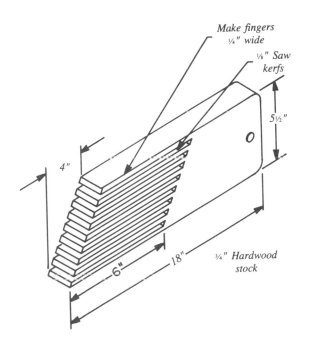

Make fingers
¼" *wide*

⅛" *Saw*
kerfs

5½"

4"

O

6"

18"

¾" *Hardwood*
stock

Fig. 17-9. Measurements for a featherboard.

the table top (Fig. 17-9). It applies pressure against the board, keeping your hands away from the blade. Position it so that it does not extend past the front edge of the saw blade (Fig. 17-10).

Raise the blade ½ inch (13 mm) and make the first cut. Turn the board end for end, keeping the same face against the fence. Saw the second edge.

Raise the blade another ½ inch, or for a total height of 1 inch (25 mm). Repeat the sawing process used for the first two cuts. Continue raising the blade and cutting until only 1 inch remains uncut. Cut this last inch on a band saw or with a handsaw.

CROSSCUTTING BOARDS TO LENGTH

Boards to be crosscut must have at least one flat face and one straight edge. A minimum of least 6 inches (152 mm) of the board must be in contact with the miter gauge. Check that the miter gauge is 90 degrees to the blade. The fastest method to check the accuracy of the miter gauge is to turn it upside down and place it in the miter gauge groove. When the face of the gauge is

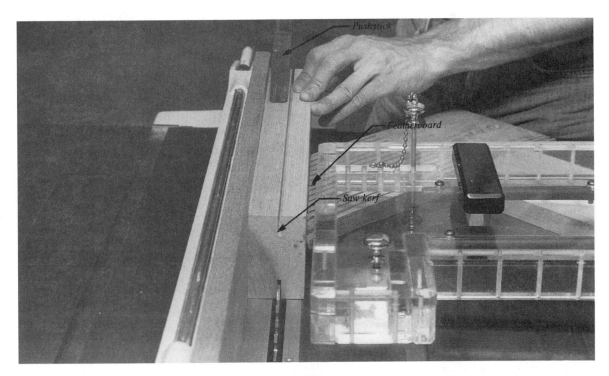

Fig. 17-10. Resawing a board with a pushstick and featherboard.

pushed against the rip fence bar there should be no space left between the two. Adjust the blade so that it is ⅛ inch (3 mm) above the face of the board.

If just a few pieces are to be crosscut, start by pushing the rip fence completely out of the way. Place the straight edge of the stock against the miter gauge, with the flat face against the table. Position the board so that the first end is cut square. Cut off about 1 inch (25 mm) by pushing the miter gauge forward. Keep both hands on the miter gauge and feed the board all the way past the blade. Slide the board away from the blade and pull it and the miter gauge back towards the operator. Do not remove the waste until the blade is completely stopped.

Measure the desired length from the squared end and place a V-shaped mark at the point where the board is to be cut. Align the point of this mark with a saw tooth that is leaning toward the miter gauge. Cut the second end using the same procedure for crosscutting the first. Cut on waste side of the line (Fig. 17-11).

When several pieces of the same length are needed, use a clearance block. This is a flat piece of scrap that is placed against the rip fence opposite the blade. Move the rip fence over until the distance between the saw tooth leaning toward the rip fence and the face of the clearance block is the same as the desired length of the stock (Fig. 17-12). Lock the rip fence in place. Slide the clearance block to the front end of the rip fence and clamp it in place with a C-clamp. Never use the rip fence as a stop; always use a clearance block.

To cut boards to length with the clearance block, square the first end by sawing the first ½ inch (13 mm). After pulling the miter gauge back to the front of the saw, slide the board over until the squared end just touches the clearance block (Fig. 17-13). Holding the board against the miter gauge, cut the second end. As long as the clearance block is not bumped, pieces of the exact same length can be cut. The stock cut to length must not be removed until the blade is completely stopped.

SAWING MITERS

A miter is an angled cut on the end of board running from edge to edge. Miters are often cut to make picture

Fig. 17-11. Crosscutting a board. Note: The guard has been removed from this photograph so you can see the cut. Always use the guard.

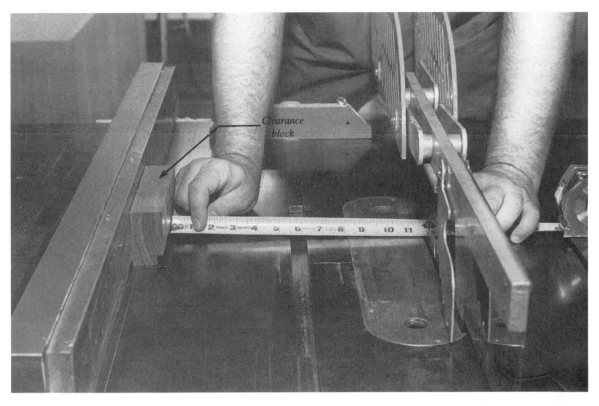

Fig. 17-12. Measuring the distance between the clearance block and tooth nearest the rip fence.

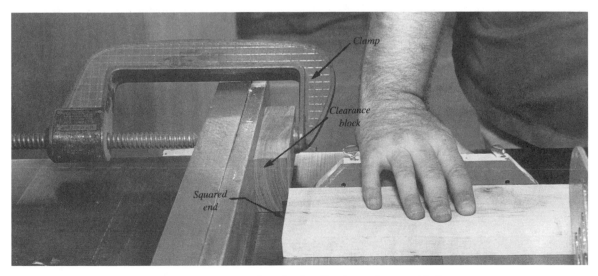

Fig. 17-13. Cutting a board to length using a clearance block.

frames or moulding. First pivot the miter gauge to the left of the desired angle. In most cases a four-sided frame is required, so the miter gauge is set at a 45-degree angle. Always check the first cut with a protractor to see if the angle is correct.

Because the board will want to move away from the blade as it is being cut, attach a long, abrasive-covered board to the miter gauge to help grip the board. Using the crosscutting procedure, cut the first end of all pieces (Fig. 17-14A). If necessary, pivot the miter gauge to the right and cut the second end (Fig. 17-14B). So that all pieces will be exactly the same length, install a stop block on the miter gauge to butt the first mitered end against.

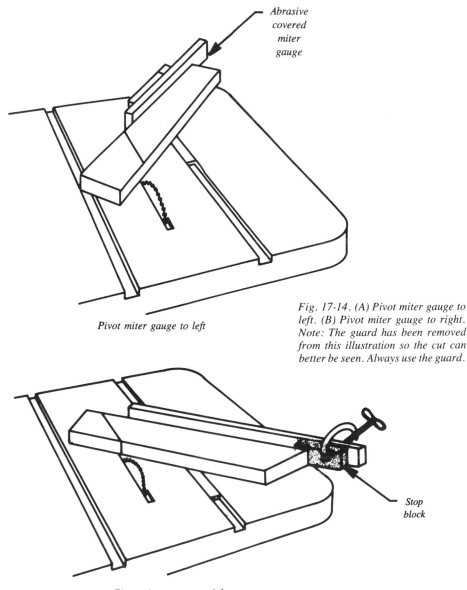

Abrasive covered miter gauge

Pivot miter gauge to left

Fig. 17-14. (A) Pivot miter gauge to left. (B) Pivot miter gauge to right. Note: The guard has been removed from this illustration so the cut can better be seen. Always use the guard.

Stop block

Pivot miter gauge to right

CUTTING CHAMFERS AND BEVELS

A chamfer is an angled cut generally made from an edge to an adjoining face. It is used mostly as a decorative cut. A bevel is an angular cut running from one face to the other. Bevels are used to join boards together on either the ends or edges.

The *tilting handwheel* is turned to change the blade to the desired angle. Turn the handwheel until the tilting gauge located below the table is at the desired angle. Use a sliding T bevel to check the angle of the blade. Use the miter gauge to chamfer or bevel narrow pieces (Fig. 17-15). The rip fence works best for guiding longer boards (Fig. 17-16). Always check the angle on the first board with a protractor before cutting any others.

CUTTING LARGE PANELS

Many pieces used in wood projects are large panels. Because plywood, particleboard, glued boards, and other panels are difficult to handle, first try cutting them rough size with a hand saw or portable electric saw. Make the finish cuts on the table saw using the rip fence. For extra-wide or long pieces have someone support the end as

it leaves the far side of the saw. If you have a sliding table, use it to more easily cut large pieces (Fig. 17-17). The sliding table can be made in a shop. It has two metal rails that slide in the left and right miter gauge grooves. It is pushed past the blade to cut the stock.

Because plywood often splinters as it is being cut across grain, use a blade with the finest teeth possible. Specialized plywood blades or carbide-tipped alternating top bevel blades will produce the best results. Cut material with the best surface facing up. Hardwood plywood might also require that masking tape be applied to the surface where the cut is to be made. Use a slow feed speed to produce an even smoother cut.

CUTTING GROOVES AND DADOES

Two types of rectangular slots are utilized in woodworking projects: grooves and dadoes (Fig. 17-18). If the rectangular slot is cut the same direction as the grain of the board, it is called a groove. A slot made across the grain is called a dado.

Both types of slots are generally cut with a dado head. For ⅛-inch (3 mm) slots, a single outside dado

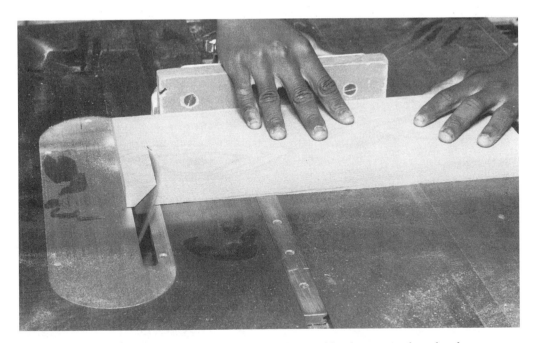

Fig. 17-15. Beveling a board with a miter gauge. Note: The guard has been removed, so that the cut can be seen. Always use a guard.

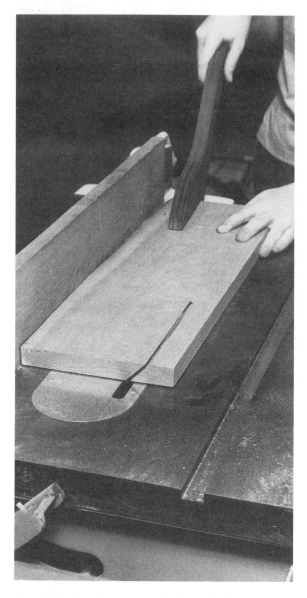

Fig. 17-16. Beveling a board with a rip fence. Note: The guard has been removed, so the cut can be seen. Always use a guard.

cutter can be used. Slots ¼ inch (6 mm) require that the two outside cutters be used together. Always mount the cutters with the teeth pointing forward. The teeth of the two cutters must not be tightened on each other. Position the teeth so that they are interlocked and so the tips are not touching each other (Fig. 17-19).

For dadoes wider than ¼ inch (6 mm), inside chippers are installed. Always use one outside cutter on each side of the chippers. Select the right combination of outside cutters and inside chippers to make the desired width of groove. For example to cut a ¾-inch-wide (19 mm) dado, use the two outside cutters for the first ¼ inch. To make up the remaining ½ inch (13 mm), select four ⅛-inch (3 mm) chippers.

After installing the first outside cutter on the saw arbor, place the first inside chipper next to it. The tooth of the chipper is centered in the gullet of the cutter (Fig. 17-20). Space the remaining chippers equally around the arbor so that the dado head will run in balance. Install the last outside cutter, collar stabilizer, and arbor nut. A special dado throat plate must be installed with a wide opening.

Always install a guard without a splitter before turning on any power. Select the miter gauge for making dados (Fig. 17-21). Because the dado head does not cut all the way through the stock, the rip fence can be used for a stop. The rip fence is used by itself if a groove is made. A pushstick will help hold the stock down. The hands of the operator must not be placed within 4 inches (102 mm) of the dado head.

CUTTING RABBETS

A rabbet is a rectangular groove cut on either an edge and face or end and face (see Fig. 17-18). The back of cabinets, for example, are often held in place in a rabbet.

Rabbets can be cut with either a dado head or single blade. With the dado head, the metal rip fence must be covered with a board (Fig. 17-22). Because the dado head will rub against the metal rip fence, the wood will protect the cutter. Utilize the same procedure to set up and cut a rabbet as described for a dado. The cut is made in one pass. Be certain to use a pushstick.

To cut a rabbet with a single saw blade, first mark out the rabbet on the end of the board (Fig. 17-23). The marks show where the cuts are to be made. Lay the board face down and raise the blade to the same level as the first layout line. Set the rip fence so the tooth set to the left is in line with the second layout line. Use a pushstick to make the first cut. Because the cut is not made all the way through the board, the splitter of the guard cannot be used. A special guard might be needed.

Make the second cut with the board standing up against the rip fence (Fig. 17-24). If necessary, readjust the height of the blade and the position of the rip fence. The waste portion of the rabbet must fall to the outside

Fig. 17-17. A sliding table aids in cutting a large panel.

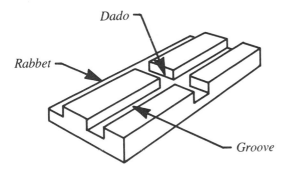

Fig. 17-18. Types of grooves.

of the blade. Install a featherboard on top of a ¾-inch (19 mm) scrap board. The fingers of the featherboard must be located in front of the blade.

CUTTING TAPERS

A tapered board will have one or more edges cut at an angle. Furniture legs are sometimes tapered to give the chair or table a more graceful look.

To cut tapers either a custom or adjustable tapering fixture is necessary. A custom tapering fixture can be cut from ¾-inch plywood using a bandsaw (Fig. 17-25). It will only cut one shape. An adjustable tapering fixture can be set to cut many different shapes (Fig. 17-26). It is made from two straight pieces of wood that have been hinged together at one end. A block glued to the outside edge of one of the legs holds the stock as it is being cut.

To cut a taper with an adjustable tapering fixture, place the amount of taper per foot between the two legs of the fixture. Measure this 12 inches (305 mm) from the hinged end. For example, if ½-inch (13 mm) taper per foot is required, swing the legs apart until there is ½

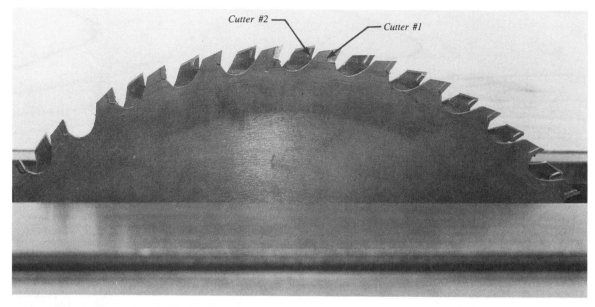

Fig. 17-19. Position of two outside cutters for a ¼-inch (3-mm) groove.

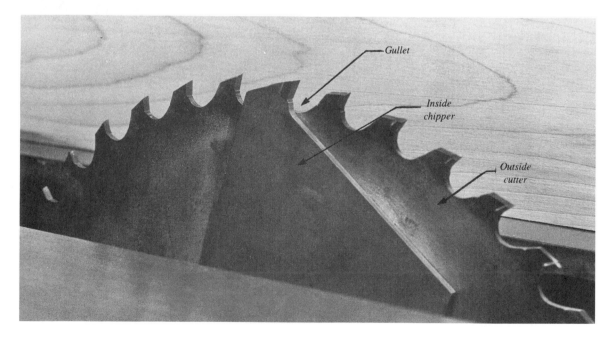

Fig. 17-20. Place the inside chipper in the gullet of the outside cutter.

Fig. 17-21. Cutting a dado with the rip fence as a stop. The miter gauge guides the board past the cutter. Note: The guard has been removed from this photo so the cut can be better seen. Always use a guard.

Push
stick

Wood covered
rip

Fig. 17-22. Cutting a rabbet with a dado head. Use a wooden covered rip fence and a pushstick. Note: The guard has been removed from this photo so the cut can be better seen. Always use a guard unless the dado head will hit it.

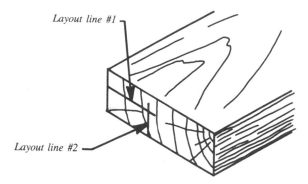

Fig. 17-23. Laying out a rabbet for a single saw blade.

inch between the inside edges of the legs of the fixture 12 inches from the hinge.

Once the fixture has been locked into position, move the rip fence over so that the blade will enter the stock at the desired spot. Making certain the guard is in position, check that the tapering fixture is against the rip fence. Hold the board on the step of the fixture and push the tapering fixture forward (Fig. 17-27). Use a push-stick if the hands of the operator get within 4 inches (102 mm) of the blade.

CUTTING TENONS

Tenons are rectangular pegs cut on the ends of boards. They are made to slip into mortises, and this makes a mortise-and-tenon joint. A mortise-and-tenon joint is an excellent way to join ends of boards to either edges or faces of other boards.

First plane all stock to the exact same thickness. Always punch the mortises before cutting the tenons. Mark out the shoulder and cheek cuts to make the tenon (Fig. 17-28). These lines show where the saw cuts are to be made.

Make the shoulder cuts by raising the saw blade to the same level as the check cut layout line. Use the rip

Fig. 17-24. Making the second cut for a rabbet.

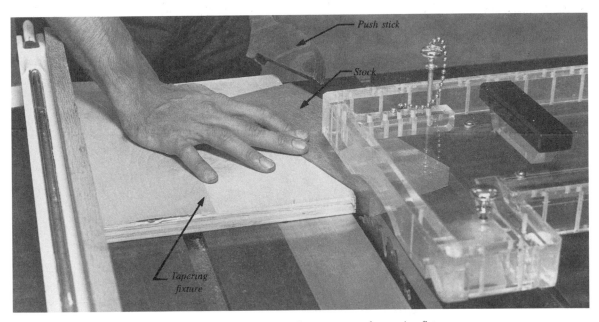

Fig. 17-25. Cutting a taper with a custom made tapering fixture.

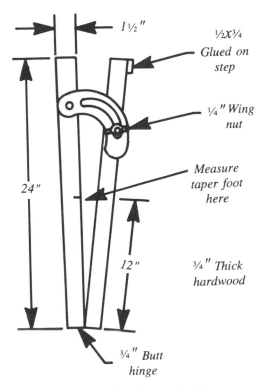

Fig. 17-26. An adjustable tapering fixture.

fence as a stop. When the board is placed against the rip fence, the saw tooth set to the left should be in line with the shoulder cut layout line. With the miter gauge, guide the stock across the blade (Fig. 17-29). Keep the board against the rip fence. Saw shoulder cuts on each side of the board.

To make a cheek cut, use the *tenoning fixture*. This device safely holds the stock on end as it is pushed pass the blade. Never make a cheek cut without using the tenoning fixture. Adjust the height of the blade to the level of the shoulder cut. The tenoning fixture must be set so that the waste will fall to the outside of the blade. After clamping the board to the fixture, guide the stock past the blade (Fig. 17-30). Make the cheek cut on each side of the board.

If a tenoning fixture is not available, tenons can be made with a dado head. Start by marking out the tenon on the end of the board. Make the cuts, using the rip fence as a stop and the miter gauge to guide the board. If the dado head is not wide enough to make the entire cut, make another pass to remove all the waste.

MAKING MOULDINGS

Mouldings can improve the appearance of a piece of furniture or cabinet. The combination of square and curved edges have a decorative effect.

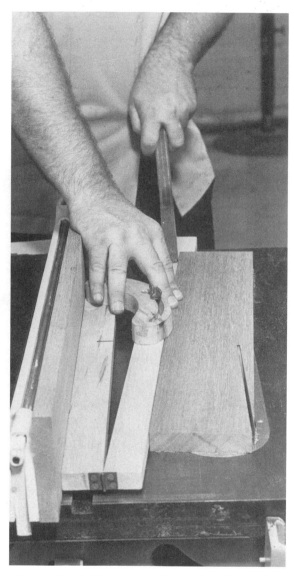

Fig. 17-27. Cutting a taper with an adjustable tapering fixture. Note: The guard has been removed from this photo so the cut can be better seen. Always use the guard.

One method of making mouldings is with a *moulding head*, which is a set of knives attached to the steel body of the head. A broad variety of shapes are available to give different effects (Fig. 17-31).

Install the moulding head on the saw arbor in the same manner as a saw blade. Double check that the knives have been tightened in the head. A special throat plate with an extra-wide opening will be needed.

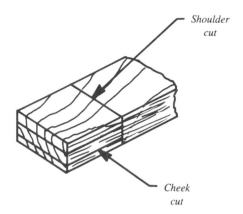

Fig. 17-28. Laying out a tenon.

Most moulding operations require the use of the rip fence. If the cutter will come close to the rip fence, attach a board to it to protect the face of the fence. After locking the fence at the desired location, feed the board at a slow, steady rate. Consider using a featherboard to help hold the stock against the table. Always use a push-stick. If many boards are to be run, stop after several pieces and check that the knives have not worked loose.

For mouldings that are thin or small, shape the edge first from a large board. Then rip the moulding from the board to produce the desired thickness.

CUTTING COVES

Cove cuts are decorative types of concave cuts that are made across the face of a board. They require that the board be fed over the blade at an angle using an auxiliary fence. A thick, stiff circular saw blade is required. An outside cutter from the dado head works best.

To establish the angle of the fence, use a shop-made parallel rule (Fig. 17-32). Adjust the legs of the rule to the same distance apart as the width of the finished cove. Raise the blade the same height as the depth of the cove. Lay the parallel rule over the blade and angle it until the front and back of the blade just touches the legs of the rule. Clamp the auxiliary fence along the rule. This is the correct angle for the fence.

Lower the blade to only 1/8 inch (3 mm) above the table (Fig. 17-33). Make the first cut using a push shoe. Keep the stock against the fence. Do not allow your fingers to come within 4 inches (102 mm) of the blade.

After the first cut, raise the blade an additional 1/16 inch (2 mm) and make a second cut. Keep repeating the process, raising the blade only 1/16 inch at a time.

Fig. 17-29. Making a shoulder cut. Note: The guard has been removed from this photo so the cut can be better seen. Always use a guard.

Fig. 17-30. Making a cheek cut with a tenoning fixture. Note: The guard has been removed so the cut can better be seen.

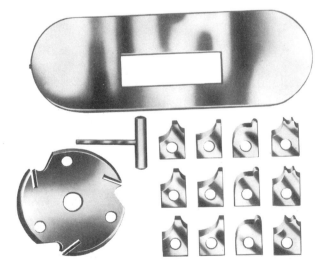

Fig. 17-31. Molding heads and molding head throat plate (Courtesy Delta International Machinery Corporation).

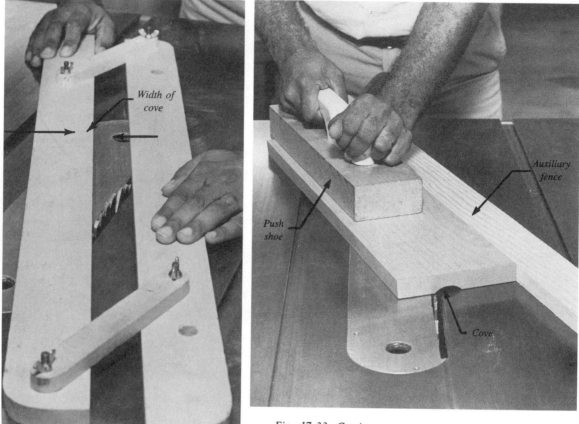

Fig. 17-32. A parallel rule for making a cove establishes the angle of the fence.

Fig. 17-33. Cutting a cove cut. Note: The guard has
been removed, so the cut can be seen. Always use a guard.

Chapter 18

Band Saw

Band saws are used mainly for cutting curves. They can also make straight cuts, but the band saw is slower and not as accurate as the tablesaw. Because of the downward cutting motion of the blade, there is little danger of a kickback, which makes the band saw easy to control. It also makes it an ideal machine for beginners.

PARTS

Inside the two wheel guards are the *band saw wheels*. One wheel is located above the table and one below. These wheels carry the steel band blade. The table can be tilted to the right, to any angle between 90 and 45 degrees, which allows the cutting of bevels and chamfers. Most tables are also equipped with a groove for the miter gauge (Fig. 18-1).

One of the most important parts of the band saw is the *upper and lower blade guides*. One is located above the table and one below. The upper blade guide above the table is mounted on a guide post and is raised up or down, according to the board thickness, by loosening the guide post knob. Always position this assembly so that it is no more than ¼ inch (6 mm) above the top surface of the board being cut.

To determine the size of a band saw, measure the distance between the blade and the inside of the column. Most band saws come in a 12-, 14-, or 20-inch (305-, 356-, or 508-mm) size.

BLADES

Band saw blades can vary in width, tooth style, type of set, and number of teeth per inch. Widths range from ⅛ inch (3 mm) to over 1 inch (25 mm). Most cuts can be made with a ⅜-inch (10 mm) blade. The *hook tooth* is the most common tooth style for cutting woods. Woodworkers prefer a *raker set*, on which every other tooth is bent to the right, the remaining bent to the left (Fig. 18-2). Four to six teeth per inch will make a fairly smooth cut at a rapid rate. For a smoother cut, use a blade with more teeth.

SAFETY

☐ Unplug the power before changing the blade or making guide adjustments.
☐ Adjust the upper blade guide assembly to ¼ inch (6 mm) above the top of the stock.
☐ Keep your hands out of the path of the blade.
☐ The surface of the stock placed against the table must be flat.
☐ Do not bind the blade in the saw kerf; use relief cuts.
☐ Turn off the power and allow the blade to stop turning before backing out of a cut.
☐ Turn off the power and stand to the left in the event the blade should break.

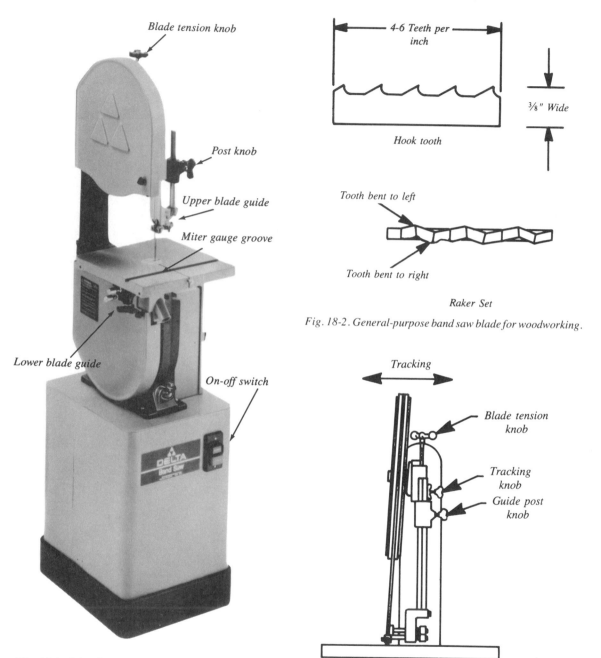

Blade tension knob

Post knob

Upper blade guide

Miter gauge groove

Lower blade guide

On-off switch

Fig. 18-1. A band saw (Courtesy Delta Machinery Manufacturing Inc.).

4-6 Teeth per inch

$3/8''$ Wide

Hook tooth

Tooth bent to left

Tooth bent to right

Raker Set

Fig. 18-2. General-purpose band saw blade for woodworking.

Tracking

Blade tension knob

Tracking knob

Guide post knob

Fig. 18-3. Tracking a band saw blade.

Changing Blades

Disconnect the power and remove the wheel guards and throat plate. To remove the old blade loosen the blade tension knob (Fig. 18-3). Coil the blade and properly store it.

Back the blade guide assemblies out of the way, then uncoil the new blade and mount it on the wheels. The portion of the blade running between the guides must have the teeth pointing downward toward the table. Tighten the blade tension knob until there is proper tension on the blade. Many saws have a tension gauge to aid in this adjustment.

Turn the wheels by hand to check that the blade is centered in the middle of the rim of the wheel. If the blade does not stay centered, turn the tracking knob a small amount and spin the wheels again. This adjustment procedure is called *tracking*.

Next, adjust the upper and lower blade guide assemblies (Fig. 18-4). Because there are two guides, be certain to make the following adjustments on each of them. Move the blade guides forward until only the teeth are showing. Place a piece of paper on each side of the blade and push the blade guides toward the blade (Fig. 18-5). Tighten them in place with the guide adjustment screws. Bring the ball bearing blade support forward until it is barely touching the back of the blade. Turn the band saw wheels one more time to check that the blade is properly tracking between the guides. Replace the throat plate and guard doors. After reconnecting the power, try the first cut on a scrap board. Check the cut for squareness.

Coiling Blades

The band saw blade is made in the form of a large loop. Because of the size of the blade it is difficult to package and store. Coiling allows the large loop to be made into three or more much smaller loops that are easier to handle.

Hold the blade out, away from you and place your foot on the blade. Teeth should be pointing towards the front. Roll the blade outwards with each hand (Fig. 18-6A). The teeth should not be pointing out. Push the thumbs downward and roll the hands inward (Fig. 18-6B). As you bend over, the blade will automatically start to form three loops.

If the blade starts to kink or bend sharply, stop coiling. Allow the blade to return to a large loop and start the procedure over again.

CUTTING SIMPLE CURVES

Select the proper width of blade for the curve to be cut. Forcing too wide of a blade around a curve will cause the blade to break. As a general rule, the narrower the blade the smaller the curve that can be cut. Figure 18-7 gives the recommended width of a blade for certain radius. Pick the blade width that matches the smallest curve in the layout.

Study the curve and decide which path the blade is to take. If a smaller radius is needed than the blade will cut, make *relief cuts* wherever the blade might bind (Fig. 18-8). Relief cuts are made through the waste portion of

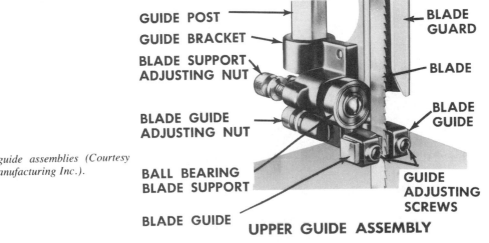

Fig. 18-4. Blade guide assemblies (Courtesy Delta Machinery Manufacturing Inc.).

GUIDE POST
GUIDE BRACKET
BLADE SUPPORT ADJUSTING NUT
BLADE GUIDE ADJUSTING NUT
BALL BEARING BLADE SUPPORT
BLADE GUIDE
BLADE GUARD
BLADE
BLADE GUIDE
GUIDE ADJUSTING SCREWS
UPPER GUIDE ASSEMBLY

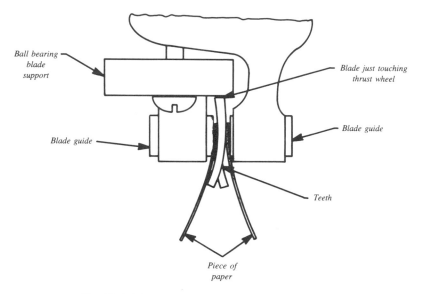

Fig. 18-5. Adjustments for blade guides and blade support.

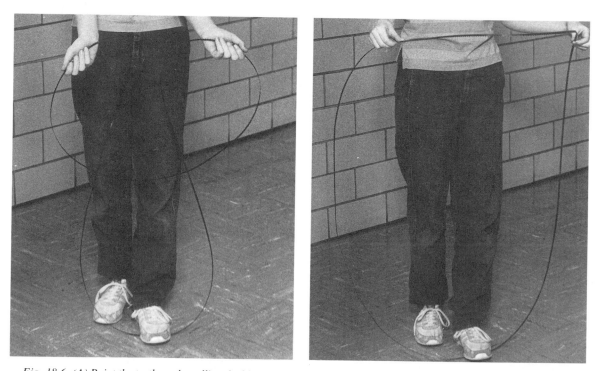

Fig. 18-6. (A) Point the teeth out by rolling the blade outward. (B) Push the thumbs downward and roll the hands inward.

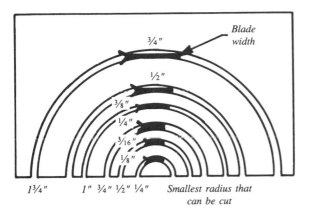

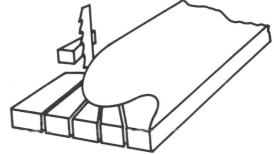

Fig. 18-8. Relief cuts allow the waste to be cut away before the blade binds in the key.

Fig. 18-7. Recommended smallest radius for different width of blades.

the board up to $\frac{1}{32}$ inch (1 mm) of the layout line. These short cuts allow the waste to fall away as the front of the blade touches them. Never back out of a curve because the blade could easily be pulled off the band saw wheels.

If there are several curves in the layout, cut the largest curves or those that are closest to the edge first (Fig. 18-9). For small circles or true curves, bore them with a drill bit before starting to saw.

Adjust the upper blade guide so that the bottom surface is $\frac{1}{4}$ inch (6 m) above the thickest part of the board. After turning on the power and allowing the blade to reach full speed, start the cut. Cut on the waste side of the line. Guide the board along the layout lines. Do not cross the layout lines—stay just outside the mark. When the cut is finished, the layout lines should still be visible. The hands of the operator must stay at least 4 inches (102 mm) from the blade. *Never* place your hands directly in line with the blade. Keep your hands clear of the blade in case you slip or the board accidentally splits.

COMPOUND SAWINGS

Compound sawings require two adjoining edges to be sawn with a band saw. Very graceful parts, such as cab-

riole legs, are made this way.

Lay the pattern out on lightweight cardboard and cut it to shape. This will serve as a template to transfer the pattern to the stock. Study the template to make certain it is the desired shape.

After squaring the material to exact size lay the template on the stock. Trace around the template. Install a narrow blade so that each side of the layout can be made in one pass. No relief cuts should be used. Carefully cut the first side. Tape the waste material back on the piece just cut. Roll the stock over and trace around the template on the adjoining surface (Fig. 18-10). Band saw this side to pattern. After all the waste has been cut away, scrape and sand the leg.

CUTTING CIRCLES

Circles can either be cut freehand, or using a circle fixture. With either, select the widest blade that will cut the desired radius (see Fig. 18-7). The freehand method is the fastest if only a few circles are needed. Use a compass to layout the circle. Start cutting on the end grain and rotate the stock around the blade.

Fig. 18-9. Method of cutting a curve.

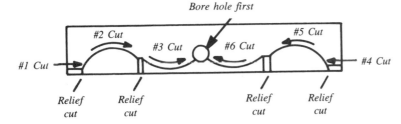

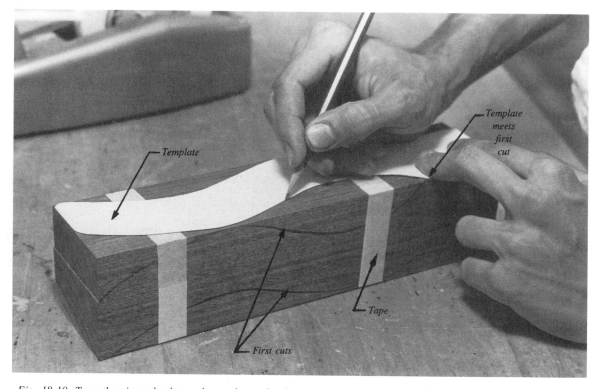

Fig. 18-10. Tape the pieces back together and transfer the template to the adjacent edge. Note the top of the template meets the first cut.

The circle fixture consists of a plywood table with a pivot point (Fig. 18-11). The pivot point is positioned the same distance from the blade as the desired radius. It must be in a straight line along the leading edge of the blade. Center the stock over the point and slowly rotate the stock into the blade. This will produce a perfect circle.

CROSSCUTTING

The band saw is capable of crosscutting both short and long boards. Because the blade cuts with a downward action, there is very little danger of a kickback.

To achieve the straightest cut, use as wide a blade as is available for crosscutting. Place the miter gauge in the miter gauge slot. Position the board against the miter gauge and align the layout mark with the blade (Fig. 18-12). Guide the stock past the blade, keeping your hands at least 4 inches (152 mm) from the blade. Check the cut with a square to make certain the cut is accurate.

RIPPING

Ripping stock on the band saw can be done with either a commercial rip fence or a shop-made fence. Use a wide blade to give a straight cut. If the blade tends to lead to one side, change to a new blade. Position the rip fence to the right of the blade. The face of the rip fence should be the same distance away from the saw tooth set to the right as the desired width of the board. As the trailing end of the board comes close to the blade, use a push-stick to clear the stock of the blade.

If a commercial rip fence is not available, clamp a straight board to the table (Fig. 18-13). It must be parallel to the miter gauge groove.

RESAWING

Resawing produces two or more thin pieces from one thick board. The bandsaw is the ideal machine for this because of the small saw kerf it makes. A wide blade at least 1/2 inch (13 mm) must be used.

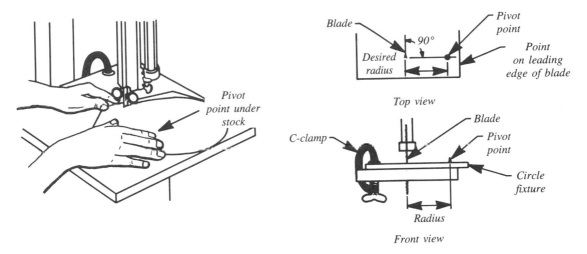

Fig. 18-11. Circle fixture for cutting circles.

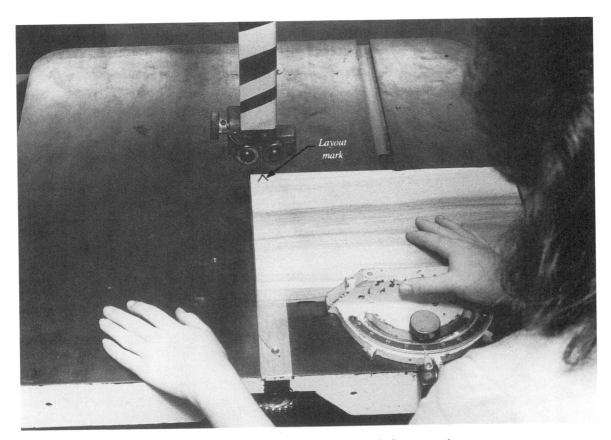

Fig. 18-12. Align the layout mark with the blade for crosscutting.

Resawing can be done with either a rip fence or a pivot block. With a rip fence, use a ripping procedure. Use a pushstick to clear the stock between the rip fence and blade.

The major advantage to the pivot block method is that the trailing end of the stock can be moved left or right (Fig. 18-14). This movement allows the operator to overcome the problem of the blade cutting towards the left or right.

To resaw with a pivot block, clamp the shop-made device to the table top. Feed the board past the blade at a slow, steady rate. Be certain that the cut remains parallel to the face against the pivot block. If it does not, move the trailing end. Never allow the hands to come closer than 4 inches (102 mm) to the blade.

CUTTING BEVELS

Bevels are often cut on the band saw when making the glue blocks to reinforce pieces or cutting corners on lathe turnings. To cut a bevel, first tilt the table to the desired angle (Fig. 18-15). Cut a scrap and check the accuracy of the angle with a protractor. Use a rip fence or miter gauge to make straight cuts.

CUTTING INSIDE CORNERS

When making inside corners, first lay out the shape. Two different methods can then be used. For the first, make the first cut along one side. Because the cut is straight, back out to the starting point. Move to the other side of the layout and start the second cut. Before reaching the corner, cut over to the end of the first cut. Remove the waste and finish cutting the layout. For the second method, inside corners are formed by first boring a hole in each corner. The hole must be large enough to turn the blade.

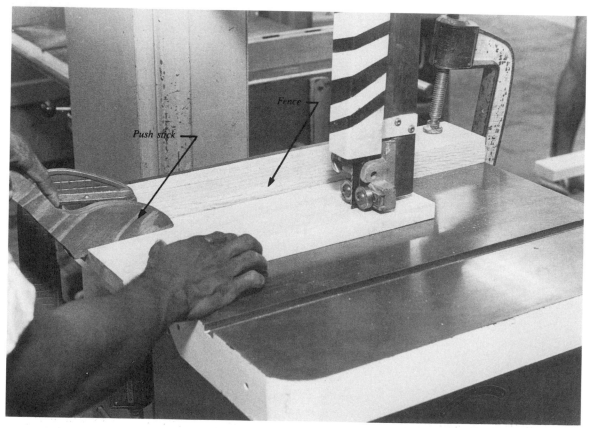

Fig. 18-13. Ripping a board with a shop-made fence that is clamped to the table.

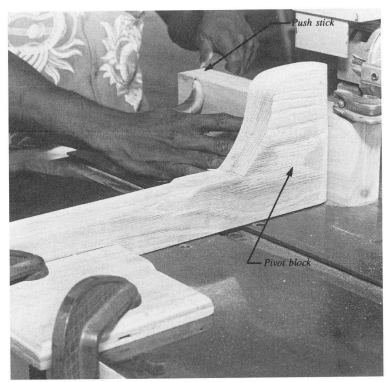

Fig. 18-14. Resawing with a pivot block.

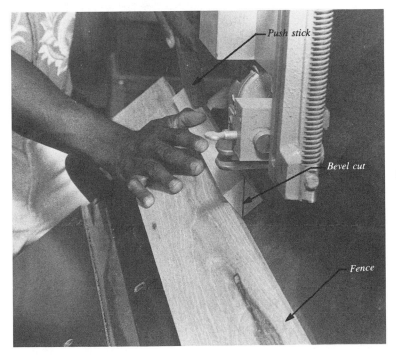

Fig. 18-15. Cutting a bevel.

Chapter 19

Scroll Saw

The scroll saw is the ideal machine for cutting small curves in thin material. It is sometimes called the *jigsaw*. It cuts with an up or down motion. This makes the saw slow cutting and a safe machine for beginners to use.

PARTS

The scroll saw has three main parts: the over arm, table, and base (Fig. 19-1). The *over arm* extends above the table and supports the *guide assembly, tension sleeve*, and *upper chuck*. Stock is placed on the table to be cut. By loosening the table tilting knob, the table can be angled left or right, up to 45 degrees.

The lower blade chuck holds the blade below the table (Fig. 19-2). The up-and-down motion of the chuck is created by the *pitman drive*. This drive changes the rotary motion of the motor into the up-and-down movement needed for cutting.

The speed the blade moves up or down is controlled by either a *cone pulley* or *variable speed pulley*. A cone pulley is the simplest and requires that the V belt be shifted to different levels to change the speed. Never change belt position with this type unless the motor is unplugged. The variable speed pulley can more easily change speeds by turning the speed adjustment crank (Fig. 19-3). The scroll saw must be running and the belt and pulley guard installed when the speed adjustment crank is turned.

The size of the scroll saw is determined by measuring from the front of the saw blade to the front of the over arm. Most scroll saws are the 24-inch size.

BLADES

Scroll saw blades vary by the type of material to be cut, and the width, thickness, and number of teeth per inch (Table 19-1). For general-purpose cutting, select a blade that is .110 inch wide × .02 inch thick and with 15 teeth per inch.

Table 19-1 gives other available blades. For sharp curves, select a narrower blade. For straight cuts, use a wider blade. Harder material requires more teeth per inch.

SAFETY

☐ Unplug the power cord before changing the blade.
☐ Keep hands out of the path of the blade.
☐ The surface placed against the table must be flat.
☐ Adjust the stock hold down to rest on the top surface of the board.
☐ Keep the belt and pulley guard in place when using the saw.

Table 19-1. Scroll Saw Blades.

MATERIAL CUT	WIDTH IN.	TEETH PER INCH	BLADE FULL SIZE	MATERIAL CUT	WIDTH IN.	TEETH PER INCH	BLADE FULL SIZE
Steel • Iron Lead • Copper Aluminum	.070	32		Plastics Celluloid	.050	15	
				Bakelite	.070	7	
Pewter Asbestos Paper • Felt	.070	20		Ivory • Wood	.110	7	
Steel • Iron Lead • Copper Brass	.070	15		Wall Board Pressed Wood Wood • Lead Bone • Felt	.110	15	
Aluminum Pewter Asbestos	.085	15		Paper • Copper Ivory Aluminum			
Wood	.110	20					
Asbestos • Brake Lining • Mica Steel • Iron Lead • Copper Brass Aluminum Pewter	.250	20		Hard and Soft Wood	.110	10	
					.187	10	
					.250	7	
Wood Veneer Plus Plastics Celluloid Hard Rubber Bakelite Ivory Extremely Thin Materials	.035	20		Pearl • Pewter Mica	.054	30	
				Pressed Wood Sea Shells	.054	20	
				Hard Leather	.054	12	

(Courtesy of Delta International Machinery Corporation).

Installing the Blade

To install a different blade, first unplug the machine. Remove the blade and table insert. Select the proper blade and pass it through the hole in the table. The teeth of the blade must point down and toward the front of the saw (see Fig. 19-2). Rotate the shaft on the motor by hand and move the lower blade chuck to the highest position. Use a guide board to align the blade with the table (Fig. 19-4). Insert the blade at least ½ inch (13 mm) into the lower blade chuck and tighten the thumb screw.

To adjust the parts above the table, loosen the tension sleeve knob. Lower the tension sleeve until it is 1 inch (25 mm) above the blade. If the blade is very narrow or thin, increase this distance to 1½ inches (38 mm). Tighten the tension sleeve knob and pull down the upper blade chuck. It must also engage the blade by ½ inch (13 mm). Tighten the thumb screw on the upper blade chuck.

Lower the guide assembly next by loosening the thumb screw on the over arm. Move the support disk and

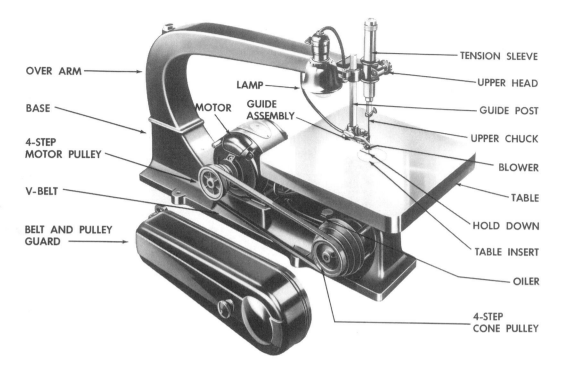

OVER ARM

BASE

4-STEP
MOTOR PULLEY

V-BELT

BELT AND PULLEY
GUARD

LAMP

MOTOR   GUIDE
ASSEMBLY

TENSION SLEEVE

UPPER HEAD

GUIDE POST

UPPER CHUCK

BLOWER

TABLE

HOLD DOWN

TABLE INSERT

OILER

4-STEP
CONE PULLEY

Fig. 19-1. Parts of a scroll saw (Courtesy Delta International Machinery Corporation).

support roller forward until only the teeth of the blade are showing (Fig. 19-5). The disk should be positioned just behind the gullets of the blade. Moving the disk too far forward will ruin the blade. Replace the throat plate.

CUTTING OUTSIDE CURVES

Lay out the curve and plan what order the cuts are to be made. If any sharp curves or corners are required, plan on making relief cuts (Fig. 19-6). These are short cuts made in the waste area that is within $1/32$ inch (1 mm) of the layout line. This allows the waste to fall free before the blade is twisted.

Place the stock on the table and lower the guide post. The stock hold down should rest on the face of the board. Turn on the power and slowly feed the board forward. Because the scroll saw cuts very slowly, feeding the board too rapidly will break the blade. The thicker and harder the material, the slower the feed rate. Always stay to the outside of the layout line. If the blade accidently crosses the layout line, back the board up and recut to the line. Hands must not come any closer than 2 inches (51 mm) to the blade.

CUTTING INSIDE CURVES

An inside curve is a design cut on the interior portion of the board that does not touch any outside edge. Because the cut cannot be started on the edge first, bore a hole inside the layout. The hole must be large enough for the blade to freely move.

Thread the blade through the bored hole (Fig. 19-7). Raise the upper blade chuck and tension sleeve. Rotate the motor shaft by hand until the lower blade chuck is at the highest position. Feed the blade through the hole. Reconnect the blade to the blade chuck and adjust the tension. Carefully make the cut following the layout lines. Once the cut is completed, reverse the procedure to remove the board.

SABER SAWING

Internal cuts can easily be made by installing a saber saw blade. This blade is held only in the lower chuck. The hole in the area to be cut is placed over the blade and the cut made in a normal manner.

A saber saw blade also requires a lower blade guide

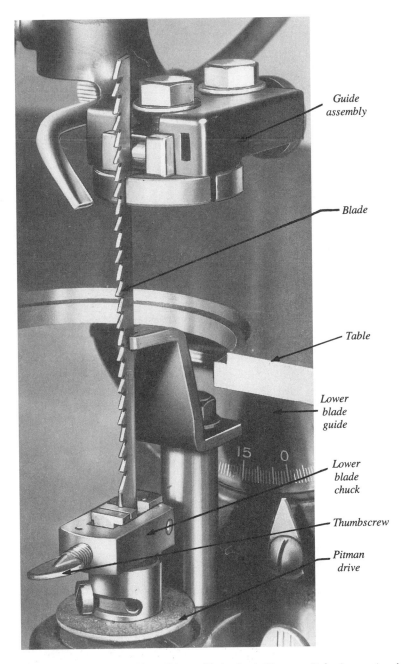

Fig. 19-2. Guide assembly and lower blade chuck (Courtesy Delta International Machinery Corporation).

Fig. 19-3. Variable speed pulley is adjusted with the speed adjustment crank. The belt and pulley guard have been removed for illustration purposes only. Do not turn on the power unless the guard is in place.

to be attached above the bottom blade chuck. Because this type of blade is only held by the bottom blade chuck, move the guide post and tension sleeve out of the way. Make the cuts using a slow, even feed rate. Do not push against the sides of the blade.

BEVEL CUTTING

To cut a bevel, first tilt the table to the desired angle by using the table tilting knob. The stock hold down must also be tilted to the same angle (Fig. 19-8). Cut the stock using only one side of the table to keep from sawing a reverse angle.

FILING AND SANDING

Because of the up-and-down motion of the scroll saw, boards can also be filed and sanded. The scroll saw files and sanding attachment are held only by the bottom blade chuck. A special throat plate is needed because of the larger size of the files and sanding attachment. Use gentle pressure to push the stock against the abrasive (Fig. 19-9).

Fig. 19-4. *(top left) A guide board aligns the blade.*

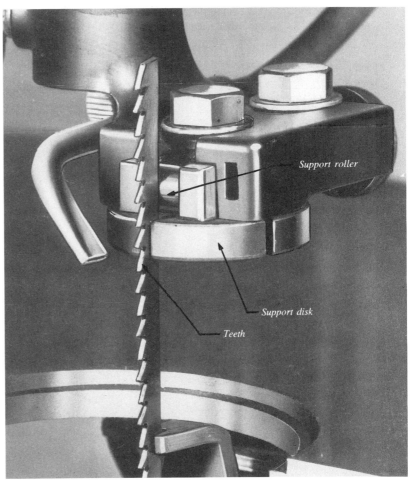

Fig. 19-5. *(top right) A properly adjusted guide assembly (Courtesy Delta International Machinery Corporation).*

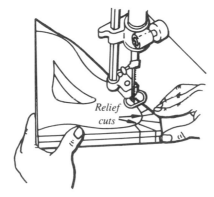

Fig. 19-6. *(bottom left) Use relief cuts when cutting sharp curves.*

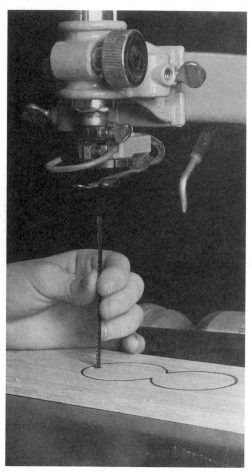

Fig. 19-7. (left) Threading a blade through a hole for an internal cut.

Fig. 19-8. Tilt the table and the stock hold down for a bevel cut (Courtesy Delta International Machinery Corporation).

Fig. 19-9. Sanding on the scroll saw.

Chapter 20

Radial Arm Saw and Miter Saw

A radial arm saw is one of the best machines for cutting boards to length. It is also used to make other cuts, such as ripping, mitering, and dadoing. The radial arm saw is different from the table saw in that it moves over the stock. One of the major advantages to this saw is that the saw blade cuts from the top side of the board, which allows the operator to see the cut as it first touches the layout lines, rather than being hidden on the bottom side of the board.

PARTS OF THE RADIAL ARM SAW

The radial arm saw has several major parts (Fig. 20-1). The *column* supports the arm and is located to the rear of the saw. The *arm* is responsible for providing a track for the *yoke* to slide. The motor is attached to this yoke. The *saw arbor* extends from the side of the motor. A *handle* is attached to the yoke and used to move the saw in and out. The table and fence provide a surface for holding the board as it is being cut.

SAFETY

☐ Unplug the power before changing the blade.
☐ Be certain the blade is installed with the teeth rotating in the proper direction.
☐ Do not use a dull saw blade.
☐ Do not cut beyond the capacity of the blade.
☐ Adjust the saw guard for each different cut.
☐ Grasp the saw by the handle and hold the stock against the table and fence.
☐ The stock to be cut must have a flat face against the table and a straight edge against the fence.
☐ Keep hands at least 4 inches (102 mm) away from the blade.
☐ Only cut one piece of material at a time.
☐ When ripping, be absolutely certain to feed the stock against the rotation of the blade, and be certain the yoke is firmly clamped to the arm and the motor to the yoke.
☐ Use a push stick when ripping.
☐ When possible, select the inboard position for ripping.
☐ When crosscutting, be absolutely certain your hands are clear of the path of travel of the saw.

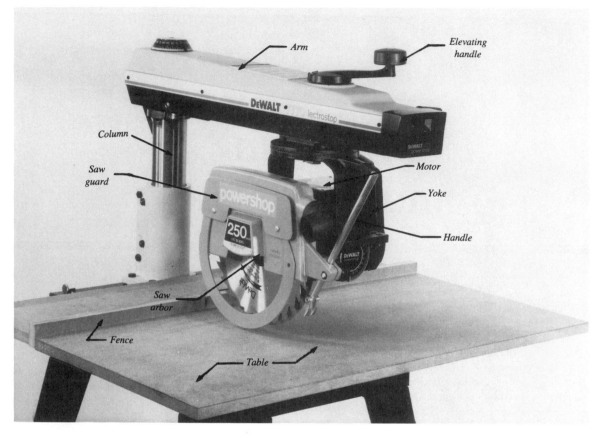

Fig. 20-1. Major parts of the radial arm saw (Courtesy Black and Decker Inc.).

Covering the blade and clamped to the yoke is the saw guard (Fig. 20-2). It has four main parts. The *saw hood* protects the top half of the blade. The two *ring guards* cover the bottom half of the blade. A *dust spout* directs and removes the flow of the dust. The *antikick-back fingers* cover the front of the blade and keep the board from being thrown.

There are several adjustment handles on the saw. Use the *elevating handle* to adjust the height of the blade. The *bevel clamp handle* allows the yoke to be tilted for beveling operations. For cutting miters, the *miter clamp handle* is used to pivot the arm. Ripping requires the use of the *yoke clamp handle* to turn the yoke into the ripping position (Fig. 20-3).

The size of the radial arm is determined by the largest blade that can be used. Most radial arm saws are

either 10 inches (254 mm) or 12 inches (305 mm). The style of saw blade is the same as used on the table saw.

CHANGING BLADES

To change a blade, first disconnect the power. Check that the power is off by turning the on/off switch on and off. Carefully remove the guard so it does not rub against the teeth. Raise the blade up so the bottom of the saw teeth is approximately 1 inch (25 mm) above the table.

The arbor must be kept from turning. Depending on the brand of saw, use either an open-end wrench or an Allen wrench. Slip the wrench onto the arbor (Fig. 20-4). Never wedge a board under the saw teeth to secure the blade; this will force the saw out of alignment. Remove the arbor nut with the arbor nut wrench. Pull the

Fig. 20-2. The saw guard contains a saw hood, dust spout, anti-kickback fingers, and ring guards.

wrench the same direction as the teeth of the saw blade point. Slide off the saw washer and blade. Properly store the blade by hanging it up.

Install the new blade with the teeth pointing the same direction as the arbor rotates. The teeth at the bottom of the blade must point to the rear of the saw. Replace the washer and tighten the arbor nut. To finish the operation, properly install the guard and reconnect the power. The blade should be lowered so it is no more than ⅛ inch (3 mm) below the table surface.

SETTING UP

Before turning on the power, make sure the blade guard is adjusted correctly. The bottom of the guard should be parallel with the table top. Adjust the antikickback fingers so the tips of the fingers are no more than ⅛ inch (3 mm) above the top of the board to be cut.

To check accuracy, make a cut on scrap stock. With a square, measure the accuracy of the cut both across the face and end of the board. If the board is not square make whatever adjustments are necessary.

CROSSCUTTING

Any stock to be crosscut must extend at least 6 inches (152 mm) to the left of the blade. Use a bandsaw or handsaw to cut shorter pieces. To cut a board to length, first cut approximately ½ inch (13 mm) off the end of the board. To control the saw, grasp the handle with the right hand and hold the board against the fence and table with the left hand. *Never* allow your hands to come any closer than 4 inches (102 mm) to the blade. Slowly pull the saw out, using the handle (Fig. 20-5). Always keep full control of the saw to keep it from grabbing at the board. Once the cut has been completed, push the saw

Fig. 20-3. Adjustments on the radial arm saw (Courtesy Black and Decker Inc.).

blade all the way back to the column. Turn off the power and screw in the rip lock. This will keep the blade from coming forward accidentally.

Measure the board to the desired length. Use a V-shaped layout line to mark the length. Align the mark with a saw tooth leaning to the left. Turn on the power and loosen the rip lock. Cut the second end the same way.

To cut several pieces the same length, use a stop block. After squaring the first end, mark the first piece to length. Align the mark with the blade. Clamp a stop block along the fence and against the squared end of the board (Fig. 20-6). After cutting the first piece, check the length of the board. If the measurement is correct, saw the remaining pieces. Be careful not to bump the stop block.

RIPPING

First raise the blade above the top of the fence so it can rotate freely. After checking that the arm is on the 90-degree setting, turn the yoke into the ripping position. Release the yoke by pulling forward on the yoke clamp handle and lifting up on the yoke pin (Fig. 20-7). The blade should be parallel with the fence. By rotating the saw blade to the right or clockwise, the saw will be locked into the inboard rip position (Fig. 20-8). Use this position for narrow boards. Rotating the saw blade to the left or counter clockwise will put it into the outboard rip position. The outboard rip position is utilized primarily for ripping extra wide pieces. Because the motor is moved out of the way, utilize the inboard position when possible.

Fig. 20-4. To remove the arbor nut, pull the wrench the same direction the teeth point (Courtesy Black and Decker Inc.).

Once the ripping position has been set, pull the motor unit out on the arm. Measure the desired width between the saw tooth leaning towards the fence and the inside surface of the fence. Tighten down the rip lock. Start the motor and lower the blade ⅛ inch below the surface of the table.

Be certain to properly adjust the guard. Lower the front end of the saw hood to ⅛ inch (3 mm) above the top surface of the board. Move the antikickback fingers so that they are ⅛ inch below the face of the board.

With a push stick, feed the board forward. Always feed the board against the rotation of the blade (Fig. 20-9). Feeding the board from the wrong direction will cause the stock to be thrown off the table. As the board is being fed, keep your hands at least 4 inches (102 mm) away from the blade. *Never* reach under the motor or behind the blade.

CUTTING DADOES

The radial arm saw is ideal for cutting dadoes. Because the dado head cuts from the top side of the board, layout lines can easily be seen. These lines are hidden on the bottom side of the board when using a table saw. Install the dado head as you would on the table saw.

After installing the dado head and adjusting the guard, raise the dado head above the board. Lower the dado head until it just touches the top of the stock (Fig. 20-10). Remove the board and determine how deep the dado is to be. Most dadoes are either ¼ inch (6 mm) or ⅜ inch (10 mm) deep. Every complete turn of the elevating crank is equal to ⅛ inch (3 mm). To cut a ⅜-inch-deep dado, turn the crank three complete turns. Always cut a scrap piece of the same thickness first and measure the depth of the dado before cutting your stock.

Fig. 20-5. Hold the board against the table and fence. Control the saw by using the handle. Caution: Keep your hands at least 4 inches (102mm) from the blade.

Fig. 20-6. A stop block aids in cutting a piece to length.

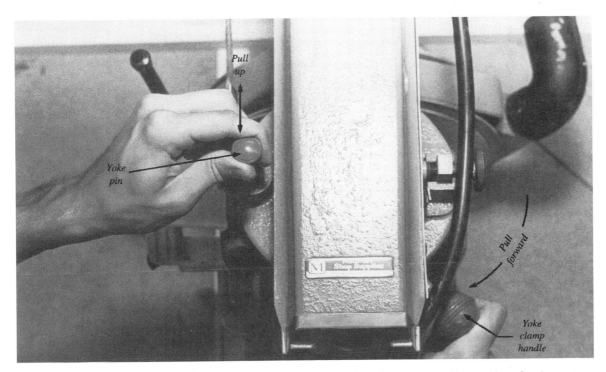

Fig. 20-7. To set the saw in the rip position, pull the yoke clamp forward and pull up on the yoke pin.

Fig. 20-8. Inboard rip position. Note direction of feed.

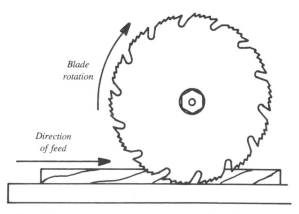

Fig. 20-9. Be certain that you always feed the board against the rotation of the blade.

After marking out where each dado is to be located, position the board next to the dado head. Install a stop block against the end of the board opposite the dado head. Firmly hold the handle and turn on the power. Slowly feed the dado head forward while holding the stock against the fence and table. Because a large cut is being made, the dado head will want to feed itself forward. To prevent an accident, you must always control the feed rate and keep your hands away from the path of the dado head.

CUTTING BEVELS

To cut bevels, rotate the motor unit in the yoke to the desired angle (Fig. 20-11). Pull the bevel clamp handle to the right and pull out on the bevel pin. Most saws will

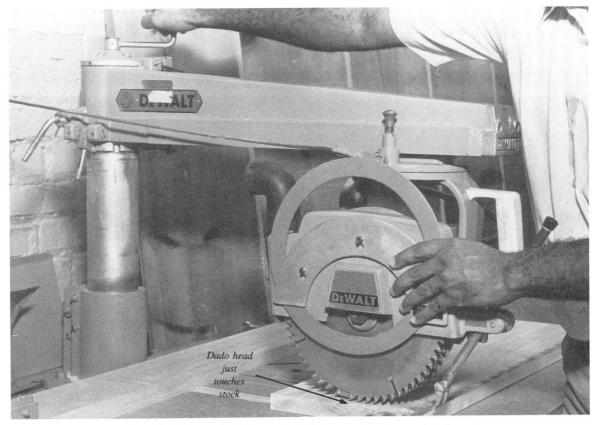

Fig. 20-10. Lower the dado head until it just touches the top of the board.

contain a positive stop for the bevel pin at 30- and 45-degree angles. Bevels can be made using either crosscutting or ripping techniques. Always check the accuracy of the first cut with a protractor.

CUTTING MITERS

Because the stock is held on the table and the blade pulled across the stationary board, the radial arm cuts accurate miters. The board does not have a tendency to slide away from the blade, as with a table saw. Swing the arm first to the right to the desired angle (Fig. 20-12). Release the arm by lifting up on the miter clamp handle and miter pin. Most saws have positive stops on the miter pin at 30 and 45 degrees. If another angle is desired, use the miter scale on the top of the arm to position the blade.

Select a piece of scrap and make a trail cut. Check the accuracy of the cut with a protractor. Cut all miters on the right end of the pieces (Fig. 20-13). Use the same procedure as recommended for crosscutting stock. Swing the arm to the left to the desired angle and cut all the miters on the opposite end.

Compound miters require not only that the arm be angled, but that the blade be tilted. To make this type of miter, determine the angle by checking the compound miter chart (Table 20-1). This cut will produce a box or frame with angled sides.

MITER SAW

Although miters can be cut using a radial arm saw, many professionals prefer a miter saw. It is compact, very accurate, and can be easily moved to the job site. With the

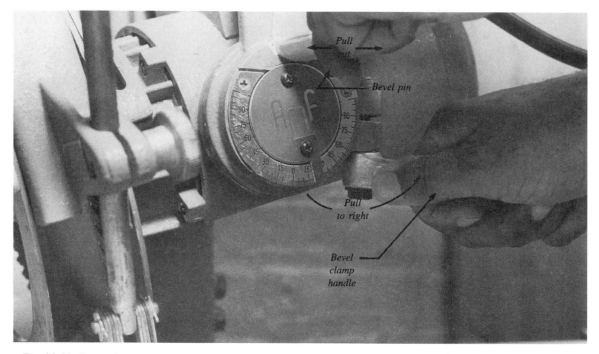

Fig. 20-11. To set the saw in the bevel position, pull the bevel clamp handle to the right and pull out on the bevel pin.

Table 20-1. Compound Miter Chart.

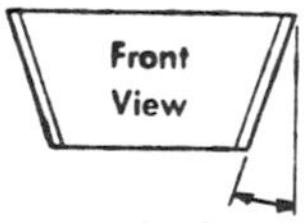

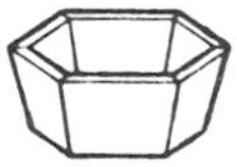

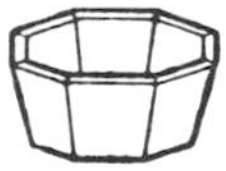

	4-SIDES		6-SIDES		8-SIDES	
ANGLE OF SIDES (DEGREES)	BLADE TILT (DEGREES)	ARM SETTING (DEGREES)	BLADE TILT (DEGREES)	ARM SETTING (DEGREES)	BLADE TILT (DEGREES)	ARM SETTING (DEGREES)
5	44¾	5	29¾	2½	22¼	2
10	44¼	9¾	29½	5½	22	4
15	43¼	14½	29	8¼	21½	6
20	41¾	18¾	28¼	11	21	8
25	40	23	27¼	13½	20¼	10
30	37¾	26½	26	16	19½	11¾
35	35¼	29¾	24½	18¼	18¼	13¼
40	32½	32¾	22¾	20¼	17	15
45	30	35¼	21	22¼	15¾	16¼
50	27	37½	19	23¾	14¼	17½
55	24	39¼	16¾	25¼	12½	18¾
60	21	41	14½	26½	11	19¼

Fig. 20-12. To set the saw in the miter position lift up on the miter clamp handle and miter pin.

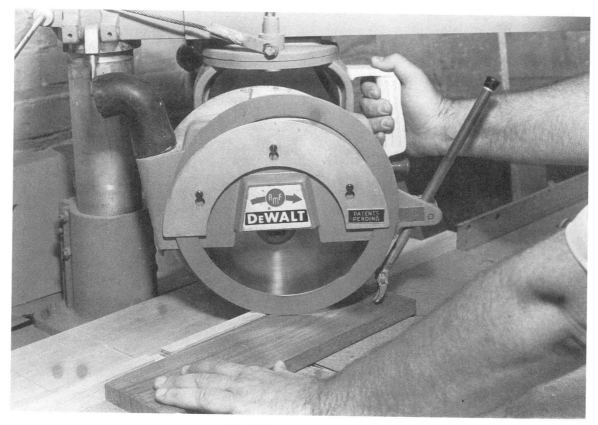

Fig. 20-13. Mitering a board.

proper blade, the saw can cut wood, plastic, and aluminum.

Parts of the Miter Saw

This relatively simple machine has few major parts (Fig. 20-14). The saw blade is mounted directly to the motor. The size of this machine is determined by the largest diameter of blade that can be mounted within the guard. You will also find the blade guard and control handle attached to this motor. The *blade guard* consists of an upper blade cover, bottom retracting ring guard, and saw dust chute. Located on the inside of the handle is the on-off switch. Some models will also contain a brake button for stopping the blade.

Stock is placed on the bed and against the *fence*. On the front of the bed is the *angle gauge*. By loosening the *angle handle* the saw blade can be moved to the desired angle.

Some models of miter saws are capable of cutting compound miters (Fig. 20-15). Not only does the blade pivot, but also tilts to the angles given in Table 20-1. This feature adds much flexibility to your saw.

Operating the Miter Saw

To operate the miter saw, first set the blade at the desired angle to the left of the angle gauge. Most models can be rotated to the left and right up to 47 degrees. You will find positive stops at 0, 22½, and 45 degrees for fast set-ups at these common settings. Make sure the miter handle is secured before proceeding.

Place the stock on the bed and against the fence. The board must be at least 10 inches (254 mm) in length. If the stock is long, be certain the free end is supported by a helper or a table. Keeping your hands at least 4 inches (102 mm) from the blade, firmly hold the stock and turn on the power. Slowly lower the turning blade

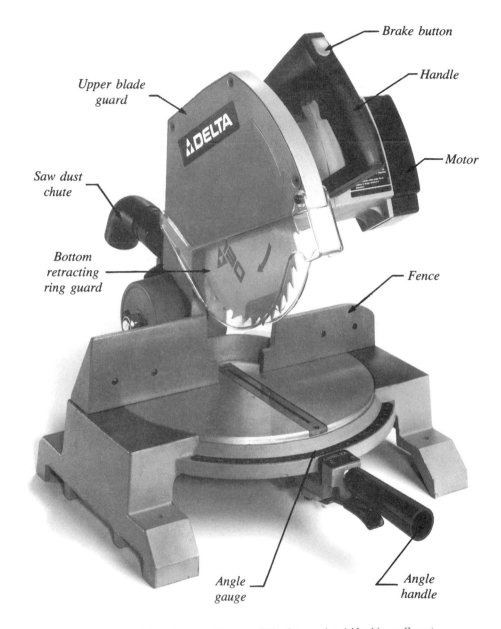

Fig. 20-14. Major parts of the miter saw (Courtesy Delta International Machinery Corp.).

through the board. When the blade has cut through the stock, let the motor unit return to the topmost position. Turn off the power and let the blade stop turning. If a very accurate miter is required, measure this first cut with a protractor or other measuring device. Cut the first end of each piece with the saw in this setting.

Set the boards end for end and measure from the newly cut end. Move the blade to the right and cut the second end. If several pieces of the same length are required, install a stop.

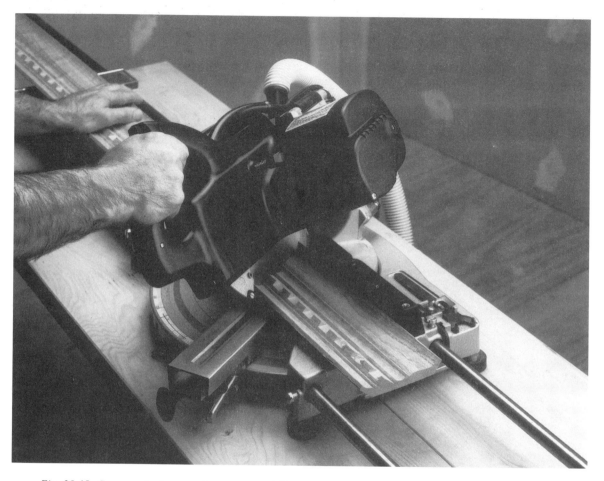

Fig. 20-15. Compound miters can be cut on specially equipped miter saws (Courtesy Black and Decker Inc.).

Chapter 21

Jointer

A *jointer* is a basic woodworking machine used primarily for smoothing, squaring, and straightening boards. With the proper setup it is also possible to make rabbets, bevels, and tapers.

PARTS

The major parts of the jointer include the tables, cutterhead, fence, and base (Fig. 21-1). The *cutterhead* contains three knives that are held in place with gibs (Fig. 21-2). To the right of the cutterhead is the *infeed table*; to the left of the cutterhead is the *outfeed table*. Both can be raised and lowered by their own handwheels. The infeed table is adjusted to the same distance below the cutterhead as the depth of cut. The *depth gauge* gives the amount of materials that will be removed in one pass. The outfeed table is set at the same height as the knives.

Extending over the tables is the *fence*. It is adjustable to any angle between 45 and 90 degrees. By loosening the fence adjusting lever, the fence can also be moved to any location across the table.

The *spring-loaded guard* covers the cutterhead. It must automatically move back over the cutterhead once the stock being jointed is pushed out of the way.

The size of the jointer is determined by measuring the length of the knives. Sizes vary from 4 inches (102 mm) to over 12 inches (305 mm). Most jointers are either 6 or 8 inches (152 mm or 203 mm).

JOINTING A FACE

Jointing the face is the first step in squaring up a board. Once the face is jointed smooth and true, it can serve as a reference plane or flat surface for squaring up the other surfaces of the board.

Select the flattest of the two faces. It must be at least 10 inches (254 mm) long. Adjust the depth of cut to

---

SAFETY

☐ Disconnect the power before working with the cutterhead.
☐ Do not use the jointer if the knives are dull.
☐ Always use the guard unless special precautions are taken.
☐ Do not take a cut deeper than $\frac{1}{16}$ inch (2 mm).
☐ Stock must be at least $\frac{1}{2}$ inch (13 mm) thick, 2 inches (51 mm) wide, and 10 inches (254 mm) long.
☐ Use a push stick or push shoes whenever possible.
☐ Never allow your hands to come closer than 4 inches (102 mm) to the cutterhead.

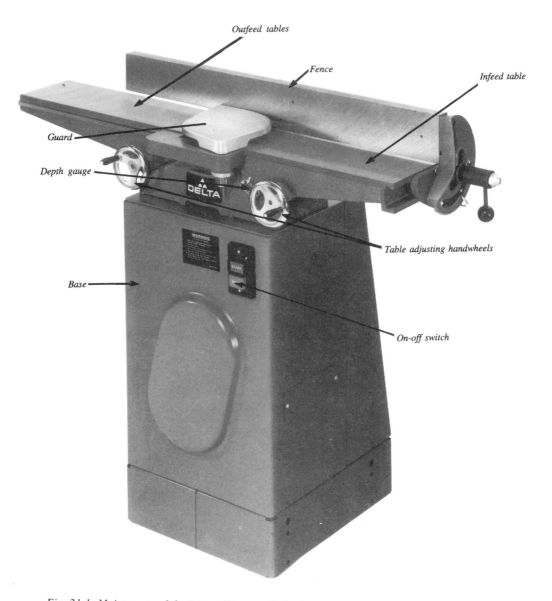

Outfeed tables

Fence

Infeed table

Guard

Depth gauge

Table adjusting handwheels

Base

On-off switch

Fig. 21-1. Major parts of the jointer (Courtesy Delta International Machinery Corporation).

no more than $\frac{1}{16}$ inch (2 mm). If the board is extra wide or the wood is hard, reduce the depth of cut to $\frac{1}{32}$ inch (1 mm). Move the fence over until just enough of the cutter is exposed to joint the board.

Position the board on the infeed table and against the face (Fig. 21-3). Make sure the material will be removed by jointing with the grain; jointing against the grain will cause severe chipping.

Using a *push shoe* as shown in Fig. 21-3, guide the stock across the cutterhead. The board must be kept from rocking. Although the board may cover the cutterhead, do not place your hands directly over the throat between the tables. Keep your hands at least 4 inches (102 mm) from the cutterhead. Use the push shoe to guide the board past the knives and out of the guard. The guard should close over the knives behind the board.

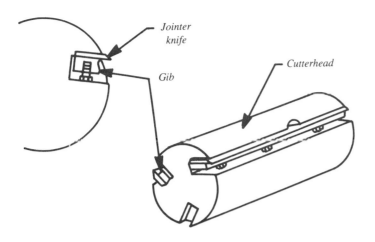

Fig. 21-2. The cutterhead consists of three knives held in place with gibs.

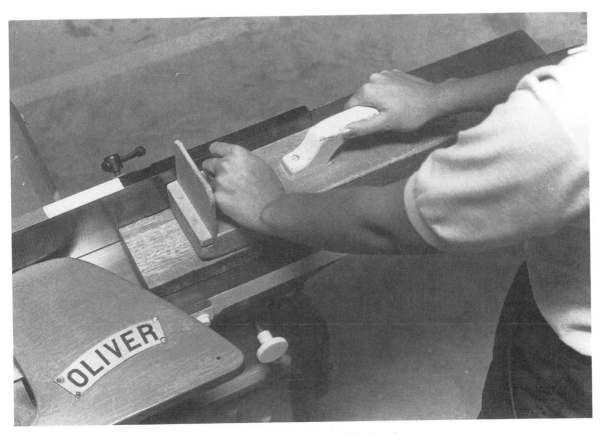

Fig. 21-3. Jointing the face of the board.

JOINTING THE EDGE

The second step after jointing the face is to joint the straightest edge. Stock must be at least 10 inches (254 mm) long. If the edge is unusually crooked, first scribe a straight line on the face and bandsaw the board.

To set up the jointer, use a square to check that the fence is at a right angle to the table. Move the fence over until just enough of the cutterhead is exposed to joint the board. Adjust the depth to no more than 1/16 inch (2 mm) deep. Be certain the stock is at least 10 inches long.

Position the board on the infeed table and against the fence. Always joint with the grain. If the board is less than the height of the fence, use a push stick to guide the board across the jointer. Push forward with the right hand. Always keep the stock against the fence with the left hand. When the left hand comes within 4 inches (102 mm) of the cutterhead, move the hand back towards the push stick. Once the board passes the cutterhead

transfer the left hand to the outfeed side. Keep both hands at least 4 inches from the cutter.

JOINTING END GRAIN
AND EDGES OF PLYWOOD

Because it is difficult to accurately joint end grain and edges of plywood, attempt to only cut the material with a fine tooth saw blade. If it is necessary to joint either of these two, make certain they are at least 10 inches (254 mm) in length. When the end grain is jointed, always joint it before jointing any edge grain.

Position the fence to expose the minimal amount of cutter. Adjust the depth to 1/16 inch (2 mm). Joint the first 1 inch (25 mm) of the end and pivot the stock off the cutter (Fig. 21-4). Turn the board around joint from the other edge. When the second cut meets the first cut, push the board on past the cutterhead. No material

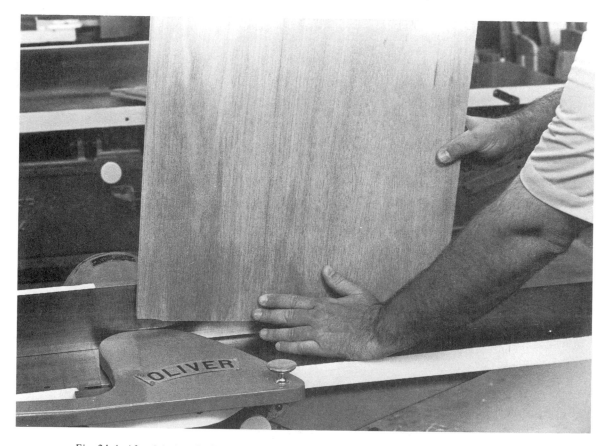

Fig. 21-4. After jointing the first 1 inch (25 mm) of end grain, pivot the stock off the cutterhead.

should be removed toward the end of the cut; this will prevent the end from chipping out.

BEVELING AND CHAMFERING

To joint either a bevel or a chamfer, the fence must be tilted to the desired angle. The angle gauge on the back of the fence will indicate the approximate angle. Use a sliding T-bevel positioned against the table and fence when a more accurate cut is desired. Most jointers have a positive stop at 30 and 45 degrees for a fast setup.

The fence can be tilted either forwards or backwards. It is recommended that the fence be tilted forward to give an inside corner to hold the board (Figure 21-5). Use edge jointing techniques to make a bevel or cham-

fer. Several passes might be necessary to produce the width of cut desired.

RABBETING

A smooth rabbet can be cut on the jointer. A jointer must have a *rabbeting arm* to be able to make this cut (Fig. 21-6). It supports the stock as the rabbet is made. First make a shoulder cut on the table saw; this will prevent the face of the board from being chipped. Remove the jointer guard and move the fence over. The face of the fence should be the same distance from the end of the knives as the width of the rabbet. Set the first depth of cut to no more than 1/8 inch (3 mm). If the rabbet is deeper than 1/8 inch, adjust the depth of cut to an addi-

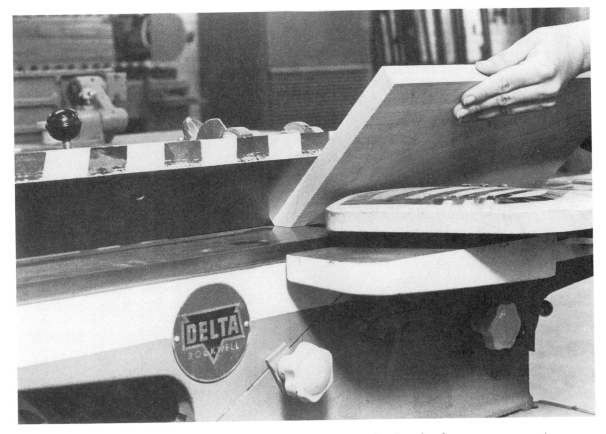

Fig. 21-5. Angle the fence forward to joint a bevel or chamfer.

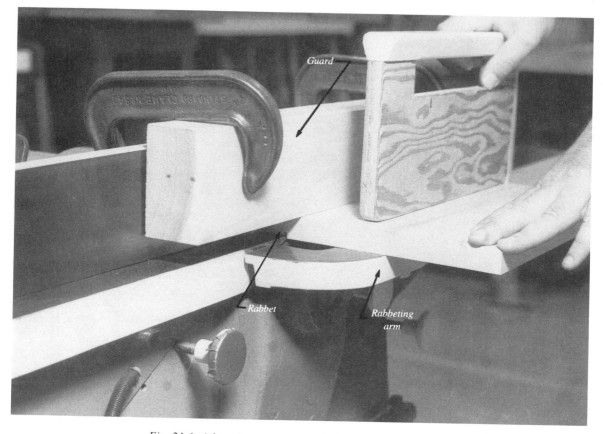

Fig. 21-6. A board serves as a guard when jointing a rabbet.

tional ¹/₁₆ inch (2 mm) and make another pass. Clamp a board on the fence the same distance from the table as the thickness of stock. This board will serve as a guard. Feed the stock using a push stick.

TAPERING

Square the material and lay out the starting point of the taper. Pulling the guard back, position the layout line directly over the lip of the outfeed table. Clamp a stop block against the trailing end of the board (Fig. 21-7). Set the depth of cut equal to the amount to be removed

from the small end of one side of the taper. For deep tapers, take ¹/₈-inch (3 mm) cuts and make several passes.

Remove the stock and turn on the power. Keep the hands away from the cutterhead and have a helper pull the guard back only enough to lower the stock. Place the board against the stop block and slowly pivot it against the table. Do not place the hands on top of the stock directly over the cutterhead. Use a push stick to guide the stock over the jointer. Because the jointer will make a small circular cut at the layout line, use a hand plane or sanding block to smooth the taper.

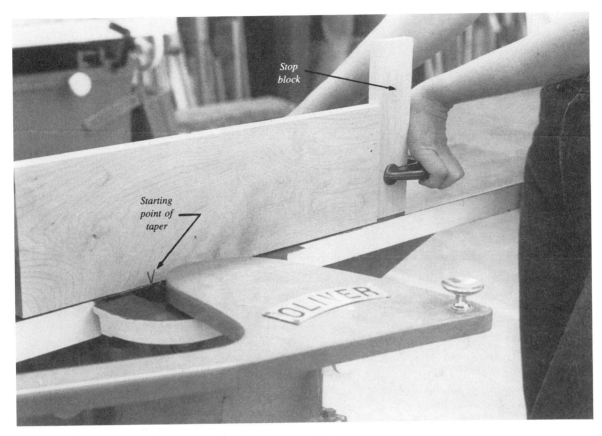

Fig. 21-7. Install a stop block for jointing a taper.

Chapter 22

Planer

The planer is a specialized woodworking machine for surfacing lumber to thickness. Some woodworkers call the planer a *surfacer*. This machine is unusual because it is one of the few pieces of equipment that automatically feeds the boards past the cutter head.

PARTS

The major parts of the planer include the bed, speed adjustment handwheel, height adjustment handwheel and base (Fig. 22-1). Inside the planer are other important parts. They include the feed rollers, chip breaker, cutterhead, and pressure bar (Fig. 22-2). The *infeed and outfeed rollers* are responsible for pushing and pulling the board past the rotating cutterhead. The *top infeed roller* is corrugated to better grip the board. To keep the cutter from chipping the stock, the *chip breaker* rests on top of the board. The cutterhead usually has three knives much like the jointer. Because the rotating cutterhead tends to lift the stock off the table, a *pressure bar* keeps the board against the bed. To pull the stock out of the planer, the outfeed rollers are located behind the pressure bar. The base is a heavy metal casting that absorbs much of the vibration created by the planing of the board.

Planers are sized by the widest and thickest board that can be surfaced. Most planers for general use are of a 13- × -6-inch (330- × -152 mm) or 24- × -9-inch (610- × -229 mm) size.

FACE PLANING

Do not face plane stock less than 12 inches (305 mm) in length. To set up the planer, first check that one face of the board is flat and true. In most cases the surface will

---

SAFETY

☐ Disconnect the power before reaching inside the planer.
☐ Do not run the planer if the knives are dull.
☐ Keep your hands at least 4 inches (102 mm) from the throat of the machine.
☐ Do not stand behind the board.
☐ Remove no more than $1/16$ (2 mm) with each cut.
☐ Never plane end grain.
☐ Boards to be planed must be at least 12 inches (305 mm) long.
☐ Use a backing board to plane stock less than $3/8$ inch (10 mm) thick.
☐ Plane only one board at a time.
☐ Never look into the machine while it is running.

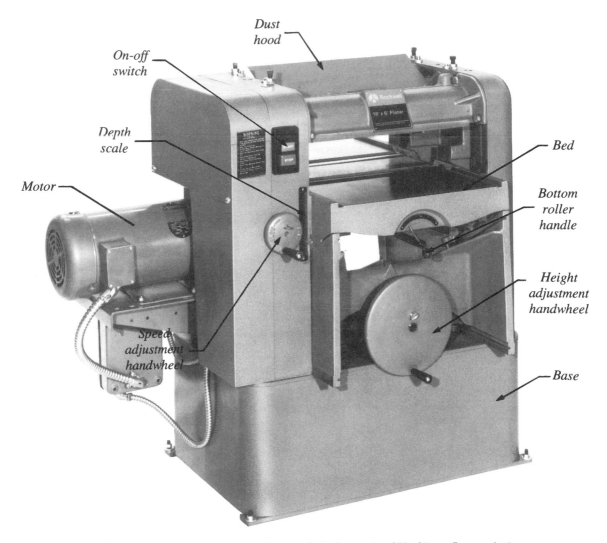

Fig. 22-1. Major parts of the planer (Courtesy Delta International Machinery Corporation).

need to be face-jointed on the jointer. Next, measure the thickest part of the board and subtract 1/16 (2 mm) from this amount. Using the *height adjustment handwheel*, move the bed to this measurement. The *depth scale* indicates the setting of the bed. Turn the speed adjustment handwheel to the proper feed rate. Use a 15–26 feet-per-minute feed rate for beginning cuts and a 48–50 feet per minute for easy-to-plane woods or finishing cuts.

Turn on the power and place the board on the edge of the bed. The flat face should be down and the grain pointing towards the operator. Push the stock forward until the infeed rollers take hold of the board. Make certain the board is started in a straight line. *Never* reach or look into the machine. Do not stand directly behind the board. If the piece becomes stuck, attempt to push the board forward. Have someone catch the stock as it leaves the machine. Support long pieces as they both enter and exit the planer (Fig. 22-3).

If several pieces of different thickness are to be planed, set the planer for surfacing the thickest piece.

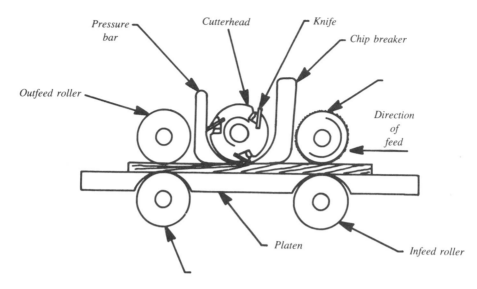

Fig. 22-2. Working parts located inside the planer which feed the board and remove the wood.

Fig. 22-3. Support the board as it is being fed into and out of the planer.

Start planing the other boards when the depth setting is adjusted to their thickness. This will save a great deal of time in adjusting the machine.

To wear the knives evenly and keep them as sharp as possible, start feeding stock on the left hand side of the planer (Fig. 22-4). Place the next board to the right of the first piece. Once the boards have reached the right side of the bed, start again on the left side.

PLANING SHORT BOARDS

Stock shorter than 12 inches (305 mm) but longer than 8 inches (203 mm) can be planed. Because each planer is built differently, however, check the owner's manual for the shortest recommended lengths. Adjust the planer as described for face planing. Start the first piece through the planer. Before the trailing end passes the throat of the planer, butt another board against it. The second board will push the first piece on through the machine. The last board must be at least 12 inches long to clear the planer by itself.

PLANING THIN BOARDS

Stock thinner than ⅜ inch (10 mm) can be surfaced using a *backing board*. A backing board should be a ¾-inch-thick (19 mm) piece of hardwood plywood at least 2 inches (50 mm) wider and longer than the piece to be planed (Fig. 22-5). After placing the stock on top of the backing board, measure the combined thickness of both. Set the depth ¹⁄₁₆ inch (2 mm) less than this measurement. Select a slow feed rate. Use the procedure recommended for face planing.

Fig. 22-4. Start feeding the first board on the left. The second board is started to the right.

Fig. 22-5. Use a backing board to plane thin boards.

Chapter 23

Drill Press

A drill press is used primarily to bore holes. It is ideal for this purpose because the drill bit is fed straight into the work, so there is little chance of the hole not being at the desired angle. The drill press can also route, mortise, sand, and even make plugs.

PARTS

The drill bit is held by the *chuck*. It is rotated by the *spindle*. In order that the spindle can be lowered and raised, the spindle turns inside the *quill*. The quill is moved up or down with the pilot wheel feed. It can be held in any position by tightening the quill lock (Fig. 23-1).

The drill press is held up by the *column*. The table is raised and lowered on this column by loosening the *table locking clamp*. Located on the floor is the *base*, which stabilizes the drill press.

The size of the drill press is determined by first measuring from the center of the bit mounted in the chuck to the front of the column. This distance is then doubled to give the drill press size. For example, if there is 7½ inches (188 mm) between the bit and column, it would be a 15-inch (381 mm) drill press. Most drill presses are either 15 inches or 17 inches (431 mm).

BORING TOOLS

Many different boring tools are used with the drill press (Table 23-1). The *twist drill* is the most common, and is generally stored in a metal box called a *drill index* (Fig. 23-2). *Spur bits* have sharp cutting lips that make very straight, smooth holes for dowel joints and other operations (Fig. 23-3).

There are several specialized tools for large diameter holes. The *forstner bit* makes a large flat-bottom hole (Fig. 23-4). Many woodworkers prefer the *multispur bit* for large diameters because of its fast boring capabilities (Fig. 23-5). When only a few large holes are needed a *spade bit* works well (Fig. 23-6). Carpenters and plumbers sometimes use a *hole saw* when making round cutouts for pipes and other rough holes (Fig. 23-7). The *circle cutter* has an adjustable arm that can be moved in or out on its center shaft (Fig. 23-8). By boring from both

SAFETY

- ☐ Unplug the power cord before changing the bit.
- ☐ Use only sharp bits.
- ☐ Always remove the chuck key from the chuck.
- ☐ Clamp small pieces and odd shapes to the drill press table.
- ☐ Hands must come no closer than 4 inches (102 mm) to the boring tool

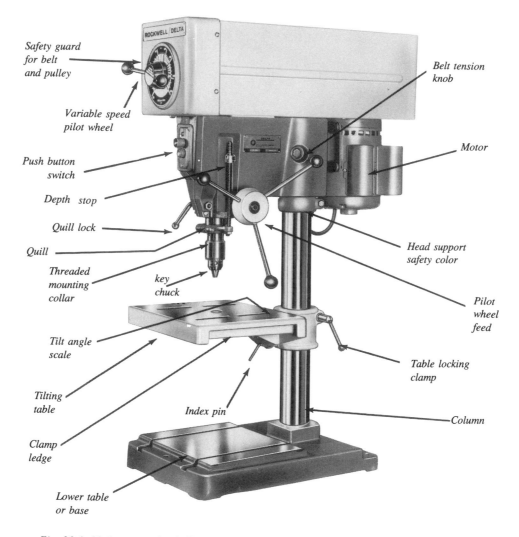

Fig. 23-1. Major parts of a drill press (Courtesy Delta International Machinery Corporation).

sides of the board the largest of all holes are made with this cutter.

Specialized boring tools are also available for working with screws. A *countersink* bores a tapered hole that fits the bottom of a flat or oval head wood screw (Fig. 23-9). *Screw bits* make the countersink, shank hole, and pilot hole all in one pass (Fig. 23-10). A *plug cutter* produces a round plug that is used to cover and hide the screw head (Fig. 23-11).

SELECTING AND CHANGING SPEEDS

Before installing the bit, select the proper drill bit speed. As a general rule the larger the bit and harder the material, the slower the bit should turn. Table 23-2 gives recommended drill speeds. If the bit is allowed to turn too rapidly, the bit will burn and might throw the stock off the table.

There are two methods of changing speeds. The

		Table 23-1. Boring Tools for the Drill Press.		
NAME OF BIT	**COMMON AVAILABLE DIA.**	**TYPE OF BORING**	**SHAPE OF BOTTOM OF HOLE**	**MAJOR ADVANTAGE**
Twist Drill	1/32″ - 1/2″	General Purpose Boring in all Materials	Tapered	Inexpensive and Widely Available
Spur Bit	3/16″ - 1 1/4″	Dowel Holes and Plywood	Flat with a Center Point	Very Clean Cutting
Forstner Bit	1/4″ - 2″	Large Diameter Flat Bottom Holes	Flat	Flattest of all Holes
Multi-Spur Bit	1/2″ - 4″	Large Diameter Flat Bottom Holes	Flat with a Center Point	Fast, Clean Cutting
Spade Bit	1/4″ - 2″	Large Diameter Flat Bottom Holes	Flat with a Very Large Center Point	Inexpensive
Hole Saw	9/16″ - 6″	Large Diameter Rough Holes	Must Bore Through Stock	Produces Circular Plug
Circle Cutter	1 1/8″ - 8-3/8″	Bores Very Large Holes	Must Bore Through Stock	Bores Largest of all Holes
Countersink	1/2″	Bores Tapered Holes for Flathead Wood Screws	Tapered	Sets Screws Below Surface
Screw Bits	Screw Sizes 3/4″ × #6 - 2″ × #12	Holes for Wood Screws	Screw Shaped	Flat Screw Holes
Plug Cutter	3/8″ - 1″	Plug to Hide Screw Holes	Round Plug	Hides Screw Heads

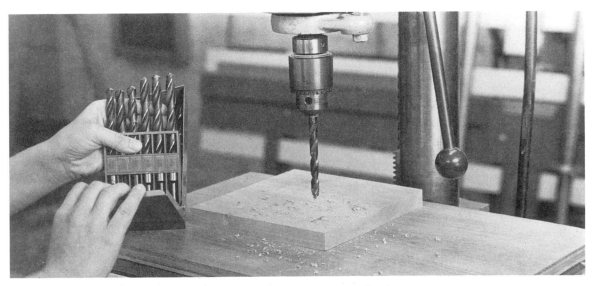

Fig. 23-2. Twist drills with the drill index.

Fig. 23-3. Spur bits have sharp cutting lips for making a smooth hole.

Fig. 23-5. A multispur bit has teeth for an aggressive cut.

Fig. 23-4. A forstner bit makes a flat bottom hole.

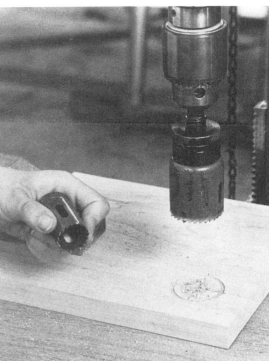

Fig. 23-6. A spade bit is used to make large-diameter holes.

Fig. 23-7. Hole saws produce a round plug.

Fig. 23-8. Circle cutters make the largest circles of all bits.

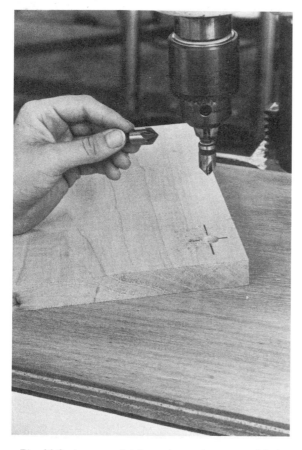

Fig. 23-9. *A countersink is used to make a tapered hole for screws.*

Fig. 23-10. *Screw bits make all the holes necessary for flat head wood screws.*

variable speed control is the simplest to operate. An operator turns on the power and then moves the variable speed control knob to the selected speed. The second method requires a V-belt to be shifted to a different level on the stepped pulley (Fig. 23-12). Never attempt moving the belt unless the power is unplugged.

SETTING UP THE BORING TOOL

Be sure to start setting up by unplugging the power. Select the bit and insert the shank of the bit at least 1 inch (25 mm) into the open key chuck. Hand tighten the chuck by turning the outside sleeve. Finish tightening the chuck by inserting and turning the chuck key in all three chuck holes. The chuck key must be removed before turning on the power.

Place a *drill pad* made of planed scrap wood or plywood on the drill press table. This will protect the table top and keep the bit from touching the metal table. Position the stock on the drill pad. Adjust the height of the table so that the end of the bit is 1 inch (25 mm) from the top surface of the stock. Loosen the elevating handle to be able to move the table. Be careful not to allow the table to drop as the handle is loosened. As the table is raised, position the hole in the drill press metal table directly under the bit. This will save the table and bit from damage if the bit accidentally bores through the drill pad.

If the stock is small or the hole is larger than ½ inch (13 mm), clamp the stock to the table. When there is a danger of the piece being grabbed by the bit, never attempt to hold the stock with just your hands. Odd-shaped pieces and metal parts might need a special holding fixture to better secure them to the table (Fig. 23-13).

Table 23-2. Drill Bit Speed Chart.	
SOFTWOODS	
WOODBIT SIZE	SPEED R.P.M.
1/8″	2000
3/16″	1800
1/4″	1800
5/16″	1800
3/8″	1800
7/16″	1400
1/2″	1400
5/8″	1000
3/4″	900
7/8″	900
1″	900
1 1/8″ & larger	700
HARDWOODS	
WOODBIT SIZE	SPEED R.P.M.
1/8″	2000
3/16″	1800
1/4″	1800
5/16″	1800
3/8″	1800
7/16″	1400
1/2″	1400
5/8″	1000
3/4″	900
7/8″	900
1″	900
1 1/8″ & larger	700

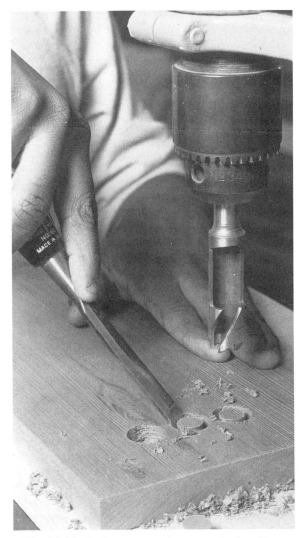

Fig. 23-11. A plug cutter makes a small plug. Use a chisel to remove the plug from the hole.

BORING THROUGH HOLES

A hole that extends completely through the stock is a through hole. To bore a through hole, select the bit and set the speed. Install the bit and adjust the table height as previously explained. Then move the drill pad to one side of the table. Raise the bit until it is slightly below the top surface of the drill pad. Lower the bit to make sure it lines up with the hole in the table.

Tighten the quill lock to keep the bit at this level. Turn the depth stop down until it is seated against the depth stop flange (Fig. 23-14). This will control how deep the bit can be lowered. Replace the drill pad and position the stock under the bit. Lower the bit just above the stock. Move the stock until the bit is centered over the layout marks. If there is a danger of the stock slipping, clamp it to the table.

Turn on the power and steady the stock with the left hand. With the right hand, slowly turn the feed lever. As the bit comes close to the stock, slow the feed rate. Feed the bit into the stock at a steady rate. The chips should be smooth and break off clean. If the hole is deep, back the bit out of the hole several times to prevent the chips from packing around the bit. Once the depth stop has reached the stop flange, return the chuck to the topmost position. Do not remove any chips until the bit has stopped turning.

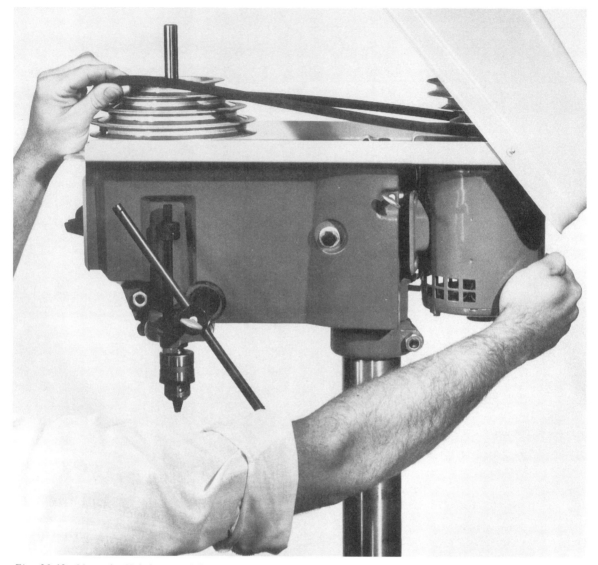

Fig. 23-12. Move the V belt to a different level to change the drill speed (Courtesy Delta International Machinery Corporation).

BORING A STOPPED HOLE

A stopped hole does not go completely through the board. It enters one face but stops before breaking through the opposite face. Stopped holes are bored very much like through holes. Set the drill press up as described for a through hole. Mark the depth of the hole, on the end of the board to be bored. With the stock on the drill pad, lower the bit even with the layout line (Fig. 23-15). Tighten the quill lock and adjust the depth stop. Loosen the quill lock and bore the hole.

BORING ANGLED HOLES

Holes bored at an angle require the table to be tilted. Using a protractor, set a sliding T-bevel to the desired an-

Fig. 23-13. Use a clamp or other holding device to secure odd-shaped pieces.

gle. After installing a bit, loosen the angle lock located under the table. Place the head of the T-bevel on the drill press table and tilt the table until the blade of the T-bevel is flat against the bit (Fig. 23-16). Tighten the angle lock.

Position the stock under the bit and clamp it to the table. The bit will have a tendency to drift sideways, so cut a scrap piece at an angle that will provide a boring surface at a right angle to the bit (Fig. 23-17). Clamp it to the top of the stock and bore through the scrap into the stock. The scrap helps hold the drill straight.

MORTISING

Mortises are rectangular holes into which a tenon fits. If a drill press is used to make mortises, it requires a mortising attachment along with the mortising chisel and bit (Fig. 23-18). The mortising attachment holds the tooling and positions the stock. The mortising bit rotates inside the mortise chisel. It cuts a round hole and moves the chips up and out of the mortise. The chisel then punches the hole square.

Because the thickness of the mortise is difficult to change, the mortise is always made before the tenon. Tenons are usually cut on the tablesaw, so it is simple to vary their size. Make certain all pieces are of the exact same thickness. Lay out the mortise on each piece (Fig. 23-19). The depth of the mortise should be $\frac{1}{8}$ inch (3 mm) deeper than the length of the tenon. This additional space at the bottom of the mortise provides a place for surplus adhesive.

Follow the instructions of the manufacturer for installing the mortising attachment, chisel, and bit. Place the stock on the drill pad and lower the chisel. When the tip of the chisel is even with the bottom layout line, tighten the quill lock. Adjust the depth stop to this level.

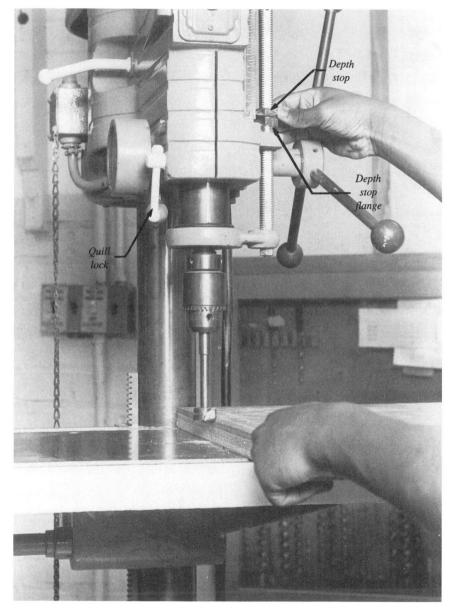

Fig. 23-14. Turn the depth stop down against the depth stop flange.

Release the quill lock and position the stock under the bit. Position the fence and hold down. If several mortises are to be punched that are the same location and size, install stop blocks. The speed of the drill press should be set to no more than 900 rpm.

After turning on the power, slowly lower the chuck. If the mortise is very deep, withdraw the chisel often to allow the bit to clean itself. Follow the punching pattern shown in Fig. 23-20 so the bit will not be broken or bent.

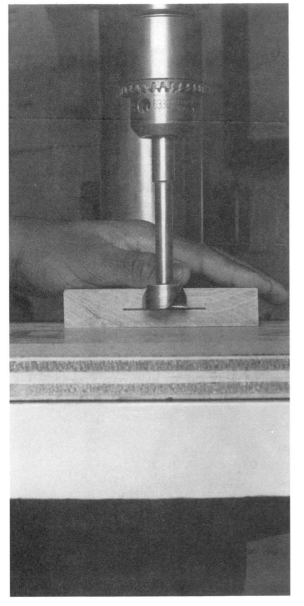

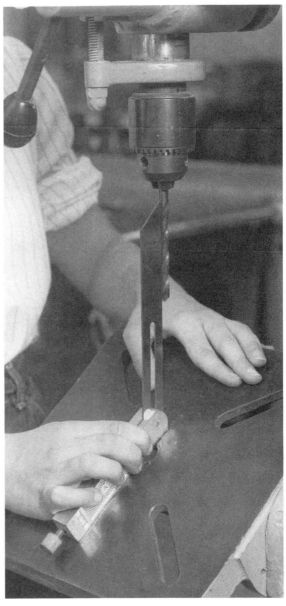

Fig. 23-15. Align the end of the drill bit with the layout line.

Fig. 23-16. Use a sliding T bevel to set the angel of the table.

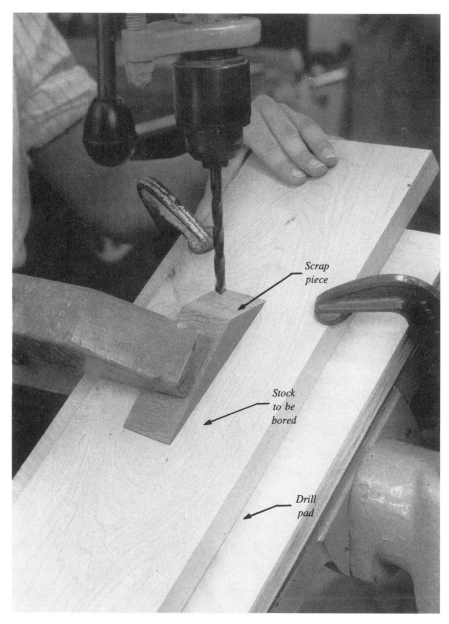

Fig. 23-17. Boring an angled hole.

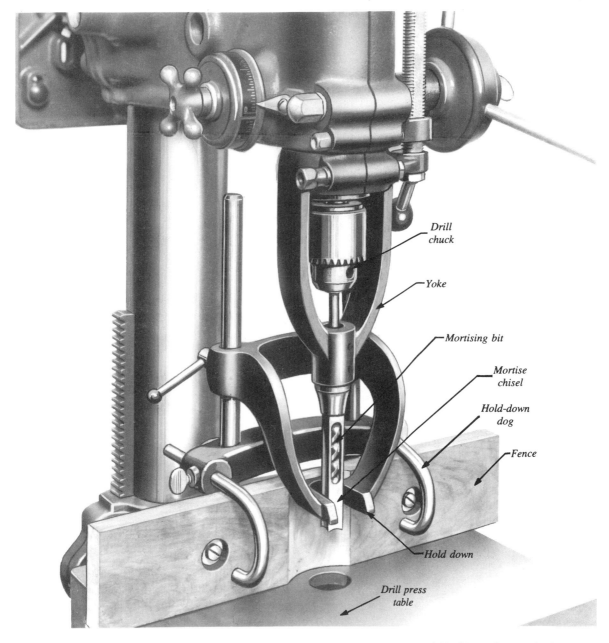

Fig. 23-18. Mortising attachment on a drill press (Courtesy Delta International Machinery Corporation).

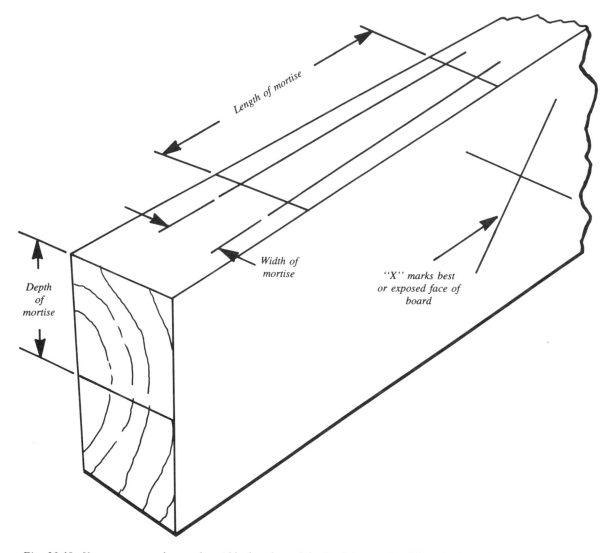

Fig. 23-19. Use a square to layout the width, length, and depth of the mortise. Place the X mark facing out when the board is placed on the drill press table.

DRUM SANDING

The drill press with a sanding drum is ideal for sanding curved pieces. An abrasive sleeve fits around the drum. Different grits or roughness of abrasives are available. For most general-purpose sanding, an 80-grit sleeve works best.

First install an auxiliary table on the drill press (see table in Fig. 23-21). It has a hole through it slightly larger than the diameter of the drum. Lower the drum through the hole and lock it into position with the quill lock. Adjust the speed to 1200 rpm and start the drill press. Always feed the stock against the rotation of the drum (Fig. 23-21). As the abrasive becomes worn, lower it farther into the auxiliary table. Once the abrasive sleeve is completely worn, replace it with a new sleeve.

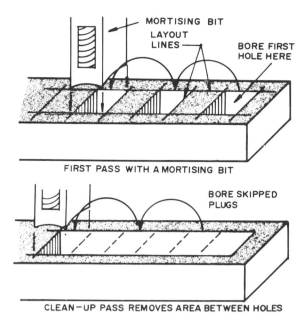

FIRST PASS WITH A MORTISING BIT

CLEAN—UP PASS REMOVES AREA BETWEEN HOLES

Fig. 23-20. Order of the punching pattern to make a mortise.

ROUTING

Do not attempt to rout on the drill press unless it is heavy duty and can rotate at least 5,000 rpm. Routing requires a large plywood auxiliary table to be screwed to the drill press table. Insert the router bit at least ½ inch (13 mm) in the chuck. Because the bit must turn at such a high speed, tighten the chuck hard. Use the chuck key in all three chuck holes to secure the bit.

Lower the bit to the desired depth and lock it into position with the quill lock. Clamp a wooden fence with a small cut out for the router bit on top of the auxilary table (Fig. 23-22). This will serve as a guide for the stock and also as a guard. Feed the stock from left to right. Use a pushstick and keep hands at least 6 inches (152 mm) from the bit. Do not attempt to route stock less than 12 inches (305 mm) long.

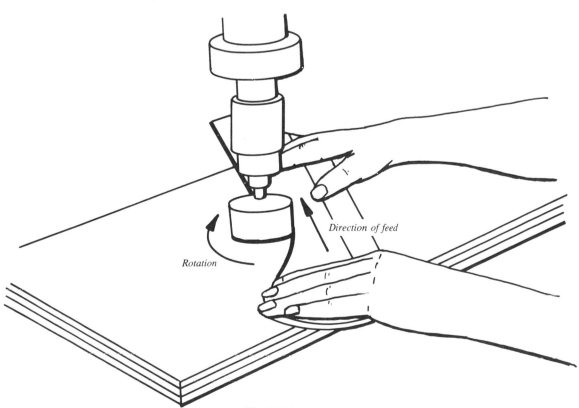

Fig. 23-21. Sanding on the drill press.

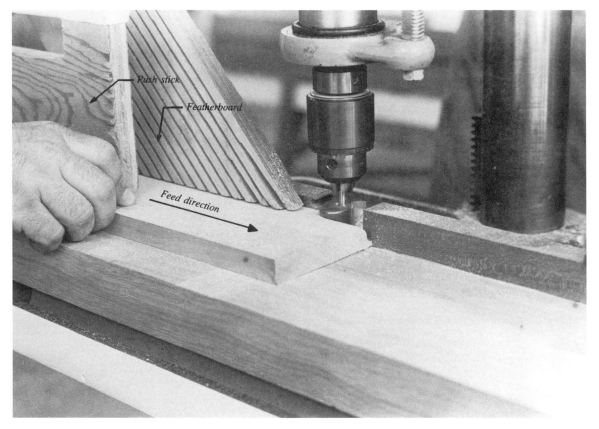

Fig. 23-22. *Routing on the drill press.*

Chapter 24

Lathe

A wood lathe is used primarily for making spindles, bowls, and other turnings. This machine is unusual because the stock is rotated while being shaped. Special cutting tools called *lathe chisels* are held against the spinning material to make the desired shape.

PARTS

The major parts of the lathe include the headstock, tailstock, tool rest, and bed (Fig. 24-1). Stock is turned by the *headstock*. The headstock contains the motor and a method to change the turning speeds. At the opposite end of the lathe is the *tailstock*. It can be moved anywhere along the bed to allow different lengths of stock to be turned. To support the lathe chisels, a *tool rest* is attached to the bed. The tool rest can also be moved to any point along the bed (Fig. 24-2). The *guard* covers the rotating stocking. It will protect the operator if a chisel is accidentally thrown or the stock comes loose.

The size of the lathe is specified by length and swing. *Length* is the longest piece of stock that can be mounted on the machine. *Swing* is the largest diameter of material that can be turned. A good general-purpose lathe can turn a 39-inch (990 mm) piece that is 12 inches (305 mm) in diameter.

EQUIPMENT

Many different pieces of lathe equipment are available to make turnings. The most important are *lathe chisels* (Fig. 24-3). These chisels have long handles and thick blades. They come in several different styles.

The *gouge* has a rounded body and a rounded cutting end. It is made in several different widths. The

---

SAFETY

☐ Disconnect the power when mounting stock.
☐ Wear a face shield, remove loose clothing, and wear a hair net if your hair is long.
☐ Stock must be sound and free from cracks and other defects.
☐ Always rotate the stock by hand before turning on the power.
☐ Stand to the side when first turning on the power.
☐ Follow the recommended turning speeds.
☐ Grasp and control the lathe chisels with both hands.
☐ Gradually change turning speeds when turning the lathe on and off.
☐ Calipers are to be used only when the stock is not turning.
☐ Remove the tool rest and post before sanding.
☐ Always lower the guard before turning on the power.

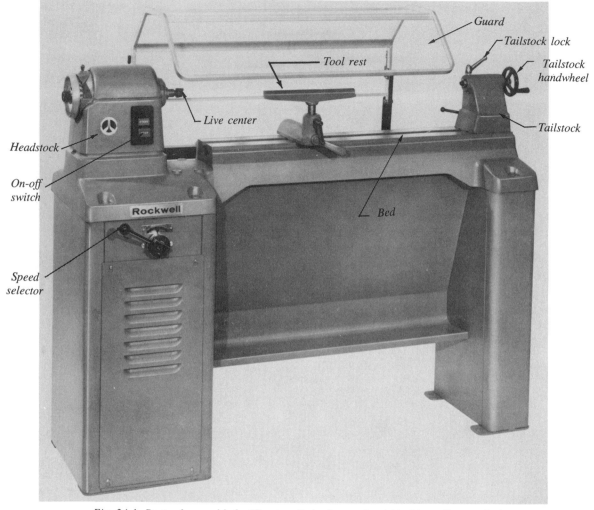

Fig. 24-1. Parts of a wood lathe (Courtesy Delta International Machinery Corporation).

gouge is used primarily for turning a rough square piece of material into cylinder.

The *skew* is a flat chisel with a beveled tip. It comes in several different widths. The skew chisel is used for smoothing a cylinder, forming beads, and making bead cuts.

A *spear point* or *diamond point* has a flat body and a pointed tip. This chisel can cut from either direction and will make the same types of cuts as the skew.

The *round nose chisel* has a flat body and a tip shaped like the rounded end of the gouge. It is available in several different widths. Most cuts made by the round nose are either for smoothing or for making a circular shape.

The *parting tool* has a diamond-shaped body and a pointed tip. It is used primarily for making narrow grooves for establishing depths of other cuts.

The *square nose* has a cutting edge much like a hand chisel. It has, however, a longer blade and handle. Use the square nose for the same type of cuts as the skew.

Outside and inside calipers are used to make measurements on lathe turnings. *Outside calipers* can check measurements on the outside of cylinder turnings (Fig. 24-4). Internal measurements can be checked with *inside calipers* (Fig. 24-5). *Dividers* have pointed arms for transferring measurements from a ruler to the turnings.

Many other lathe accessories are available. A *face-*

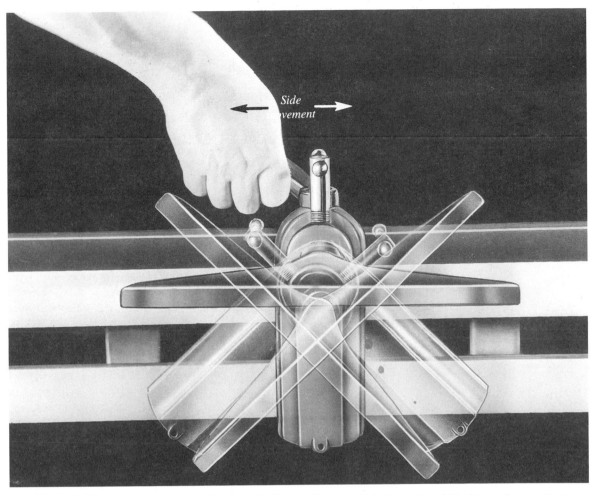

Fig. 24-2. The tool rest can be angled or moved sideways (Courtesy Delta International Machinery Corporation).

plate is used to hold large-diameter stock when the live center is not used (Fig. 24-6). Faceplates come in several diameters and are used to turn such items as bowls. *Drill chucks* hold drill bits for boring holes in lathe turnings. A *steady rest* supports long slender turnings and keeps them from flexing (Fig. 24-7). To sand curves, a *sanding drum* can be used on the lathe (Fig. 24-8).

MOUNTING STOCK

Prepare the stock by first selecting a piece of high-quality sound material. If a solid piece is not available, glue several pieces together with a thermoset adhesive.

The glue joints must be tight and strong. Square the material at least ¼ inch (6 mm) larger than the largest diameter of the turning. For turnings with exposed ends, make the squared piece at least 1 inch (25 mm) longer than the finished length. To save time on extra-thick squares, plane the corners with a hand plane, making a rough cylinder.

The steps to prepare the square for the lathe are as follows: Locate the center of each end by drawing a diagonal line from one corner to the opposite corner. On the end against the headstock, use a backsaw to cut a ⅛-in-deep (3 mm) kerf along the diagonal lines. Bore a ⅛-inch hole ¼ inch deep where the two saw cuts cross.

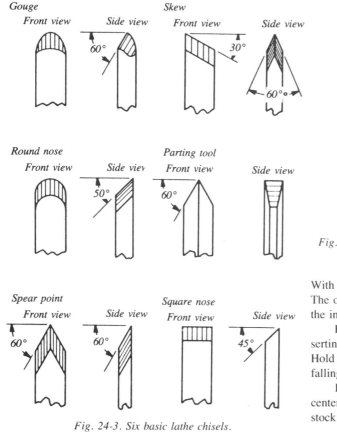

Gouge

Front view   Side view

60°

Skew

Front view   Side view

30°

60°

Round nose

Front view   Side view

50°

Parting tool

Front view   Side view

60°

Spear point

Front view   Side view

60°   60°

Square nose

Front view   Side view

45°

Fig. 24-3. Six basic lathe chisels.

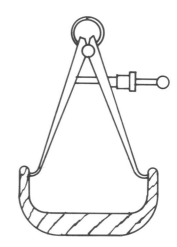

Fig. 24-5. Inside calipers are used on faceplate turnings.

With a mallet, drive the live center into the saw kerfs. The opposite end should also have ⅛-inch hole bored at the intersecting lines.

Remove the live center from the headstock by inserting a knockout rod through the headstock spindle. Hold the center as it is being removed to prevent it from falling to the floor.

Insert the live center in the headstock. The dead center should be slipped into the tailstock. Place the stock into the live center and bring the tailstock within 1

Fig. 24-4. Outside calipers are used on spindle turnings.

Fig. 24-6. Faceplates come in several sizes.

Fig. 24-7. A steady rest supports thin turnings.

Fig. 24-8. A sanding drum sands curves.

inch (25 mm) of the other end. Lock the tailstock to the bed with the locking wrench. Turn the tailstock handwheel until the dead center has gripped the stock. Back the dead center out and place a few drops of oil on the center. Retighten the tailstock handwheel and secure it with the tailstock lock.

Adjust the tool rest so that it is ⅛ inch above center and ⅛ inch away from the nearest corner (Fig. 24-9). Secure the tool rest in place with the locking handle. Always turn the stock by hand so it does not hit the tool rest.

REMOVING STOCK

Two methods of removing stock on the lathe can be used: cutting and scraping. Scraping is the most accurate and easiest way. A scraping cut is made with a lathe chisel held parallel with the floor. As the chisel scrapes, stock is removed in the form of fine powder.

The cutting method is more difficult than scraping but does make a smoother cut. Only gouges and skews can be used. These chisels are held so the handle is at a 30–60-degree angle to the floor. Stock is removed in the form of shavings.

MAKING A CYLINDER

The cylinder or round rod is usually the first shape that is made for any turning. After the cylinder is turned, other shapes can be produced. To make a cylinder, mount the turning square and position the tool rest as recommended in the section entitled "Mounting Stock." Before turning on the power, always rotate the square by hand to check that the corners of the stock will not strike the tool rest.

Do not initially rotate the stock any faster than listed under the roughing column in Table 24-1. With a wide skew placed on edge, make a nick in the rotating square

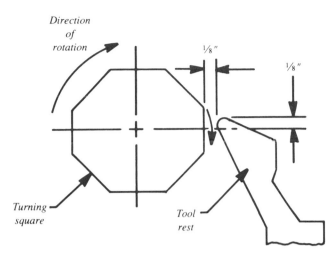

Fig. 24-9. Adjustments for the tool rest.

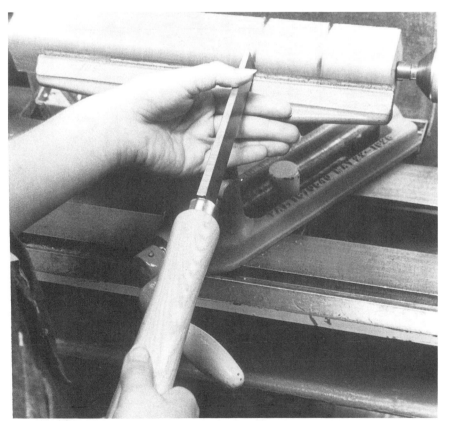

Fig. 24-10. Nicking the corners with a skew. Note: The guard has been removed so the cut can be seen better. Always use the guard.

Table 24-1. Turning Speeds for the Lathe.

SIZE OF SQUARE	ROUGHING	GENERAL CUTTING	SANDING
Under 2″	900 to 1300 R.P.M.	2400 to 2800	3000 to 4000
2″ to 4″	800 to 1000 R.P.M.	1800 to 2400	2400 to 3000
4″ to 6″	600 to 800 R.P.M.	1200 to 1800	1800 to 2400
6″ to 8″	400 to 600 R.P.M.	800 to 1200	1200 to 1800
8″ to 10″	300 to 400 R.P.M.	600 to 800	900 to 1200
Over 10″	300	300 to 600	600 to 900

every 2 inches (Fig. 24-10). This will prevent long splinters from being formed.

Use the largest gouge to start forming the cylinder. With the left hand, hold the tip down against the tool rest. Slide the index finger along the tool rest to control the depth of cut. Hold the handle of the chisel with the right hand. When moving the gouge from left to right, lower the handle and swing it slightly to the right. This will expose a small area of the tip that gives the best cut.

Bring the chisel against the stock about 1 inch (25 mm) from the left end. Move the chisel towards the tailstock, taking a light cut. Never start cutting right on the ends because the chisel might be knocked out of your hands. Continue to make light passes until there is $\frac{3}{8}$ inch (10 mm) between the stock and tool rest. Turn off the power and move the tool rest closer to the stock.

After the cylinder is round, adjust the outside calipers to $\frac{1}{16}$ inch (2 mm) over the finished diameter. Take the parting chisel and turn the cylinder down to this setting every 2 inches (51 mm) along the length of the stock. This will make a series of small grooves. Always stop the stock before measuring with the calipers. To give a smoother cut, increase the speed, then use a wide skew to level the surface until the grooves just disappear.

It is recommended that beginners try a scraping action when using the skew. Place the chisel flat against the tool rest, the handle parallel with the floor. Angle the chisel slightly so that the leading corner does not touch the cylinder. Push the chisel along the cylinder, taking a light cut. Once the skew reaches the end of the stock, turn the chisel over and push it back the other direction.

Once the entire cylinder is turned to the setting of the calipers, start to sand the last $\frac{1}{16}$ inch with a piece of old 100-grit sanding belt (Fig. 24-11). Remember to remove the tool rest and tool post. Use the speed recommended in the sanding column of Table 24-1. Hold the sanding belt with the tips of the fingers only. Do not wrap the belt around your hands. After removing all of the major defects, change to 120-grit abrasive paper.

Finish sanding with 150- and then 180-grit abrasive paper. Be careful not to sand away too much material.

With a ruler, measure the length of the cylinder. Mark the end points by placing the pencil on the cylinder and rotating the stock by hand. Turn on the lathe, and

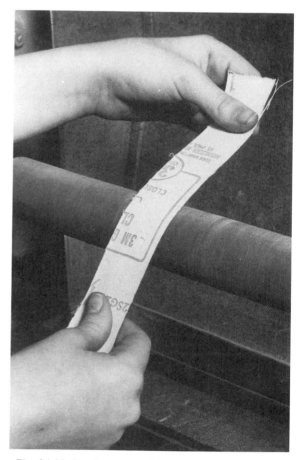

Fig. 24-11. Sanding a turned cylinder. Note: The guard has been removed so the cut can be seen better. Always use the guard.

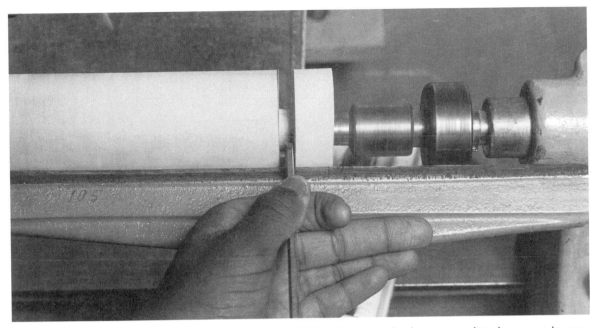

Fig. 24-12. Cutting a cylinder to length with a parting tool. Note: The guard has been removed so the cut can be seen better. Always use the guard.

with the parting chisel, cut into the rotating stock along the layout lines (Fig. 24-12). Leave ¼ inch (6 mm) of material. Remove the stock from the lathe and cut the last ¼ inch with a backsaw.

TURNING A TAPER

First turn a cylinder to the same diameter as the large end of the taper. Lay out the taper on a piece of paper as shown in Fig. 24-13. Transfer the layout points onto the cylinder with a pencil. Set the outside calipers to the first step from the paper and add an additional ¹⁄₁₆ inch (2 mm). With a parting tool, cut down to this diameter along the first layout line. Follow the same procedure for each step. Use a roundnose chisel to remove excess material until the surface reaches the grooves. Start from the end that will have the most material removed and work in a series of passes to the other end. Select a large skew to make the finish cut. Do not cut any deeper than the depth grooves.

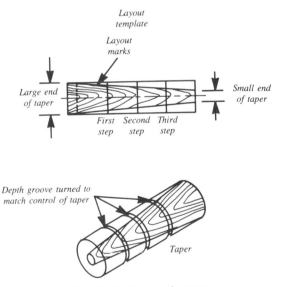

Fig. 24-13. Layout of a taper.

MAKING A V CUT

After turning a smooth cylinder, lay out the ending points and center the V-cut (Fig. 24-14). Use the spear point chisel, placing the point of the chisel on the center line. Gently push the spear point straight into the rotating stock. Stop the lathe often to check when the smallest diameter at the point of the V is the right size. If the cut is wider than the spear point will first cut, use a skew or the side of the spear point to widen the V.

MAKING A COVE CUT

Cove cuts are concave cuts that have rounded bottoms (Fig. 24-15). Lay out the cove cut on a finished cylinder. Mark the ending points and the center of each cove. With a parting tool, cut down to the smallest diameter along the center line. Use a roundnose chisel to round the cove out. Slowly push the chisel in until the groove made by the parting tool disappears. Pivot the roundnose chisel from side to side, but stay within the layout lines to widen the cove cut.

MAKING A BEADING CUT

Bead cuts are convex cuts that have rounded tops (Fig. 24-16). After turning a cylinder, lay out the ending points and center of the bead. Using a parting tool, cut each side of the bead to the smallest diameter. With a skew, round the bead over, leaving the center line. Keep the chisel on the tool rest and pivot it from the center line into the groove.

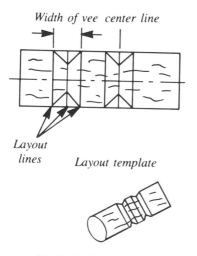

Fig. 24-14. Layout of a V.

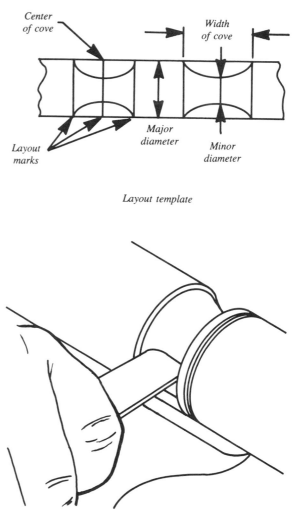

Layout template

Use a roundnose to make a cove.

Fig. 24-15. Turning a cove.

DUPLICATE TURNINGS

Two or more turnings the same shape and size are often required. To save time and costly mistakes, make a full-sized paper pattern. Cut the pattern in half along the center line. With the first half of the pattern, draw a line at a right angle to each point where a measurement is to be made (Fig. 24-17). This part of the pattern can then be laid on the tool rest to transfer key points onto the cylinder.

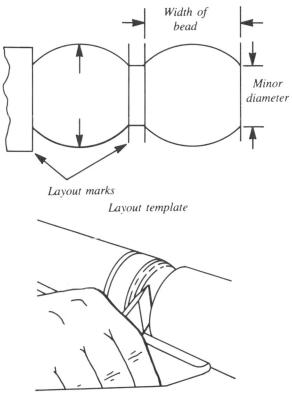

Width of bead

Minor diameter

Layout marks

Layout template

Use a skew to shape a bead.

Fig. 24-16. Turning a bead.

The second half of the pattern is used as a template (Fig. 24-18). Cut the paper along the outline of the turning. Once the turning has been turned to rough shape, place the template against the turning to see if any additional material needs to be removed.

Another method of making duplicate turnings involves the use of a *duplicator* (Fig. 24-19). It is a lathe accessory that is bolted onto the bed of the lathe. First turn stock into a cylinder using regular lathe chisels. Make a template with the same shape as the desired finish turning. Mount the template on the duplicator and the stock on the lathe. With the stylus of the duplicator, trace around the template. Make light repeated cuts until the stylus meets the template. After the shape is roughed in, use regular lathe chisels and the tool rest to make final finish cuts.

FACEPLATE TURNING

Faceplate turning allows both the side and face of the stock to be turned. Circular shaped stock is attached to a faceplate that is then screwed onto the spindle of the headstock. Products including fruit bowls, plates, and candlesticks can be made using a faceplate.

After gluing up the material to the desired thickness, use the bandsaw to cut a circle. The circle must be at least 1/4 inch (6 mm) larger than the finished diameter. Mount the faceplate exactly in the center of the stock. Use flathead wood screws to attach the faceplate.

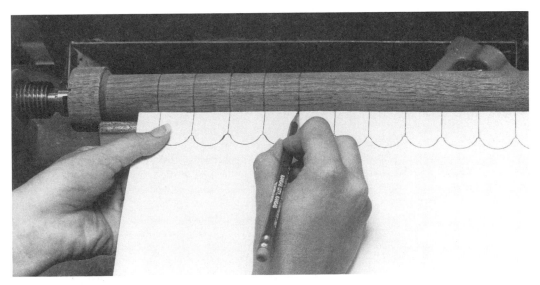

Fig. 24-17. Transferring key points from a pattern.

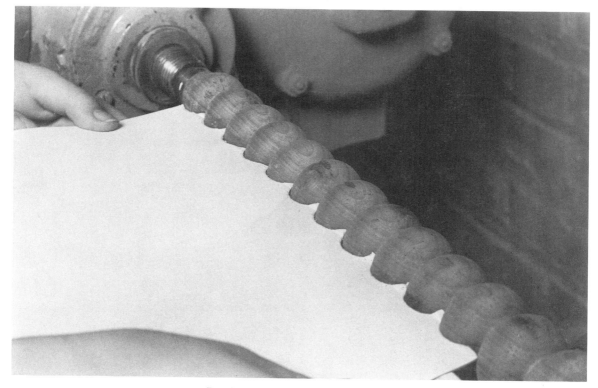

Fig. 24-18. Checking the fit of a template.

If the bottom of the finished turning is to be exposed, first glue a piece of wood to the bottom of the stock. Before gluing the two pieces together, insert a glossy magazine cover into the glue joint. This will allow the extra piece glued to the bottom to be easily removed. Once the turning is completed, use a wide wood chisel to drive between the two pieces. The glue joint will split.

Screw the faceplate onto the headstock. Use the faceplate wrench to tighten the faceplate. The spindle lock will secure the spindle while the faceplate is tightened. To give the stock additional support, adjust the tailstock so the dead center enters the face of the turning.

Start the lathe at the slowest available speed. Use a roundnose chisel to scrape the turning stock into a round cylinder. Stop the lathe often and move the tool rest in towards the stock. With a pair of outside calipers and a parting chisel, make several grooves to 1/16 inch (2 mm) larger than the final desired diameter. Use the roundnose

chisel or skew to connect the grooves made by the parting chisel (Fig. 24-20). Cut a template to the shape of the outside turning to check when the final shape has been reached. Increase the turning speed as in Table 24-1. Make the final finish cuts with either a very sharp roundnose or skew.

After the outside is completed, bore a hole in the center of the face to the depth of the finish turning. This serves as a guide so you know when the proper depth has been reached. Adjust the tool rest so that it is now parallel to the face of the turning. The only safe place to cut is on the front half of the stock. The work must rotate down upon the chisel (Fig. 24-21). Placing it on the back half will cause the chisel to be thrown. Use a roundnose chisel to scrape away the inside. If the faceplate screws were driven into the bowl itself, be careful that you do not cut deep enough to hit them. It is safer to glue a piece on the bottom of the bowl and drive the screws into it.

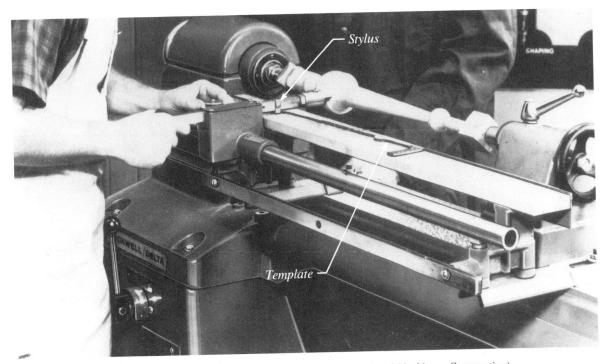

Fig. 24-19. Using a duplicator (Courtesy Delta International Machinery Corporation).

As the inside of the turning takes shape, stop and slant the tool rest more to the inside. Keep the tool rest as close as possible to the turning. If too much space is developed between the tool rest and stock, the chisel will be difficult to control.

Once the shape is formed, remove the tool rest and tool post. Sand the turning.

BORING HOLES ON THE LATHE

Holes can be bored using the lathe by first installing a drill chuck. For boring holes in the face of the faceplate turning, mount the bit and chuck in the tailstock. For spindles, the drill chuck and bit is placed in the headstock. Support the spindle with one hand while the rotating bit enters the stock.

Set the turning speed to the slowest speed. Slowly turn the tailstock handwheel to bring the stock and bit together. Continue to turn the handwheel until the desired depth is reached. Back the bit out often to prevent it from grabbing.

SANDING LATHE TURNINGS

Once the turning has been made 1/16 inch (2 mm) over the finished diameter, it should be sanded. To prevent the fingers from being pinched, remove the tool rest. Set the turning speed as given in Table 24-1.

Start sanding with an old 100-grit sanding belt that has been torn into a strip. Hold the abrasive strip on the top side of the turning, gripping the strip only by the fingertips. Wrapping the abrasive around your hands could cause a serious accident.

Continually move the abrasive strip from side to side. Holding it in one spot will cause a low spot. Be careful not to sand too long because too much material will be removed. Continue to sand with 100-grit abrasive until all tool marks and torn grain are removed.

To remove the circular sanding scratches put in the wood by the coarse abrasive, change to 120-grit. After the surface is smooth and glossy, progress to 150-grit abrasive paper. Turn off the power and, while the turning is still mounted on the lathe, sand with 180-grit abrasive paper. Sand with the grain to remove any circular scratches.

Fig. 24-20. Turning the outside of a bowl. Note: The guard has been removed so the cut can be seen better. Always use a guard.

Fig. 24-21. Turning the inside of a bowl. Note: The guard has been removed so the cut can be seen better. Always use a guard.

Chapter 25

Shapers

Shapers can produce molding and jointery cuts. A decorative edge around a tabletop, for example, can be made with this machine. The shaper can also make smooth rabbets and small grooves.

PARTS

The major parts of the shaper include the spindle, fence, table, and base (Fig. 25-1). The *spindle* is a threaded shaft where the cutter is mounted. Although several spindle sizes are available, ½ inch (13 mm) is the most common for smaller machines. A *fence* is bolted to the table top and is used to guide the stock. Stock can also be guided with a miter gauge that fits into a groove in the table. Mounted inside the base is the motor and height adjustment mechanism. The cutter mounted on the spindle can be raised and lowered with the *height adjustment handwheel*. On most shapers the direction of the motor can be reversed, which allows stock to be fed from either direction.

SHAPER CUTTERS

Shaper cutters are available in many different styles and sizes (Fig. 25-2). Most cutters have three *wings*, or cutting edges. For general cutting, the cutters are made of high-speed or carbon steel. Shaping hard-to-cut materials such as particleboard requires carbide-tipped cutters.

INSTALLING THE SHAPER CUTTER

Disconnect the power and remove the fence. Select the cutter or combination of several cutters that will make the desired shape. Hold the cutter against the end of the board and trace around it (Fig. 25-3).

First mount a collar on the spindle (Fig. 25-4). Slip the cutter on the spindle next, with the largest part of the

---

SAFETY

☐ Unplug the power cord before working around the cutter.
☐ Use only sharp cutters.
☐ Hands must come no closer than 6 inches (152 mm) to the cutter.
☐ Use the recommended featherboards, pushstick, and guards.
☐ Feed the material opposite the direction the cutter rotates.
☐ Shape from the bottom surface of the board.
☐ Stock must have at least 10 inches (254 mm) in contact with the fence.
☐ Use several light cuts if the pattern is large.

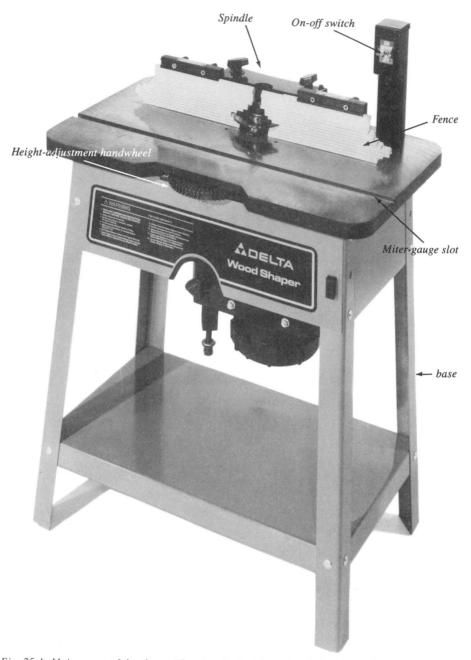

Fig. 25-1. Major parts of the shaper (Courtesy Delta International Machinery Corporation).

cutter towards the bottom. With the cutter mounted in this position, the stock can be rerun if the material accidentally lifts off the table. It is also safer than having the cutter on top of the board. Place another collar on top of the cutter. To keep the spindle nut from turning loose, place a keyed washer on top of the collar. Hand tighten the spindle nut. Secure the spindle with the spindle wrench and tighten the spindle nut.

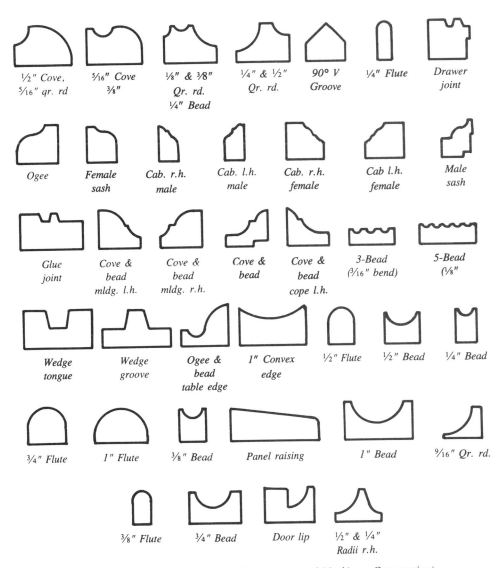

½″ Cove, 5/16″ qr. rd   5/16″ Cove 3/8″   1/8″ & 3/8″ Qr. rd. ¼″ Bead   ¼″ & ½″ Qr. rd.   90° V Groove   ¼″ Flute   Drawer joint

Ogee   Female sash   Cab. r.h. male   Cab. l.h. male   Cab. r.h. female   Cab l.h. female   Male sash

Glue joint   Cove & bead mldg. l.h.   Cove & bead mldg. r.h.   Cove & bead   Cove & bead cope l.h.   3-Bead (3/16″ bend)   5-Bead (1/8″

Wedge tongue   Wedge groove   Ogee & bead table edge   1″ Convex edge   ½″ Flute   ½″ Bead   ¼″ Bead

¾″ Flute   1″ Flute   3/8″ Bead   Panel raising   1″ Bead   9/16″ Qr. rd.

3/8″ Flute   ¾″ Bead   Door lip   ½″ & ¼″ Radii r.h.

Fig. 25-2. Shaper cutters (Courtesy Delta International Machinery Corporation).

ROTATION OF CUTTER

Once the cutter has been mounted, the rotation of the cutter can be determined. Most spindles can be rotated from either direction. Always rotate the cutter so that the sharp edge of each wing will cut the wood first (Fig. 25-5). The beveled edge should trail.

Always feed against the rotation of the cutter. If the cutter is rotated clockwise, feed the stock from left to right. A cutter that turns counterclockwise must be fed from right to left.

SHAPING A STRAIGHT EDGE

To shape a straight edge, first install the cutter. Next set the height of the cutter by turning the height adjustment handwheel. Place the stock on the table and raise or lower the spindle until the outline of the cutter is at the

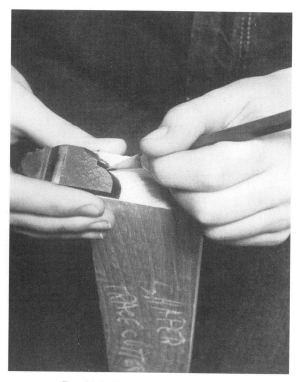

Fig. 25-3. Tracing around the cutter.

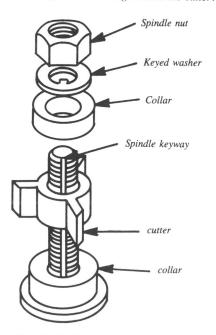

Fig. 25-4. Correct setup for the shaper cutter.

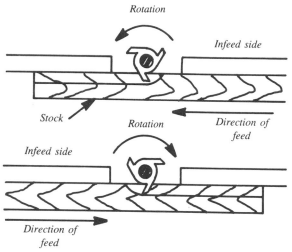

Fig. 25-5. The infeed side of the fence will depend upon the direction of rotation for the cutter.

same level as the pattern previously drawn on the end of the board.

Install the fence using the fence studs, which are screwed into the table (Fig. 25-6). Based on the information given in the previous section, determine which side of the fence will be the infeed side. With the stock placed against this infeed side of the fence, move the fence in or out until the cutter is again aligned with the marked pattern. Tighten the fence stud on the infeed side. If only part of the edge is to be shaped, use a straight edge to align the outfeed side of the fence with the infeed side. Tighten the fence stud on the outfeed side.

To shape the entire edge, turn on the power and shape the first 2 to 3 inches (51 to 76 mm). Shut off the power and hold the board completely still until the cutter has stopped turning. Turn the depth-adjustment knob to bring the outfeed side of the fence up to support the newly shaped edge (Fig. 25-7). Tighten the fence stud.

Never shape any board unless featherboards are properly installed. Place the stock against the fence. With C clamps, secure a featherboard on each side of the fence (Figure 25-8). Bring the featherboards as close together as possible to cover the space between the fence halves. These featherboards will not only help hold the board down, but also aid in guarding the cutter. Turn the cutter by hand to check that it does not strike the featherboard.

Turn on the power and make sure the rotation of the

Fig. 25-6. Raise or lower the spindle until the cutter is aligned with layout.

cutter is correct. Feed the board forward, going against the rotation of the cutter. Use a pushstick to keep the board moving and against the fence. Hands must not come any closer than 6 inches (152 mm) to the cutter. Shape the end grain first, before the edges. Any chipping caused by machining across the end grain will then be removed when the edges are shaped.

SHAPING CURVED EDGES

If a curved edge is to be shaped install a contact collar on top of the cutter (Figure 25-9). This contact collar is either a solid steel or ball bearing collar. The curved stock is guided against this collar and no fence is used.

The distance from the tip of the cutter to the edge of contact collar equals the depth of cut. The larger the diameter of the contact collar, the lighter the cut. If a large

amount of material is to be removed, first use a bandsaw to cut to rough shape and then shape the piece with a large-diameter contact collar. Change to the desired size collar to make the final pass.

A *starting pin* is a steel pin in the table that acts as a pivot point against which to position the stock (Fig. 25-10). Install a starting pin on the infeed side of the cutter. Place the starting pin on the right side if the cutter is rotating counterclockwise. To protect the operator from the cutter, always use either a ring guard or plastic shield.

Prepare the stock, making sure the edge is perfectly smooth. Because the edge is guided against the contact collar, any low or high spots will be reflected in the shaped edge.

Turn on the power and position the stock against the starting pin. Pivot the stock slowly into the cutter. The

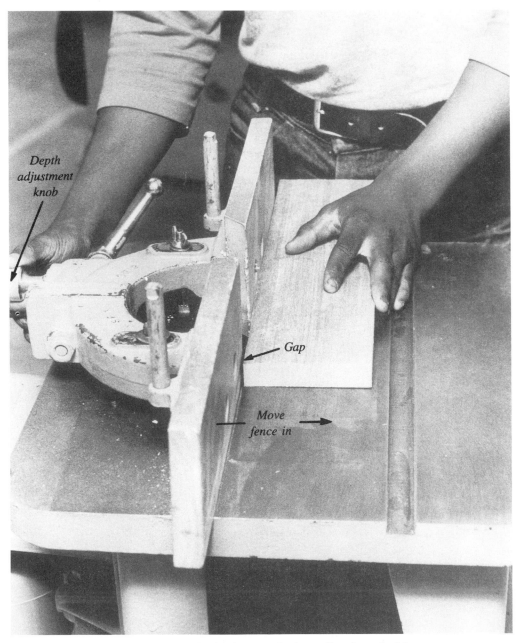

Depth
adjustment
knob

Gap

Move
fence in

Fig. 25-7. Turn the depth adjustment knob to adjust the outfeed fence.

cutter must first come in contact with the stock 1 inch (25 mm) from the end. It cannot touch a corner first. If it does, it will cause kickback.

Once the cut is begun, move the stock away from the starting pin. Maintain just enough pressure against the stock to keep it next to the contact collar. Too much pressure will cause the stock to wear and burn. Keep hands *at least* 6 inches (152 mm) from the cutter (Fig. 25-11).

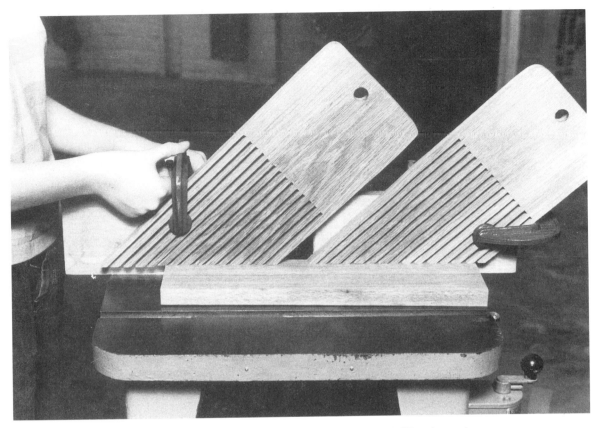

Fig. 25-8. Featherboards serve as a guard and aid in holding the stock.

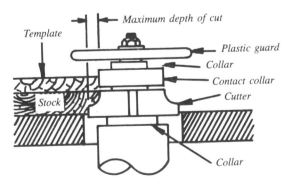

Fig. 25-9. Proper setup for shaping a curve.

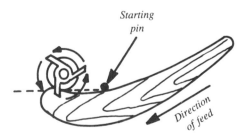

Fig. 25-10. The starting pin serves as a pivot point for shaping curves.

Fig. 25-11. Shaping a curve.

Chapter 26

Stationary Sanding Machines

Stationary sanding machines remove material with abrasives instead of metal cutters. These machines sand wood quickly and save much hand sanding.

Several types of stationary sanding machines are available. These include the stationary belt sander, disc sander, and spindle sander. Each serve special functions but are designed to sand a variety of shapes.

STATIONARY BELT SANDER

The stationary belt sander has an abrasive belt that is run between a top and bottom pulley (Fig. 26-1). On most of these sanders, the belt is 6 inches (152 mm) wide. The *platen*, positioned directly behind the belt, supports the abrasive belt.

The stationary belt sander has a tiltable table. To sand miters and other angles, the table can be tilted up to a 45-degree angle. The table contains a groove for the miter gauge.

To use the sander, first decide where the belt is to be positioned. It can be placed in the horizontal, vertical, or angle position. The horizontal position is used for sanding flat surfaces and curves (Fig. 26-2). In the vertical position, outside or *convex* curves and straight edges can be sanded. To sand inside or *concave* curves, remove the top guard to expose the pulley (Fig. 26-3). Angles are sanded by tilting the belt (Fig. 26-4).

Once the sander table has been positioned, turn on the power. Check that the material is large enough to keep the fingers at least 2 inches (51 mm) from the belt. If not, build a holding fixture to secure the stock. Take light passes and keep the board moving to prevent burning. Replace the belt whenever it becomes torn, clogged, or burned.

STATIONARY DISC SANDER

The stationary disc sander has a large metal disc covered with abrasive (Fig. 26-5). This sander is ideal for sanding convex curves. The size of the sander is determined by the diameter of the disc. Most disc sanders have a 12-inch (305 mm) disc. A tiltable table is mounted in front of the disc to support the stock. It contains a groove for guiding the miter gauge.

Because the disc sander removes material rapidly, first mark a line to locate the finished edge. Do not sand

---

SAFETY

☐ Unplug the power cord when changing the abrasive.
☐ If the material cannot be safely held in your hands, use a clamp or holding fixture to hold the board.
☐ Replace the abrasive when it becomes worn or torn.
☐ Use light pressure to feed the board into the abrasive.
☐ Wear a face shield and respirator.

Top guard

Tracking
knob

Belt

Table

Angle
lever

Miter gauge
groove

Base

Fig. 26-1. Major parts of the stationary belt sander (Courtesy Delta International Machinery Corporation).

past the layout line (Fig. 26-6). Only sand on the downhill side of the disc. Place stock against the rotating disc and keep it moving, using light pressure. If a great deal of material needs to be removed, cut the material before starting to sand. This will prevent burning of the abrasive. The miter gauge will be a helpful guide when sanding angles or end grain.

Once the abrasive disc becomes worn it needs to be replaced. Pull the old abrasive off. Recoat the metal disc with a special stick adhesive. Stick the new abrasive on the metal surface and firmly press.

SPINDLE SANDER

The spindle sander has a rubber spindle covered by an abrasive sleeve. It has a tiltable table, base, and sanding spindle (Fig. 26-7). This sander is primarily designed for sanding convex curves. Sleeves and spindles are available in various diameters.

To use the sander, select the desired spindle. Pick the size of spindle that comes closest to matching the diameter of the curve. If the sleeve needs to be changed, remove the nut on top of the spindle. Slide the old sleeve off and the new sleeve on. Tighten the nut.

To operate the spindle sander, turn on the power. The spindle will revolve and might move up and down. The up-and-down motion will make the abrasive last longer. Place the stock on the table and bring it in contact with the rotating spindle. Move the stock from right to left (Fig. 26-8). Apply only light pressure. Do not sand past the layout lines. If a spindle sander is not available, a drill press with a sanding drum can perform the same sanding job.

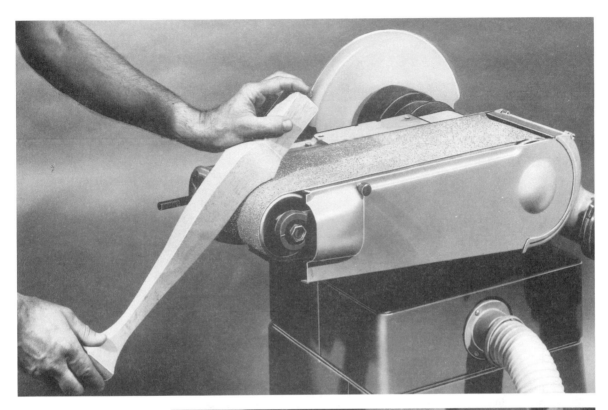

Fig. 26-2. (top) Sanding in the
horizontal position (Courtesy
Delta International Machinery
Corporation).

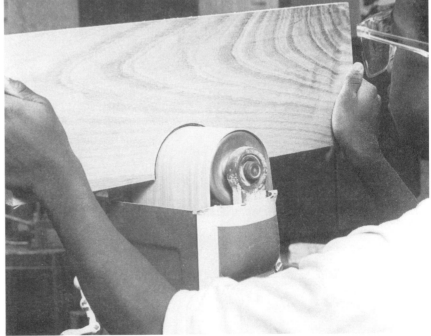

Fig. 26-3. (bottom) Sanding in
the vertical position.

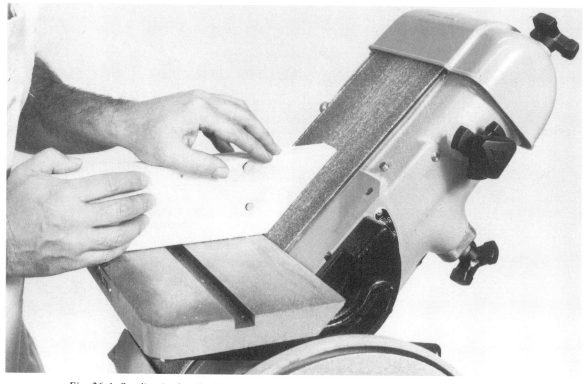

Fig. 26-4. Sanding in the tilted position (Courtesy Delta International Machinery Corporation).

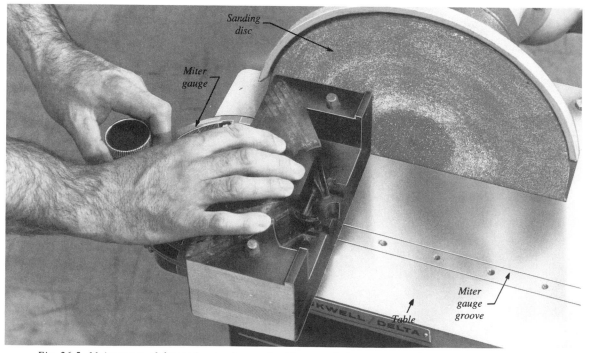

Fig. 26-5. Major parts of the stationary disc sander (Courtesy Delta International Machinery Corporation).

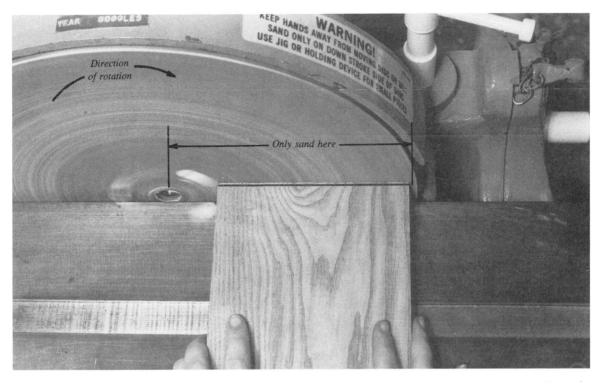

Fig. 26-6. (above) Sand to a layout line only on the downhill side of the disc.

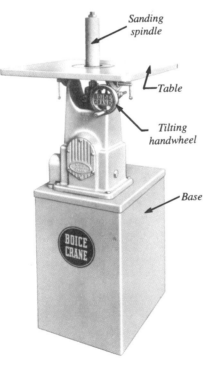

Fig. 26-7. (left) Major parts of a spindle sander (Courtesy Boise Craine).

Fig. 26-8. Sanding on a spindle sander.

Chapter 27

Preparing the Surface

Preparing the surface is one of the most important steps in the finishing process. Without proper scraping and sanding, even the best constructed piece of furniture will have a poor appearance.

Proper surface preparation requires time, effort, patience, and the proper sanding techniques, but will add much to the finished piece.

SCRAPING

Once the boards have been planed to the desired thickness, use a cabinet scraper. The *cabinet scraper* removes torn or unusual grain. (Refer to chapter 5.) Frequently check the surface with a framing square to see that no low spots develop.

If the surface is free from marks, a hand scraper is all that is needed to remove minor defects. It takes off less material with each pass than the cabinet scraper. The hand scraper is less likely to make an uneven surface. Continue using the hand scraper until all defects have been removed and the surface is level.

SANDING

After the surface is scraped, use either a pad sander or a hand sanding block. Power sanders will remove material more quickly, but might leave cross scratches on the surface. (Refer to chapter 16.)

ABRASIVES

Coated abrasives, better known as sandpaper, are used for many different jobs. Coarse or rough abrasives can remove large amounts of material. Fine abrasives smooth material more slowly and leave the surface ready for finishing.

Several different natural and man-made materials are used to make coated abrasives. *Flint* is a natural, whitish-colored abrasive and the least expensive. It is used to sand paint and for other jobs where the sandpaper does not need to last. *Garnet* is another natural abrasive, reddish in color. It is the best and most common abrasive for hand sanding.

Synthetic or man-made abrasives are made in a furnace. They include aluminum oxide and silicon carbide. *Aluminum oxide* is a brown substance. It is the abrasive used most often for woods, because it is heat resistant and does not break down when used with power sanders. *Silicon carbide* is black and used primarily for sanding between coats of finish.

Backing Materials

Coated abrasives are glued to some type of backing material, usually paper, cloth, or synthetic materials. All three come in several weights or thicknesses. The lightest weight of paper is A, and paper is available in weights A through D. The C weight is called *cabinet paper*, and should be used for hand sanding and for portable pad sanders.

Cloth backing lasts much longer than paper but is more expensive. It is used primarily for sanding machines. Cloth comes in either J or X weights. J is the lightest weight and most commonly used. Synthetic materials are the newest form of backing and are also used for machine sanding. They are less expensive than cloth but just as strong.

Grits

Abrasives come in various sizes or *grits*. The most common method of rating the size of the abrasive particles is with the number system (Table 27-1). The smaller the number, the larger the diameter of each abrasive particle. For example, 60-grit has larger particles than 120-grit. Large particles make deep scratches but remove material quickly. Small particles give a fine finish.

Two other rating systems are also sometimes used. The aught system includes abrasives from very fine—12/0—to very coarse—4½. Flint is sized by the word system: from "very fine" to "very coarse."

Selecting Coated Abrasives

A number of things must be taken into consideration when selecting abrasives. Most of the necessary information can be found on the back of the abrasives (Fig. 27-1). Abrasives are available in many different forms. Although 9-x-11-inch sheets are the most common, sanding machines might require belts, discs, or sleeves (Fig. 27-2).

Select the grit size that best suits the task. A medium grit such as 80 is a recommended grit for initial rough sanding. A board might be finish sanded with 180-grit.

Abrasive particles are spaced closer together or farther apart. When most of the backing is covered with abrasive, it is labeled "close coat." This kind of backing is recommended for sanding hardwoods. Close coat will load or clog, however, if used to sand resinous woods such as pine. When only 50 to 70 percent of the backing is covered it is called "open coat." Open coat should be used for softwoods and where clogging can be a problem (Fig. 27-3).

Select the backing material next. Most hand sanding and pad sanders use a paper backing. C-weight will wear

	SILICON CARBIDE	ALUMINUM OXIDE	GARNET	FLINT
Very Fine	600	600-12/0	—	—
(Sanding	500	500-11/0	—	—
between	400	400-10/0	—	—
coats of	360	—	—	—
finishing	320	320-9/0	—	—
or	280	280-8/0	280-8/0	—
polishing)	240	240-7/0	240-7/0	—
	220	220-6/0	220-6/0	Very Fine
Fine	180	180-5/0	180-5/0	—
(Final	150	150-4/0	150-4/0	—
sanding)	120	120-3/0	120-3/0	Fine
Medium	100	100-2/0	100-2/0	—
(Rough	80	80-1/0	80-1/0	Medium
sanding)	60	60-1/2	60-1/2	—
Coarse	50	50-1	50-1	Coarse
(Abrasive	40	40-1½	40-1½	—
planing)				
Very	36	36-2	36-2	Very
Coarse				Coarse
(Grinding	30	30-2½	30-2½	—
or rough	24	24-3	24-3	—
shaping)	20	20-3½	20-3½	—
	16	16-4	—	—
	12	12-4½	—	—

Table 27-1. Abrasive Grit Sizes.

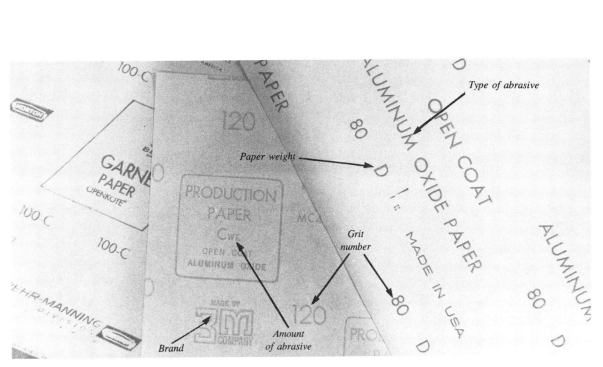

Fig. 27-1. Refer to the back of the abrasive paper for detailed information.

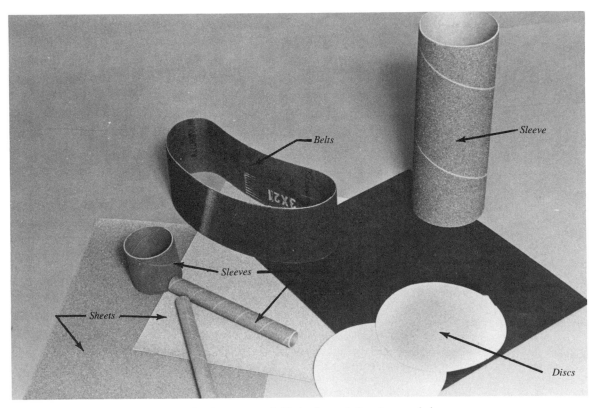

Fig. 27-2. Abrasives are available in sheets, belts, discs, and sleeves.

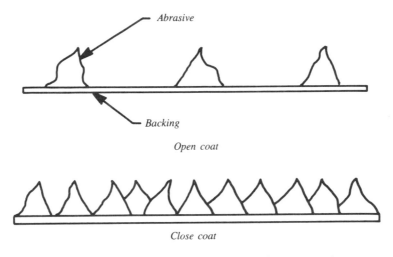

Open coat

Close coat

Fig. 27-3. Open coat abrasives have fewer abrasive particles
than close coat.

well in most applications. Cloth backing is recommended
for belt sanders and in other applications where there will
be much stress.

Preparing the Abrasive Paper

Abrasive paper is sold in a standard sheet size. The
sheets must therefore be cut to fit either a hand sanding
block or a power sander.

Before cutting the paper, *flex* or bend it over a sharp
edge (Fig. 27-4). The edge of a metal machine top works
well. Pull the paper back and forth several times. Flexing
will keep the particles from falling off and will allow the
abrasive paper to fit into corners and sand other unusual
shapes.

After flexing the abrasive paper, cut to size. Fold
the paper to the desired size with the abrasive on the inside. Use a knife and straightedge to cut from the back
side of the abrasive backing (Fig. 27-5).

Most sanding blocks require one-fourth of a sheet.
Pad sanders vary according to the size of pad. Sanders
require either one-fourth or one-third of a sheet.

Never use just your hand to hold the abrasive paper
when sanding flat surfaces. This will sand away the
softer part of the wood, giving a wavy surface.

Always sand with the grain. Move the abrasive in a
straight line, in the same direction the growth rings
point. Sanding across the grain will produce scratches
running at right angles to the grain. These scratches will
be very noticeable when the finish is applied. For end
grain, sand across the width of the board.

Start sanding with 100-grit abrasive paper. Sand
evenly over the entire surface. If you only sand the
defects, low spots will form. After all of the deep mill
marks or scraper and planer marks have been sanded
away, sand with 120-grit abrasive paper. Use the 120-
grit to remove the deep sanding scratches made by the
first 100-grit paper. Progress next to 150-grit, then finish
and with 180-grit. Do not skip one of the grits, because
sanding scratches will be difficult to remove.

SANDING IRREGULAR SURFACES

Surfaces that are not flat require special attention. You
will need to use a sanding block that matches the shape
you are sanding. Short pieces of dowel rods, tin cans,
and hand tools can serve as sanding blocks. Select a
shape that matches the diameter or shape of the piece
to be sanded. Wrap abrasive paper around the sanding
block and sand with the grain (Fig. 27-6).

For very fine details the abrasive paper can serve as
its own sanding block. Fold the paper several times,
making a rigid edge. This works well on inside corners
of moldings (Fig. 27-7). Abrasive cloth cut into narrow
strips works for sanding inside grooves and other small
radiuses. Pull the cloth back and forth as if it were a shoe
shine cloth (Fig. 27-8).

INSPECTING THE SURFACE

After rough sanding the piece with 100-grit abrasive paper, inspect the entire project under a strong light. A

Fig. 27-4. *Flexing a piece of abrasive paper.*

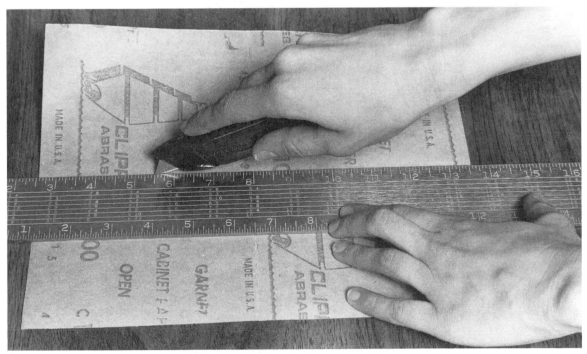

Fig. 27-5. *Cutting abrasive paper to size.*

Fig. 27-6. Use a dowel for sanding inside curves.

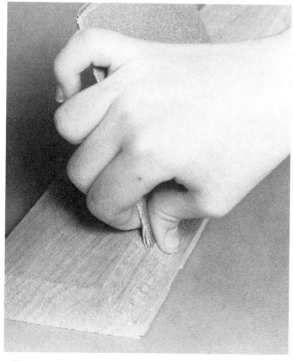

Fig. 27-7. A folded piece of abrasive paper sands detailed moldings.

Fig. 27-8. Sand a turning by pulling the abrasive cloth back and forth.

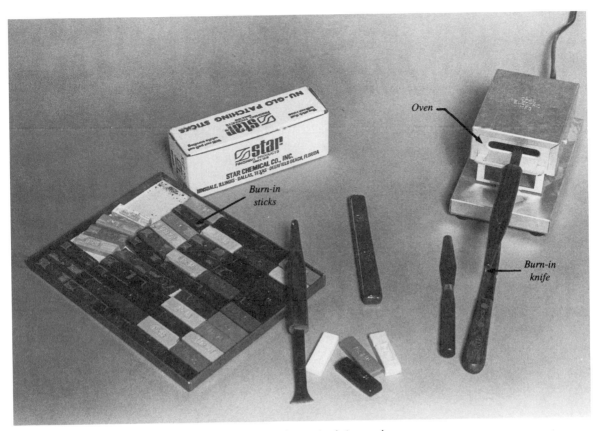

Fig. 27-9. Burn-in sticks require knives and an oven.

handheld spotlight is ideal. Note dents, cracks, or digs in the wood; these will usually need to be repaired.

Make certain all glue has been scraped and sanded away. Any adhesive left on the surface will prevent stain or finish to penetrate. Glue spots will appear as very noticeable light areas in the finished piece.

REMOVING DENTS

Inspect the dent carefully and see if the wood fibers have actually been broken, or if they are still attached. If the fibers are attached, the dent can often be raised. If the dent contains broken fibers, however, it will have to be filled with some type of wood filler.

To raise a dent, first put a moist clean rag directly over the top of the dent. Place a heated clothes iron or soldering iron on the rag. Keep the iron moving at all times. Steam will be produced and cause the wood fibers to swell. Remove the rag occasionally and inspect the

dent. If it requires additional raising, remoisten the rag and repeat the process. After steaming, allow the area to dry overnight before sanding.

WOOD FILLERS

These fillers are used for defects that cannot be raised by steaming. There are several fillers to select from. Do not confuse this type of filler with the thinner-bodied paste wood fillers that are specifically used for filling the open pores in ring porous woods.

Wood Dough

The most common method of filling a defect is with wood dough. This material is usually sold in small containers. It is premixed to match the color of the wood being filled. Wood dough, for example, is available in colors to match pine, cherry, walnut, and many other common woods.

To use wood dough, first clean the defect with a brush and pressurized air. With a putty knife, work a small amount into the opening in the wood. Any time filler is not being removed from the can, keep the lid on the container closed because the wood dough dries out rapidly. The more filler worked into the defect, the better it will stick. Leave the wood dough slightly mounded above the surface, because as the filler dries, it will shrink. Do not smear the wood dough over any area except the defect. If the defect is large, use several applications of filler instead of filling the dent all at once. Allow the wood dough to dry at least 12 hours. With a sanding block, sand the surface thoroughly. Do not leave any excess filler on the surface or in the surrounding wood. Excess filler will not accept stain and will call more attention to the defect.

Putty Sticks

Putty sticks are another method of filling small defects. They consist of a wax containing a pigment or color. The sticks are available in many more colors than wood dough. Two or more colors can be mixed to more closely match the finished piece.

To use this type of filler, first apply all of the finish. Work the putty stick into the recess by rubbing the stick back and forth. Take a soft cloth and wipe off any excess.

Burn-in Sticks

Burn-in sticks are a third method of filling defects. They require the most practice to apply. Most burn-in sticks are either a shellac base or a lacquer base. Use shellac sticks on resin varnishes and lacquer sticks on lacquer. Burn-in sticks are available in a wide variety of colors.

Select the stick or sticks that match the finished piece of wood. Use a burn-in knife that has been heated in an oven to melt the stick into the defect (Fig. 27-9). After the burn-in is cooled, sand the excess off with 280-grit abrasive paper and a sanding block.

Water Putty

Water putty is another type of wood filler. It comes as a light tan powder that is mixed with water. The mixture makes a thick paste. Although dry pigments can be added to match the wood, it is most often left natural and used on projects to be painted.

Apply the water putty using the same technique as used for wood dough. Because the mixture cannot be kept for any length of time, only mix a small amount at one time. If you have not made a sufficient amount, mix another small quantity. Throw away any that is left over. Do not place the extra mixture back into the water putty container.

Chapter 28

Methods of Applying Finishes

There are three primary methods of applying a finish. They include wiping, brushing and spraying. Each method has its advantages. Check the label on the finish cans for recommended methods of application.

WIPING

The simplest and least expensive method of applying a finish is wiping. The only equipment required is a soft, lint-free cloth. To wipe on a finish, fold the cloth into a pad approximately 4 to 6 inches square. Dip the pad into the finish and place it on your project. Using a circular motion, rub the finish into the wood. The more rubbing, the better the finish will penetrate. Some finishes, penetrating oils for example, should be left on the surface to soak in even more. Always use a clean cloth to wipe with the grain to remove the surplus finish before the finish has dried. To complete the task, properly dispose of the rags. Never leave the finish-soaked rags in your shop. They are highly flammable and could easily start a fire.

BRUSHING

Brushing a finish is one of the most popular methods of application. It is relatively fast and does not require expensive spray equipment. Using a brush, however, does require skill. Unless the proper brushing technique is uti-

lized, for example, brush marks will be left in the finish and leave a "washboard" appearance.

Brush handles are made of wood or plastic. The shape of the handle varies, so when choosing a brush, make sure it comfortably fits your hand. The bristles of the brush transfer the finish onto the surface. Ideally, the bristles should form a chisel edge. To form the chisel edge, longer bristles are located in the center and become shorter towards the outside. In the middle of the brush is the plug and ferrule. The plug holds the bristles in place. The metal ferrule is wrapped around the handle and connects the plug and handle (Fig. 28-1).

Selecting a Brush

There are many points to consider when selecting a brush, including type of brush, shape of handle, and width of the brush. Different brushes are designed for different jobs. Choosing the correct brush for the job is important to getting a good finish.

Start by selecting the correct type of bristle. Pure bristle brushes should be used for varnishes and oil base stains. They are made from animal hair. The very best pure bristles, but also the most expensive, are china boar bristles. These should not be used on water-based materials. Other bristles are made from synthetic materials; nylon and polyester are the most common. Brushes made of nylon bristles work well for water-based materials. Polyester bristles can be used for either oil-, water-, or

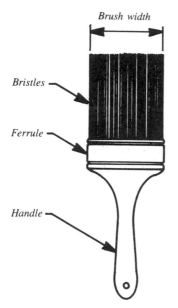

Brush width

Bristles

Ferrule

Handle

Fig. 28-1. Parts of a brush.

lacquer-based materials. Both the nylon and polyester bristles outwear pure bristle brushes.

A high-quality brush should have bristles with flagged ends (Fig. 28-2). These bristles will be split to hold more finish. The fine ends leave fewer brush marks.

Brushes are sized by the width of the bristles. Widths range from ½ inch to 8 inches (13 to 203 mm). Select a narrow brush to reach into small areas and to coat narrow pieces. To speed the finishing process, utilize a wide brush for large surfaces.

Brushing a Finish

After the surface is sanded, remove dust with a tack cloth. Mix the finish completely, then brush it onto the project. Dip the bristles of the brush into the finish, not more than one-third to one-half their length. Dipping the brush any deeper will cause the finish to soak into the plug and make the brush difficult to clean.

Lift the brush out of the finish and lightly draw it against the strike wire (Fig. 28-3). Turn the brush over and draw the opposite side past the wire. This will keep the brush from dripping.

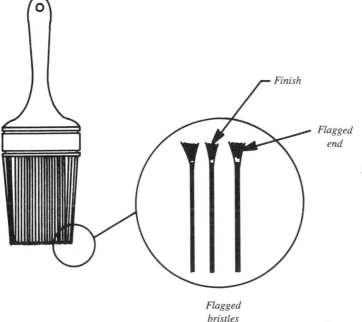

Finish

Flagged end

Flagged bristles

Fig. 28-2. Flagged bristles hold more finish.

Strike
wire

surface. Place the full brush on the dry surface and move the brush towards the wet area. Always draw the brush parallel to the outside edges or ends of the project.

Projects require a variety of brushing techniques. Start at the top and brush each piece as you work toward the bottom. Coat pieces that are horizontal. Cover the entire piece or section before moving onto the next. Apply finish to the inside of a project before moving to the outside surfaces. For inside corners, carefully place the brush in the corner and move the brush toward the center of the board. Although a thick coat is usually desirable, be careful not to develop runs. It is better to brush on another coat than to apply too much wet finish. Pieces that are round can be brushed using a circular pattern (Fig. 28-5).

Cleaning a Brush

After using a brush it must be properly cleaned. Failing to remove all the finish will shorten the life of the brush. As the finish dries in the brush it hardens, which causes the bristles to stick together and become rigid.

To clean a brush, remove as much finish as possible by drawing it back and forth over the strike wire. Repeat this several times.

The label on the finish can will give the correct solvent. Set up a three-container wash system (Fig. 28-6). Fill the first can with slightly used solvent, and the second and third with clean solvent. Work the brush back and forth in container number one. Move to the second can and bend the bristles back and forth on the bottom many times. Repeat the process in the third container. Properly dispose of the solvent in the first container. Save the solvent from the last container separately for future cleaning. Cover the cans tightly.

To complete the cleaning process, comb the bristles as they dry. A special brush comb will straighten the bristles. If the brush has pure bristles, work in a small amount of turpentine. Wrap the dry bristles in paper or the original packaging. Brushes are usually stored by hanging them by their handles.

Fig. 28-3. Draw the brush over the strike wire to remove excess finish from the brush.

Hold the brush loosely in your hands. Grip the ferrule with your fingers. Place the bristles on the project and apply light downward pressure. The bristles should slightly bend. Angle the brush approximately 60 degrees (Fig. 28-4). Move the brush back and forth across the

SPRAYING

Most woodworkers believe that spraying produces the best surface finish. Because the finishing material is sprayed rather than brushed or wiped, it produces a smoother coat. Spraying is also much faster. This method does, however, require specialized equipment to develop the pressurized air needed to spray the finishing

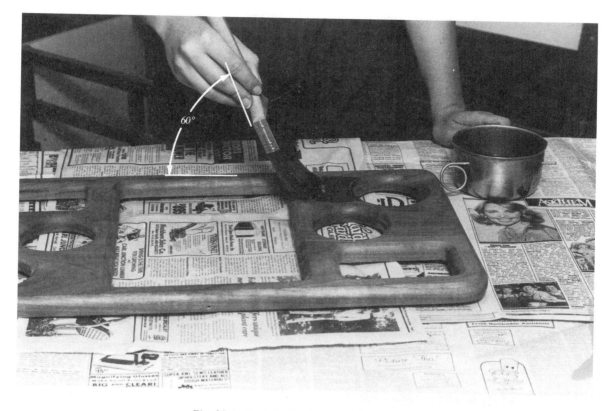

Fig. 28-4. Hold the brush at a 60-degree angle.

Equipment

The equipment necessary for spraying includes an air compressor, oil and water extractor, air hose, and spray gun. Each must be maintained following the instructions of the manufacturer.

An *air compressor* contains a pump, motor, and air storage tank (Fig. 28-7). The pump turned by the motor compresses the air and develops pressurized air, which is then stored in the air tank. Either a pipe or hose is utilized to move the pressurized air to the *oil and water extractor* (Fig. 28-8), which removes oil or water in the air that will harm the finish. It also regulates the amount of air pressure fed to the spray gun. An *air hose* connects the extractor to the spray gun.

The *spray gun* is used to atomize or break up the finish into a mist or tiny droplets (Fig. 28-9). Most schools and small shops use a *suction-fed* gun for spraying lacquers. The gun creates a vacuum that sucks the thinned finish up and out of the cup. At the very front of the gun is the air cap. With an external mix air cap the air and finish are combined outside the nozzle.

Another piece of equipment needed is a *spray booth*, a metal enclosure that confines the spray. It will contain a fan to exhaust the finish vapors away from the operator and give the proper amount of ventilation to keep the finishing area clean. A spray booth usually contains filters that should be cleaned or changed frequently.

A *respirator* is required whenever you are spraying. It will filter out any harmful vapor not removed by the exhaust fan. Be certain it has been approved for the type of finish that is being applied. Fit the respirator to your face so that no air will leak between your face and the mask.

material. This makes it much more expensive than other methods.

through the air cap. By screwing this valve in or out, the spray fan coming from the air cap can be adjusted.

The finish enters the gun through the fluid inlet. It is channeled to the air cap, past the fluid-adjusting valve. Screwing the fluid-adjusting valve in or out controls the amount of finish material passing through the gun.

To start air through the gun, pull the trigger slightly to the rear. Pulling the trigger all the way will start the finish. Letting go of the trigger will stop both the air and finish.

Spraying a Finish

Before the project is brought into the finishing area, clean it with pressurized air. After it is inside the finishing area and just before moving it into the spray booth, wipe it down with a clean tack cloth. Cover the spray table with paper and position the project in the spray booth.

Before the finish is sprayed, fill the cup with a thinner that is recommended for the finishing material. Adjust the air pressure at the oil and water extractor to between 40 to 50 pounds of pressure.

Attach the hose to the gun and aim the air cap toward a piece of paper taped to the wall of the spray booth (Fig. 28-11). Pull the trigger of the spray gun and observe the pattern of the spray. It should be 6 inches (152 mm) wide when the gun is held 6 to 8 inches (152 to 203 mm) from the wall (Fig. 28-12). Use the pattern adjusting valve to adjust the width of the spray pattern and the fluid control valve to regulate the amount of finish that comes out of the gun. Screwing the valve in will allow less finish to go through the gun.

Empty the solvent from the cup. Mix the finish and thinner following the recommendation on the label of the finish can. Refill the cup 1 inch (25 mm) from the top. If a small project is to be sprayed, use less finish.

Position the gun to the side of the project. Pull the trigger and immediately start moving the gun to the opposite corner of the project. At the end of each pass, move the gun off the project. Move the gun in a slow, smooth motion. If the gun is moved too slowly, runs will occur; too fast and it will not deposit the desired amount of material. Reposition the gun and again pull the trigger. The gun must move in a straight line. Keep the nozzle parallel with the work (Fig. 28-13).

Before the surface is coated, band each piece along its edges (Fig. 28-14). This is a separate pass that will deposit finish along the edges. Because the corners are sharp, finish does not stick to them as well as a flat sur-

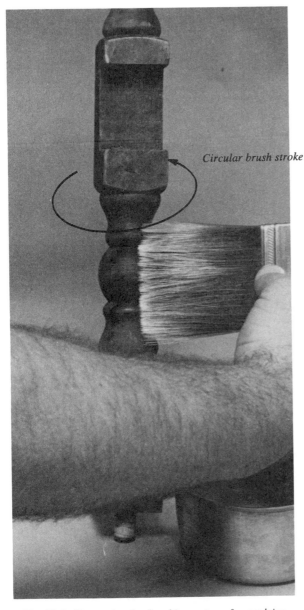

Circular brush stroke

Fig. 28-5. *Use a circular brushing pattern for applying finish to a round piece.*

Parts of a Spray Gun

There are several parts to a spray gun (Fig. 28-10). Air enters the guns at the bottom of the gun through the air inlet. It is channeled to the pattern-adjusting valve and

Fig. 28-6. Use a three-container wash system to clean a brush.

Fig. 28-7. An air compressor produces pressurized air for the spray gun (courtesy The Campbell Group).

Pressure
gauge

Pressure
regulator

Air
valve

Air
valve

Filter

Fig. 28-8. The oil and water extractor removes any liquid from the air and regulates the amount of air pressure (Courtesy Binks Manufacturing Company).

face. Banding allows extra finish to build up in the corners.

Overlap each pass of the gun by 50 percent, or half of the previous pass (Fig. 28-15). This will give the surface an adequate coat. Do not attempt to apply too much finish with one coat. Start by spraying the inside areas or those surfaces that are seen the least. Save the top and sides of the most visible surfaces for last.

Position the gun at a right angle, 6 to 8 inches (152 mm to 203 mm) from the top edge of the project. Moving the horns of the air cap will change the position of the spray gun. Turn the horns horizontally when moving the gun from side to side (Fig. 28-16). Rotate the horns vertically when spraying up and down (Fig. 28-17).

After the finish has dried, the surfaces should be sanded lightly with 320-grit wet-or-dry abrasive paper.

Do not sand near the corners. Spray another coat of finish. Repeat the spraying and sanding as many times as necessary to build up the desired thickness of finish. Usually one coat of sealer and three coats of lacquer will be sufficient. Rub the final coat down with pumice and rottenstone.

See Fig. 28-18 for tips on troubleshooting spraying problems.

Cleaning the Spray Gun

The spray gun must be cleaned immediately after each use. If even a small amount of finish is left in the spray gun passages, it will harden and result in severe spraying problems.

To clean the gun, empty all the finish from the cup.

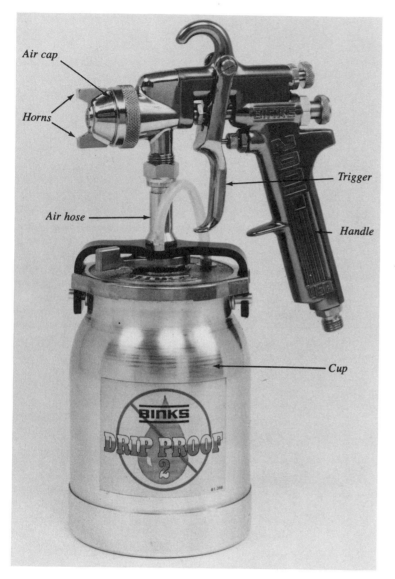

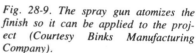

Fig. 28-9. The spray gun atomizes the finish so it can be applied to the project (Courtesy Binks Manufacturing Company).

Fill with about 1 inch of thinner. After putting the cup back on the gun, aim the air cap towards the exhaust fan. Pull the trigger and spray about ¼ cup of thinner through the gun. Move the horns of the air cap in several positions as the thinner is sprayed.

Use a rag soaked in thinner to clean the outside of the gun and cup. Leave the air cap in the bottom of the cup with a small amount of thinner. Leave the thinner in the cup until used again. Clean the vent hole with a toothpick. Store the gun in a fireproof cabinet.

Spraying with Aerosol Cans

Many finishes are available in aerosol cans. Although finishes packaged this way are expensive, it is a very easy method of applying a finish. Aerosol cans contain a

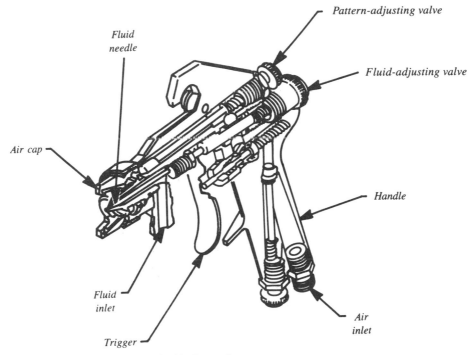

Fluid needle

Pattern-adjusting valve

Fluid-adjusting valve

Air cap

Handle

Fluid inlet

Air inlet

Trigger

Fig. 28-10. Parts of a spray gun.

Fig. 28-11. Check the pattern of the spray by aiming at a piece of paper.

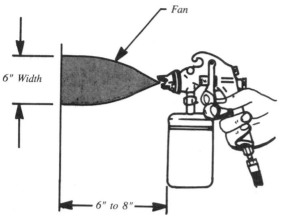

Fig. 28-12. *Adjust the width of the fan to 6 inches (152mm) when the gun is held at 6 to 8 inches from the surface.*

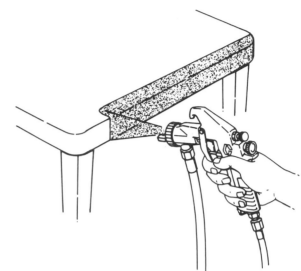

Fig. 28-14. *Band the project with a coat of finish along its edges (Courtesy Graco Inc.).*

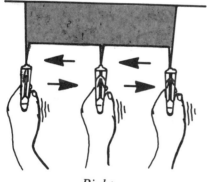

Right

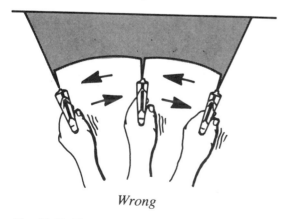

Wrong

Fig. 28-13. *The gun must be moved in a straight line across the surface (Courtesy Graco, Inc.).*

propellant gas, finish, and agitation balls (Fig. 28-19). The propellant keeps the finish under pressure and forces the finish out through the nozzle. Before spraying, always shake the can vigorously to make the agitation balls stir the finish.

To use aerosol finish, hold the can 10 inches (250 mm) away from the project. Push down on the spray nozzle and move across the project. Use back and forth passes keeping the can parallel with the work. Stop the flow of finish at the end of each stroke. Do not apply too much finish with one coat. A second or third coat can always be applied to achieve the desired coverage.

To clean the spray nozzle, turn the can upside down and push in on the spray nozzle until the finish no longer sprays out. Failure to clean the nozzle will cause the finish to harden in the passages and could ruin the nozzle.

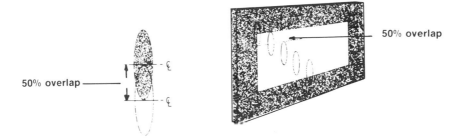

50% overlap

50% overlap

Fig. 28-15. Overlap each pass of the spray by 50 percent of the last pass (Courtesy Graco Inc.)

Horns horizontal

Gun movement

Fig. 28-16. When the gun is directed sideways the horns are to be in the horizontal position.

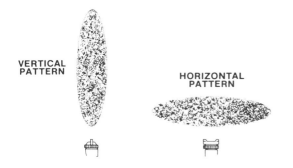

VERTICAL PATTERN

HORIZONTAL PATTERN

Fig. 28-17. Move the horns up and down for a vertical pattern (Courtesy Graco Inc.).

Problem: Heavy Pattern on Top or Bottom

When there are problems with the spraying pattern, it will generally involve two areas:
1. Air cap   **2.** Fluid tip

To determine if it is one or the other, first spray the problem pattern. Then invert the air cap and spray again. If the pattern inverts itself, the problem is with the air cap. If the pattern stays the same, the problem is usually with the fluid tip.

The following are some common spray pattern problems, and possibilities for correction.

HEAVY PATTERN ON TOP

HEAVY PATTERN ON BOTTOM

CAUSE
1. Horn holes plugged on air cap.
2. Fluid tip obstructed or damaged.

REMEDY
1. Clean off air cap.
2. Clean/replace the fluid tip and needle.

Problem: Heavy Left or Right Side Pattern

HEAVY LEFT SIDE PATTERN

HEAVY RIGHT SIDE PATTERN

Fig. 28-18. Troubleshooting guide for spraying (Courtesy Graco Inc.).

CAUSE
1. Opposite side horn holes plugged.
2. Dirt on the fluid tip.

REMEDY
1. Clean off the air cap.
2. Clean off the fluid tip.

Problem: Fluttering or Spitting Spray

CAUSE

1. Insufficient fluid in material container.
2. Dry or worn fluid needle packings, and loose packing nut permitting air to get into fluid passage (siphon feed).
3. Loose fluid tip or damaged tip seat and needle.
4. Dirt between fluid tip, taper seat and body.
5. Loose or cracked coupling at fluid inlet. (Siphon feed only.)
6. Loose fluid tube in the cup or tank.

REMEDY

1. Fill container.

2. Lubricate or replace packing, or tighten packing nut.

3. Tighten or replace tip and needle.
4. Clean.

5. Tighten or repair.

6. Tighten.

Problem: Split Bell-Shaped Pattern

Split Bell-Shaped Pattern

CAUSE

1. Insufficient paint.

2. Too much atomizing air pressure.

REMEDY

1. Turn fluid adjusting valve open (counter clockwise) or increase fluid pressure.
2. Reduce air pressure or correct by using air adjusting valve.

Fig. 28-18. (continued)

Problem: Heavy Center Pattern

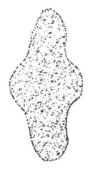

Heavy Center Pattern

CAUSE
1. Atomizing air is too low.
2. Material too thick.
3. Too much material.

REMEDY
1. Increase air pressure.
2. Reduce viscosity.
3. (a) Lower fluid flow at fluid adjusting valve.
   (b) Reduce fluid pressure.

Problem: Finish Has Streaks.

Streaked Pattern

CAUSE
1. Last coat applied too wet.

2. Too much air pressure.
3. Insufficient air.
4. Spray pattern not uniform.
5. Improper overlap technique.

REMEDY
1. Apply drier finish with multiple strokes.
2. Use least air pressure possible.
3. Increase air pressure.
4. Clean or replace air cap.
5. Use 50% overlap technique.

Problem: Material Leaking From the Gun.

CAUSE
1. Worn or damaged fluid needle, tip or spring.
2. Packing dry, loose or worn.
3. Incorrect needle.

REMEDY
1. Replace with matched, lapped tip and needle.
2. Lubricate, tighten or replace.
3. Replace with proper needle.

Fig. 28-18. (continued)

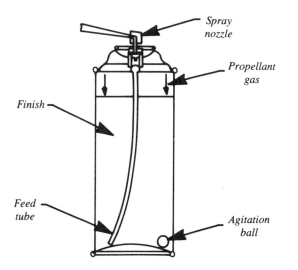

Spray
nozzle

Propellant
gas

Finish

Feed
tube

Agitation
ball

Fig. 28-19. An aerosol can contains several parts.

Chapter 29

Selecting and Applying Finishes

Selecting a finish is a job that is often overlooked and many woodworkers devote little attention and effort to finishing the project. This is unfortunate, because a beautifully made project can have its appearance ruined if the proper finish is not applied. Plan your project schedule so there is time to perform each needed finishing step. Finishing should bring out the natural beauty of the wood and add to the craftsmanship of your project.

Before applying a finish make sure you know which finish is to be applied and how the finish should be applied. There are a number of choices.

(*Note*: Finishing materials can be harmful to your skin and other parts of your body. They are also highly flammable and can easily start a fire. Follow the warnings on the finishing containers and the following safety rules.)

CONSIDERATIONS

When selecting the finish consider where the project is to be used and how you would like it to look. The environment in which the project is to be used might limit your selection of finishes. For example, outdoor items require finishes that withstand sun and rain. Also consider the

---

SAFETY

☐ Read and follow the instructions given on the finishing can label.

☐ Wear eye protection at all times.

☐ Wear long sleeves, rubber gloves, and a shop apron whenever there is danger of getting a finish on your skin.

☐ Wear an approved respirator when working with chemicals of finishing materials.

☐ Only work with finishes in a well-ventilated area.

☐ Mix thinners and solvents following the instructions from the manufacturer.

☐ Smoking, sparks, and other open flames are not allowed in the same room as finishing.

☐ Keep finishing containers tightly covered when not in use.

☐ Know where fire extinguishers are located and how to use them.

☐ Keep finish materials, particularly aerosol cans, away from any heat.

☐ Keep all finishing areas and equipment clean.

☐ Properly dispose of unused finish and solvent.

☐ Throw finish soaked rags and paper in an approved safety can.

amount of wear. For example, a coffee table top requires a finish that will resist moisture and abrasion.

The appearance of a finish is also important. Some finishes soak into the wood and do not develop a surface layer, and so leave the wood natural looking. Other finishes penetrate the wood but also build up on the surface, which gives the wood a deep luster.

Another consideration is whether a stain or paste wood filler will be used. Stain will change the color of the wood and is often used to make an inexpensive wood appear better looking. It also tends to bring out the grain. Filling the pores of the wood with a paste wood filler will produce a smooth base for the transparent or clear finish. Some woodworkers prefer not to fill the wood but leave it with more of a natural look.

Thousands of different finishes are available. Fortu-

Table 29-1. Characteristics of Finishing Materials.

FINISH MATERIAL	THINNER	RECOMMENDED USES	METHOD OF APPLICATIONS	MAJOR ADVANTAGES
Pigmenting Oil Stain	Mineral Spirits or Turpentine	Beginner Projects	Wipe or Brush	Easy to Apply
Penetrating Oil Stain	Mineral Spirits or Turpentine	Small Projects	Wipe or Brush	Readily available
Nongrain Raising Stain (N.G.R.)	Alcohol, glycol, acetone or toluol	Projects needing deep penetration	Spray-large project Wipe-small project	Clarity—does not cover the grain and fast drying
Water Stains	Water	Small projects with true colors	Spray-large project Wipe-small project	Fades the least
Paste Wood Filler	Mineral Spirits or Naptha	Ring porous woods	Brush	Levels surface by filling in pores
Waxes	None	Small inexpensive projects	Wipe	Inexpensive and fast
Danish Oil	Mineral Spirits	Natural looking projects	Wipe or brush	Does not require dust free finishing room
Resin Finish	Mineral Spirits	Small projects	Wipe	Wipe on finish that develops a surface layer
Shellac	Denatured Alcohol	Sealer	Brush or spray	Fast drying
Spar Varnish	Mineral Spirits	Outdoor projects	Brush or spray	Resistant to water and sunshine
Polishing Varnish	Mineral Spirits	Furniture and cabinets	Brush or spray	Polishes well; easy to purchase
Polyurethane	See label of finish can	Furniture and cabinets	Brush or spray	Durable and resistant to heat and water
Brushing Lacquer	Lacquer thinner	Small projects	Brush	Fast drying
Spraying Clear Lacquer	Lacquer thinner	Furniture and cabinets	Spray	Resist heat, alcohol and water and wide range of lusters
Colored Lacquer	None	Small project with opaque finish	Aerosol can	Convenient
Oil-Based Paint	Mineral Spirits	Heavy wear area	Brush or spray	Durable
Water-Based Paint	Water	Houses and trim	Brush or spray	Low odor and easy to clean-up

nately they can be grouped into a few families, which makes selection much easier. They each have specific characteristics you should consider (Table 29-1). First decide if you want to hide or expose the wood grain. If the grain is an important feature, you will want to use a *transparent* or clear finish. *Opaque* finishing hides the wood grain.

Several steps are required to complete the finish. Table 29-2 gives a few possible combinations. Make sure that each coat of finish is compatable with the other finishing materials; some finishes will soften other layers of finish. Carefully read the instructions before applying anything and allow the proper drying time.

STAINS

Wood is left its natural color with only a clear finish applied, or the color of the wood can be changed by applying a stain. A stain contains a pigment, or color, that will tint the wood.

Stains bring out the grain of the wood and can be used to make the wood a more uniform color. Sapwood, for example, may be lighter in color than heartwood. Staining will make these two types of woods similar in color. If an inexpensive wood such as willow is used to build a project, staining the willow a walnut color will make the project look like it was constructed from more expensive material. Stain can make two different woods appear the same. A pine faceframe, for example, is sometimes used on birch plywood cabinets, and the two will look like the same wood with the right stain.

There are three common types of stains: oil, non-grain raising, and water. Each stain has a different type of vehicle or solvent. The vehicle evaporates from the wood, leaving the color.

Oil Stains

There are two types of oil stains: pigmenting and penetrating. Pigmenting oil stain is the easiest of all stains to apply, and is best for beginning woodworkers. The stain is applied on the surface with a clean soft rag. It is then

---

Table 29-2. Recommended Steps for Applying Finishes.

Clear Finish with Surface Build-Up (Lacquer and Varnish)
1. Sand and clean
2. Stain-if additional color is desired
3. Fill pores with paste wood filler (open grain woods only)
4. Sealer or thinned coat of finish
5. Very lightly sand with 320 grit wet or dry abrasive paper and water
6. First coat of finish
7. Sand lightly with 320 grit wet or dry abrasive paper and water
8. Additional coats of finish—sand between each coat except last
9. Flow on last top coat
10. Rub the last coat with pumice stone and rubbing oil
11. Polish with rotten stone and rubbing oil

Oil Finish (Danish Oil)
1. Sand and clean
2. Stain—if additional color is desired or use pigmented oil stain
3. First coat of oil
4. Lightly sand if grain is raised
5. Additional coats of oil
6. Wax if desired

Painted Finish
1. Sand and clean
2. Primer—if oil based paint
3. Sand lightly to remove raised grain
4. Additional coats of paint
5. Flow on last coat of paint

wiped off after a period of time. Start by leaving the stain on the surface five minutes. The longer the stain lays on the surface, the darker the wood will become. It is better to wipe the stain off too soon than leave it on too long.

Pigmenting oil stains give an even color but somewhat hide the wood grain. Another major disadvantage to this type of stain is that it tends to fade when exposed to direct sunlight. If it is not covered with a coat of sealer the stain might bleed into the remaining finish.

The penetrating oil stain is more difficult to apply evenly. It should not be used by inexperienced woodworkers. Unless the proper technique is used different colored streaks will develop.

Non-Grain Raising Stains

Non-grain raising stains—or, as they are more commonly known, NGR stains—produce one of the most transparent colors. The grain of the wood shows through and is not covered over as with a pigmenting oil stain. The primary reason for this clarity is that the color is produced by a dye rather than a pigment. NGR stains do not raise the grain as much as water stain and they dry rapidly. Because they do streak easily, large projects should be sprayed with a spray gun. If wiped or brushed on large projects, the stain might produce light and dark areas. Small projects can be wiped if applied with the grain. Much practice is needed to apply these stains evenly.

Water Stains

Water stains produce the clearest colors of all stains. They fade the least of all stains in direct sunlight. They are more difficult than oil stains to evenly apply. When using these stains the grain of the wood must be raised, which makes the surface rough so it will require sanding. Water stains are sold in dry powdered form. Follow the instructions of the manufacturer when mixing the powder with warm water.

Before applying this type of stain, raise the grain of the wood by dampening the surface with a wet sponge. Allow it to dry and then sand off the raised wood fibers. Now apply the water stain—with a spray gun, ideally. Small projects can be stained using soft cloth and light strokes. Wipe with the grain to minimize streaking. After the water stain has dried, sand the surface lightly with

280-grit abrasive paper. Be careful not to sand through the stain at the corners.

Applying Stains

Always read the manufacturer's instructions on how to apply stain. The printed information on the container will give a step-by-step procedure. Be sure to accomplish the following:

1. Carefully sand and prepare the surface. Stains will not cover up scratches, but will cause the scratches to darken and to become even more noticeable.

2. Make sure there is enough stain to complete the entire project. If a small amount of stain remains in one container, mix it with a full can to achieve one uniform color.

3. Any stain must be thoroughly mixed with a stiring stick because the color in the stain will settle to the bottom of the can. Also, occasionally stop during the staining and restir the stain or the stained wood will become darker the closer you get to the bottom of the can.

4. Try the stain on a scrap piece of wood before starting to stain your project. The scrap should be of the same wood as your project. Allow it to completely dry before judging the color: Many stains change color as they dry.

5. Because the end grain exposes the ends of the wood cells, it tends to stain darker. To seal off the end grain and prevent this darkening, coat the end grain with a wash coat of the shellac or the same vehicle used in the stain. A wash coat of shellac can be made by diluting the shellac 60 percent with denatured alcohol.

6. Disassemble your project and remove any hardware. The stain will color the hinges, pulls, and drawer slides. Doors and other parts can then also be laid flat, which makes staining easier and prevents runs.

7. Wear rubber or plastic gloves to keep your hands free of stain.

8. Start staining on the back, drawer side, or an area that is not easily seen. This allows some experimentation and final checking of the color.

9. Always apply the stain by brushing, rubbing, spraying with the grain (Fig. 29-1). Going across the grain will create dark and light streaks.

10. Start at one edge and work to the opposite edge. Work no more than a 2-foot square area at one time. If a piece is larger than this, divide it into smaller sections. Complete one section before going on to the next. Runs will create dark streaks.

Fig. 29-1. Apply the stain by wiping with the grain.

PASTE WOOD FILLERS

Paste wood fillers are used to fill the small openings or pores in hardwoods. Filling the pores will give a flatter, smoother surface on which to apply the finish (Fig. 29-2). Some hardwoods have extra-large pores and are called *ring porous*. Examples of ring porous woods include oak, mahogany, and ash. These require a paste wood filler. Hardwoods with the smaller pores are called *diffuse porous*. Examples include willow, birch, and gum. These require a liquid filler. Table 29-3 lists woods that are filled with paste wood filler, liquid filler, or do not require a filler. For example, softwoods such as pine do not contain pores and are not filled.

Paste wood filler is primarily silex. *Silex* is a white powder made from finely ground rock. To make the thick paste, silex is mixed with a liquid vehicle. The vehicle can be one of several liquids, including boiled linseed oil, turpentine, or benzine. A japan drier is also added to aid in the drying of filler. In most cases, however, the paste wood filler is purchased with these ingredients premixed.

For ring porous woods—those containing large pores—the filler is usually used directly from the container. Woods having smaller pores will need to have the filler thinned. Use the liquid thinner specified on the paste wood filler can to thin or reduce the filler. Greatly thinned filler is often called *liquid filler*. Occasionally

Table 29-3. Wood Filler Requirements.		
WOODS REQUIRING PASTE WOOD FILLER	WOODS REQUIRING LIQUID FILLER	WOODS REQUIRING NO FILLER
Ash	Alder	Basswood
Elm	Birch	Beech
Mahogany	Cherry	Maple
Oak	Gum	Most Softwoods
Pecan Hickory	Poplar	
Walnut	Willow	

the filler will become too thick even for ring porous woods. Add small amounts of thinner and stir thoroughly until it is the desired thickness.

The natural color of paste wood filler is a light tan or cream color. This filler will work well for blonde woods such as ash and oak. For dark woods such as cherry and walnut, use a colored filler. Some manufacturers make precolored fillers specifically tinted for these woods. By adding oil stains or concentrated oil pigments, the natural filler can also be colored to match the wood. When mixing your own fillers, be certain the color is completely mixed. Always apply the filler on a scrap piece of the same type of wood to check the color. Allow it to dry before judging the color.

Barrier Coat

Barrier or "wash" coat is used after the stain has dried and before the filler is applied. It is designed to seal the stain and keep it from bleeding into the clear finish. It will also make it easier to rub the filler into the sealed surface and will prevent the filler from turning a gray color.

Always check the finish container for the correct barrier coat. Most often it will be either a shellac or lacquer sealer. Mix one part lacquer sealer to six parts lacquer thinner for lacquered finishes. Shellac is used primarily for varnishes. Mix it using one part shellac to seven parts denatured alcohol.

Applying Fillers

For best results follow these instructions when using paste wood filler:

1. Clean the surface completely with pressurized air and a tack cloth. If the surface is to be satined, apply the stain. Allow it to dry.

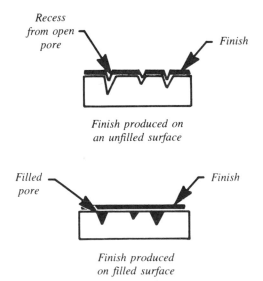

Recess from open pore — *Finish*

Finish produced on an unfilled surface

Filled pore — *Finish*

Finish produced on filled surface

Fig. 29-2. A filler will level the pores and give a flat surface for applying a finish.

2. Select the proper barrier coat and apply it by brushing or spraying. The barrier coat must be one that can be used with the clear finish. After the coat is dried, sand the surface lightly with 280-grit abrasive paper.

3. Decide which thickness of filler you need. The larger the pores, the thicker the paste wood filler should be. Completely stir the mixture, making certain the color is completely dispersed.

4. Using an old paint brush, work the filler into the wood. First apply the filler by brushing with the grain, then brush back across the grain several times. If the area to be filled is large, divide it into sections and complete a section at a time. A 24-×-24-inch (610-×-610 mm) area works well.

5. Use the palm of your hand to rub the filler further into the pores. Wear rubber gloves if you do not want your hands to become stained. Use circular motion to drive in the filler (Fig. 29-3). The more filler worked into the wood, the better.

6. Allow the filler to dry for about five minutes. The filler has dried enough when the glossy wet surface turns flat and dull. The filler should ball up under your finger when it is ready to be wiped off. Leaving the filler on too long will create smudges and discoloration.

7. Use burlap, sawdust, or a loosely woven cloth to wipe off the excess filler. Wipe across the grain (Fig. 29-4).

8. After the surface has been completely wiped, finish cleaning the project using a soft cloth. Rub with the grain to remove excess filler on the surface. Any filler left on the surface will turn hard and give a chalky appearance.

9. A sharpened dowel rod with a rag wrapped around the tip works well for removing filler from inside corners (Fig. 29-5).

10. Allow the filler to dry at least 24 hours. If the pores are not quite filled, repeat the process with a thinned filler.

WIPE-ON FINISHES

Wipe-on finishes are among the most popular materials for finishing a project. They have several advantages. Many woodworkers prefer them because they are easy to apply. Most wipe-on finishes are applied with a clean soft cloth. Although brushes or spray guns can be used, they are not necessary. The cloth can be thrown away in an approved fireproof container after use, which saves time and equipment.

Another important advantage is that wipe-on fin-

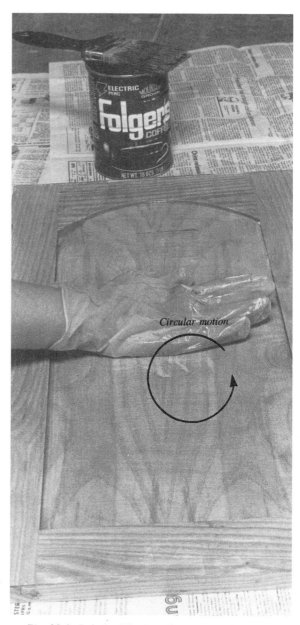

Fig. 29-3. Rub the filler into the pores of the wood.

ishes can be applied in the shop area and do not need a separate clean finishing room, as required for lacquers and varnishes. Although wipe-on finishes do not build up a thick layer on the surface, they do penetrate and preserve the wood.

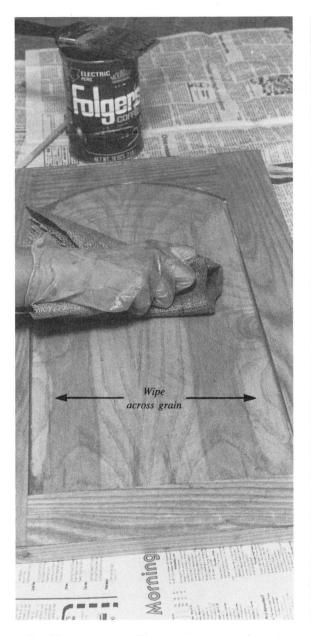

Fig. 29-4. Remove the filler by wiping across the grain.

Fig. 29-5. A rag wrapped around a sharpened dowel removes filler in corners.

Wipe-on finishes can be divided into three major types: waxes, oils, and resin finishes. Each type is made from different materials and will give a different appearance.

Waxes

The most common wax used for wood finishing is paste wax (Fig. 29-6). Most waxes are a blonde color and leave a natural appearance. Paste waxes that contain a

Fig. 29-6. Paste wax used for finishing wood.

pigment are also available. These will lightly tint the surface as they are applied. Pigmented waxes are used on darker colored woods. Most have a carnauba wax base. Any of these finishes can be applied on either stained or natural wood.

Waxes give the wood a soft shine. Although they do not build up on the surface, they will leave a natural hand-rubbed appearance. Two or three coats can be applied for extra protection. Wax is often used as the last step, applied over the top of varnishes, lacquers, and other top coats. This gives added protection and a higher shine, but will make it difficult to apply additional coats of finish.

Oils

Oil finishes give a project a contemporary appearance. Because they do not build up on the surface, the wood appears very natural. Although the finish hardens with age, the wood can be reoiled at anytime. If a scratch is made after the oil is applied, the surface can be lightly sanded and the area coated with oil. Oil resists water spotting, alcohol, and damage from heated objects.

There are several types of oil finish (Fig. 29-7). The most common is Danish oil. It can be purchased in natu-

ral as well as several pigmented colors. The pigmented Danish oil finishes will stain and finish the piece in one step. For maximum protection, work as much oil as possible into the wood. This requires a great deal of rubbing. Let it penetrate for at least 30 minutes before wiping off the surface. Several coats are recommended.

Do not use Danish oil on items that will come in contact with food; instead select mineral oil or an FDA-approved finish that are non-toxic. Work as much of this oil as possible into the wood for more protection.

Resin Finishes

Resin finishes develop more of a shine than wax or oil; they come close to matching a lacquered finish. Resin finishes can be applied with a rag, and at least the last coat should be applied in a dust-free environment.

Applying a Wipe-On Finish

Wipe-on finishes require patience and work. They are, however, easier to apply than most finishes. Start by completely cleaning the surface and corners with pressurized air. If compressed air is not available, use an old paint brush to do the job. Complete the cleaning process

Fig. 29-7. Oil finishes.

with a clean tack cloth. A *tack cloth* is a sticky piece of fabric that picks up and holds dirt.

Select a soft, clean, lint-free cloth. Fold it into a pad and dip it into the finish. Using a circular motion rub the finish into the wood. The more material worked into the surface, the better. Keep dipping the cloth into the wipe-on finish to get as much finish as possible into the wood.

Follow the instructions on the container concerning how long the finish should be rubbed. After the recommended time, wipe off the excess from the surface with a clean dry cloth. Let the finish dry the suggested amount of time and repeat the process. Apply as many coats as desired. Buff the finish with a clean soft cloth to remove any streaks (Fig. 29-8). Move the cloth with the grain.

A light coat of paste wax can be applied over the top of oil and resin finishes. This should be done only after the finish has completely dried. The wax will add luster.

VARNISHES

Varnishes have been used for hundreds of years on wood products. Because there are over 200 types, you will find a specific varnish for almost any application. This wide selection makes the finish very popular.

Varnishes will penetrate into the wood, but if enough coats are applied, they will produce a thick layer on the surface. This adds much depth to the finish and gives a glass-like appearance. It is, however, a slow-drying finish, so varnished finishes must be protected from dust.

The three major families of varnishes include spirit varnishes, linseed oil varnishes, and synthetic varnishes. Several types of varnishes can be found in each family. These varnishes are made from either a natural or synthetic base. Spirit varnishes and linseed oil varnishes both have a natural base.

Spirit Varnishes

The spirit varnish family dries into a hard film as the solvent evaporates. The most common type is shellac. It is considered not to be the best finish when used by itself. Disadvantages include yellowing with age, watermarking, and a short shelf life.

Some woodworkers do use shellac as a sealer and barrier coat. This keeps the material under the shellac from reacting with other coats of finish. Usually an orange shellac is selected. Denatured alcohol is used to thin the shellac and clean equipment.

Linseed Oil Varnishes

Linseed oil varnishes dry by oxidation, which is a slow process but builds a thick protective layer. There are two

Fig. 29-8. Buffing the finish to remove streaks.

major types in common use: Long oil and medium oil (Fig. 29-9).

Long oil or "spar" varnish contains a high percentage of linseed oil. It is used primarily on exterior surfaces such as lawn furniture and exterior doors. This type of varnish is also very resistant to water. It will give a finish that appears very thick amber or yellow in color.

Medium oil varnish contains less linseed oil than the long oil varnish. It is commonly used on furniture. Although slow in drying it hardens faster than long oil varnish. It is sometimes called rubbing and polishing varnish.

Both linseed oil varnishes are thinned and equipment cleaned with mineral spirits. Surfaces to be coated with linseed oil varnishes are sealed with a thinned coat of the varnish.

Synthetic Varnishes

Synthetic based varnishes are the newest varnish family. They dry much faster than the natural types and harden through *polymerization*, a chemical reaction. Most generally they are named by the plastic from which the base is made.

Polyurethane is the most common of the synthetic varnishes. It develops one of the toughest of all finishes. Polyurethane should be applied only on a completely sealed and clean surface. The surface is normally sealed with a medium oil varnish or another finish recommended by the manufacturer. Some types of this varnish are meant to be used only on interior products while others work well on exterior finishes. Use the solvent recommended on the container for cleaning the equipment.

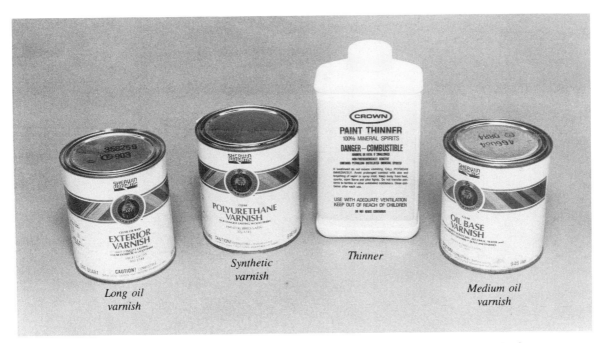

Fig. 29-9. Different types of linseed oil and polyurethane varnishes. Mineral spirits is used as the thinner.

Under the image, labels read:

Long oil varnish

Synthetic varnish

Thinner

Medium oil varnish

Applying Varnish

Varnishes can either be brushed or sprayed on the surface, but are usually brushed. Start by cleaning the surface completely with pressurized air and a clean tack cloth. Because they are slow drying, only apply varnishes in a dust-free room. Procede as follows:

1. Carefully stir the finish, attempting to avoid air bubbles. Slowly pour a small amount into a brushing container. Do not apply the varnish directly from the original can because the brush picks up dust particles and transfers the foreign material back into the can, and eventually onto other projects. For the first coat, thin the varnish by 25 percent. Gently stir again. This first coat will seal the wood.

2. Select the proper brush and dip it one-third the length of the bristles into the varnish. Wipe off the excess on the strike wire on the brushing container—not on the edge of the can. This will minimize air bubbles. (Fig. 29-10).

3. Flow the varnish onto the wood by brushing across the grain (Fig. 29-11). Start in the center of the piece and brush towards the edges. Divide a large sur-

Fig. 29-10. Pour the varnish with the can very close to the cup to reduce the air bubbles. Always use the strike wire, as shown, to remove excess varnish from the brush.

Strike wire

Fig. 29-11. Flow the varnish onto the surface by first brushing across the grain.

face into sections and apply varnish to each section before going onto the next.

4. After the first area is covered, wipe off the brush on the strike wire. Using the tips of the bristles, lightly brush back over the surface. Now move the brush with the grain. Do not over brush or brush marks will develop. Inspect the surface carefully for any runs or sags; these must be brushed out. As the varnish is drying, be sure no dust is allowed to get on your project.

5. Complete the job by cleaning your brush thoroughly.

After the varnish has thoroughly dried, sand the surface with wet-or-dry abrasive paper. Dip the 320-grit paper into water and sand lightly with the grain (Fig. 29-12). Do not sand through the finish. Be especially careful along outside corners: It is easy to sand the finish completely away from these corners.

Apply a second and third coat, following the same procedure. Do not, however, thin the varnish. After the last coat, polish the surface with pumice stone and rottenstone, which are powdered natural abrasives. They are very fine and do not remove a great deal of material.

Fig. 29-12. Lightly sand with 320-grit wet-or-dry abrasive paper and water.

Use a rubbing oil on a felt pad as a lubricant. Rub the pad with the grain. First rub the surface with pumice stone. Wipe off the pumice, then rub with the finer rotten stone. The more polishing you do, the deeper the finish will appear (Fig. 29-13).

LACQUERS

Lacquer is one of the most common finishes used on wood projects. Its popularity is due to the fast drying time and durability. Some lacquers are perfectly clear, while others are opaque. Opaque lacquers completely hide the surface. Many lacquers can be sprayed on the surface.

Lacquers have several advantages and few disadvantages. The finish dries to a hard, durable coating. Because of this hardness, however, lacquer might crack as the wood moves. Lacquer dries much faster than most finishes, which allows more coats to be applied in a shorter period of time. Fast drying will make the finish difficult to brush. The sheen varies greatly. Sheens are available from flat to a super high gloss. Lacquers cannot be mixed with other finishes. Never apply them over the top of other finishes or they could become soft.

Many companies make lacquers and each manufacturer has several different types. They can be purchased in sizes from 16-ounce spray aerosol cans to 55-gallon barrels.

Lacquer Sealers

Lacquer sealer is applied to wood before the finish top coat of clear lacquer. It penetrates the wood and can be easily sanded. The sealer also forms a barrier that prevents stains from bleeding or soaking into the rest of the finish. Lacquer sealer is sometimes called "sanding sealer."

Clear Lacquers

Clear lacquers are usually applied after the lacquer sealer. They are used to build up the thickness of the finish. Clear gloss lacquers accumulate the fastest and give the highest luster. Other lusters are also available, including semi-gloss and dull. The dull clear lacquers will give a flat, hand-rubbed appearance.

Brushing Lacquers

Brushing lacquers are designed to be applied with a brush rather than with a spray gun. Use a good-quality varnish brush for best results. Brushing lacquers dry more slowly than spraying lacquers. The slow drying time helps the coat flow and reduces the brush marks in the surface. Drying usually takes two hours.

Colored Lacquers

Colored or pigmented lacquers contain a colored pigment. They completely hide the wood grain or any surface detail. In this way they are similar to oil and latex paints. This lacquer is usually sold in aerosol spray cans.

Shading Lacquers

Shading lacquers are used to add color to the finish. When sprayed on they will slightly hide any differences on the surfaces. Sapwood, for example, will blend with the heartwood. Sometimes these laquers are only sprayed on the edges to give a piece an antique look.

Fig. 29-13. Polish the surface with pumice stone and rubbing oil.

Lacquer Thinner

Lacquer thinner is the recommended solvent for lacquer. It is used to thin lacquer so it can be sprayed. The thinner is also used to clean equipment. Not all lacquer thinners will work with every lacquer. Follow the instructions of the manufacturer for the recommended lacquer thinner.

Spraying Lacquer

The smoothest of all lacquered finishes is achieved by spraying. Spraying will apply an even coat that contains no brush marks. Because lacquer might blush or become cloudy on humid days, spray only when the conditions are right. Apply laquer following the proper procedure.

Carefully sand and prepare all surfaces. If the project is to be stained, follow the steps given in this chapter. For ring porous wood, apply paste wood filler.

Thin the lacquer sealer following the instructions of the manufacturer. Just before spraying the sealer, clean the surface with a clean tack cloth. Use up to 50 pounds of air pressure and the spraying procedure given in chapter 29. After spraying, clean the gun and any equipment with lacquer thinner.

When the sealer has dried, sand the surface lightly with 320-grit wet-or-dry abrasive paper. Use water to keep the abrasive paper lubricated. Be careful not to sand through into the stain and do not sand the corners. It is easy to sand into the raw wood.

Wipe the surface with a clean tack cloth and pressurized air. Thin the clear lacquer following the instructions of the manufacturer. Spray a light even coat (Fig. 29-14). Allow the lacquer to dry for at least two hours. Sand lightly with 320-grit wet-or-dry abrasive paper and water.

Apply as many coats as desired. The number of coats will depend on how heavy a layer is applied with each coat and how thick a finish is desired. Three to four coats will be sufficient in most cases. After the last coat of clear lacquer is dry, rub the surface down with pumice stone and rottenstone.

Brushing Lacquers

Be certain to select a brushing type lacquer. Prepare the project and carefully clean the surface with a clean tack cloth and pressurized air.

Fig. 29-14. Spraying a project with laquer.

After dipping the brush into the lacquer, start on an edge and brush towards the center. Flow the finish on the surface. Always brush with the grain. Keep the brush wet by only covering a small area and then redipping the brush. Do not overlap the brush strokes. Do not return to the project and rebrush the freshly applied lacquer; rebrushing will cause brush marks.

Sand lightly between the coats with 320-grit wet-or-dry abrasive paper and water. Rub the last coat with pumice and rottenstone.

PAINTS

Paint refers to finishes that are opaque. Because they contain pigment they totally hide the wood grain. Paints are often more protective than clear varnishes or lacquers. The color used in the paint blocks the harmful rays from the sun. Most often paints are used on exterior projects and on buildings. However, painted interior projects also have their place.

Paint is made from a pigment and a vehicle. The pigment gives the finish its color, the vehicle makes the pigment into a liquid and allows the paint to be brushed, rolled, or sprayed on the surface. By varying the amount of vehicle and pigment and adding other chemicals, many types of different paints can be made for various applications. Read the label on the paint can for recommended applications.

A common term used with paints is *enamel*. Enamel can be either oil or water base. In most cases enamel is very glossy and is more durable than other paints.

All paints can be purchased in several different sheens or amount of shine. Although each manufacturer has a different set of terms, flat, semi-gloss, and gloss are most often used to describe sheen. Flat is the least durable and has no shine. It does, however, cover up defects the best. Semi-gloss is the most popular. Because it can be easily washed, it is often used for woodwork. Gloss paint is the shiniest and gives a glossy appearance.

Paints will be either oil-based or water-based.

Oil-Based Paint

Oil-based paints have been on the market a long time and are considered very durable. Trim around a door or kitchen cabinets are sometimes coated with this finish because of the hard use. Oil-based paint produces a heavy odor and special solvents such as turpentine or mineral spirits are required to clean equipment. Most of these paints also require a separate paint primer to seal the surface.

Water-Based Paint

Water-based paints have a latex base. They are also durable and have some advantages oil-based paints do not. Advantages include lower price, equipment that can be cleaned with warm water, and little odor. It can also be thinned with water. Most water-based paints do not require a separate primer. The first coat of latex paint serves as the sealer.

Applying Paint

Start by making certain the surface is clean and free from dirt or loose paint. If the surface has been previously painted, use a paint scraper to remove any loose finish. Lightly sand the project to remove any glossiness in the oil finish. If possible, blow the surface off with pressurized air and then wipe with a clean cloth.

Although paint can be rolled, brushed, or sprayed, it is usually brushed on small woodworking projects.

1. Select a brush and primer according to recommendations on the label of the paint can. Stir the primer thoroughly without producing bubbles. Do not apply the primer directly from the can; use a paint pan to keep the paint clean. Paint your project in a dust-free environment.

2. Allow the primer or first coat to dry. Sand the surface with 280-grit abrasive paper to remove the raised grain. Clean the surface again and wipe with a tack cloth.

3. Apply a second coat if necessary. Use long, light strokes running with the grain. Be careful not to apply the paint too thickly. This will cause runs and a longer drying time. A third coat might be required. If so, sand and clean the surface before applying.

4. Always clean the equipment immediately after each coat has been applied. Use the recommended solvent given on the paint can to clean the paint pan and brush. Properly store the equipment.

Chapter 30

Table and Chair Construction

The key to successful table and chair construction is the type of joints used. Tables and chairs are subject to heavy downward loads, which cause the legs to spread apart. The leg and rail jointing used for tables and chairs must resist these pressures. (Review chapters 12 and 13 for information on joint construction).

TABLES

There are many different types of tables. Their size and design depends upon the purpose they serve. Typical among these are dining tables, end tables, coffee tables, and workbenches. Tables are made in many shapes, such as square, rectangular, or oval. Some have drawers, drop leaves, shelves, or are built so that they can be expanded in size. Quality tables and chairs are built using leg and rail construction (Fig. 30-1).

LEG AND RAIL CONSTRUCTION

Rails are usually joined to legs with a mortise-and-tenon or a dowel joint (Fig. 30-2). The mortise-and-tenon joint is the strongest. The tenon enters the mortise and provides gluing surfaces with the leg. The shoulders add to the stiffness.

A mortise is difficult to cut by hand. Mortises can be made with a portable router, then the tenons cut on the tablesaw.

The dowel joint is easier to make by hand. However, it has less gluing surface so is not as strong as the mortise-and-tenon—but is quite satisfactory. When using this joint, legs and rails can be reinforced with wood

corner blocks or metal corner braces. In fact, in low-quality furniture this metal corner brace is often used alone to hold the rails and legs together and the rail simply butts the leg: No dowel or mortise and tenon joint is used (Fig. 30-3).

While rails usually run perpendicular to the legs, on some designs they run on a diagonal (Fig. 30-4). Tables with two pedestals are also popular (Fig. 30-5). Some use a stretcher to connect the pedestals to resist horizontal forces. A *stretcher* is a horizontal member running between the legs, located near the floor (Fig. 30-6). A single pedestal table has several feet forming a base (Fig. 30-7).

In addition to the typical mortise-and-tenon joint and dowel joint, rails can be joined to legs in a variety of other ways. If the rail is to be flush with the outside of the leg, a barefaced tenon is used. Dowels or wood screws can be set through the rail into the leg. Screws can be hidden by counterboring them and gluing a wood plug in the hole (Fig. 30-8).

Rails can be straight or curved. They can meet a leg on an incline or be perpendicular to it (Fig. 30-9). It is easier to use dowel joints to join round rails to legs. Most chairs are narrow in the back and will require inclined rails. Inclined rails can use dowels or mortise-and-tenon joints, but remember that the mortise-and-tenon is very difficult to make. Rails can also meet legs in a sculptured joint. The leg is usually formed to have a curved section meeting the rail. This is very attractive and not difficult to cut (Fig. 30-10).

Rails can have their bottom edge shaped or have

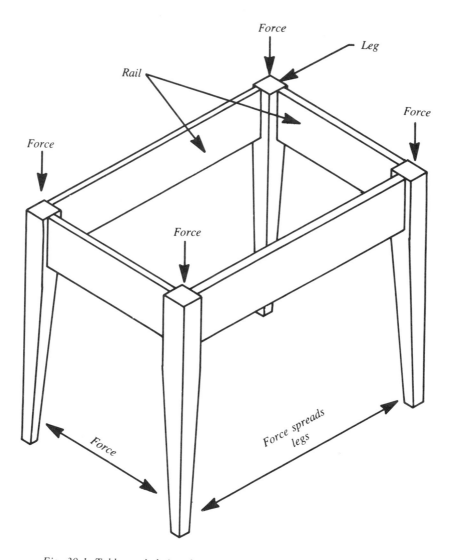

Fig. 30-1. Tables and chairs often are built using leg and rail construction.

molding applied to their face or bottom edge. They can also have designs recessed into them with a router (Fig. 30-11).

The stretcher strengthens the chair or table, and also serves a decorative function. Sometimes a shelf is used instead to serve the same purposes. The shelf can be secured by notching it around the legs and joining at these points with a dowel. An alternate method is to cut a dado in the leg to receive the shelf (Fig. 30-12).

Some tables have drawers. (Drawer construction and installation is explained in chapter 32.) The rail must be changed to receive the drawer. The design could include a pierced rail, one small rail below the drawer, a dust panel below the drawer, or omit the rail entirely. (Fig. 30-13).

CHAIRS

Chair construction is similar to table construction in that leg and rail construction is commonly used. Strength is

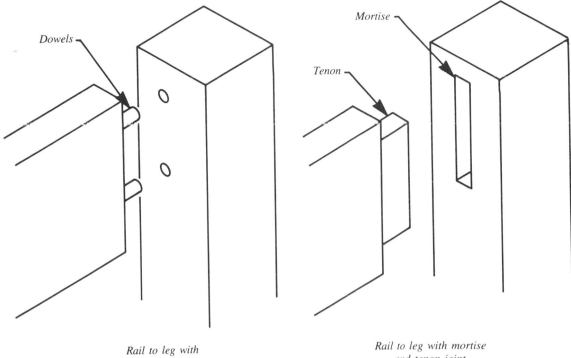

Rail to leg with
a dowel joint

Rail to leg with mortise
and tenon joint

Fig. 30-2. Legs and rails are usually joined with dowel or mortise-and-tenon joints.

very important when building a chair. The chair is subject to downward forces on the legs and rails, and also to a backward thrust (Fig. 30-14).

When designing chair legs, consider the load the bottom end of each leg must carry. The total weight to be imposed on a chair is divided equally among the four legs. If, for instance, a 200-pound person uses the chair, each leg will have to carry 50 pounds. If the end of the leg is ¾ inch square, the force on the floor is 200 divided by 3 square inches (area of all four legs together —which equals 66.67 pounds per square inch. If the wood to be used has a low compressive strength, or you think this small leg surface might damage the finish floor, enlarge the area of the end of the legs. If the legs were enlarged to 1½ inches square, the load per leg would be 33.3 pounds per square inch.

Stretchers are very important to chair design. If they are not used the leg and rail joint might have to be larger to resist the forces. Corner blocking, as shown for tables, is vital to strong chair construction.

Chairs can have arm rests. These can be built in

many ways; some simple designs are shown in Fig. 30-15.

Seat construction varies considerably. One easy design involves a plywood seat panel resting on cleats that are secured to the chair rails. A foam rubber seat pad can be placed on this and covered with material (Fig. 30-16).

TABLETOP CONSTRUCTION

Tabletops are generally made from solid wood, plywood, or particleboard. Other materials such as glass and slate —although heavy—provide attractive design possibilities.

Solid Wood Tops

Solid wood tops are difficult to build and often have warping problems. They are not widely used in furniture construction, especially on units that have large tops, as a dining table has. For small tables, such as end or bedside tables, sold wood tops can be used satisfactorily.

To work correctly the tops must be made from kiln-

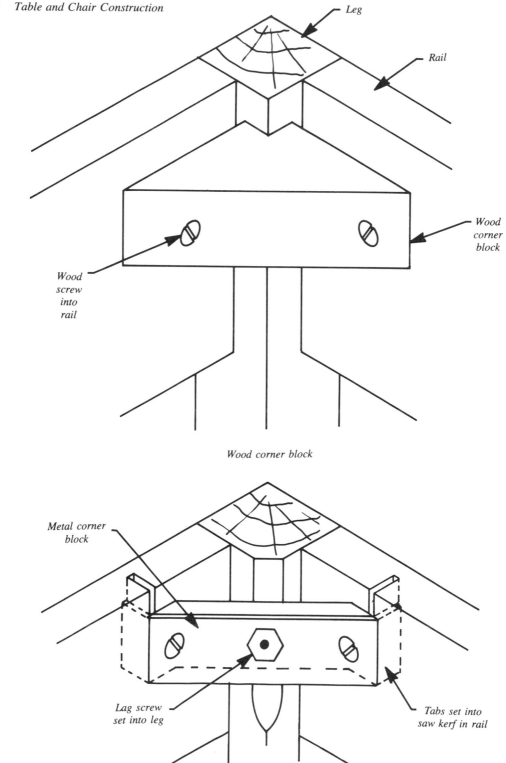

Wood corner block

Fig. 30-3. Corner blocks are used to strengthen tables and chairs.

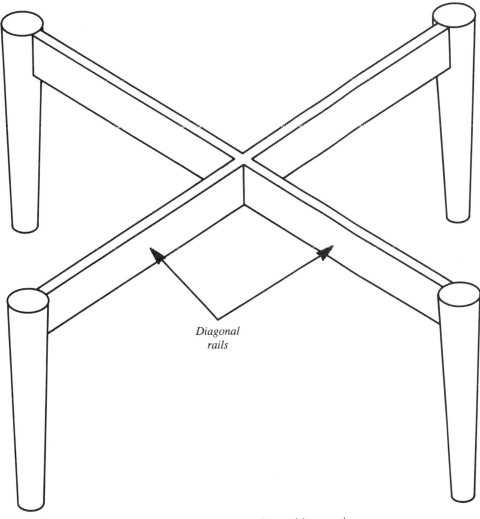

Fig. 30-4. Rails can run on a diagonal between legs.

Diagonal
rails

dried wood with a moisture content of 6 to 8 percent. The boards must be assembled as described as follows:

Select the boards to be used for the top, examining for grain and flatness. If they are warped, do not use them. The boards are joined edge to edge with an edge dowel or a milled glue joint (Fig. 30-17). The milled joint can be made with standard shaper cutters. Wide boards tend to warp more than narrow boards, so use strips approximately 4 inches wide. When gluing the pieces, alternate them so the heart side is up on every other piece (Fig. 30-18). The grain must run the same direction in each piece.

Sometimes end boards are used to help keep the solid wood top flat. These can be joined with a tongue-and-groove or dovetail joint, although the dovetail joint is preferable. Cut a small V groove in the joint between the end board and the top, so if a crack develops it will not be noticeable. (Fig. 30-19).

A solid wood top can be strengthened and made to appear thicker by gluing strips below it (Fig. 30-20). To match the grain and color, make the top 4 inches longer and wider than the desired finished size. Then cut off 2-inch strips from each edge, rotate them under, and glue to the bottom of the top. The bottom surface of the top

Fig. 30-5. This table has two pedestals (Courtesy Gold Medal, Inc.).

should have a sealer coat of finish applied to keep out moisture.

Plywood Top Construction

Because plywood is made by laminating veneers together, it is very strong and resists warping. Plywood is available in large sheets, so tops can be made as one piece with no glue joints. Usually ¾-inch-thick plywood is used for table tops.

Hardwood plywood is often used because it has a beautiful veneer on the one side. However, careful finishing is necessary to protect the finished top from stains caused by moisture from drinks and from scratches. A sealer coat of finish should also be applied on the bottom.

Plywood with an inexpensive top veneer can be covered with a sheet of plastic laminate or a hardwood veneer. The plastic laminate is available in a wide range of colors and wood grains. Wood veneers are sold with matched grain patterns, so special designs can be formed

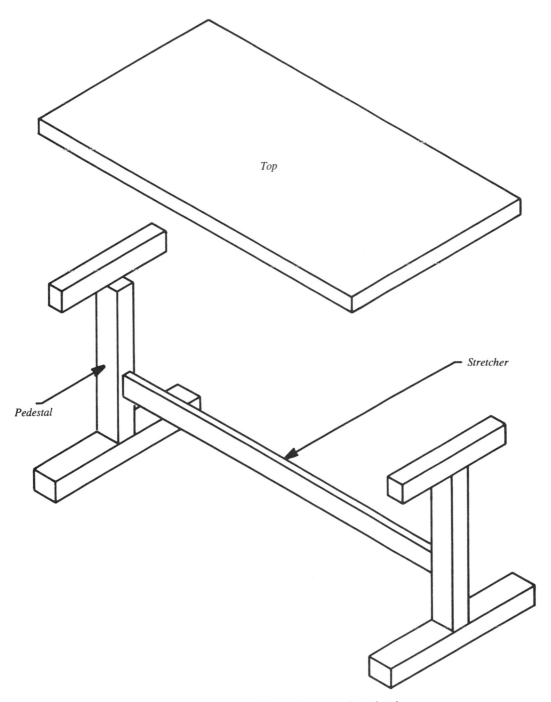

Top

Stretcher

Pedestal

Fig. 30-6. Stretchers are often used to connect the pedestals.

Fig. 30-7. This table uses a single pedestal that has several feet (Courtesy Hekman Furniture Company).

on the plywood substrate. The edges of plywood tops must be banded in some way, as described below.

Particleboard Tops

Particleboard is used more and more as the substrate for furniture tops. It is solid, strong, and resists warping. It can be covered with wood veneers or plastic laminates. Special screws are necessary when fastening legs or other pieces to it. The edges must be banded to improve appearance.

Banding Plywood and Particleboard Tops

The way the edges are banded depends to some extent upon the design of the furniture. The easiest alternative is adhesive-backed real wood edging. It is available by the roll in various widths. Cut the edging to fit, press into position, and iron on with an ordinary household iron. Other methods are given in Fig. 30-21. Solid wood

banding can be made wide enough so that it can be shaped with a router or shaper after it is glued to the top. Plastic and metal edging is also available.

EXPANDABLE TABLES

Two basic types of expandable tables include those on which the legs remain stationary and the top slides larger, and those that have the top secured to the legs, with the top and legs sliding out together (Fig. 30-22). A variety of wood and metal table top slides are available from woodworking supply houses for each of these types of expandable tops.

DROP-LEAF TABLES

Many traditional styles of tables used drop leaves, which permit the table to fit into a small space yet open up, with the addition of the leaves, to a larger size. Often the

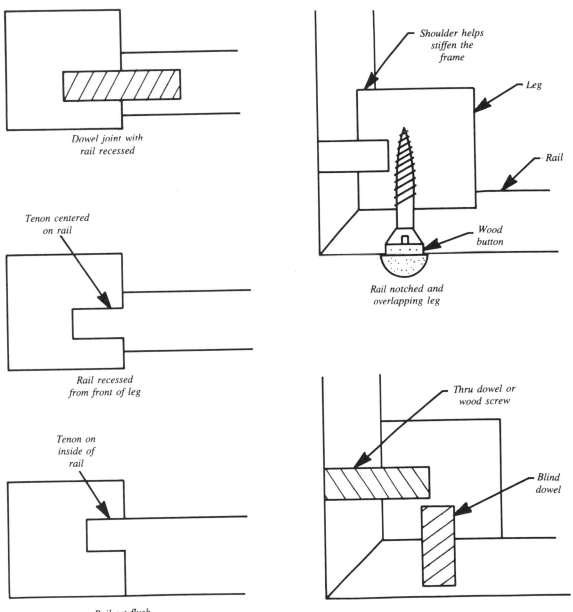

Dowel joint with
rail recessed

Tenon centered
on rail

Rail recessed
from front of leg

Tenon on
inside of
rail

Rail set flush
with front of leg

Shoulder helps
stiffen the
frame

Leg

Rail

Wood
button

Rail notched and
overlapping leg

Thru dowel or
wood screw

Blind
dowel

Fig. 30-8. Other ways rails can be joined to legs.

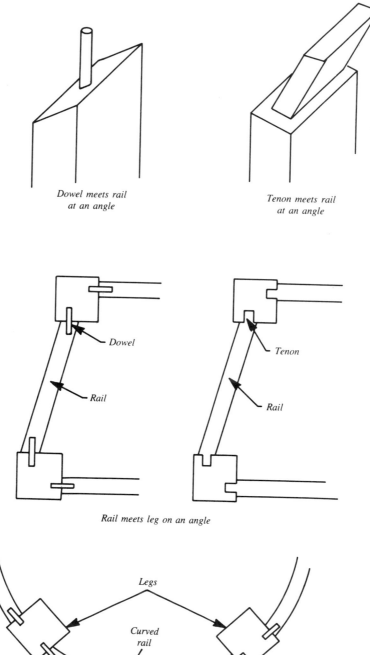

Dowel meets rail
at an angle

Tenon meets rail
at an angle

Dowel

Rail

Tenon

Rail

Rail meets leg on an angle

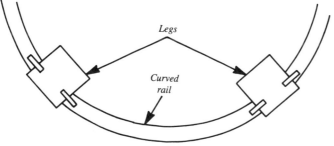

Legs

Curved
rail

Fig. 30-9. Rails are made in several shapes.

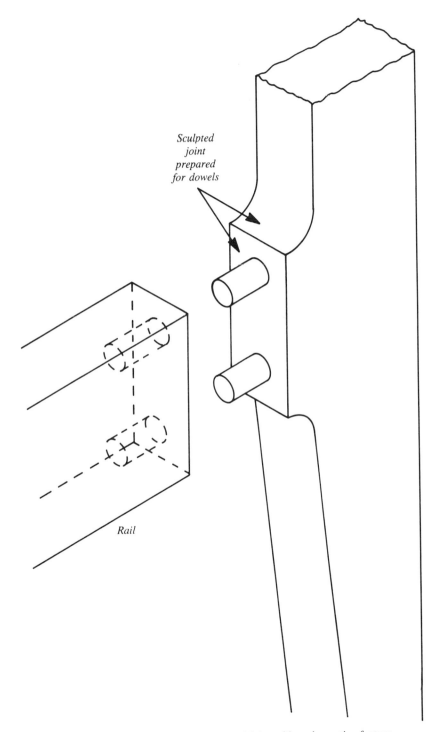

Sculpted
joint
prepared
for dowels

Rail

Fig. 30-10. A curved section at a dowel joint adds a decorative feature.

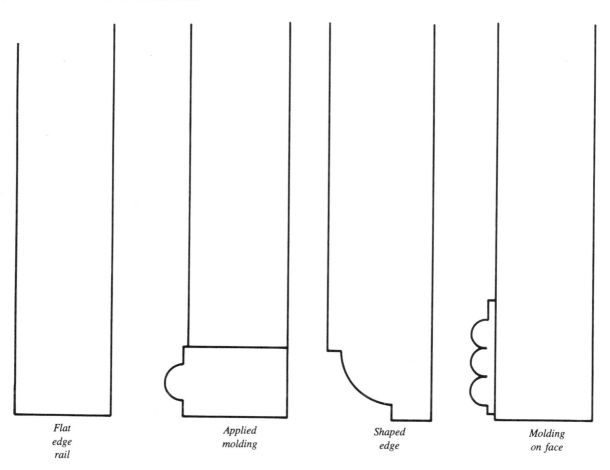

| Flat edge rail | Applied molding | Shaped edge | Molding on face |

Fig. 30-11. Rails can have decorative features added.

style of furniture dictates the type of joint used to form the drop leaf. The simplest way is to use a butt table hinge and square edge top and leaves (Fig. 30-23). When the leaf is up it is flush with the top; when it is down it sticks out beyond the end of the top. Notice the long leaf on the butt table hinge is fastened to the drop leaf.

A special drop-leaf hinge for square joints can also be used. Notice in Fig. 30-24 how it swings the leaf below the edge of the top. It also is a leaf support that holds the leaf in a horizontal position.

Many traditional styles of tables require the rule joint to be used for drop leaves. This joint gives a decorative appearance when the leaf is down. It is cut using a matched set of cutters on a shaper (Fig. 30-25). It is very important that the joint be cut exactly as shown, otherwise the top and leaf might not be flush or the leaf might

bind on the curved edge of the top. A drop-leaf hinge must be used, and one leaf will be longer than the other. Install as shown in Fig. 30-26. Notice the groove cut in the bottom of the top that holds the knuckle of the hinge.

Drop-Leaf Support

There are several ways to support a drop leaf in the up position. The easiest involves a metal drop-leaf support, which is available from woodworking supply companies (Fig. 30-27). It must be installed exactly as shown. Notice the short arm is fastened to the drop leaf. A small leaf can be held with one support; larger leaves will require two.

Figure 30-28 illustrates a metal leaf support for use on tables that do not have rails between the legs. It fastens to the bottom of the top and to the drop leaf.

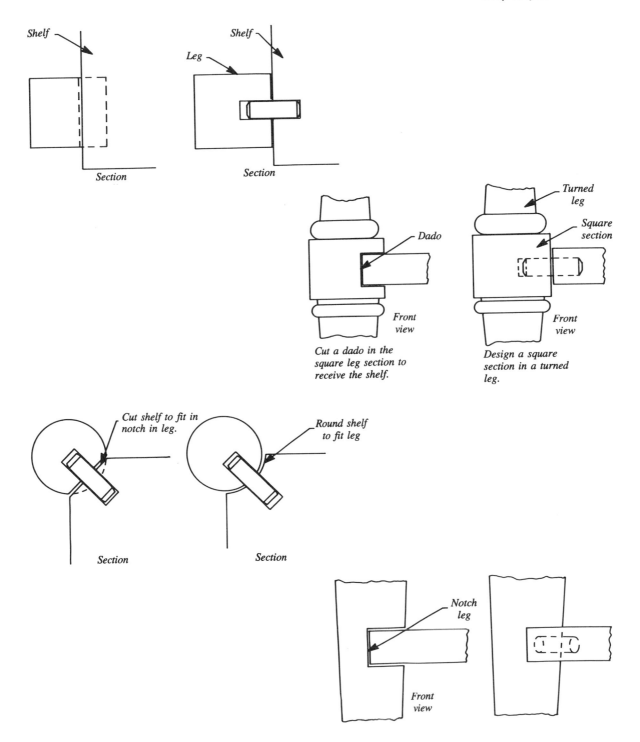

Fig. 30-12. Shelves can be joined to legs with dowels or dadoes.

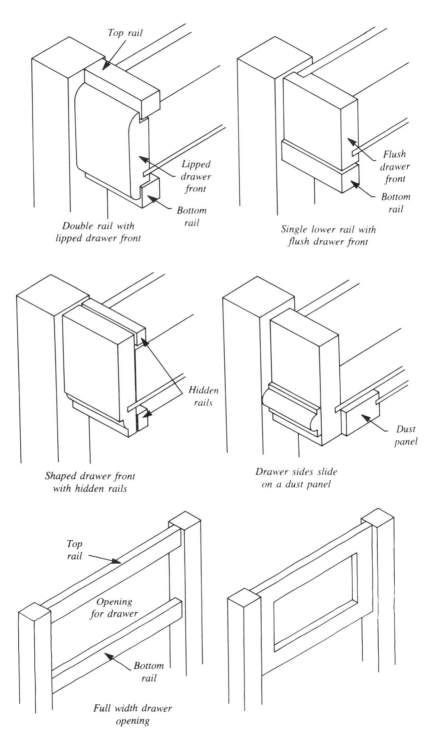

Fig. 30-13. Drawers can be installed using a variety of rails or a dust panel.

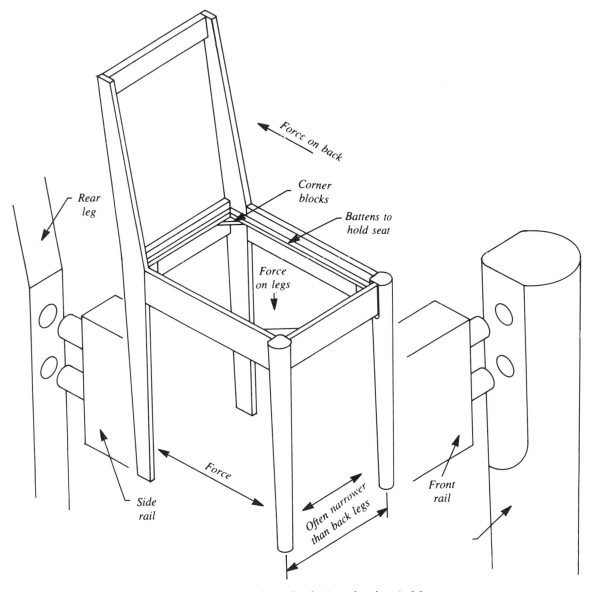

Fig. 30-14. Chairs are subjected to horizontal and vertical forces.

Various types of sliding supports have been used for a long time. A commercially available metal slide is shown in Fig. 30-29. One slide will hold small leaves; large leaves will need two slides. A wood slide design is shown in Fig. 30-30.

A butterfly wing is used on certain traditional tables. Each leaf requires a wood wing that rotates on wood dowels set in each end. When the leaf is down, the wing folds back against the table rail.

SECURING TABLETOPS TO THE BASE

Among the devices to fasten a tabletop to the base are shop-made and factory-made devices. A rabbeted wood block is easy to make and works well. A metal clip is sold to do the same job (Fig. 30-31). Other methods are shown in Fig. 30-32.

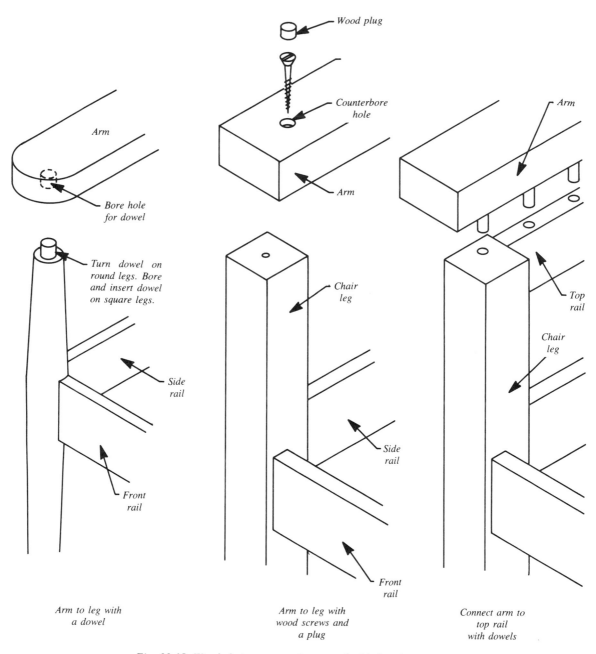

Fig. 30-15. Wood chair arms can be secured with dowels or screws.

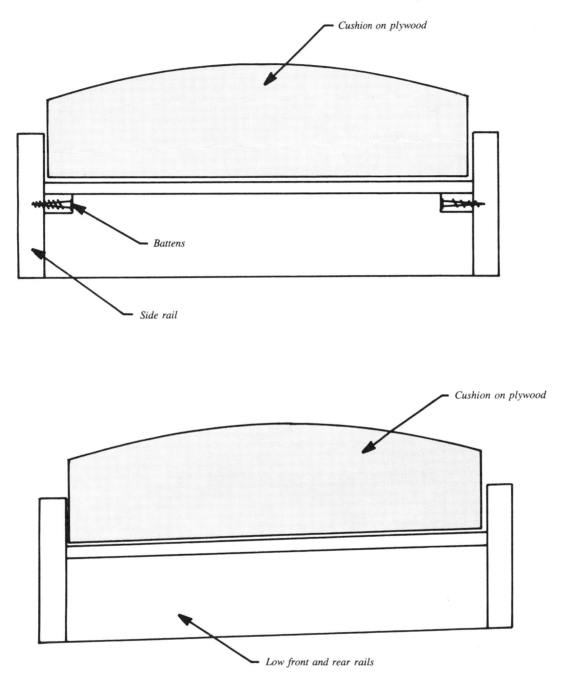

Fig. 30-16. Two easy ways to build a simple upholstered chair seat.

Fig. 30-17. A milled joint used when gluing solid wood stock edge to edge.

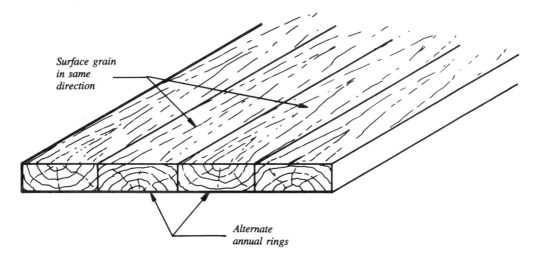

Fig. 30-18. Alternate the heartwood side to minimize warping.

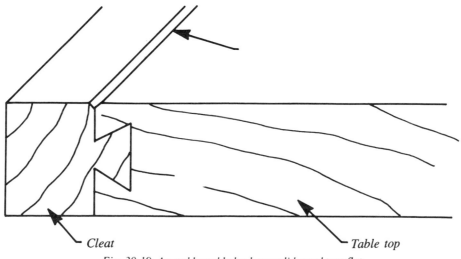

Fig. 30-19. An end board helps keep solid wood tops flat.

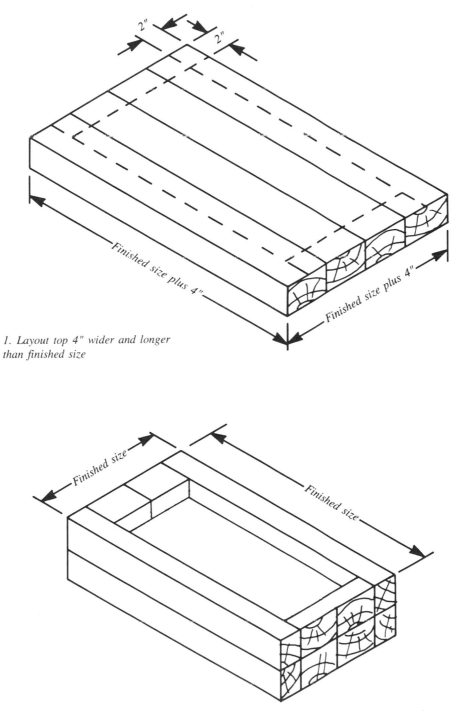

1. *Layout top 4" wider and longer than finished size*

Fig. 30-20. *Solid wood tops can be stiffened and made to appear thicker by gluing strips to their bottom surface.*

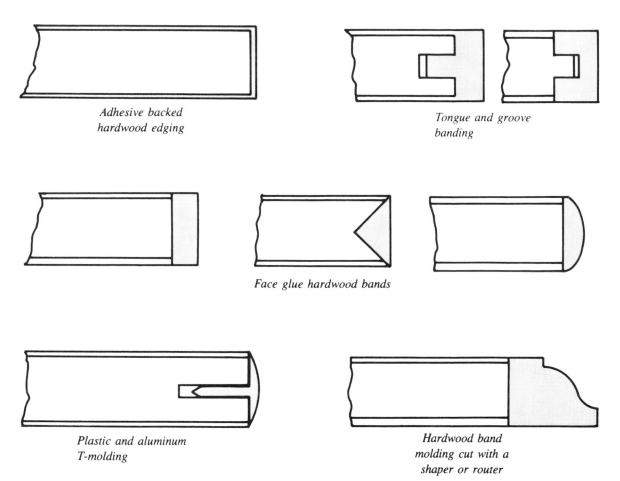

Adhesive backed
hardwood edging

Tongue and groove
banding

Face glue hardwood bands

Plastic and aluminum
T-molding

Hardwood band
molding cut with a
shaper or router

Fig. 30-21. A few ways to band edges of plywood and particleboard.

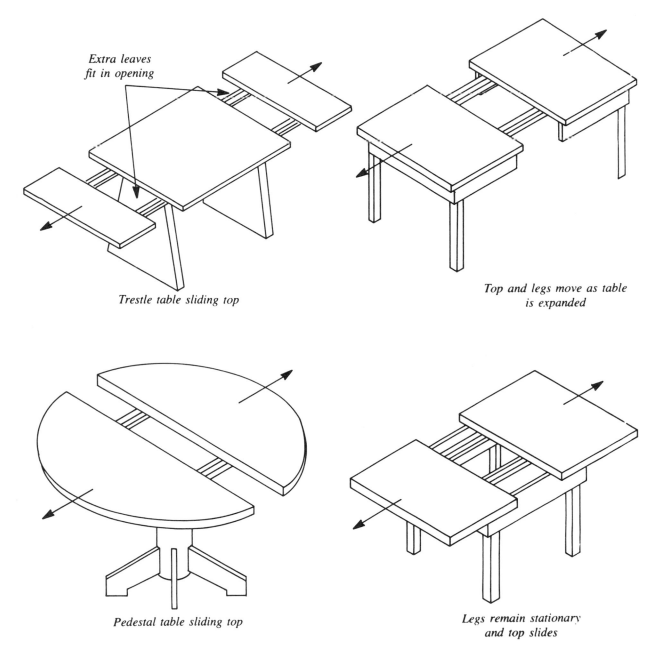

Extra leaves
fit in opening

Trestle table sliding top

Top and legs move as table
is expanded

Pedestal table sliding top

Legs remain stationary
and top slides

Fig. 30-22. Types of expandable tables.

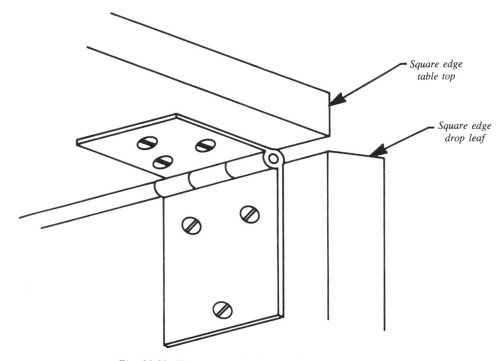

*Square edge
table top*

*Square edge
drop leaf*

Fig. 30-23. The square edge drop leaf is the easiest to make.

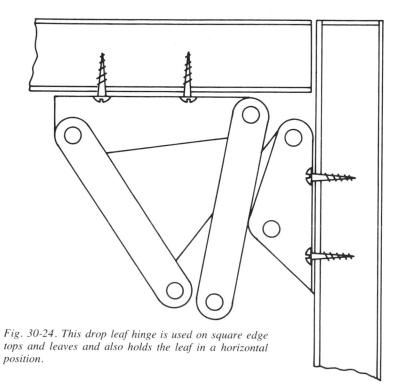

*Fig. 30-24. This drop leaf hinge is used on square edge
tops and leaves and also holds the leaf in a horizontal
position.*

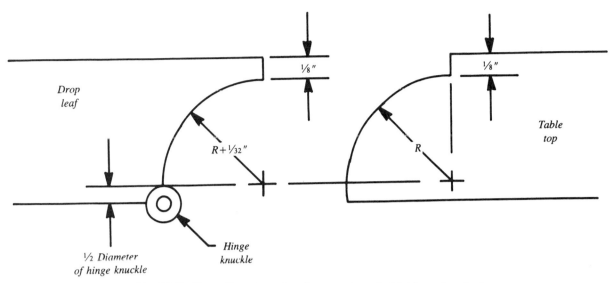

Fig. 30-25. *These dimensions show how to cut a rule joint for a drop leaf.*

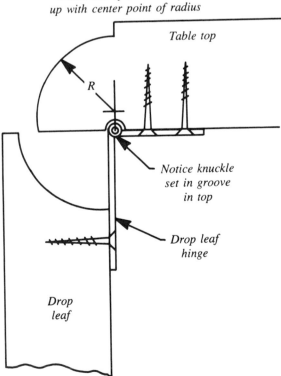

Fig. 30-26. *The rule joint assembled with a drop leaf hinge.*

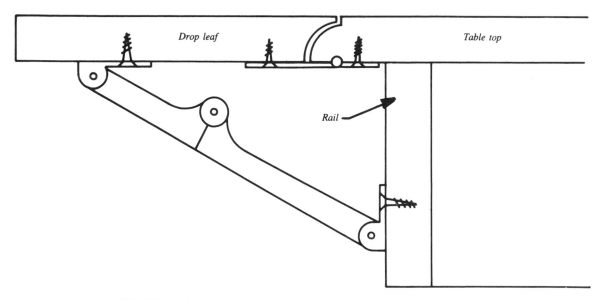

Fig. 30-27. This support is used to hold drop leaves in a horizontal position.

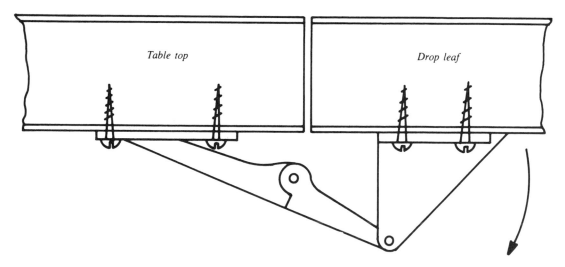

Fig. 30-28. This leaf support and hinge is used on tables that do not have a rail between legs.

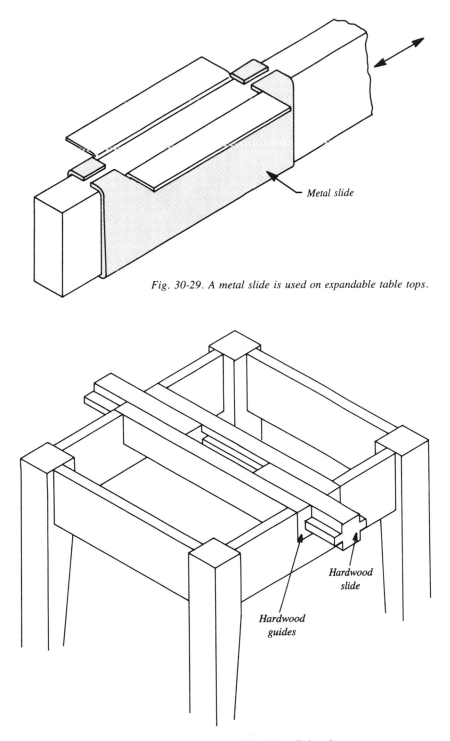

Fig. 30-29. A metal slide is used on expandable table tops.

Fig. 30-30. A hardwood slide will hold small drop leaves.

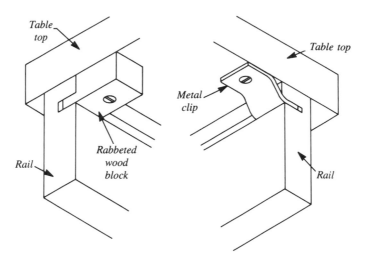

Fig. 30-31. Two methods of securing wood table tops to the base.

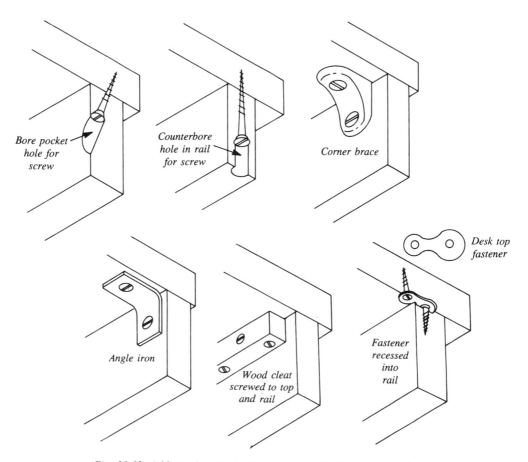

Fig. 30-32. Additional methods of securing wood table tops to the base.

Chapter 31

Furniture and Cabinet Construction

The basic box forming a cabinet or unit of furniture is called the *carcass*. It can be a simple box with butt joints, or a better-quality piece using dust panels and any of a variety of jointing at the corners and tops.

CARCASS CONSTRUCTION FOR FURNITURE UNITS

Carcass construction is used to build furniture units that are boxlike and have an opening for doors, shelves, or drawers. A dresser is an example (Fig. 31-1). The carcass is made up of side panels called *bulkheads*, plus back, top, and dust panels and a faceframe. The unit in Fig. 31-2 has legs raising it off the floor. In Fig. 31-3, notice that the bulkhead extends to the floor and a toeboard is used across the front.

BULKHEADS AND PARTITIONS

Bulkheads, or end panels of furniture units, are made from solid wood, wood panel construction, plywood, or particleboard.

Solid wood bulkheads are made by edge gluing wood strips 3 to 4 inches wide. Panel construction uses a solid wood frame with inset panels (Fig. 31-4). Shaped edges and moulding applied on the face of the panel produce very attractive results. Typical panel details are shown in Fig. 31-5. The panels can be $1/4$-to-$3/8$-inch-thick plywood, solid wood, glass, metal, plastic, or other material. The rails and stiles are joined with dowel, mortise-and-tenon, or stuck joints.

Bulkheads can also be made from plywood or particleboard. Plywood and particleboard bulkheads are more stable than those made from solid wood. Plywood bulkheads usually are made from hardwood plywood because it has an attractive face veneer. Particleboard bulkheads are covered with wood veneer or plastic laminate.

Partitions are vertical dividers inside the carcass used to support drawer slides and shelves. They stiffen long cabinets and provide a place to secure the faceframe. They are usually made of plywood, but panel construction can also be used (Fig. 31- 6).

DUST PANELS

Dust panels are made using the same construction used for partitions or bulkheads. They are located under each drawer and between drawers and a section having doors. They strengthen the carcass and control the filtration of dust within the unit. On less expensive furniture, the frame is installed but the panel is omitted. Dust panels are not visible on the finished unit so they are made from cheaper wood and the panel insert is usually hardboard (Fig. 31-7).

CONSTRUCTING THE CARCASS

Corner joints for flush top construction can be rabbet, half-blind tongue and rabbet, splined miter, through dovetail, half-blind dovetail, butt joint with dowels, off-set miter, and lock miter (Fig. 31-8). The butt joint is the easiest to make. The shoulder on the rabbet joint provides additional stiffness. These corners are stronger and stiffer if a glue block is used. A glue block is a triangular

Fig. 31-1. This furniture unit was constructed using carcass construction.

wood strip that is glued and nailed or stapled to the top and bulkhead.

Vertical corners can be joined using a solid wood corner piece. There are many possible designs; two are shown in Fig. 31-9.

Partitions and fixed shelves can be installed using a dado, rabbet and dado, blind dado and tongue, dovetail, butt joint with nails, dowels, or spline and battens (Fig. 31-10). Joints such as the through dado or rabbet and dado are hidden if the carcass has a faceframe. If it is frameless, use a blind joint. A blind joint is one that is not cut through the front of the bulkhead or partition. Stop the joint about ½ inch from the front edge.

When rails are required they can be joined to the bulkhead as shown in Fig. 31-11.

Cabinet Backs

Cabinet backs can be set in a rabbet or in a groove. The rabbet is cut about ¼ inch deeper than the thickness of the back, providing a slight recess (Fig. 31-12). If a groove is used, the back panel should be slightly smaller than the groove-to-groove distance to allow for expansion (Fig. 31-13).

Faceframes

Faceframes are solid wood frames that are attached to the front of the unit to provide door and drawer openings. Door hinges are screwed to the faceframe. The parts of a faceframe are the stiles, rails, and mullions. *Rails* are the horizontal members and *stiles* are vertical members.

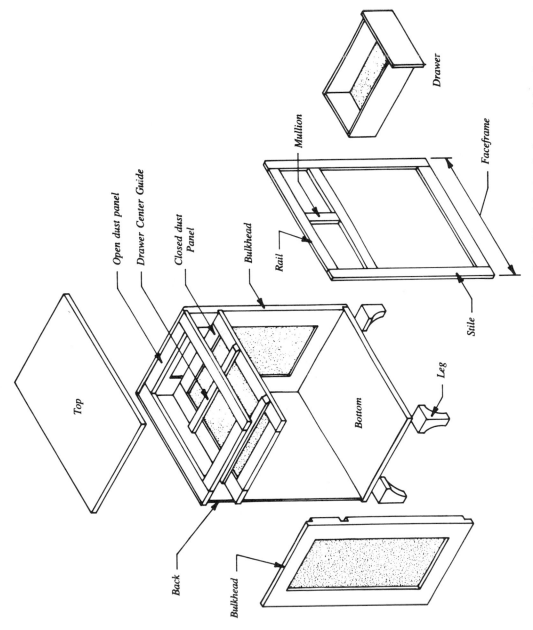

Top

Open dust panel

Drawer Center Guide

Closed dust Panel

Bulkhead

Back

Bulkhead

Bottom

Leg

Rail

Mullion

Stile

Faceframe

Drawer

Fig. 31-2. A carcass uses box-like construction. Note the individual legs joined to the bottom of the unit.

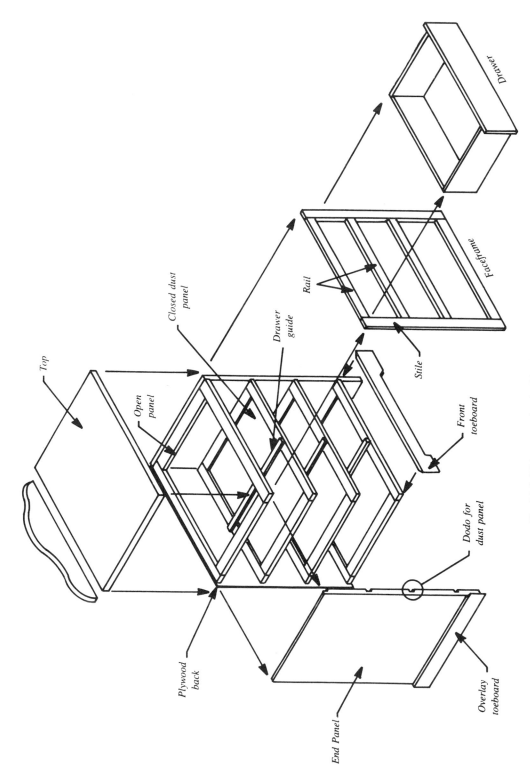

Fig. 31-3. This carcass has bulkheads that run to the floor.

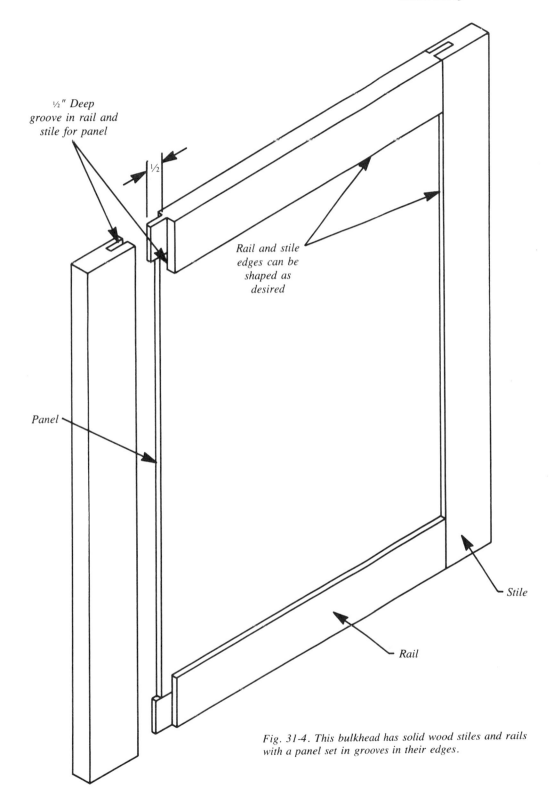

½" *Deep
groove in rail and
stile for panel*

½

*Rail and stile
edges can be
shaped as
desired*

Panel

Stile

Rail

Fig. 31-4. *This bulkhead has solid wood stiles and rails
with a panel set in grooves in their edges.*

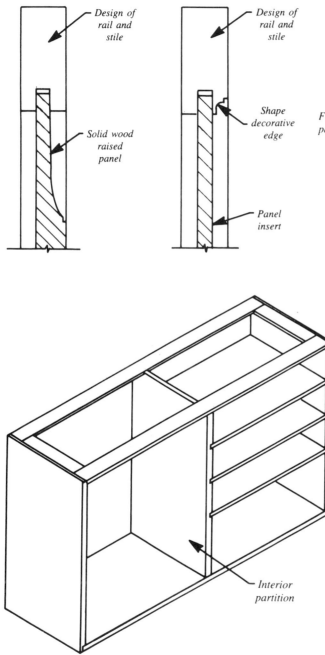

Design of rail and stile

Solid wood raised panel

Design of rail and stile

Shape decorative edge

Panel insert

Fig. 31-5. Designs for enhancing the stiles, rails, and panels in a bulkhead.

Fig. 31-6. Interior partitions are used to stiffen the carcass and support drawers and shelves.

Interior partition

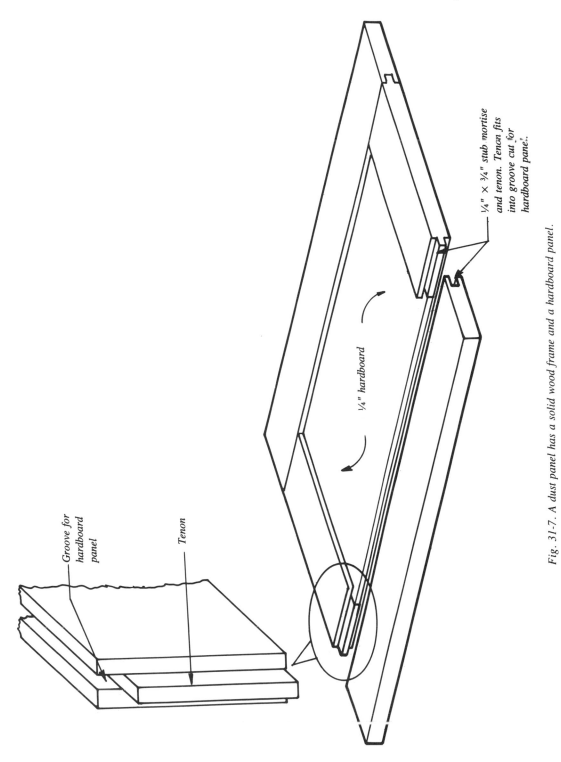

Groove for hardboard panel

Tenon

¼" hardboard

¼" × ¾" stub mortise and tenon. Tenon fits into groove cut for hardboard panel..

Fig. 31-7. A dust panel has a solid wood frame and a hardboard panel.

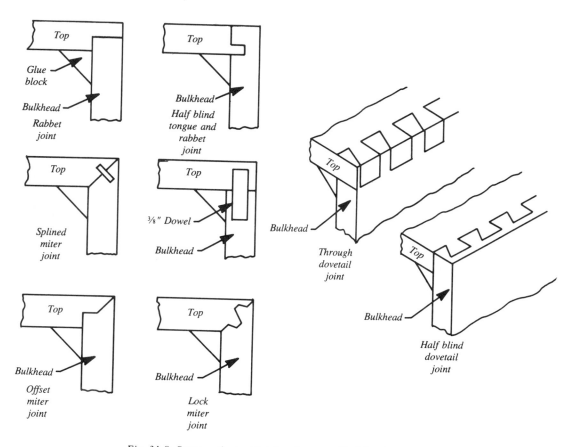

Fig. 31-8. Some methods of joining the top and bulkhead.

Mullions are vertical parts that separate drawers and doors (Fig. 31-14).

The parts of a faceframe are joined using dowel, mortise-and-tenon, or stub tenon joints. The assembled faceframe is glued to the edges of the bulkheads, bottom, and partitions. The parts can be nailed and the nails set and hidden.

Tops

The tops on furniture units made with carcass construction are often made of the same material as the carcass. If this is plywood or particleboard, the edges must be banded (see previous chapter).

Tops may be flush with or overhang the front and sides of the carcass (Fig. 31-15).

Base

A variety of bases can be used on furniture units. The base should fit the design of the piece. Those most often used are leg and rail construction, legs attached directly to the carcass, plinth, and a recessed toeboard.

An example of leg and rail construction and individual legs is shown in Fig. 31-16. Two variations of a plinth are shown in Fig. 31-17. The plinth is assembled and then joined to the base unit. Some variations on the toeboard are in Fig. 31-18.

CABINET CONSTRUCTION

Commercially made cabinets are available from many cabinet manufacturers in a wide range of sizes and de-

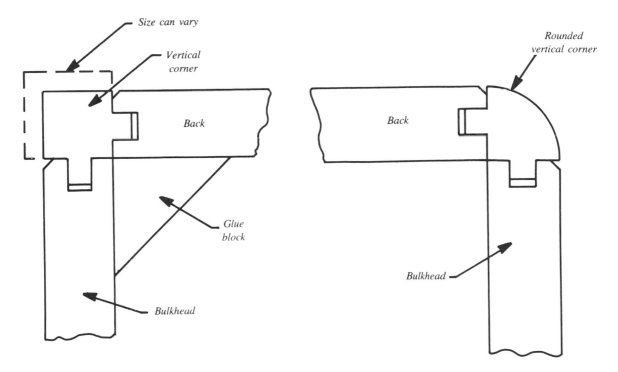

Fig. 31-9. Vertical corners can be joined using a solid wood corner.

signs. The cabinets are sold completely assembled and finished; the homeowner must simply install them.

Some people prefer to have cabinets built to suit their individual needs and sized to exactly fit their rooms. The designs that follow are suitable for mass production or custom construction.

Standard Cabinet Types and Sizes

Standard types of kitchen cabinets include wall, base, vanity, tall oven and utility cabinets. Their standard widths and heights are shown in Fig. 31-19. Notice that these units are made up of drawers, doors, faceframes, sides, backs, tops, shelves, bases, and a wide variety of hardware.

The members of the National Kitchen Cabinet Association have agreed upon these standards. Across the country cabinet manufacturers and custom builders tend to observe these sizes. Especially important are the heights, because if a base cabinet is too low or too high, it is very inconvenient to use. Wall and shelves that are too high are also inconvenient. Detailed design sizes are

in Fig. 31-20. Sizes for cabinets for the handicapped shown are in Figs. 31-20 and 31-21.

KITCHEN PLANNING

Before designing the cabinets it is necessary to plan the kitchen layout. The kitchen is planned around the three major areas: food storage, cooking and preparation, and cleanup. The storage involves placement of canned goods, fresh foods, and frozen foods. This requires shelving, wire bins, and a refrigerator-freezer. The cooking area includes the stove and oven and a microwave. The preparation and cleanup area includes a sink, compactor, dishwasher, and disposal.

The cabinet arrangement depends to a certain extent upon the shape and size of the kitchen. The commonly used shapes include the I-shape, L-shape, U-shape, and corridor (Fig. 31-22).

It is recommended that the kitchen be planned around a working triangle. The distance should not exceed 22 feet. The purpose of this is to improve efficiency

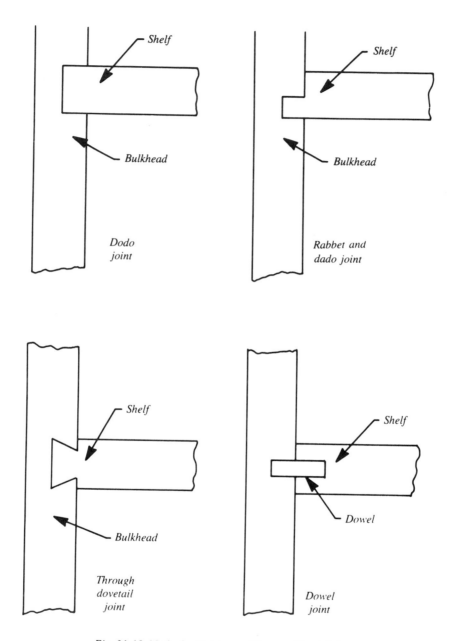

Fig. 31-10. Methods of joining partitions and fixed shelves.

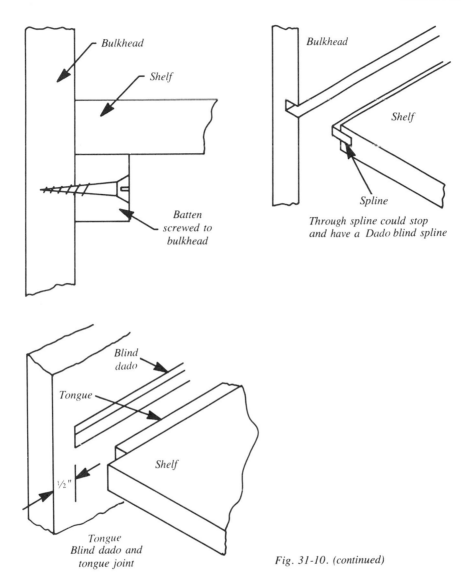

Batten
screwed to
bulkhead

Through spline could stop
and have a Dado blind spline

Tongue
Blind dado and
tongue joint

Fig. 31-10. (continued)

by reducing the amount of walking necessary (see Fig. 31-22).

After the major appliances are located, check to see that there is sufficient countertop surface by each. There should be 3 to 4 feet on each side of the sink, 2 feet on each side of the cooking unit, and at least 1 foot beside the refrigerator-freezer. The minimum amount of base cabinet plus appliance surface should be 15 lineal feet, not including corners.

Drawing the Kitchen Layout

Make a drawing of the kitchen and show all doors, windows, pipes, or other obstructions. As you study the space, locate the appliances in various places. The easiest way is to make scale paper templates for each so you can move them around. After a satisfactory arrangement has been reached, draw the cabinets and appliances on the plan as shown in Fig. 31-23. A scale on which ¼ inch or ½ inch equals 1 foot is convenient.

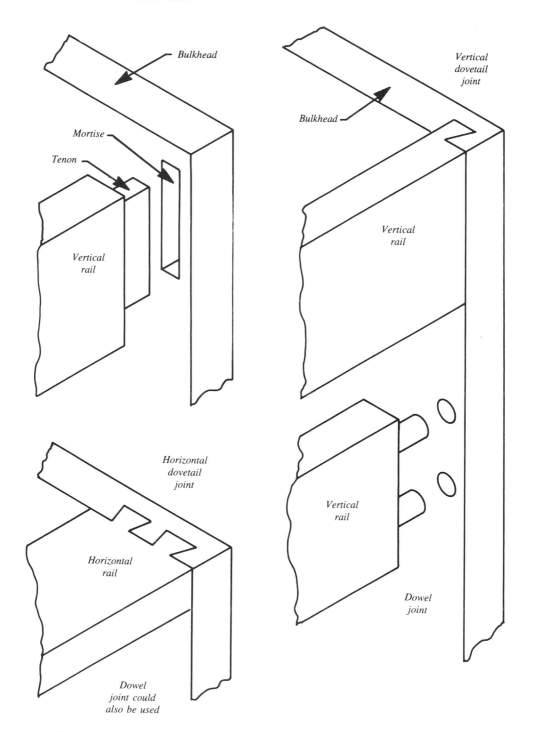

Fig. 31-11. Vertical and horizontal rails can be joined to the bulkhead with these joints.

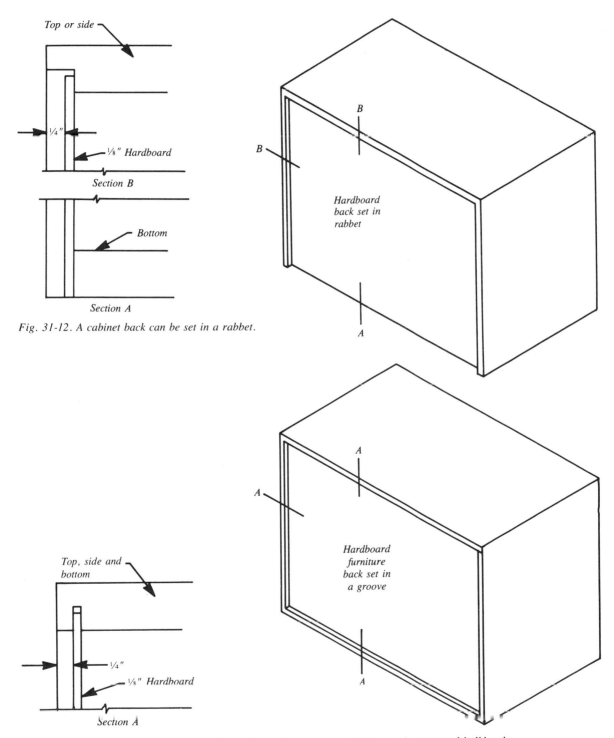

Top or side

¼"

⅛" *Hardboard*

Section B

Bottom

Section A

Fig. 31-12. *A cabinet back can be set in a rabbet.*

B

B

Hardboard back set in rabbet

A

A

A

Hardboard furniture back set in a groove

A

Top, side and bottom

¼"

⅛" *Hardboard*

Section A

Fig. 31-13. *Cabinet backs can be set in grooves cut in the top, bottom, and bulkheads.*

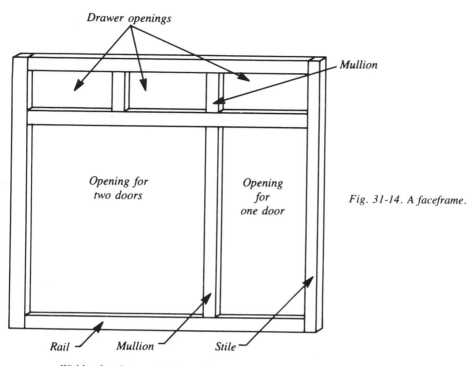

Drawer openings

Mullion

Opening for
two doors

Opening
for
one door

Fig. 31-14. A faceframe.

Rail ⌐   Mullion ⌐   Stile ⌐

*Width of rail to suit design. Common to
use 1¼" to 1¾"*

Now draw the elevations of each wall, showing the location of drawers and doors and the linear sizes of the cabinets. Remember, long cabinets are built in shorter sections and joined on the job (Fig. 31-24). It is helpful to study kitchens shown in magazines and in advertising materials from kitchen cabinet manufacturers. These drawings will illustrate the size of each cabinet and the use of the space.

Constructing Cabinets with a Faceframe

Cabinets can be built with or without a faceframe. The latter will be covered later in this chapter.

The carcass of the faceframe cabinet is ¾-inch plywood or particleboard. The faceframe is solid wood. The doors and drawer fronts may be solid wood or plywood.

Study the construction details in Fig. 31-25. Exterior bulkheads are those that are visible and must be of hardwood plywood or covered with veneer or plastic laminate. Interior bulkheads and partitions are not visible and can be of less costly plywood or particleboard. The interior bulkhead is one that meets a wall or another cabinet. The faceframe is glued or glued and nailed to the bulkheads. Wood cleats are used to secure the top to the

carcass. The back adds a great deal to the rigidity of the unit. It is usually ⅛-to-¼-inch hardboard.

When considering faceframe construction, also decide on the type of door and drawer construction to be used. For years the use of a lipped door was standard. The lip is normally ⅜ × ⅜ inch. Other styles now used are the reveal overlay and the overlay. These require the use of special hidden hinges. Another style involves setting the doors and drawers flush with the faceframe. This presents special difficulties because it is necessary to get the crack the same size on all sides. These styles are shown in Fig. 31-26.

Building Cabinets for Turning Corners

There are three commonly used ways to build cabinets to turn a 90-degree corner. The easiest is to butt two cabinets together and fill the space between them with a filler strip. This, however, wastes the entire corner (Fig. 31-27).

A second method involves building a rectangular cabinet, allowing it to fill the corner space. The adjoining cabinet then butts up against it (Fig. 31-28).

A third method provides the most useful space. It

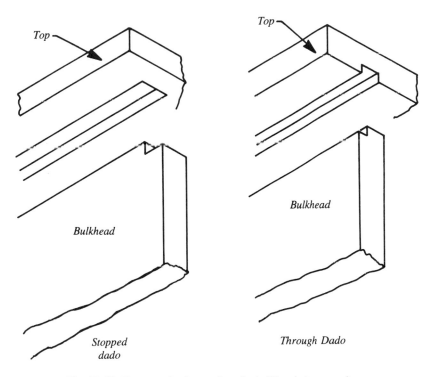

Fig. 31-15. Tops can be fastened to the bulkheads in several ways.

involves building a corner cabinet with a door on a 45-degree angle (Fig. 31-29) or a square corner with a 90-degree door (Fig. 31-30). The adjoining cabinets from both sides butt up against this corner unit.

When building the base unit, cut the pieces to size. Locate and cut dadoes for fixed shelves and notches for the toeboard and the rigid back. Figure 31-31 illustrates a typical set of bulkheads and partitions. Cut a dado in the bottom for interior partitions. Remember the partition and interior bulkhead are ½ inch narrower than the exterior bulkhead because the back nails directly on to them. Cut a ⅜-×-½-inch rabbet in the back edge of the interior bulkhead.

ASSEMBLING THE BASE UNIT

The base unit can be assembled by using butt joints and nails. However, dadoes give a stronger cabinet. The best grade cabinets are assembled with glue and a few nails. No nails are used on the exterior bulkhead.

To assemble the base unit, mark the location of the partitions on the bottom. If they are set in dadoes, cut them at those locations. Place the bottom on its back

edge on the floor, slide the partitions in place, and nail to the bottom (Fig. 31-32). Place the shelves into the dadoes and nail in place. Nail the cleat in place on the front. Turn the cabinet over and nail the rear rigid back in place. Now square the cabinet by measuring its diagonals and adjusting it until they measure the same length. Carefully keep it square and nail the back in place. It can be secured with 2d common nails or ¾-inch staples. Turn the unit over and nail the toeboard in place, then apply the faceframe.

Assembling the Faceframe

The faceframe is made using rails, or horizontal members, stiles, or vertical members, and mullions, which are the vertical members between doors or drawers (Fig. 31-33). The faceframe members are joined using ⅜-inch-diameter-×-2-inch-long dowels. Use two dowels at each union. A tongue set in a short groove can also be used.

Lay the faceframe members on the floor and assemble dry to make certain the joints will close easily. Put glue in the dowel holes and insert the dowels. Begin by

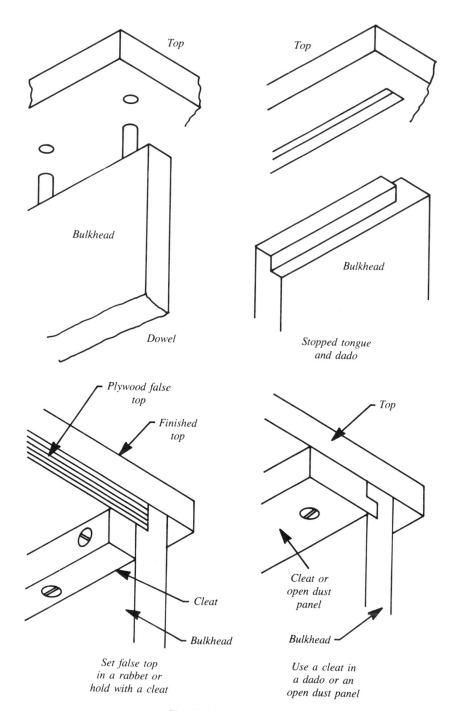

Top

Top

Bulkhead

Bulkhead

Dowel

Stopped tongue
and dado

Plywood false
top

Finished
top

Top

Cleat

Cleat or
open dust
panel

Bulkhead

Bulkhead

Set false top
in a rabbet or
hold with a cleat

Use a cleat in
a dado or an
open dust panel

Fig. 31-15. (continued)

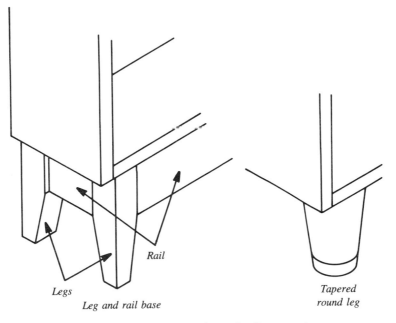

Rail

Legs

Leg and rail base

Tapered
round leg

Fig. 31-16. A base can use leg and rail construction.

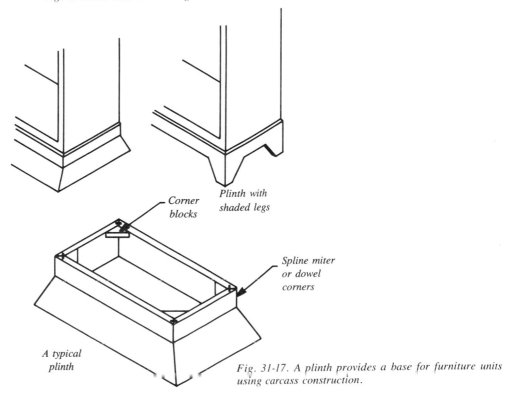

Corner
blocks

Plinth with
shaded legs

Spline miter
or dowel
corners

A typical
plinth

Fig. 31-17. A plinth provides a base for furniture units
using carcass construction.

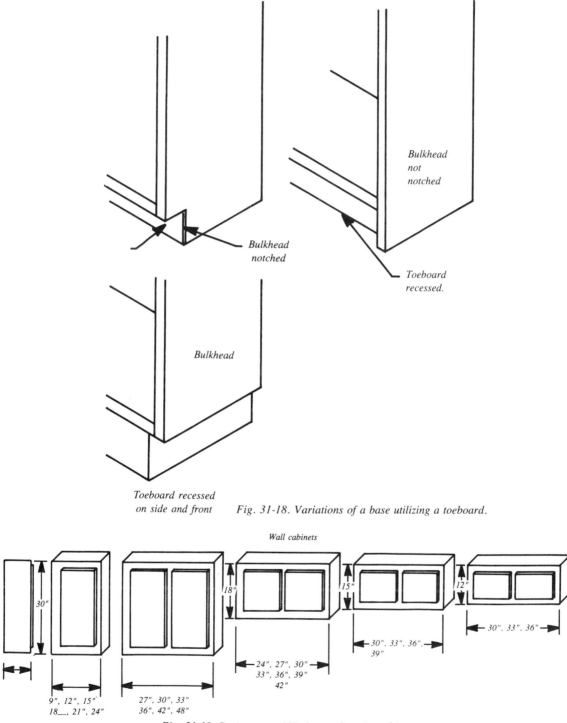

Bulkhead
not
notched

Bulkhead
notched

Toeboard
recessed.

Bulkhead

Toeboard recessed
on side and front

Fig. 31-18. Variations of a base utilizing a toeboard.

Wall cabinets

30"

18"   15"   12"

24", 27", 30"
33", 36", 39"
42"

30", 33", 36",
39"

30", 33", 36"

9", 12", 15"
18__, 21", 24"

27", 30", 33"
36", 42", 48"

Fig. 31-19. Basic types of kitchen and vanity cabinets.

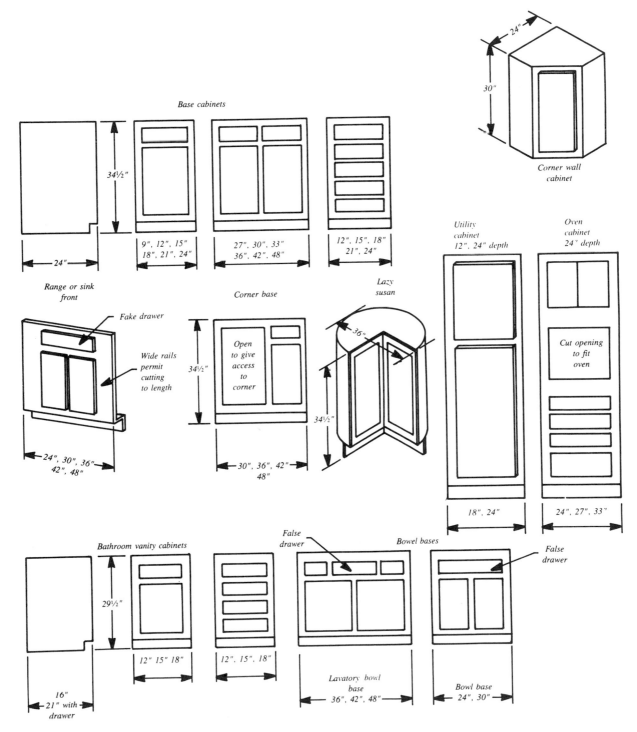

Base cabinets

34½"

24"

9", 12", 15"
18", 21", 24"

27", 30", 33"
36", 42", 48"

12", 15", 18"
21", 24"

Corner wall cabinet

24"

30"

Range or sink front

Corner base

Lazy susan

Fake drawer

Wide rails permit cutting to length

Open to give access to corner

34½"

34½"

36"

34½"

24", 30", 36"
42", 48"

30", 36", 42"
48"

Utility cabinet
12", 24" depth

Oven cabinet
24" depth

Cut opening to fit oven

18", 24"

24", 27", 33"

Bathroom vanity cabinets

False drawer

Bowel bases

False drawer

29½"

16"
21" with drawer

12" 15" 18"

12", 15", 18"

Lavatory bowl base
36", 42", 48"

Bowl base
24", 30"

Fig. 31-19. (continued)

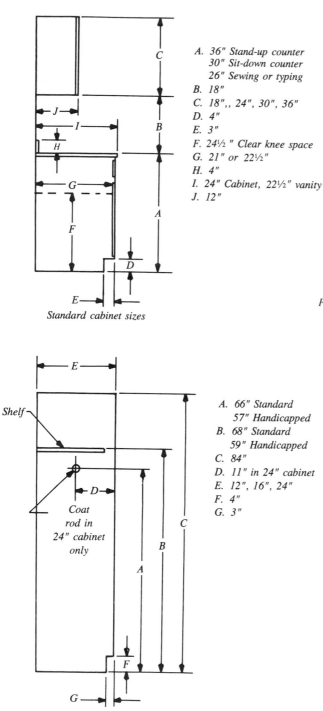

A. *36" Stand-up counter*
   30" Sit-down counter
   26" Sewing or typing
B. *18"*
C. *18",, 24", 30", 36"*
D. *4"*
E. *3"*
F. *24½ " Clear knee space*
G. *21" or 22½"*
H. *4"*
I. *24" Cabinet, 22½" vanity*
J. *12"*

Standard cabinet sizes

Fig. 31-20. Standard sizes for kitchen and vanity cabinets.

Shelf

A. *66" Standard*
   57" Handicapped
B. *68" Standard*
   59" Handicapped
C. *84"*
D. *11" in 24" cabinet*
E. *12", 16", 24"*
F. *4"*
G. *3"*

Coat
rod in
24" cabinet
only

Tall cabinets

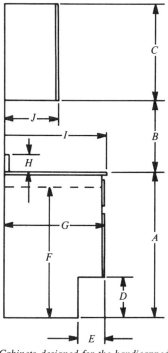

Cabinets designed for the handicapped

A. Counter must be able
   to be adjusted to 28",
   32" and 36"
   31" Bath vanity
B. 15" to 20"
C. 18", 24", 30"
D. 10"
E. 7"
F. 29½" Clearance for a
   wheel chair
G. 22½" maximum
H. 4"
I. 24" maximum, 22½" vanity
J. 12"

Fig. 31-21. Design sizes for cabinets for the handicapped.

joining the inside pieces first and work to the outer members (Fig. 31-34). Clamp carefully so the joints close but do not tighten too much; excess pressure can twist the faceframe. Measure the diagonals to see if they are square. If not, clamp along the long diagonal until it is square.

Joining the Faceframe to the Base

The easiest way to join the faceframe to the base is to nail it with 6d finishing nails, set the nails, and fill the holes. On quality work it is best to glue the faceframe in

place. Set the unit up on sawhorses, apply glue to the faces of the base, place the faceframe on it, and clamp. Use as many clamps as necessary to get the faceframe touching the base at all points (Fig. 31-35).

NONFACEFRAME CABINETS

Cabinets made without faceframes use flush, flush overlay, and reveal overlay construction. Flush construction is much the same as used with faceframe cabinets. The elimination of the faceframe reduces cost and gives a different appearance. It lends itself to economical use of plastic laminates on exposed surfaces (Fig. 31-36).

The flush overlay construction completely hides the bulkheads and partitions. Plastic laminates may be effectively used on this style. It can use conventional and concealed hinges. (Fig. 31-37).

Reveal overlay construction provides an accent between doors and drawer fronts. The reveal can be made on all horizontal and vertical joints or it can be combined to use flush overlay in some places to provide additional styling. This style permits the use of conventional or concealed hinges (Fig. 31-38).

INSTALLING CABINETS

Before installing cabinets, make certain the wall is free of irregularities and obstructions. If it is a remodeling job, remove the old baseboard. If the wall is not straight it might be necessary to do some preliminary work to correct it.

Mark the studs on the wall surface. Check to see if the floor is level or if it has highspots. Either plane down the high spots or shim up the base cabinet so it will be horizontal and steady. Then draw a horizontal line on the wall 34½ inches above the highest remaining spot on the floor.

Installing Base Cabinets

Base cabinets are installed first. Begin by installing the unit in the corner and work out in each direction from there. Proceed as follows:

Place the corner unit in place and shim it up at the floor until it lines up with the horizontal 34½-inch mark (Fig. 31-39). Check it with a level and adjust the shims until it is horizontal. Drill holes through the rigid back at each stud and fasten to each stud with wood screws. Place a washer under the head of each screw. The screw should go at least ¾ inch into the stud.

Place one of the base units next to the corner unit.

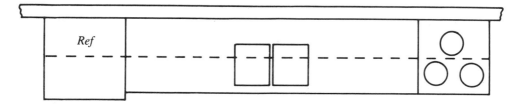

I-shaped kitchen

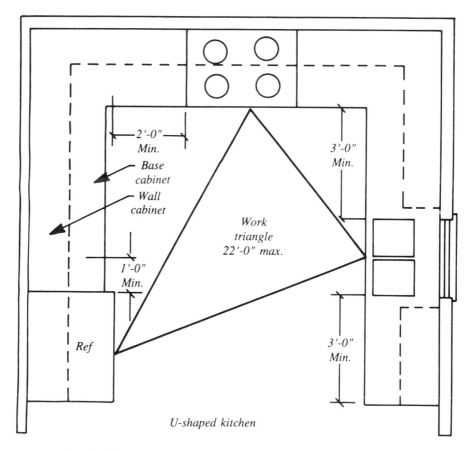

U-shaped kitchen

Fig. 31-22. Frequently used arrangements of kitchen cabinets.

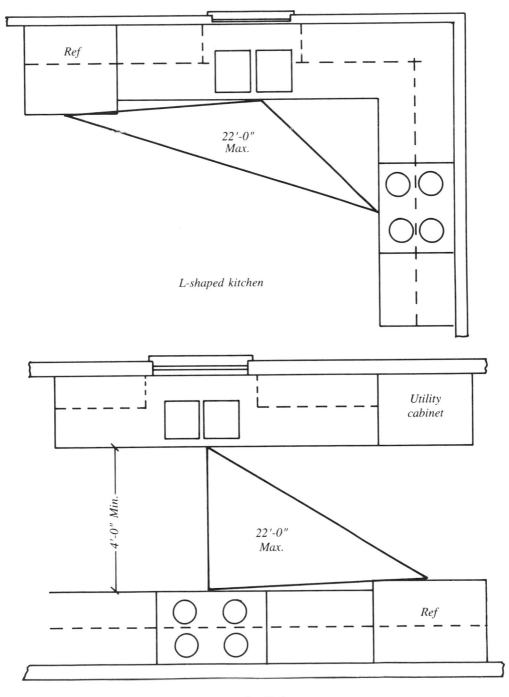

L-shaped kitchen

Corridor kitchen

Fig. 31-22. (continued)

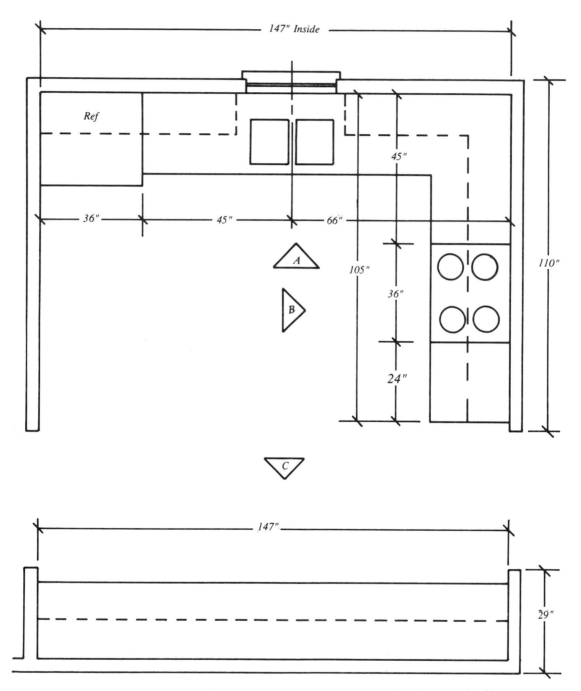

Fig. 31-23. A plan view showing a proposed solution to the location of appliances and cabinets.

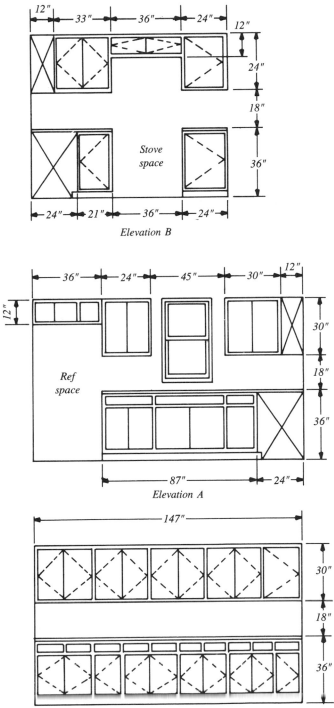

12"

| 33" | 36" | 24" |

12"

24"

18"

Stove
space

36"

24" — 21" — 36" — 24"

Elevation B

36" — 24" — 45" — 30"

12"

12"

30"

Ref
space

18"

36"

87" — 24"

Elevation A

Fig. 31-24. Wall elevations show drawer and door details. These are elevations for the plan in Fig. 31-23.

147"

30"

18"

36"

Elevation C

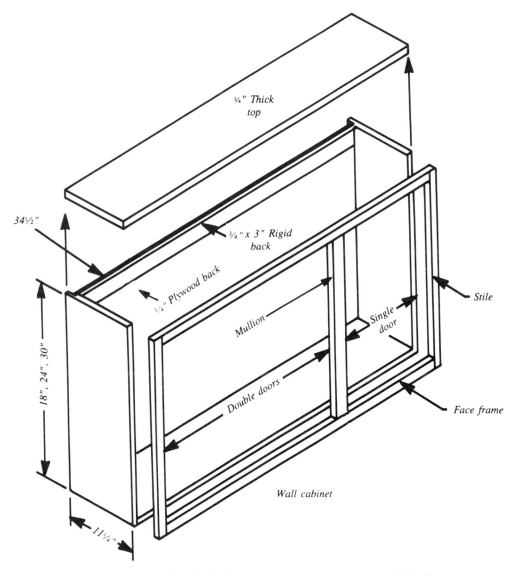

*Fig. 31-25. Construction details for a conventionally built
kitchen base and wall cabinets with faceframes.*

Clamp the two units together with C clamps or hand-screws. Shim it at the floor to bring it into a horizontal position and in line with the 34½-inch line on the wall. Drill pilot holes in the frame of one cabinet and anchor holes in the other. Drill these about 6 inches from the top and bottom of the cabinet. Fasten the cabinets together with wood screws.

Now fasten this unit to the studs in the wall as ex-

plained above. Repeat this for each unit. If the wall is crooked, it might be necessary to shim the cabinets along the wall. The cabinet units should be kept straight even though the wall is crooked (Fig. 31-40).

Check to see if the corner is 90 degrees. If it is more than or less than 90 degrees, it will have to be shimmed as shown in Fig. 31-41.

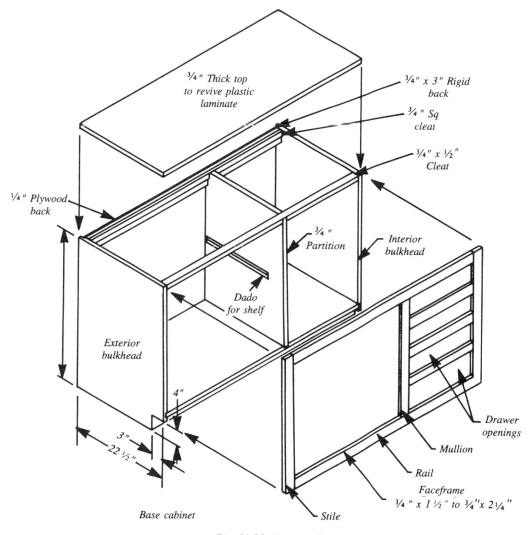

3/4" Thick top
to revive plastic
laminate

3/4" x 3" Rigid
back

3/4" Sq
cleat

3/4" x 1/2"
Cleat

1/4" Plywood
back

3/4"
Partition

Interior
bulkhead

Dado
for shelf

Exterior
bulkhead

4"

3"

22 1/2"

Drawer
openings

Mullion

Rail

Faceframe
3/4" x 1 1/2" to 3/4" x 2 1/4"

Base cabinet

Stile

Fig. 31-25. (continued)

Installing the Countertop

The countertop is placed on the assembled and installed base unit and secured to it with either wood screws through the corner blocks or cleats secured to the rigid back and bulkheads.

Installing the Wall Cabinets

Before installing wall cabinets, check the walls to be certain they are straight and that they meet adjoining walls at 90 degrees, as shown for base cabinets. Then check to see if they are plumb (Fig. 31-42). *Plumb* means the wall is vertical or meets the floor at a 90-degree angle. Now proceed as follows:

Mark a line 54 inches above the floor on the wall. The bottom of the wall cabinet is to align on this line. Place the corner cabinet in place, using some type of stand to hold it above the base cabinet. A carpenter-built box is as good as anything (Fig. 31-43). Fasten the cabinet to the wall with wood screws placed through the rigid back into each stud. The wall cabinet will have a rigid back at the top and bottom of the cabinet.

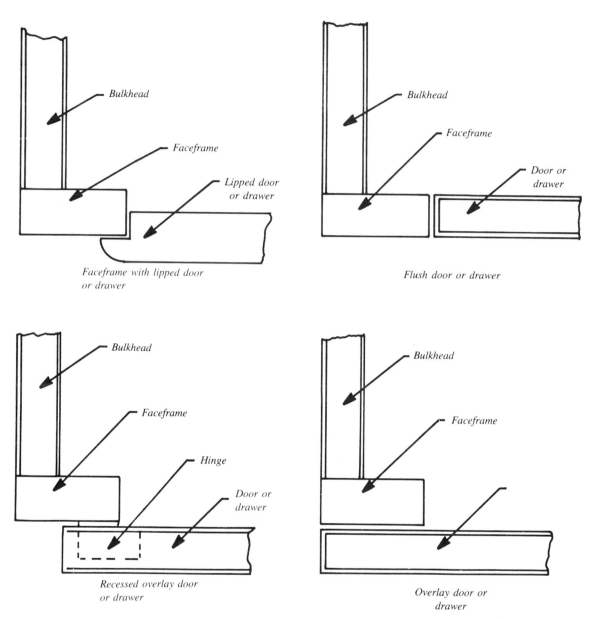

Bulkhead

Faceframe

Lipped door
or drawer

Faceframe with lipped door
or drawer

Bulkhead

Faceframe

Door or
drawer

Flush door or drawer

Bulkhead

Faceframe

Hinge

Door or
drawer

Recessed overlay door
or drawer

Bulkhead

Faceframe

Overlay door or
drawer

Fig. 31-26. The placement of doors in relation to the faceframe provides design variations.

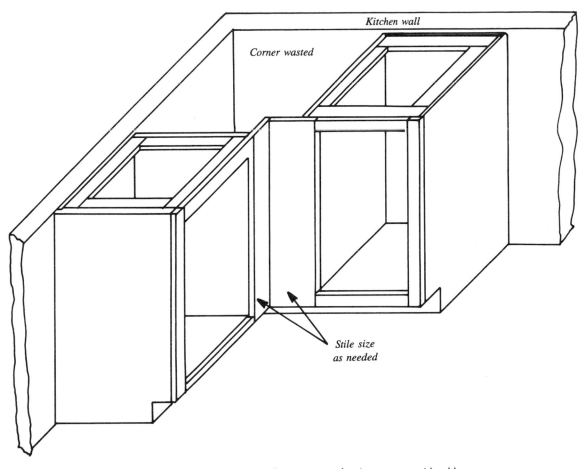

Fig. 31-27. This is the easiest way to form a corner but it wastes considerable space.

Place the next cabinet on the boxes and butt it to the corner unit. Join with wood screws as explained for the base unit. Fasten the cabinet to the wall, and continue until all cabinets are in place. Remember to keep them in line with the mark on the wall. Check them with a level to be certain they are horizontal.

CASEWORK USING MECHANICAL FASTENERS

An increasing number of furniture and cabinet units are being built using some form of mechanical fastener. These require that a butt joint be made and holes of various sizes be bored. In addition to ease and speed of assembly, the furniture unit can be shipped unassembled and put together by the purchaser using only a screwdriver or Allen wrench. Following are examples of some of these fasteners.

One-piece fasteners are used in low-stress locations, such as lightweight partitions. While they may be removed and reinstalled several times, they are generally used in locations that do not require disassembly. This fastener requires that a through hole be bored in the panel and a pocket hole bored in the material which will anchor the screw. The screw cuts threads in the side of the anchor hole. Joints made with this fastener do not have to be glued (Fig. 31-44).

A two-piece fastener has a threaded insert that is screwed into a hole in the anchoring material. A decorative head countersunk machine screw is run through a

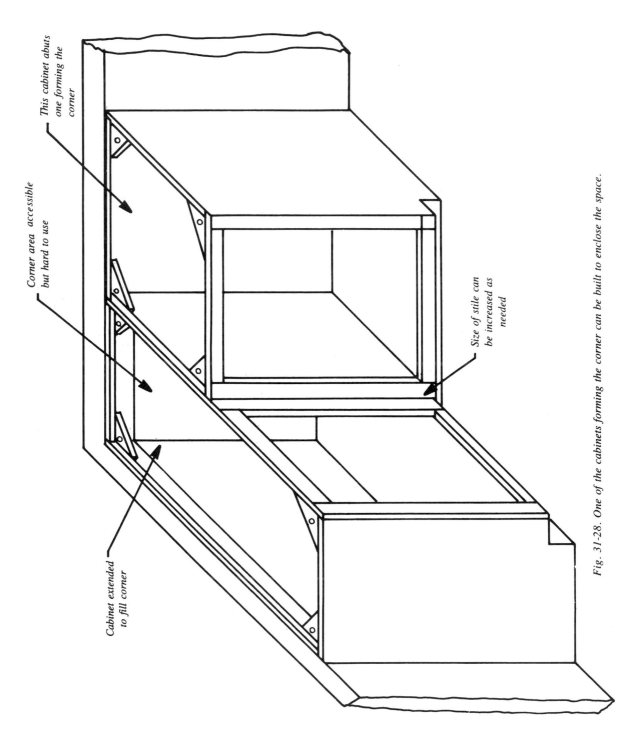

This cabinet abuts one forming the corner

Corner area accessible but hard to use

Size of stile can be increased as needed

Cabinet extended to fill corner

Fig. 31-28. One of the cabinets forming the corner can be built to enclose the space.

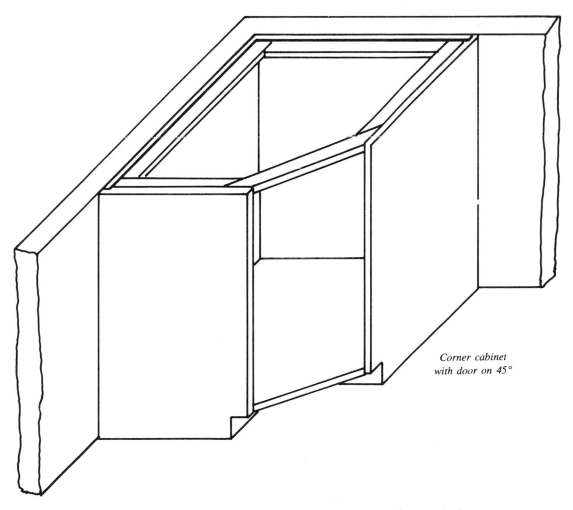

Fig. 31-29. Corner cabinets with a 45-degree angle door give easy access to the space in the corner.

hole bored in the panel and screws into threads inside the insert (Fig. 31-45).

Another two-piece fastener uses a counterbored cylinder lead machine screw that screws into a cross nut, which is set in a hole in the anchoring material (Fig. 31-46).

An eccentric type fastener develops high tightening forces and is used on units that require occasional disassembly. The eccentric casing is forked-shaped. The bolt engages the center and holds the pieces together as the eccentric is turned (Fig. 31-47). Another eccentric type of fastener is shown in Fig. 31-48. It is used to join shelves to the sides of the carcass. The housing is in-

serted into a hole in the shelf. The connecting bolt is screwed into the bulkhead or partition.

A fastener using a lock spring with a mating element is in Fig. 31-49. This hardware is easily inserted and permits easy assembly.

A type of slide-on hardware is shown in Fig. 31-50. The metal wedge is fastened to the edge of the shelf. The shelf can have a groove in the edge if a close-fitting joint is desired. The wedge slides on to a collar screw that is screwed into the partition or bulkhead. Another type of concealed wedge fastener is in Fig. 31-51. It can be used to secure horizontal rails to the partitions or bulkhead.

Another dowel type fastener used for joining shelves

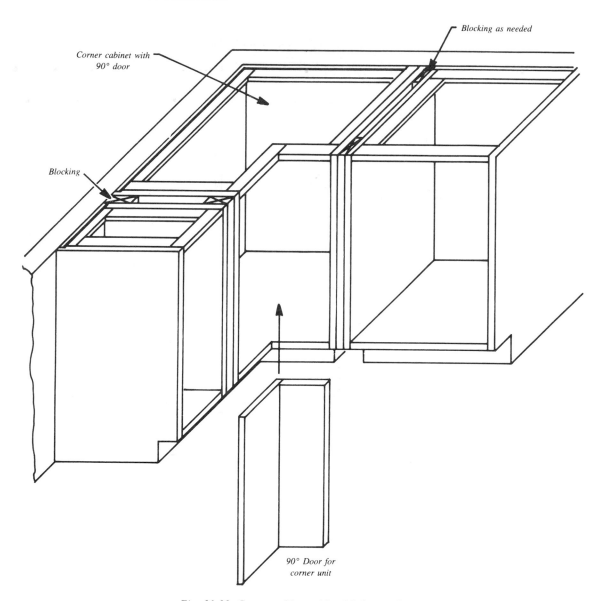

Fig. 31-30. Corner cabinet with a 90-degree door.

and structural panels produces a concealed, releasable joint (Fig. 31-52). The rounded edge-mounted fitting is secured to the shelf by a screw. A threaded fastener with a cone shaped head is screwed into the partition or bulkhead.

One last example uses a universal hook-in bracket. The bracket is joined to one panel with screws. Matching screws in the mating panel fit into the recesses provided (Fig. 31-53).

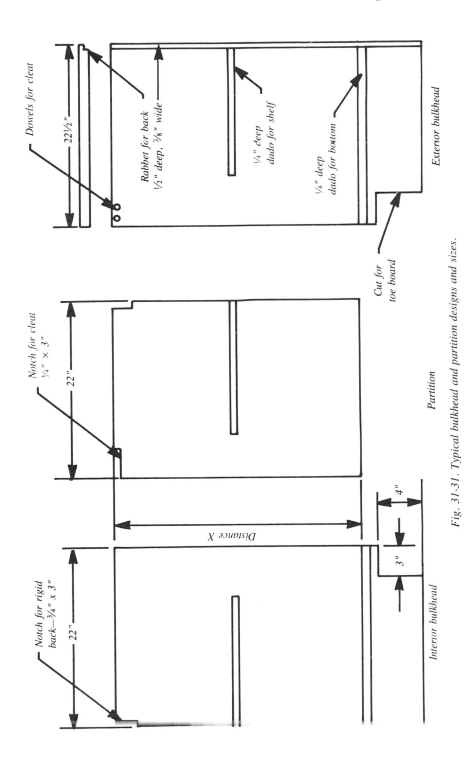

Fig. 31-31. Typical bulkhead and partition designs and sizes.

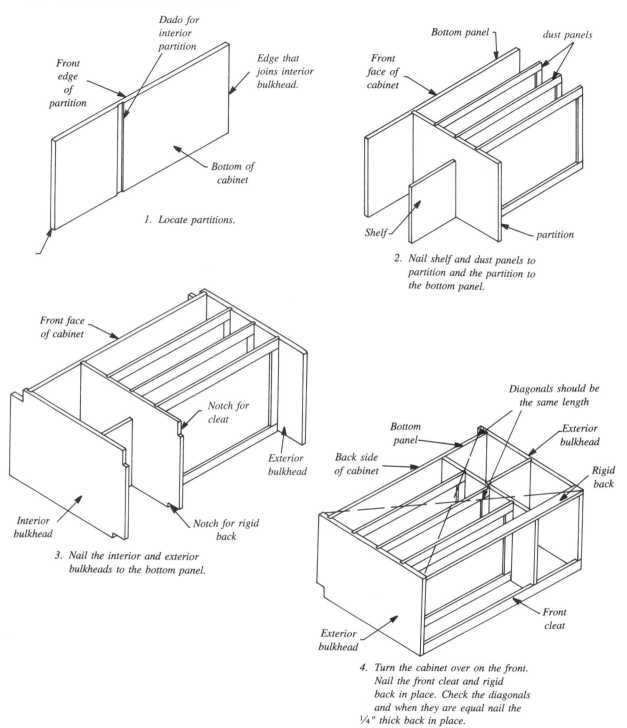

1. Locate partitions.

2. Nail shelf and dust panels to partition and the partition to the bottom panel.

3. Nail the interior and exterior bulkheads to the bottom panel.

4. Turn the cabinet over on the front. Nail the front cleat and rigid back in place. Check the diagonals and when they are equal nail the 1/4" thick back in place.

Fig. 31-32. This is how to assemble the cabinet.

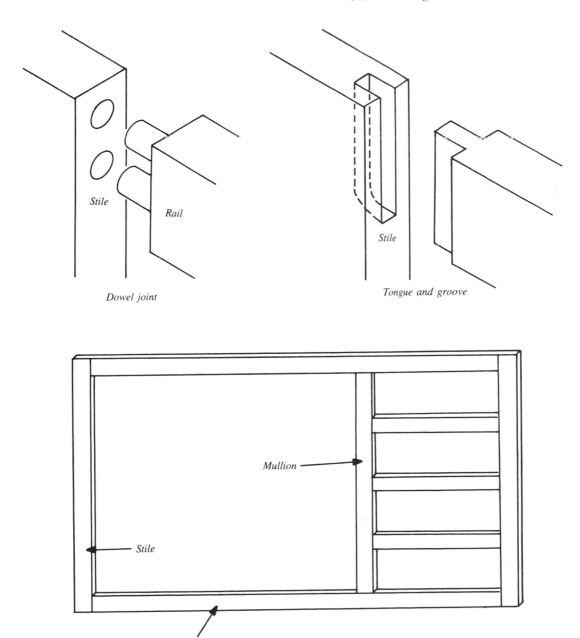

Dowel joint

Tongue and groove

Mullion

Stile

Rail

Fig. 31-33. Parts of a faceframe.

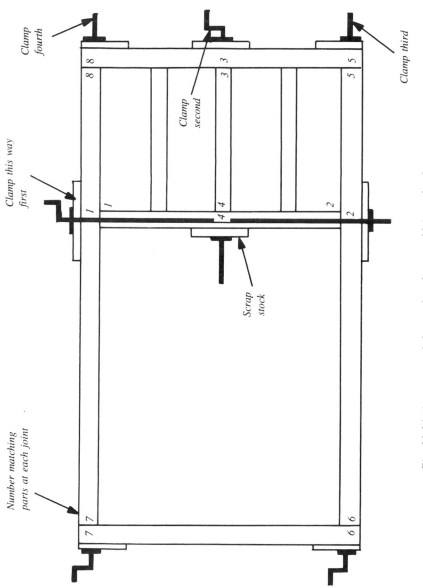

Clamp
fourth

Clamp third

Clamp
second

Clamp this way
first

Scrap
stock

Number matching
parts at each joint

Fig. 31-34. A recommended procedure for assemblying a faceframe.

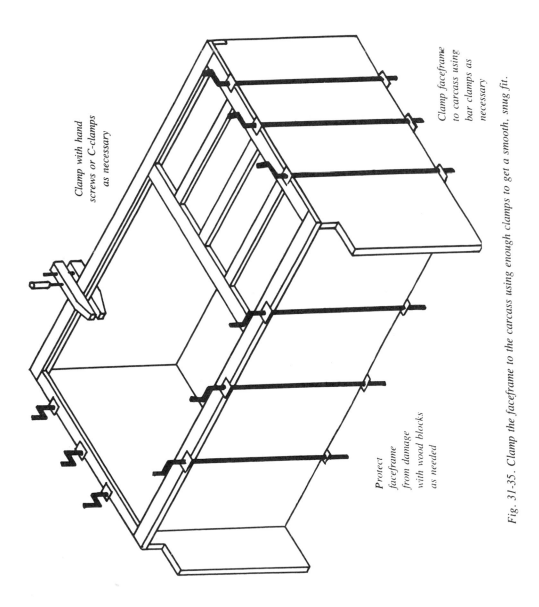

Clamp with hand
screws or C-clamps
as necessary

Clamp faceframe
to carcass using
bar clamps as
necessary

Protect
faceframe
from damage
with wood blocks
as needed

Fig. 31-35. Clamp the faceframe to the carcass using enough clamps to get a smooth, snug fit.

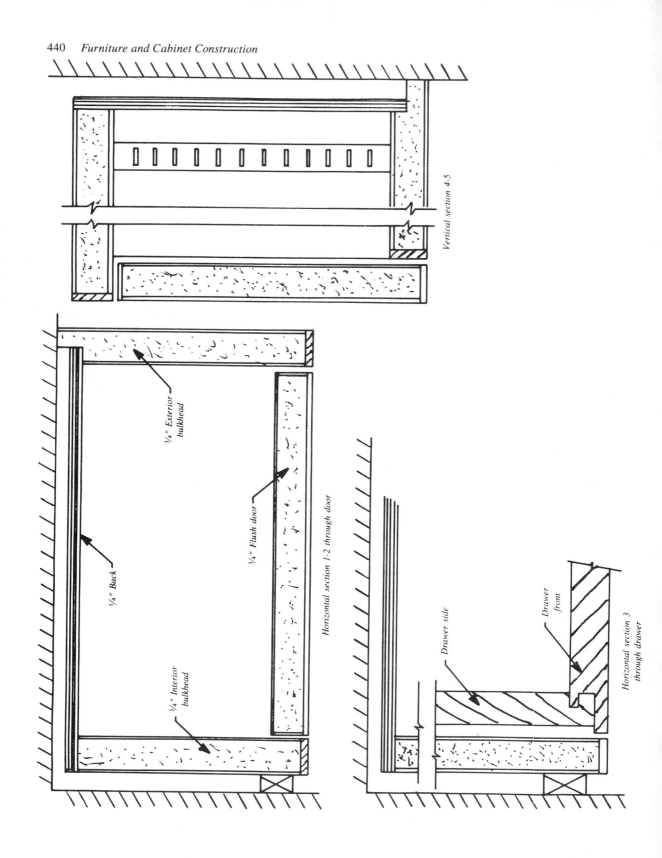

Vertical section 4-5

¾" Exterior
bulkhead

¾" Flush door

¼" Back

Horizontal section 1-2 through door

¾" Interior
bulkhead

Drawer side

Drawer
front

*Horizontal section 3
through drawer*

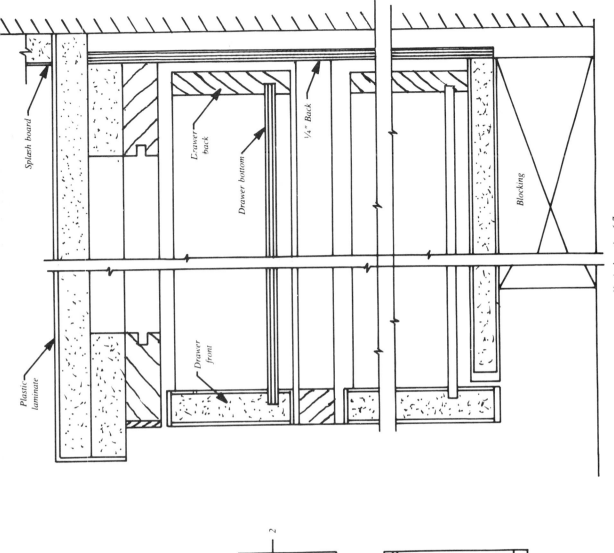

Splash board

Plastic laminate

Drawer back

Drawer bottom

1/4" Back

Blocking

Drawer front

Vertical section 6-7

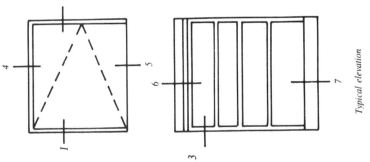

Typical elevation

Fig. 31-36. Details of flush cabinet construction without a faceframe.

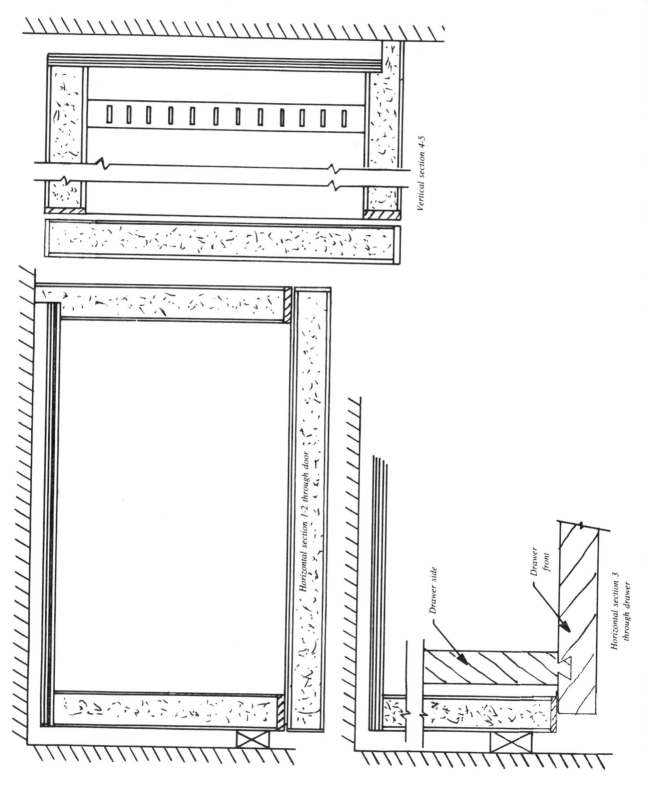

Vertical section 4-5

Horizontal section 1-2 through door

Drawer side

Drawer front

Horizontal section 3 through drawer

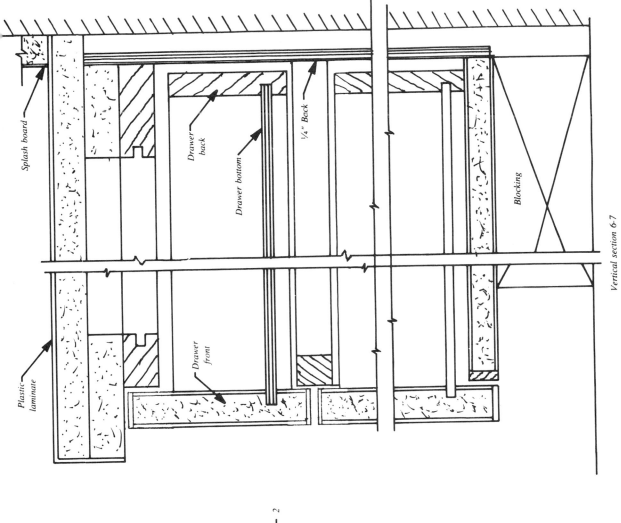

Splash board

Plastic
laminate

Drawer
back

Drawer bottom

1/4" Back

Drawer
front

Blocking

Vertical section 6-7

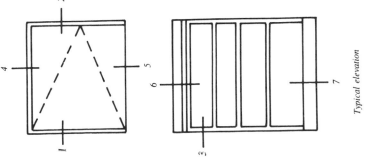

Typical elevation

Fig. 31-37. Flush overlay construction without a faceframe hides the edges of the bulkheads and the top and bottom panels.

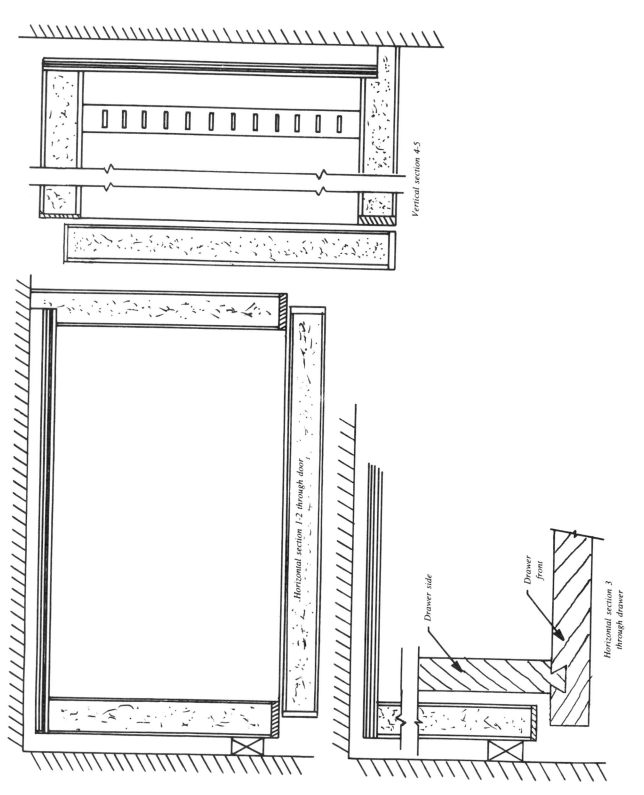

Vertical section 4-5

Horizontal section 1-2 through door

Drawer side

Drawer front

Horizontal section 3 through drawer

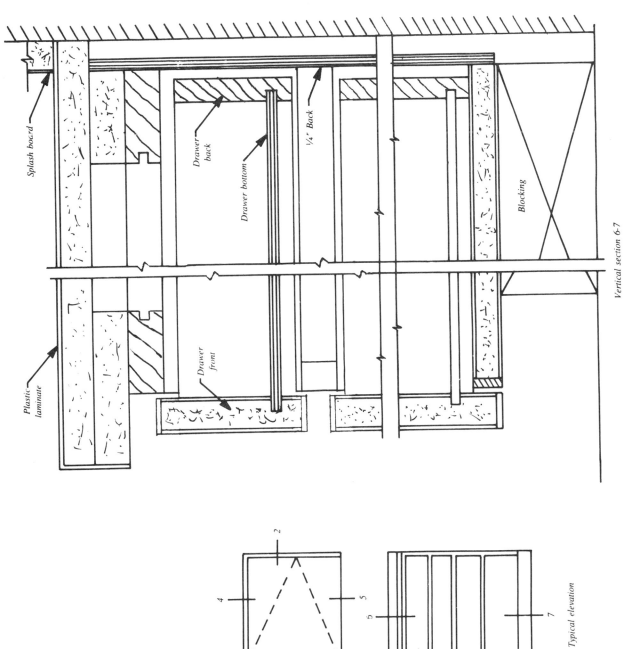

Fig. 31-38. Reveal overlay construction without a faceframe partially exposes the edges of the bulkheads and the top panel.

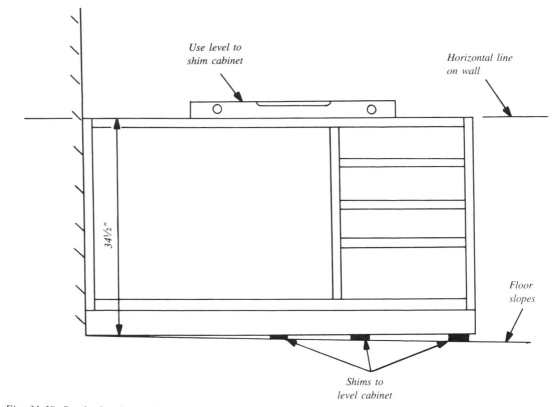

*Use level to
shim cabinet*

*Horizontal line
on wall*

34½"

*Floor
slopes*

*Shims to
level cabinet*

Fig. 31-39. Set the first base cabinet next to a corner. Get it level and mark horizontal line on wall.

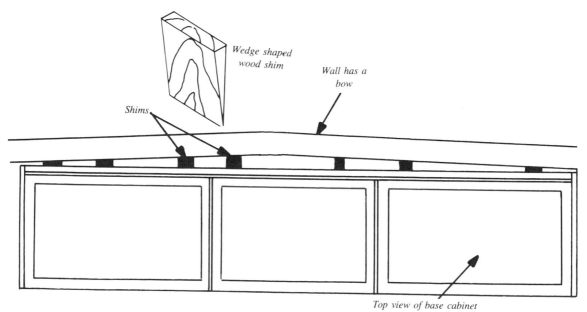

*Wedge shaped
wood shim*

*Wall has a
bow*

Shims

Top view of base cabinet

Fig. 31-40. If the wall is crooked, shim the cabinets so the assembled cabinets are straight.

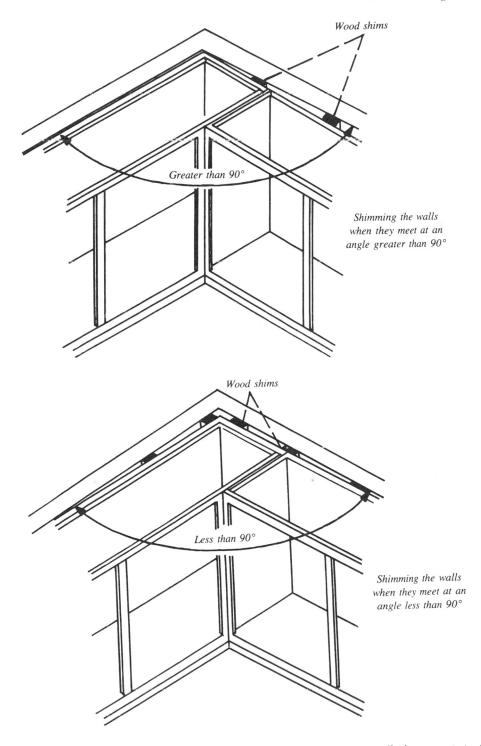

Wood shims

Greater than 90°

Shimming the walls
when they meet at an
angle greater than 90°

Wood shims

Less than 90°

Shimming the walls
when they meet at an
angle less than 90°

Fig. 31-41. This is how to shim cabinets at a corner when the walls do not meet at a 90-degree angle.

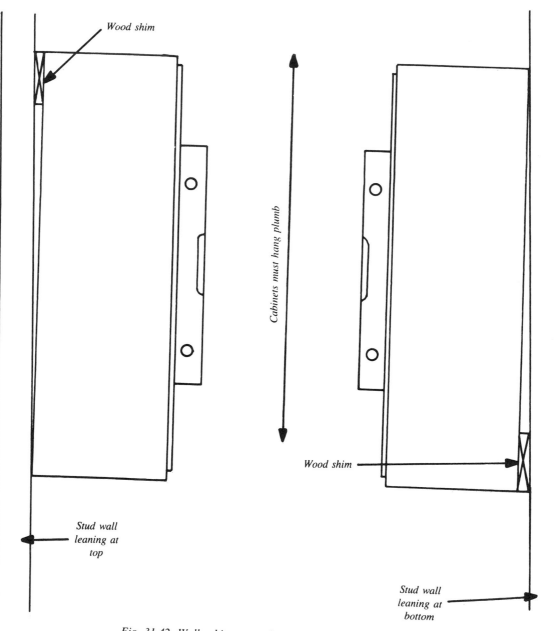

Fig. 31-42. Wall cabinets are shimmed out so they hang plumb.

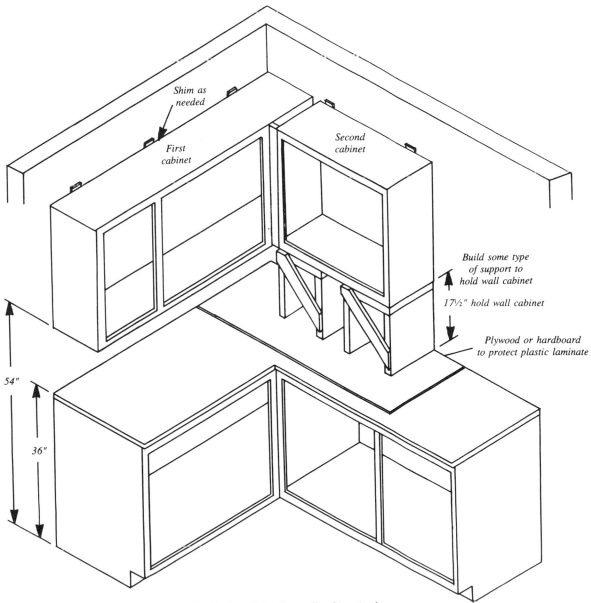

Shim as needed

First cabinet

Second cabinet

Build some type of support to hold wall cabinet

17½" hold wall cabinet

Plywood or hardboard to protect plastic laminate

54"

36"

Fig. 31-43. Install the first wall cabinet in the corner.

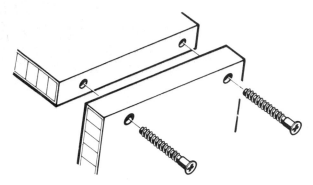

Fig. 31-44. *This one-piece fastener cuts threads in the wood (Courtesy Hafele America Co.).*

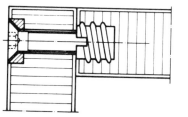

Fig. 31-45. *This two-piece fastener has a treaded insert that is set into the panel (Courtesy Hafele America Co.).*

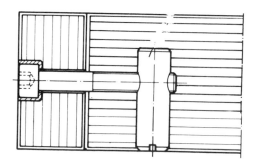

Fig. 31-46. *This two-piece fastener uses a cross nut set in a hole in the panel (Courtesy Hafele America Co.).*

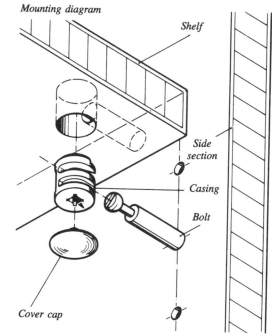

Fig. 31-47. *The bolt fits into the casing that, when turned, will secure it (Courtesy Hafele America Co.).*

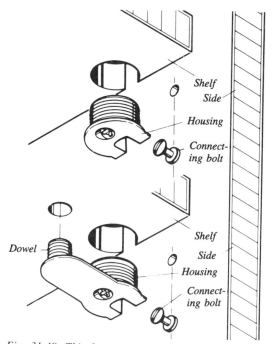

Fig. 31-48. *This fastener is strong and is used to join shelves to the bulkhead (Courtesy Hafele America Co.).*

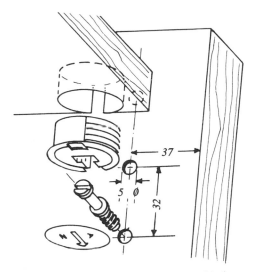

Fig. 31-49. A lock spring is used to secure this fastener. It is easily assembled and disassembled (Courtesy Hafele America Co.).

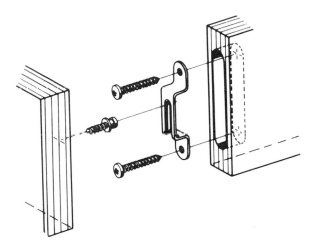

Fig. 31-51. This fastener is used to join horizontal rails to legs and partitions (Courtesy Hafele America Co.).

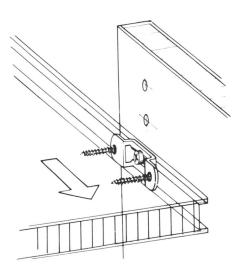

Fig. 31-50. This fastener slides on the screw and wedges on the collar of the screw (Courtesy Hafele America Co.).

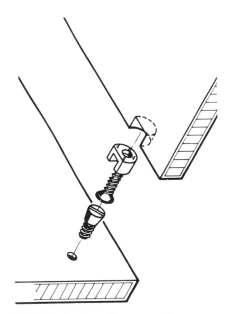

Fig. 31-52. This dowel type fastener produces a concealed, releasable joint (Courtesy Hafele America Co.).

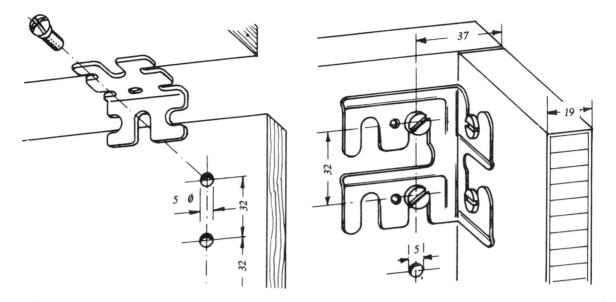

Fig. 31-53. Two types of hook-in brackets that seat on screws (Courtesy Hafele America Co.).

Chapter 32

Doors, Shelves, and Drawers

Cabinets and many types of furniture use doors, shelves, and drawers. While their main function is to provide storage, they also greatly influence the appearance of the unit. The previous two chapters revealed the variety of ways doors, shelves, and drawers are used. This chapter will show how to build and install the basic types.

DOORS

The types of doors are: flush, overlay, lipped, and sliding (Fig. 32-1). The flush, lipped, and overlay doors can be made of solid wood or plywood or have a flat or raised panel (Fig. 32-2).

Hinged Doors

Butt hinges are generally used for flush doors. Some types are decorative and are mounted on the face of the cabinet. Semiconcealed hinges are used on lipped doors. One part of the hinge is visible while the largest part is concealed in the lip. (See Chapter 3 for detailed information on hinges.)

Most doors used on furniture and cabinets require only two hinges. They must be carefully installed so the door is square on the frame and swings freely. Work carefully when locating them.

Butt Hinges. Butt hinges are installed as follows for flush and overlay doors (Fig. 32-3).

Be certain the door fits the frame. If it is a flush door it should have a 1/16-inch (1.5-mm) gap on all sides. If it is an overlay door it should be flush with the outside of the frame.

Mark the location of the hinges on the edge of the door. For most doors, keep them the same distance from the top and bottom, which is usually 1 to 2 inches (25 to 50 mm). Place the hinge on the edge of the door. Let the barrel stick out beyond the face of the door. Use a try square to position the hinge square with the edge of the door. Mark around the leaf of the hinge.

Mark the thickness of the hinge on the face of the door to outline the area that is to be cut away to receive the leaf of the hinge. This area is called a *gain*. The depth of the gain depends upon the hinge; a swaged hinge requires less depth than a plain hinge (Fig. 32-4).

Stand a sharp wood chisel on the marks and cut into the wood, keeping the bevel side facing into the gain. Slant the chisel and remove the wood forming the gain.

Place the hinge in the gain. Drill an anchor hole and install the center screw. This permits the hinge to be moved a little when the door is fastened to the frame. The other screws will be put in later.

Place the door in position on the frame. If it is a flush door, hold it in place with wood shims. This keeps the spacing equal on all sides. Mark the location of each hinge on the frame. Remove the door and mark the gains on the frame. Cut to depth with a wood chisel. Now fasten the door to the frame, using one screw on each hinge.

Check the door to see if it swings easily and is in the proper location. A common error is to cut the gains too deep. If this happens, the door will not close. To correct this, remove the hinges and place pieces of cardboard or veneer in the gain. When the door fits properly, install the remaining screws. Finally, install the knob and door catches.

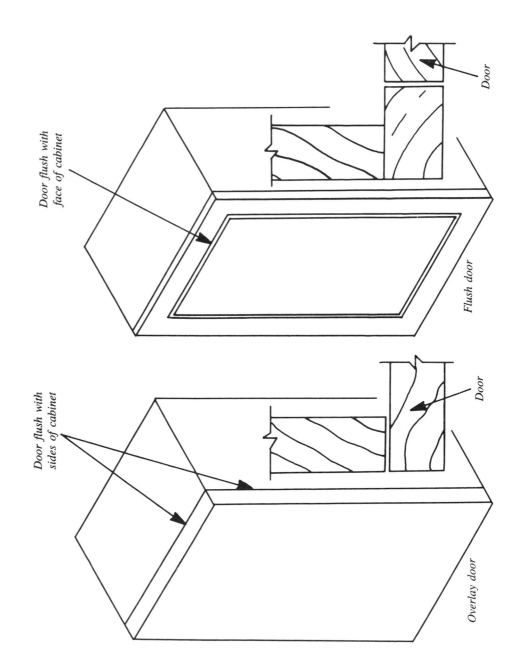

Door

Door flush with
face of cabinet

Flush door

Door flush with
sides of cabinet

Door

Overlay door

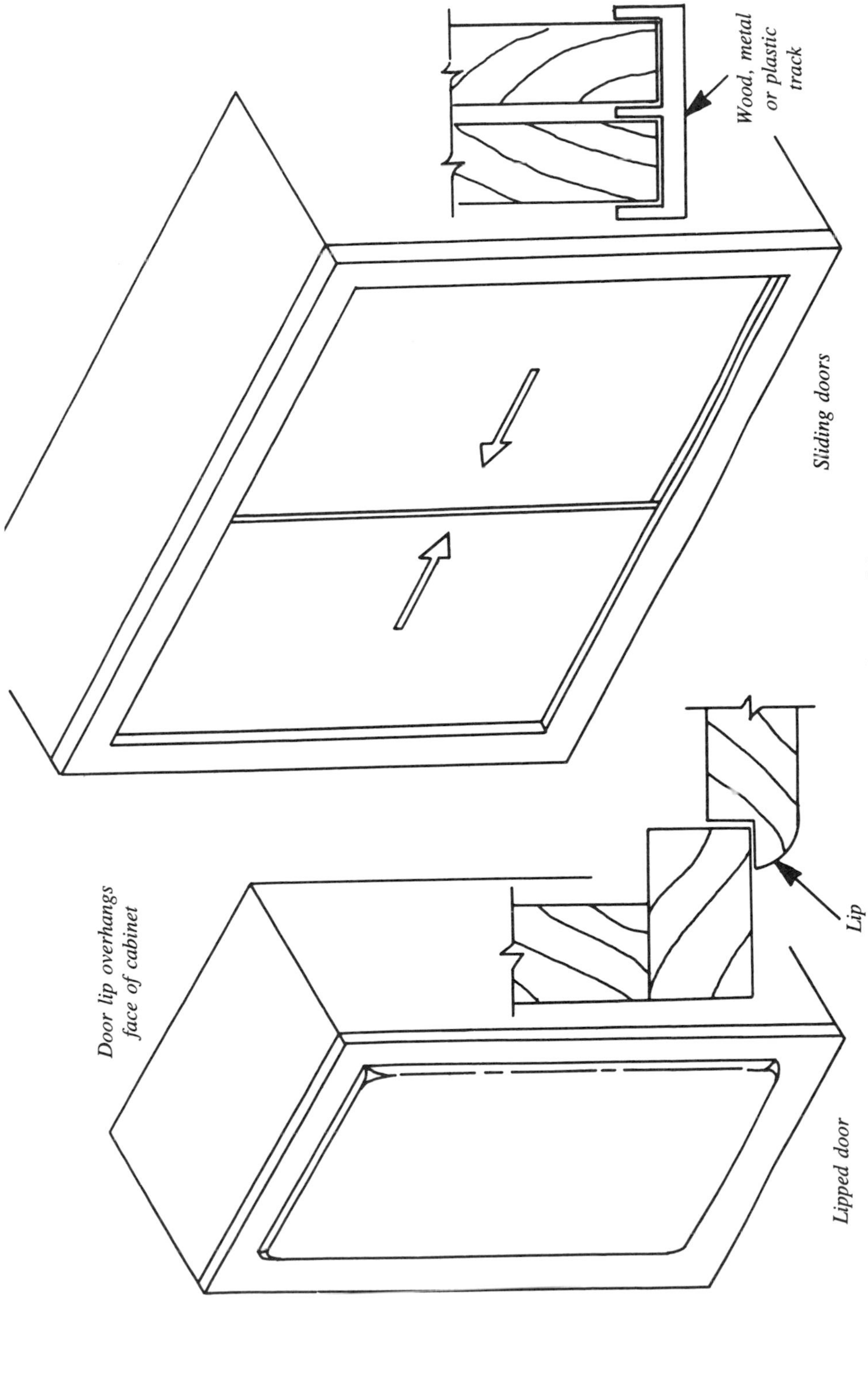

Wood, metal or plastic track

Sliding doors

Door lip overhangs face of cabinet

Lip

Lipped door

Fig. 32-1. The types of doors.

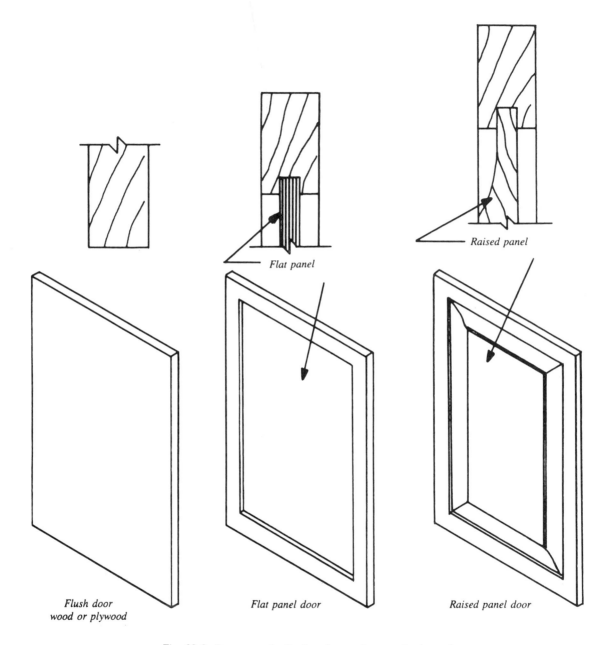

Flat panel

Raised panel

Flush door
wood or plywood

Flat panel door

Raised panel door

Fig. 32-2. Doors may be flush or have a flat or raised panel.

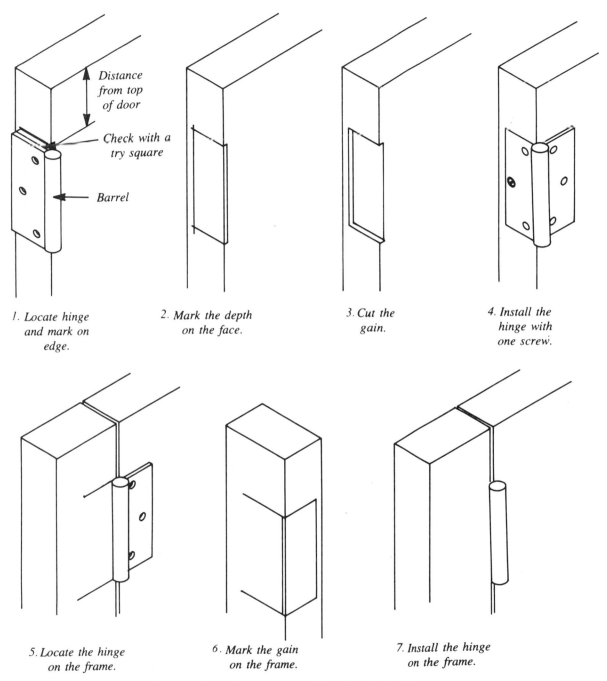

1. Locate hinge
   and mark on
   edge.

2. Mark the depth
   on the face.

3. Cut the
   gain.

4. Install the
   hinge with
   one screw.

5. Locate the hinge
   on the frame.

6. Mark the gain
   on the frame.

7. Install the hinge
   on the frame.

Fig. 32-3. The steps to cut a gain and install a butt hinge.

Semiconcealed Hinges. Semiconcealed hinges are used to install lipped doors. They are surface-mounted, so it is not necessary to cut gains. Proceed as follows to install semiconcealed hinges:

Measure the desired distance from the top and bottom of the door. Place the hinge in the lip and install the screws (Fig. 32-5).

Place the door on the frame. Line it up so it fits properly. Fasten the surface-mounted leaf to the frame. Put only one screw in each leaf, then check the door to see if it swings properly. Adjust as needed and install the other screws.

Sliding Doors

The two types of sliding doors are straight and tambour. Straight doors can be made of almost any material, such as wood, plywood, hardboard, glass, or metal. Tambour doors are flexible and made of many small slats. Solid wood slats are most often used.

Straight Sliding Doors. Straight sliding doors can use several types of tracks. Manufactured tracks are made of metal or plastic. For heavy doors, tracks often have a bottom piece that rolls on ball bearings (Fig. 32-6).

Straight sliding doors can also run in wood tracks. Grooves can be cut into the surface of the cabinet, or wood strips an be glued and nailed to form a track. (Fig. 32-7). The space between the strips or the width of the groove should be at least $1/16$ inch (1.5 mm) wider than the part of the door that is to fit into them. This keeps the doors from binding in the tracks.

If you use grooves, remember to cut them before the cabinet is assembled. The grooves on the top should be at least twice as deep as those on the bottom in order to install the door. Slip the top of the door in the top groove and push it all the way up. Hold the door over the bottom groove and lower it into place.

Sliding doors must have flush handles. Thin doors can have a $3/4$-inch (13-mm) hole bored through to form a finger hold. Thicker doors use recessed metal handles (Fig. 32-8). See chapter 3 for more information on handles.

Tambour Doors. Tambour doors are made from narrow wood strips glued to heavy canvas, which makes the door flexible so it can roll around corners. The wood strips can be shaped as desired, or preshaped wood moulding can be used (Figs. 32-9 and 32-10).

Tambour doors slide in a groove cut in the base and top (Fig. 32-11). When using a groove, cut it $1/16$ inch (1.5 mm) wider than the part of the door that will fit into it. Remember to cut the top groove deeper so the door can be installed. To build a tambour door, proceed as follows:

Cut the wood strips to the proper length and shape the surface as desired. Cut a rabbet on each end of each strip. The size will vary depending upon the thickness of the door strip. Strips are generally $3/8$ to $1/2$ inch thick and $5/8$ to $3/4$ inch wide. The bottom rabbet should be $1/16$ inch (1.5 mm) longer than the depth of the groove, and the top rabbet should be twice as long as the bottom rabbet.

The end strip at the bottom of the door is often made wider than the rest to provide a better place to fasten a handle.

Lay the strips on a bench with the back side up. Carefully line up the ends. Coat the canvas strips with glue; polyvinyl adhesive works well. When the glue is tacky, place the canvas strips across the wood strips and clamp in place. Keep it clear of the ends so it does not interfere with the sliding of the door. Let it dry thoroughly.

Now construct the tracks. Cut the groove with a power router, following a template. The template can be made from hardboard. Clamp the template to the wood, and use a router with a straight bit set to the correct depth. Run the router along the edge of the template (Fig. 32-12). The rounded corners in the track should have as large a radius as possible. Be certain the door can be installed later.

Assemble the project and install the doors after everything is finished.

SHELVES

Shelves are built into many pieces of furniture. Some are adjustable while others are fixed. Fixed shelves are held by cleats, metal shelf brackets, a mechanically made butt joint, and dadoes (Fig. 32-13). Adjustable shelves are held with metal strips having metal clips, long adjustable brackets, or pins set into holes in the side. The metal strips holding clips or brackets can be mounted on the surface or recessed into the side.

When planning shelves, the width is an important factor. The actual width depends upon the size of the piece of furniture and the purpose it will serve. For normal size books, a $7\frac{1}{2}$-inch (190-mm) width is adequate. The distance between fixed shelves is also important. Lower shelves are usually spaced wider apart than upper shelves. Normal spacing is about 10 inches (254 mm) for

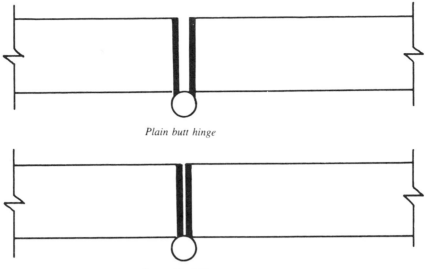

Plain butt hinge

Swaged butt hinge

Fig. 32-4. A plain butt hinge requires a deeper gain than a swaged hinge.

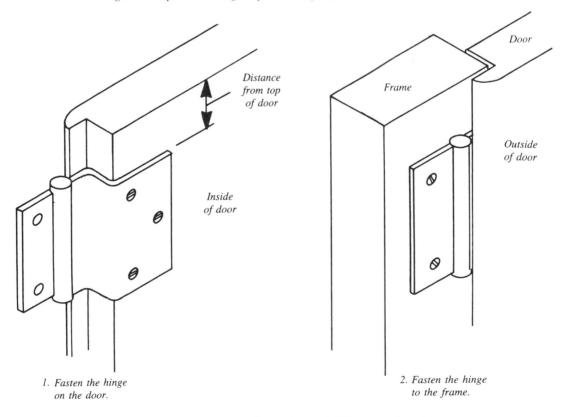

Distance
from top
of door

Inside
of door

Door

Frame

Outside
of door

1. Fasten the hinge
   on the door.

2. Fasten the hinge
   to the frame.

Fig. 32-5. The steps to install a semiconcealed hinge on a lipped door.

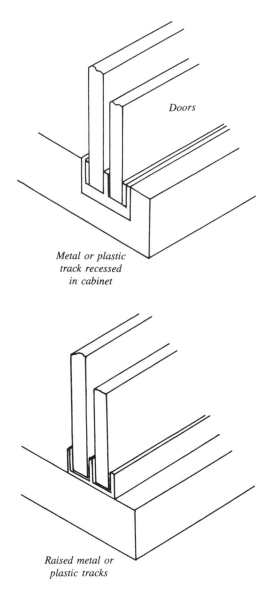

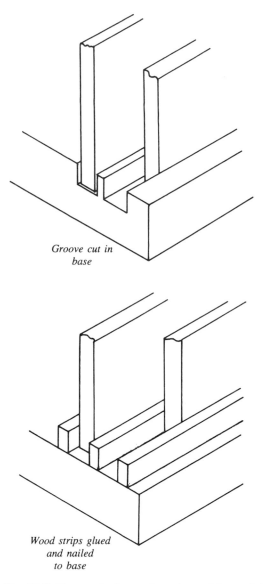

Fig. 32-6. Hardware for straight sliding doors.

Fig. 32-7. Grooves in the wood can be used for straight sliding doors.

upper shelves, 13 to 14 inches (330 to 355 mm) for lower shelves.

If the shelves are plywood and the edges are visible, they are usually banded. They can be covered with wood veneer, a thicker wood strip, or plastic laminate (Fig. 32-14).

DRAWERS

Drawers are a common item in cabinet and furniture design. They are made in a wide variety of sizes. A drawer has five parts: a front, two sides, a back, and a bottom (Fig. 32-15).

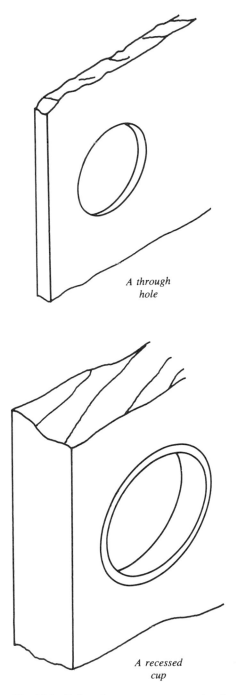

A through
hole

A recessed
cup

Fig. 32-8. Sliding doors require recessed pulls.

The two types of drawers are flush and lipped (Fig. 32-16). A flush drawer has a front that fits inside the cabinet frame. When the drawer is closed the outer face is flush with the face of the frame. A lipped drawer has a rabbet cut on its edges. The lip extends up over the cabinet frame, which hides the space between the drawer and the frame. This type of drawer can be made with a looser fit than the flush drawer.

Drawer fronts are usually made of the same material as the cabinet frame. Because they are visible, they are made from the best quality wood. Fronts are usually ¾ inch thick. The drawer sides and back are not seen, so can be made from cheaper woods, such as poplar or pine. In quality furniture, drawer sides and backs are made from oak or maple. Sides are usually ⅜ to ⅝ inch thick. Drawer bottoms are made from ¼-inch-thick plywood or hardboard. On small drawers, ⅛-inch material can be used.

The joints used to form a drawer are a key to its long life (Fig. 32-17). Several different types are used (see Chapter 12). The strongest joint for fastening the sides to the front, and the most popular on quality furniture, is the dovetail. It is difficult to cut with hand tools, and is usually cut with a power router and a dovetail template.

The rabbet dado joint (sometimes called a lock shoulder) is also a strong joint and should be used on large drawers when dovetailing is not possible. The rabbet joint is the easiest to make but is the weakest. The rabbet and rabbet dado joints are secured by glue and nails or screws.

The back is joined to the sides with a dado, rabbet, or butt joint (Fig. 32-18). The dado is the strongest and is easy to cut. All three are joined by glue and either nails or screws.

The bottom is set into a ¼- × -¼-inch groove in the sides, front, and back (see Fig. 32-15). The bottom should fit loosely in the grove and is not glued. The bottom is not bonded to the sides, therefore the drawer can expand and contract with temperature and moisture changes and not twist or warp.

Making a Drawer

First, study the drawing and determine the size of each piece. Remember to allow for the joints (Fig. 32-19).

Cut the front to size. Allow extra for planing to finished size. The finished size of a flush drawer front should have ¹⁄₁₆ inch (1.5 mm) clearance on all sides to allow for expansion of the wood. If it is a lipped drawer,

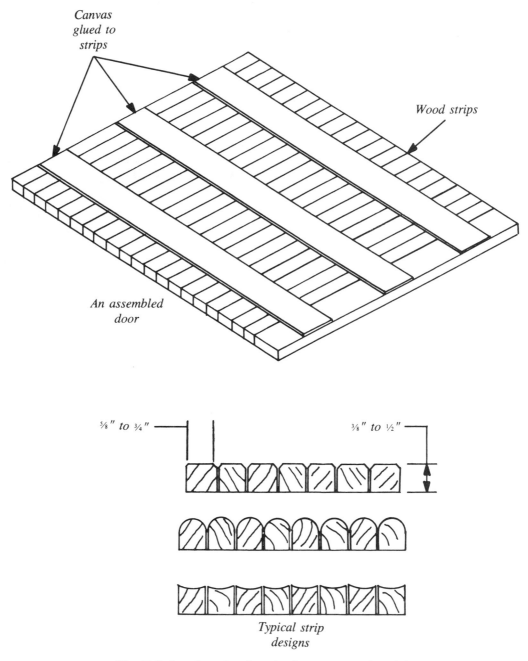

Fig. 32-9. A tambour door is made of many narrow shaped slats.

Fig. 32-10. A typical tambour door.

the front is larger than the frame opening. A ⅜-inch (9 mm) lip on all sides is common (Fig. 32-20).

Cut the sides and back to size, then plane to finished size as shown on the working drawing. Cut the grooves for the bottom in all pieces, cut the dadoes in the sides for the back and cut the rabbet or (rabbet dado) in the front. If the rabbet dado is used, cut it in the side pieces also. Cut the bottom to size.

Now assemble the drawer without glue to see if it fits. Adjust the joints until they fit together without forcing. Take the drawer apart and sand the parts. Sand the top edges of the sides and back round.

Apply glue to the joints, holding the front, back, and sides together. Do not glue in the bottom (Fig. 32-21). Join the front, one side, and the back, then slide in the bottom. Finally, put the other side in place. Clamp it and check for squareness. This can be done by measur-

ing across the diagonals, or you can use a try square inside to check the corners.

Let the glue dry and remove the clamps.

Drawer Guides

A drawer guide is a track used to guide the drawer into the cabinet frame. Good guides are important if you want drawers to operate properly. Guides not only keep the drawer running straight but provide a means for sliding easily.

The choice of drawer guide is part of the working drawings. Because the various drawer guides have special space requirements, the guides must be planned at the same time as the cabinet and drawer.

The common types of guides are center guides, side guides, corner guides, and metal and plastic manufactured guides.

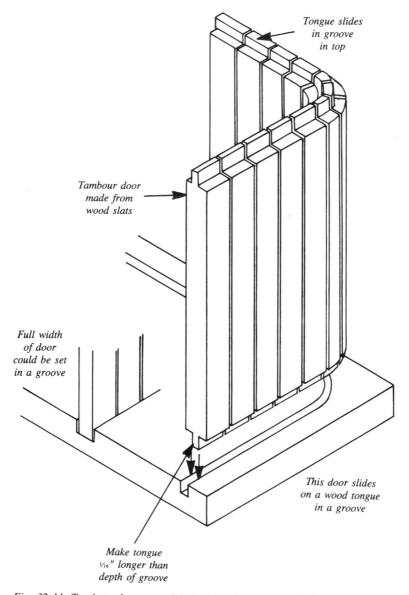

Tongue slides in groove in top

Tambour door made from wood slats

Full width of door could be set in a groove

This door slides on a wood tongue in a groove

Make tongue ¹⁄₁₆" longer than depth of groove

Fig. 32-11. Tambour doors can slide in curved grooves cut in the base and top.

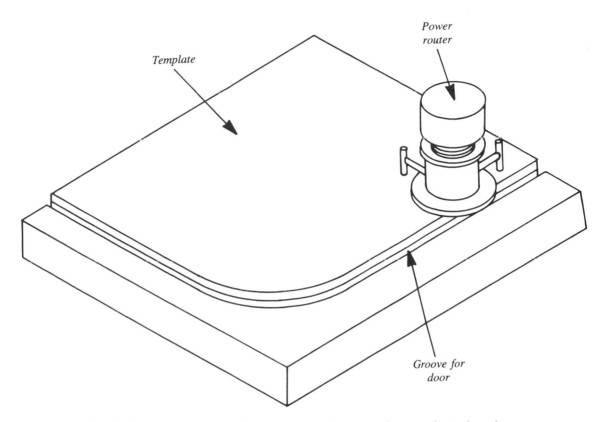

Fig. 32-12. A template is used with a power router to cut curved grooves for tambour doors.

Center guides are a good choice because they reduce the chance that a drawer will bend. They are especially useful on wide drawers. A guide strip, usually ¾ inch wide, is placed in the frame of the cabinet. A guide channel is mounted on the bottom of the drawer (Fig. 32-22). With this type of guide the drawer bottom is set deeper into the drawer. At least ½ inch is needed for the channel on the bottom of the drawer.

Side guides are used in cabinets with solid wood sides. If lipped drawer fronts are used, a dado is cut in the cabinet side (Fig. 32-23). A matching wood strip is glued and screwed to the side of the drawer. This strip should be of smooth hardwood, such as maple, so it will slide easily. If a flush drawer front is used, the groove is cut in the drawer side and the wood strip is fastened to the cabinet wall. In this case the drawer side should be ¾ inch thick so the groove can be ⅜ inch deep. This type of slide is satisfactory for small drawers, but tends to bind with large, heavy drawers.

Corner guides support drawers at the bottom edges of the sides (Fig. 32-24), and can be adapted to carry the drawer from the top edge (Fig. 32-25). The guides are L-shaped wood runners that are joined to the cabinet frame. The bottom edge of the drawer slides on the guide. If the drawer is hung from the top, a wood strip is glued and screwed to the drawer and the L-shaped hanger is fastened to the top. This type of guide does not work well for heavy drawers.

There are many types of manufactured guides, usually involving metal tracks and rollers. They run easily and can carry heavy drawers. Some types fasten to the cabinet side and drawer side, others act as a center guide and have plastic wheels below the sides of the drawers (Fig. 32-26).

Kickers, Stops, and Pulls

When drawers are pulled out past their mid point, the front drops and the back moves upward. A *kicker* can

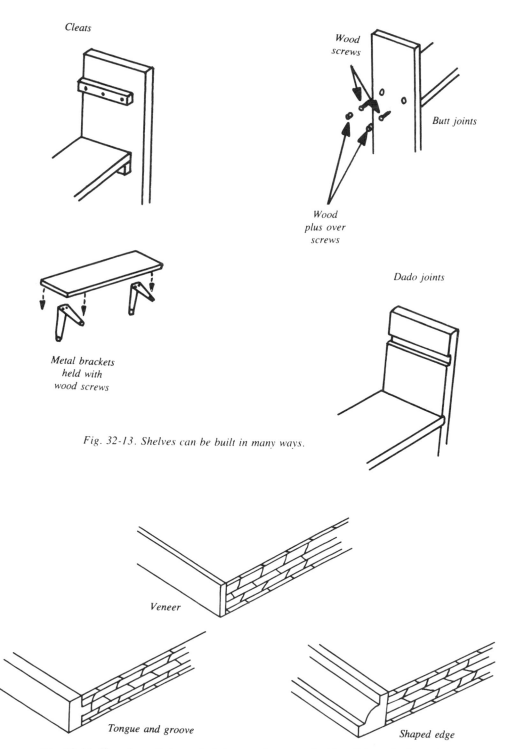

Cleats

Wood
screws

Butt joints

Wood
plus over
screws

Metal brackets
held with
wood screws

Dado joints

Fig. 32-13. Shelves can be built in many ways.

Veneer

Tongue and groove

Shaped edge

Fig. 32-14. The edges of plywood shelves can be covered with solid wood edge strips.

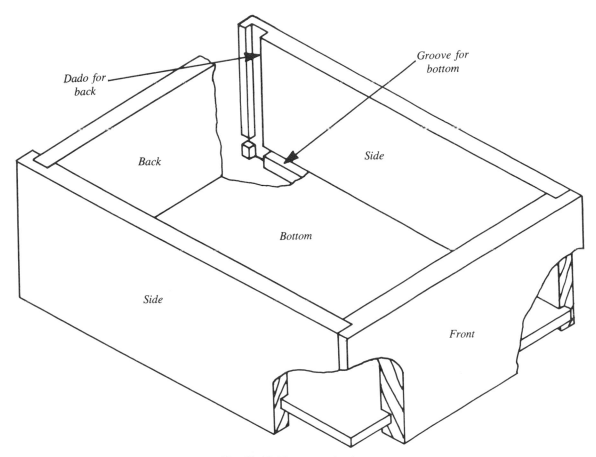

Fig. 32-15. The parts of a drawer.

prevent this tilting. It is installed above the drawer in the center of the frame. Usually ¾-inch-thick wood is used (Fig. 32-27).

Drawer sides are cut a little shorter than the total depth of a cabinet. If the drawer has a flush front, a stop is required. The *stop* is a wood piece placed behind the drawer. It is adjusted so that when the drawer back hits the stop, the front is flush (Fig. 32-28). Stops can also prevent a drawer from being accidentally pulled com-

pletely out of the cabinet. A wood piece can be screwed to the back of the drawer that sticks up far enough to hit the front frame.

There are many styles of drawer pulls and handles made from metal, wood, ceramics, and plastic. These are usually secured to the drawer with a screw or bolt (Fig. 32-29). Many designs can also be made from wood (Fig. 32-30).

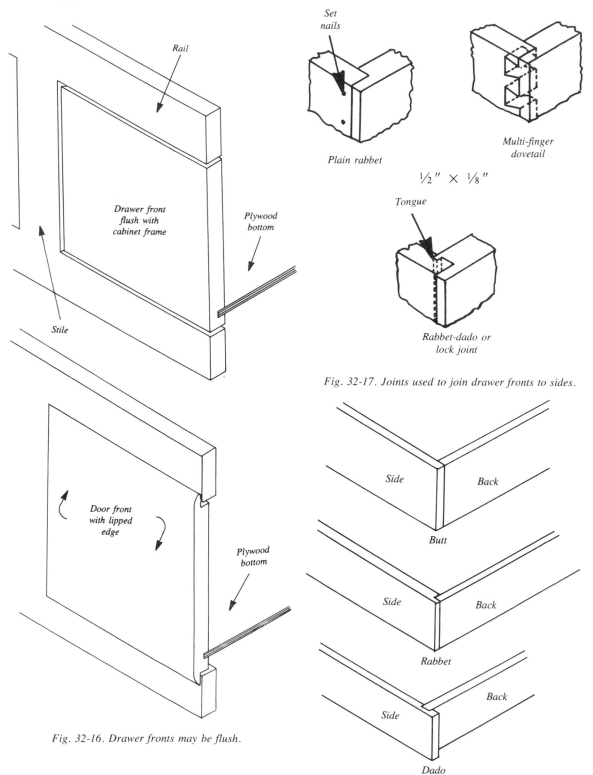

Rail

Drawer front
flush with
cabinet frame

Plywood
bottom

Stile

Set
nails

Plain rabbet

Multi-finger
dovetail

$\frac{1}{2}''\ \times\ \frac{1}{8}''$

Tongue

Rabbet-dado or
lock joint

Fig. 32-17. Joints used to join drawer fronts to sides.

Door front
with lipped
edge

Plywood
bottom

Side   Back

Butt

Side   Back

Rabbet

Side   Back

Dado

Fig. 32-16. Drawer fronts may be flush.

Fig. 32-18. Joints used to join drawer backs to sides.

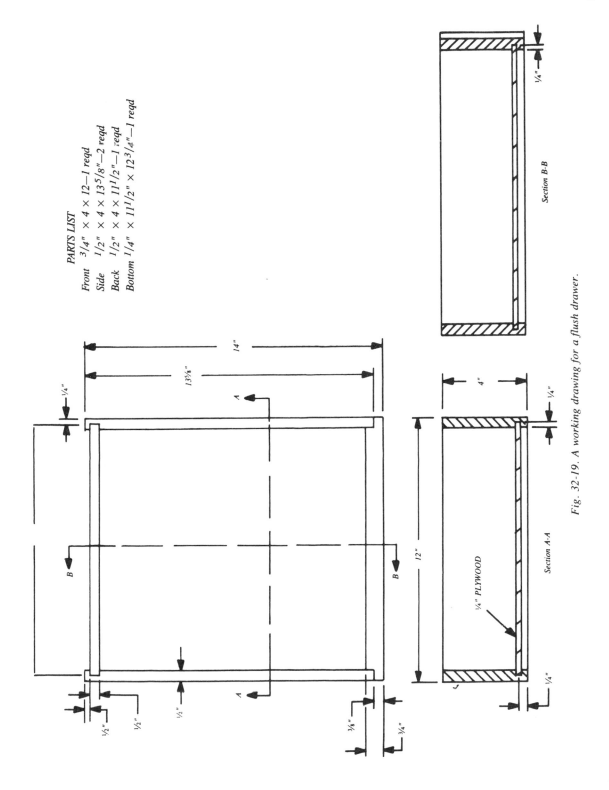

PARTS LIST

Front $3/4" \times 4 \times 12$—1 reqd
Side $1/2" \times 4 \times 13^5/8"$—2 reqd
Back $1/2" \times 4 \times 11^1/2"$—1 reqd
Bottom $1/4" \times 11^1/2" \times 12^3/4"$—1 reqd

Section B-B

Section A-A

$1/4"$ PLYWOOD

Fig. 32-19. A working drawing for a flush drawer.

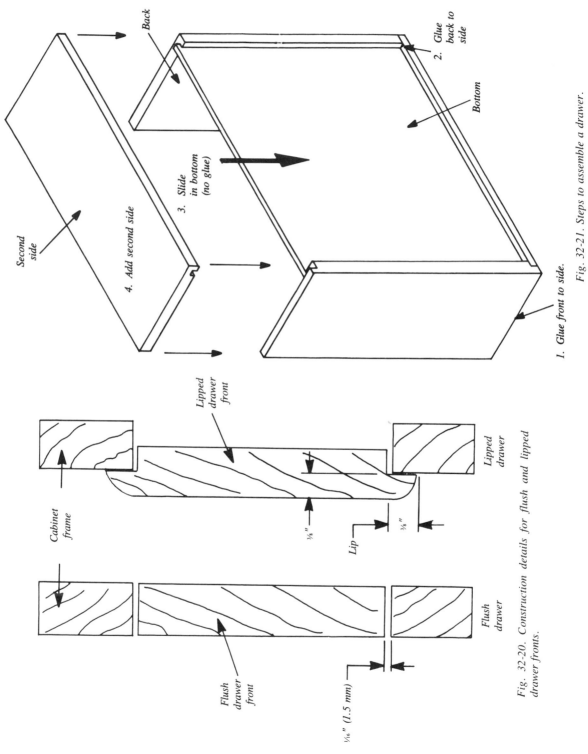

Back

2. Glue back to side

Bottom

3. Slide in bottom (no glue)

4. Add second side

Second side

1. Glue front to side

Fig. 32-21. Steps to assemble a drawer.

Lipped drawer front

Cabinet frame

Lipped drawer

⅜"

Lip

¼"

Flush drawer front

Flush drawer

1/16" (1.5 mm)

Fig. 32-20. Construction details for flush and lipped drawer fronts.

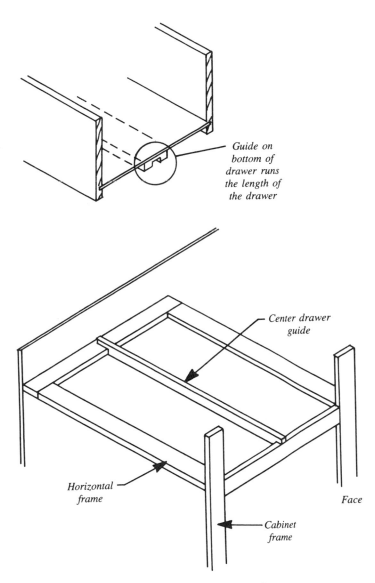

Fig. 32-22. A center drawer guide.

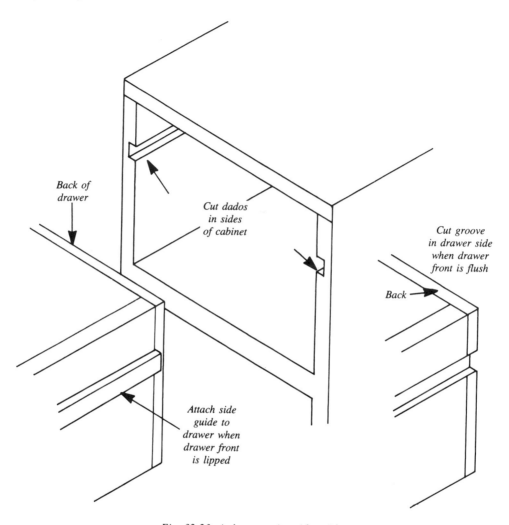

Fig. 32-23. A drawer using side guides.

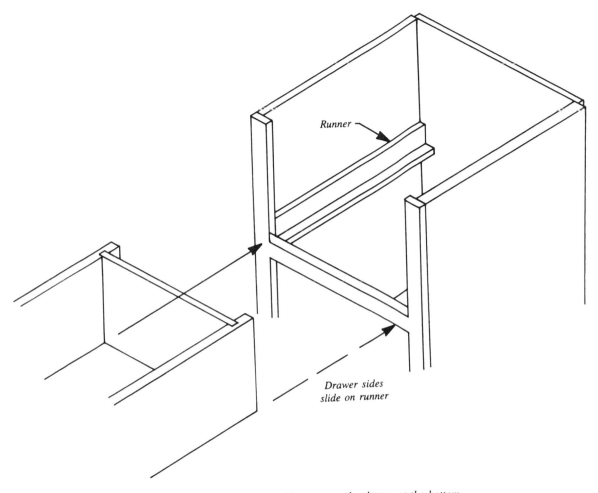

Fig. 32-24. Corner drawer guides support the drawer at the bottom.

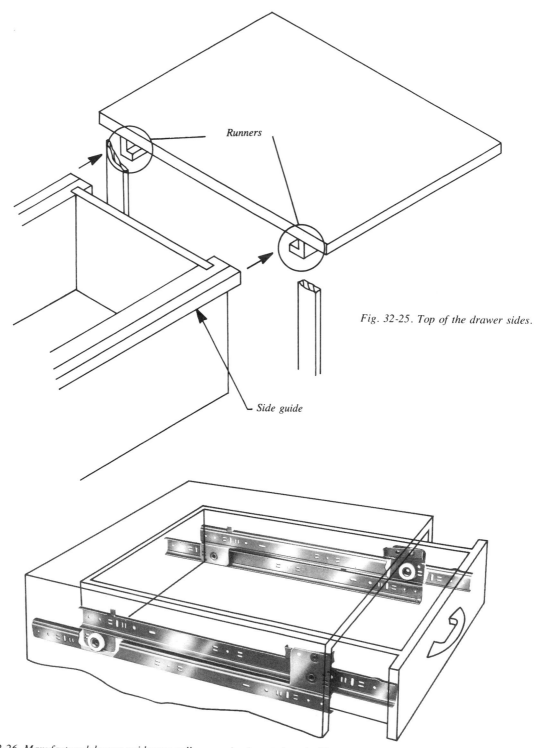

Runners

Side guide

Fig. 32-25. *Top of the drawer sides.*

Fig. 32-26. *Manufactured drawer guides use rollers running in metal tracks (Courtesy Knape and Vogt Manufacturing Co.).*

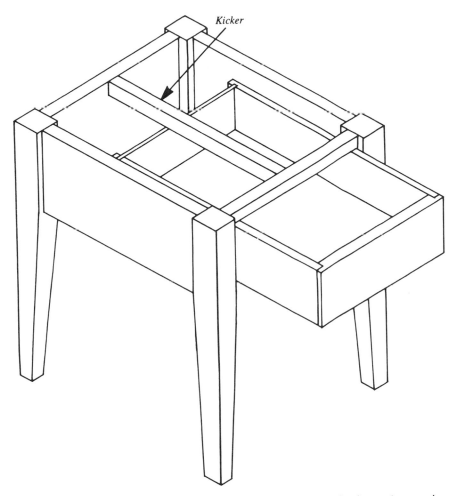

Kicker

Fig. 32-27. A kicker keeps the back of the drawer from lifting up as the drawer is opened.

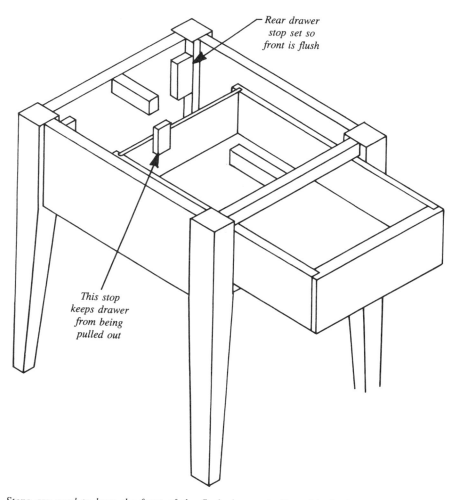

Rear drawer stop set so front is flush

This stop keeps drawer from being pulled out

Fig. 32-28. Stops are used to keep the front of the flush drawer in line with the frame. A stop on the back of the drawer keeps it from being accidentally pulled out of the frame.

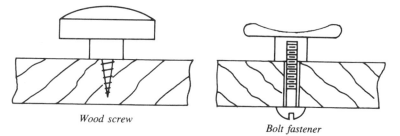

Wood screw

Bolt fastener

Fig. 32-29. Knobs and drawer pulls are fastened with wood screws or bolts.

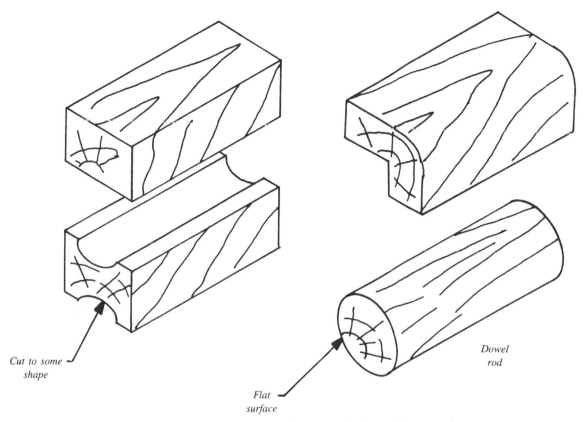

Cut to some
shape

Flat
surface

Dowel
rod

Fig. 32-30. Wood pulls and handles can easily be made from wood.

Chapter 33

Applying Veneers
and Plastic Laminates

Wood veneers and plastic laminates are glued to a substrate such as particleboard or plywood. Veneers provide an attractive finished surface. Technical information about veneers and plastic laminates was provided in chapter 3; the information given here explains how to **bond them to the core material.**

VENEERS

Veneers are thin pieces of wood. They can be cut using regular woodworking tools, but because they are thin and easily broken, special cutting tools should be used.

Cutting Veneers

Veneers are cut with a veneer saw, utility knife, or sheetmetal shear. The veneer saw has fine teeth with no set. It is used to cut with and across the grain. Veneers are cut from each edge, toward the center. Cutting toward the center reduces splintering on the edge (Fig. 33-1).

The veneer saw must be guided against a straightedge. A framing square or straight piece of hardwood is a good tool to use. Because the veneer saw cuts through the veneers, cover the bench top with a scrap piece of plywood.

Veneers can also be rough cut to size with a utility knife or a sheetmetal shear. Use light cuts.

Making Edge Joints

Larger pieces of veneer are formed by gluing narrow pieces together along their edges. First, however, the pieces are laid side by side and the grain matched as desired. It is important that the joining edges be cut straight. Clamp the two edges to be joined between two straight boards. The veneer should stick out about 1¹/₁₆ inch (2 mm). Remove this with a plane or laminate-trimming router bit (Fig. 33-2).

Gluing Edge Joints

After the edge joint is cut, place the veneer on the bench with the good side up. Check the joint to make certain it is perfect. Apply short pieces of masking tape across the joint every 6 inches (150 mm), then apply tape the full length of the joint (Fig. 33-3).

Turn the veneers over and fold one piece back. Apply white glue to the edges with a small artist brush (Fig. 33-4). Place them flat on the table and apply tape over the length of the joint (Fig. 33-5). This holds the veneers as the glue dries. Let the project dry overnight. After drying, it is ready to be glued to the backing sheet.

Gluing Veneer to the Substrate

Veneers can be glued with contact cement or a polyvinyl adhesive. Contact cement requires no clamping, but polyvinyl adhesive must be clamped for three or more hours.

When using polyvinyl, spread it uniformly over the substrate. Use a brush or roller to get a thin, uniform coating. Lay the veneer on the adhesive with the good face up and line it up so it parallels the edge of the backing board. Cover the surface of the veneer with several layers of paper; newspaper or brown wrapping paper

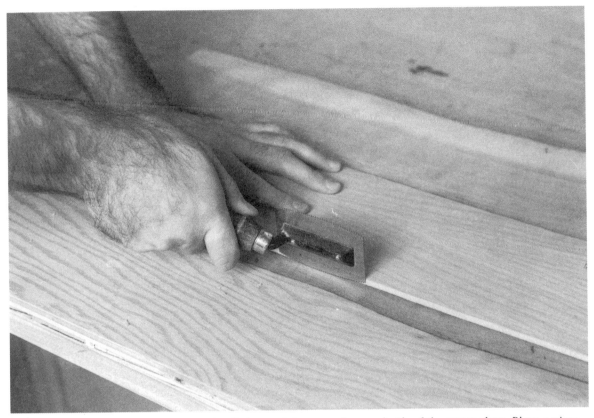

Fig. 33-1. The veneer saw is pushed and pulled toward the center from each side of the veneer sheet. Place a piece of scrap wood below to protect the bench.

work well. Place a piece of plywood the size of the area being glued over the newspaper. Use handscrews on all edges. Be certain to get uniform pressure on each clamp (Fig. 33-6). Special veneering presses can also be used.

PLASTIC LAMINATES

Plastic laminates are used to cover furniture and cabinet doors, tops, and sides. They resist stains and heat and are easy to clean. Laminates are bonded to a substrate such as plywood or particleboard.

Cutting Plastic Laminates

Plastic laminates are hard and will dull regular steel woodworking cutters. Cut laminates with power saws, using carbide-tipped blades. Laminates can also be cut by scoring with an awl then snapping them along the score line.

Cut the piece to be used about ½ inch (12 mm) larger than the area to be covered. This allows it to be trimmed after it is bonded to the backing board.

To cut plastic laminates on the table saw, clamp a piece of wood to the fence to keep the laminate from slipping under the fence. Feed the laminate slowly into the blade with the good side up. If you cut with a saber saw, support the laminate below with wood. Laminates are brittle and will break. Place the good side down and use a fine-tooth blade (Fig. 33-7).

To cut by scoring, clamp two pieces of wood along the line to be cut. Cut a score mark with an awl on the good face (Fig. 33-8). Push the laminate down toward the back until it snaps along the score line.

Gluing Plastic Laminates to the Backing Sheet

Plastic laminates are bonded with contact cement. Read the instructions on the can for proper use. Because some are flammable, do not use near an open flame.

Fig. 33-2. Clamp the veneer between two straight pieces of wood and plane the edges straight.

When applying laminates to edges and face, apply the sides first, then the front and back edges, and the face last. This produces the fewest visible joints.

Apply contact cement to the edges of the core and the plastic laminate edge strips. Use a brush or roller. Let the contact cement dry. To test it, place a piece of brown paper against it. If the paper does not stick, it is dry.

Place the end strips against the edges of the backing sheet (Fig. 33-9). Position them exactly before they touch the surface. A small roller can be used to press on the laminate (Fig. 33-10). Then bond the front and back edges. Trim the excess laminate so it is flush with the substrate as explained in the next section.

Apply contact cement to the wood top and the back of the plastic laminate. After the cement dries, align the laminate on the top by placing ⅜-inch (10-mm) dowels across the surface (Fig. 33-11). Place the laminate on top, moving it until it is in the desired position. Remove the dowel on one edge and push the laminate against the top, then work across the surface removing one dowel at a time (Fig. 33-12). Bond the laminate to the surface with a roller. Finally, trim the excess laminate.

Trimming Plastic Laminates

Plastic laminates can be trimmed with a power router, an electric laminate trimmer, or a hand-operated laminate trimmer. The power router uses a laminate trimming bit. It has a ball bearing pilot tip that touches the edge of the product to control the trimming cut. The electric laminate trimmer is lighter and smaller than a router, but works in the same manner. The edge of the laminate can also be dressed to size using a file designed especially for smoothing plastic laminates (Fig. 33-13).

Fig. 33-3. With the good side up, place tape along the joint between the sheets of veneer.

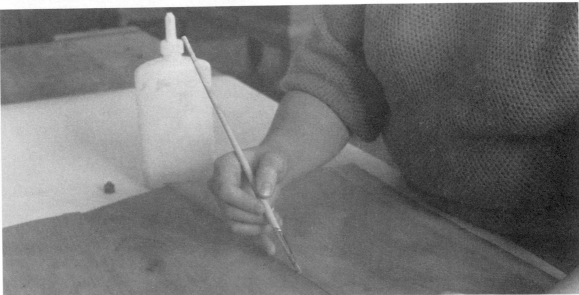

Fig. 33-4. Turn the veneers over and place white glue in the joint.

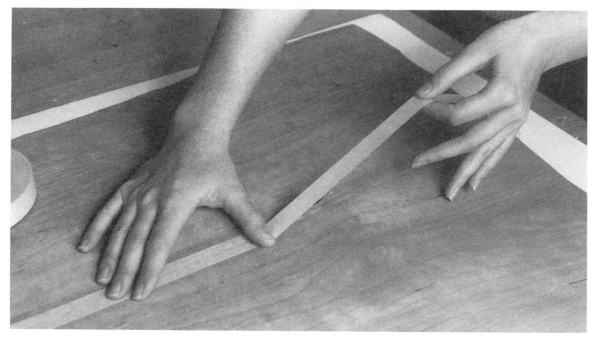

Fig. 33-5. Press the veneers flat and place tape over the joint on the back side.

Fig. 33-6. Use a piece of plywood as a top form when gluing veneers to the backing board.

Fig. 33-7. When cutting plastic laminates with a saber saw, place the good side down. Use a board below to keep from breaking the laminate.

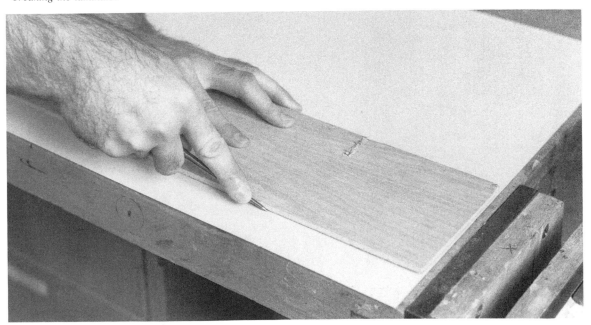

Fig. 33-8. Plastic laminates can be cut by scoring and breaking.

Fig. 33-9. Center the plastic laminate on the edge before making contact. Stick one end first and work toward the other end.

Fig. 33-10. Role the laminate to assure a tight bond.

Fig. 33-11. Place dowel rods on the surface to keep the plastic laminate from touching.

Fig. 33-12. (top) Begin by removing the center dowels, allowing the laminate to make contact with the surface.

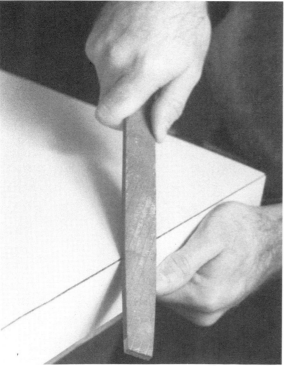

Fig. 33-13. (left) Remove the router cutter marks with a file. Be careful not to file into the edge strip of laminate.

Index

Index